ECHOES OF

A SHAAR PRESS PUBLICATION

GLORY

THE STORY OF THE JEWS IN THE CLASSICAL ERA 350 BCE-750 CE

BEREL WEIN

© Copyright 1995 by Rabbi Berel Wein and Shaar Press
First edition – First impression / December 1995
Second impression / February 1996
Third impression / January 2001
Fourth impression / October 2003

ALL RIGHTS RESERVED

No part of this book may be reproduced **in any form,** *photocopy, electronic media, or otherwise – even FOR PERSONAL, STUDY GROUP, OR CLASSROOM USE – without* **written** *permission from the copyright holder, except by a reviewer who wishes to quote brief passages in connection with a review written for inclusion in magazines or newspapers.*

THE RIGHTS OF THE COPYRIGHT HOLDER WILL BE STRICTLY ENFORCED.

Published by SHAAR PRESS
and Distributed by MESORAH PUBLICATIONS, LTD.
4401 Second Avenue / Brooklyn, N.Y 11232 / (718) 921-9000

Distributed in Israel by SIFRIATI / A. GITLER
6 Hayarkon Street / Bnei Brak 51127 / Israel

Distributed in Europe by LEHMANNS
Unit E, Viking Industrial Park, Rolling Mill Road / Jarrow, Tyne and Wear, NE32 3DP/ England

Distributed in Australia and New Zealand by GOLDS WORLD OF JUDAICA
3-13 William Street / Balaclava, Melbourne 3183 / Victoria Australia

Distributed in South Africa by KOLLEL BOOKSHOP
Shop 8A Norwood Hypermarket / Norwood 2196, Johannesburg, South Africa

Printed in the United States of America by Noble Book Press
Custom bound by Sefercraft, Inc. / 4401 Second Avenue / Brooklyn N.Y. 11232

Contents

Prologue
Up From Despair / Focus on the Land of Israel / An International Faith / The Centrality of the Oral Law   xiii

Section I   The Beauty of Japheth and the Tents of Shem

1   Going Home
A Hostile Welcome / Rebuilding of the Temple Is Halted / In the Wake of Purim / Ezra / The Second Temple / Building a New Community / Nechemiah / Persian Tolerance / The "Great Assembly" / A Vital Partnership   1

2   Greece and Hellenism
The Beginning of Greek Dominance / Alexander the Great / Division of the Greek Empire / Division of the Commonwealth / A Corrupting Alliance / Translation of the Seventy / Hellenism / The Spread of Greek Culture / The Development of Philosophy / Three Schools of Thought / The Philosophic Challenge / The Ravages of Hellenism   17

3   Twin Hellenism — Ptolemaic And Seleucid
The Jews of Alexandria / Parallel Governments / The Sadducees / Tax Collection / Division of Power / The Persistence of Hellenism / Antiochus III / An Attempt to Rob the Temple   35

4   Economic and Social Life in Judah in Second Temple Times
The Basis of the Economy / Agriculture / Produce / Other Resources / The Trades / Slavery / Population Centers   45

5   Chanukah and the Hasmoneans
The Greek Notion of Sports / Jason's Decline / Menelaus and Lysimachus / Civil War / Persecution / Mattisyahu and His Sons / Yehudah HaMaccabee / The Miracle of Chanukah / Significance of the Miracle / The Hasmonean Kingdom / Lysias and Philip / Yehudah Defeats the Syrians   59

6 The Hasmonean Dynasty
A Clouded Destiny / Alexander Balas / Yonasan's Rise / Changes of Power / Tryphon's Treachery / Shimon's Victory / A Tragic Breakdown / The Extermination of a Family / Jewish Independence Regained / Enlarging Judah's Borders / Dissent from Within / Efforts of the Pharisees / A Troubled End / The Essenes / Yehudah Aristobulus / Opposition to the Hasmoneans / Two Brothers Die / Shlomis Alexandra / Alexander Yannai / Alexander Yannai and the Pharisees / A School System / Sacrilege in the Temple / Civil War / Alexander Yannai's End / A Period of Healing / Shlomis Loses Power   73

Section II Edom Ascendant

7 Rome the Colossus
Julius Caesar / A Conflict of Approaches / Tiberius / Caligula / Claudius / Nero   105

8 Aristobulus, Hyrcanus and Antipater
Brother Against Brother / The Rabbis Withdraw from Politics / A Pig on the Temple Mount / Pompey's Intervention / Second Siege of the Temple / Pompey's Regime / Alexander's Escapes / Disbanding of the Sanhedrin / Caesar and Pompey / Antipater's Ascension / Herod / Herod's Trial / Antipater's Wiles / Herod's Persistence / Hillel / A New Focus / The Houses of Hillel and Shammai / Further Atrocities of Herod / Family Murders / Herod's Temple / Hillel's Legacy   114

9 The End of the Second Commonwealth
A Respite from Cruelty / Corruption in the High Priesthood / The Zealots / Pontius Pilate / Gaius and Agrippa / Claudius / The Path to Revolt / Florus / Inner Strife / A Fatal Triumph / Josephus Flavius / Vespasian's Campaigns / The Year of the Four Emperors / Three Factions in Jerusalem / A Meeting with Vespasian / Yavneh / Titus Attacks Jerusalem / Tishah b'Av   142

Section III Response to Exile

10 Yavneh and Its Wise Men
The Sanhedrin / Preserving the Oral Law / A Smaller Community The Synagogue / Five Disciples / Titus and Domitian / The Leadership in Yavneh / The New Nasi / Changes in Yavneh / Nerva   175

11 The Rise of Christianity
     Roots of the Religion / Paul / A Series of Paradoxes / Too Much the Same / A Widening Gap / One Good Word 191

12 Bar Kochba
     Yavneh Disbanded / Lod / Roman Fury Unleashed / The Jews Revolt / Hadrian / The Sanhedrin Reconvenes / A Third Rebellion / High Hopes / The Fall of Beitar / A Failed Promise 199

13 Rabbi Akiva and the Aftermath of Bar Kochba's Defeat
     A True Martyr / Rabbi Akiva's Disciples / Acher / Ambivalence Towards Rome / Hope for Peace / The Power of the Nasi / Antoninus and Rabbi 213

Section IV Torah Remains Eternal

14 Mishnah
     Rabbi's Project / Notebooks of the Scholars / Sections of the Mishnah / Migration from the Homeland / Rabbi Chiya / Rabbi's Legacy 229

15 The Valley of Babylonia
     Rav / The Sidra / Hutzal / Nehardea / Sura / The Mantle Passes to Babylonia / Rav's Work / Rav's Prayers / Rav's Disciples / The Sassanian King / Sura and Pumbedisa / The Exilarch / Rav Huna and Mar Ukva / Rabbi Yochanan 238

16 Rome Declines and Dies
     The Yeshivos in Tiberias and Caesarea / Decline of the Samaritans / Destruction of Nehardea / Growth of Pumbedisa / Constantine / Decline of the Jews in Israel / The Jewish Calendar / The Christian Calendar / Babylonian Leadership / Abbaye and Rava / A Warring Family / "Julian the Apostate" / The Empire Weakens / Shifting of the Yeshivos / Rav Ashi / Reviving the Yarchei Kallah / Truce with Parthia / Leader of Pumbedisa / Leaders in Sura / Declining Fortunes in Babylonia 255

17 The Talmud — The Book of the Jews
     Talmud Yerushalmi / Talmud Bavli / Aggadah / The Power of the Talmud / Toward Deeper Understanding 279

Section V New Challenges, New Lands

18 The Era of Byzantium
The New Rashei Galusa / The Savoraim / Life Under the Byzantines / Jews in the Western Empire / Jewish Life Under Christianity / The Synagogue / Monastic Living   289

19 Islam and the Jews
The Founding of Islam / The Influence of Judaism / The Rule of the Sword / The Spread of Islam / Sunnis and Shiites / Omayyads and Abbasids / The Jews and Islam / The Effects of Islam   299

20 The Era of the Geonim
Bustenai / Bustenai and the Geonim / The Courts / The Role of the Babylonian Geonim / Chisdai and Shlomo / The Abbasids / Anan and the Birth of Karaism / The Waning Power of the Reish Galusa / The Legacy of the Geonim   309

21 Epilogue   319

Bibliography   325

Index   327

Preface

This book forms the third and final part of a trilogy describing the story of the Jewish people from the post-biblical period until the present, modern era. My first book, *Triumph of Survival*, told the story of the Jews in the modern era, the period from 1650 until 1990. I then devoted my second book, *Herald of Destiny*, to describing Jewish life in medieval times (750-1650). With this book, I back up even further to write about the Jews of classical antiquity (400 B.C.E.-750 C.E.).

I believe that these three books in conjunction provide a continuous picture of the past 2,400 years of Jewish and world history. This picture and perspective is essential for viewing the events and challenges of current Jewish and general life intelligently and wisely.

People need heroes to identify with, historical events to remember and a feeling of continuity to gain the security necessary for productive and meaningful lives. The story of the Jewish people over the millennia will provide these requisite heroes, events, challenges and lessons. Thus, although the chronology of the writing of these books is backwards, I hope the message of Jewish history will be viewed as straightforward, progressive and relevant, even if at times painfully so.

The difficulty of writing accurate history increases geometrically as one retreats in time. Modern history has photographs, newspapers, diaries and other artifacts upon which an accurate portrayal of the past few centuries may be based. Even the medieval world, though far removed from our society in time, mindset and circumstance, may yet be glimpsed, albeit fuzzily and inexactly, and recognized. However, the world of classical antiquity, of Greece, Rome, Persia and Babylonia, is much more difficult to describe and appreciate.

Although much of that period has been preserved in its surviving books, art and architectural ruins, few moderns have any real concept of ancient life. The decline in popularity of classical studies in modern universities, the fact that such studies are no longer deemed to be requirements for graduation, the reality that Latin truly has become a dead language and that the study of Greek culture and philosophy is now an anachronism in modern academia, all contribute to a continuing ignoring, and resulting ignorance, of the societies where our ancient roots were nurtured. Thus, all attempts to make this period more understandable and meaningful to modern society are haunted by the perception of irrelevance that now shrouds the world of classical antiquity. But to Jews, who are compelled daily to face their roots and ancestors of classical antiquity in order to appreciate their tradition, the knowledge of the events, forces and people of that long-ago era is a necessity. This book attempts to meet that need.

A peculiar problem arises regarding the dating of events in this early part of Jewish history. Baldly put, it is very difficult to reconcile the generally accepted system of historical dating — and therefore the times of certain events within that system — with the traditional Jewish system of dating those very events.

General world history considers 586 B.C.E. as the year that Judah was conquered and the First Temple was destroyed. Since we know the Jews built the Second Temple seventy years later, it would follow that it was constructed in 516 B.C.E; and since the Talmud and other Jewish sources state that the Second Temple stood for 420 years, it would then follow further that it was destroyed in 96 B.C.E. However, both general and Jewish history agree that the destruction of the Second Temple took place not in 96 B.C.E., but in 70 C.E. This discrepancy of 166 years has perplexed Jewish scholars for a long while. Many innovative, ingenious and sometimes even far-fetched theses have been proposed to bridge the gap and explain away the discrepancy.[1]

I have nothing new to add to the debate regarding this problem. I accept the traditional Jewish system of dating the events of this period, and thus in this book, the First Temple's destruction is dated not 516 B.C.E., but 423 B.C.E. (3338 since Creation); and Ezra, who supervised the Second Temple's construction seventy years later, is assumed to have lived circa 350 B.C.E. It is the combination of my faith in the collective memory of the Jewish people and the convenience of following such a dating system that has led me to adopt this time sequence system in this book.

There is actually a major philosophical undercurrent involved in this matter. In my opinion, this conflict regarding the historical dating of the beginning of the Second Commonwealth is representative of a deeper issue of faith which lies at the core of differing perspectives of Jewish history.

The prophet Hosea (14:10) concludes his mission of prophecy by stating, "For the ways of the Lord are straight and the righteous should walk upon them, and the wayward shall stumble over them." I believe that in no field of knowledge is this dichotomy of "paths" so apparent as it is in the field of Jewish history. History, unlike mathematics and other exact sciences, always contains a bit of error, bias, misinformation, disinformation and selective reporting. Yet somehow there always emerges from this inexact subject called history a clear and informative pattern of civilizations rising and falling, of shifting circumstances of life and events, of changing directions and value systems. The existence of some discrepancies or conflicting evidence, therefore, is a "problem," but it does not refute the entire structure. So too in the traditional Jewish chronology. Even if particular historical problems or errors of fact or calendar would be found in the traditional view of the story of the Jews, this in no way should impugn the great general thrust and truths this view of the history provides. Nevertheless, almost with a perverse glee, secular Jewish historians and many non-Jewish historians, upon encountering problems such as this 166-year Second Commonwealth dis-

---

1. See the appendix, "The Traditional Jewish Chronology," p. 211, in *History of the Jewish People: The Second Temple Era* by Rabbi Hersh Goldwurm (Mesorah Publications, New York, 1982), for a short review of the problem, possible solutions and scholarly sources.

crepancy, have rejected as inauthentic and inaccurate the entire traditional and Talmudic-oriented view of Jewish history.

One's view of Jewish history depends upon one's own personal agenda of life. Therefore, people of faith and belief, who view the Jewish story in its miraculous totality, will walk upon the paths of the Lord and will be able to live with apparent inconsistencies, inexact recollections and the possibility of particular factual errors which, nonetheless, in no way change the overall story of God and Israel. But Jews fleeing from their heritage, frightened of their past and unsure of their future, rejecting the notion of Providence in the affairs of humans, will naturally fall and trip upon discovering any inexactitude and discrepancy in traditional sources. The great Yiddish aphorism about life in general is that "no one dies because of a contradiction." If only this would be the attitude toward Jewish history as well!

Upon reflection, I must reiterate that the difficulties of reporting on this period of history are enormous. Besides the difficulties I have already mentioned due to the removal in time, society and circumstances, and the relative scarcity of accurate historical documents, artifacts and records, there is another dimension of Jewish life in classical antiquity which challenges our way of thinking — the spiritual and intellectual standing of the figures of Jewish history of that time.

As a traditional Jew I have been trained to believe, and I do so believe, that the Jewish scholars and leaders of that time were immensely greater spiritual beings than we are. We simply are not in the same league as Ezra, Mordechai, Hillel, Rabbi Akiva and Rabbi Judah the Prince. Therefore, the main difficulty that I found in writing this book is in portraying these greater-than-life figures while somehow dealing with them in the mundane, almost pedestrian fashion that a history book of this nature demands. Perhaps readers will sense the awe and trepidation I feel in writing about this era of Jewish history. In any event, I hope the readers' learning the story of Israel in the times of classical antiquity will indeed lead them to appreciate the greatness of those people and inspire the feelings of wonder and destiny inherent in the saga of the Jews.

Acknowledgments

Amongst the pains, tribulations, and frustrations of writing a book, there are also many rewards that have come to this author even before the book's publication. I have met and benefited from people of intellect, taste, and humor who have helped me in the writing of this work of history. Their contributions are herewith thankfully acknowledged and gratefully recognized.

Rabbi Tzvi Lampel was an expert editor and insightful critic. Professor Sid. Z. Leiman, one of the world's leading authorities in the field of Jewish studies, was kind enough to read the manuscript and make cogent and incisive comments. Rabbi Moshe Gans was a sensitive reader whose comments added much to the book. I cannot thank them enough.

The professional staff at *Shaar Press* has done their usual beautiful work on the graphics and layout of the book. Of the *Shaar Press* staff, I would particularly like to thank Mrs.

Bassie Gutman and Rochel Leah Ross who worked so hard to turn my manuscript into a book, and Fayge Silverman for her proofreading and insights.

Several individuals made their personal collections of photographs available for use in this volume, particularly Eli Kroen, Shmuel Margareten and Avrohom Biderman. I am grateful for their assistance.

Finally, I must once more state the debt I owe my beloved wife, Jackie, for all of her help and patience over the years of endless writing. I am truly fortunate to have been blessed with such a great woman as my spouse.

I have attempted to be as fair and accurate as possible in the text of this work. However, human failings are part of the makeup of even this author. Any errors of the facts and /or judgment in this book are solely my responsibility. I hope that they are few and easily forgiven by the reader.

As I have noted in my other history books, the story of the Jews does not occur in a vacuum. The backdrop of general world events, of civilizations and societies rising, flourishing and declining, of wars and pestilence, commerce and scholarship, personalities and leaders, is absolutely necessary for an understanding of the Jewish story.

The period of history covered by this book demands a basic understanding of Persian, Greek and Roman civilizations. The rise of two large monotheistic religions, Christianity and Islam, both derived from Jewish roots and sources, requires some study of their antecedents, philosophies, goals and dynamics. The progress of humankind in medicine, science, the arts, mathematics and architecture during this time also begs our attention. Only when there is some broader view of the full tapestry of world history can the uniqueness and singularity of the Jewish component be appreciated and treasured.

I hope this book will provide the reader with both that broad view and singular appreciation. If it does, then I am amply rewarded for the struggle inherent in writing this volume.

Dedication

Dedicated to the memory of my beloved mother, Esther Rubinstein Wein, ז״ל, who taught me how to attempt to appreciate and treasure the past.

Prologue

hen Solomon's Temple was sacked and burned by the hordes of Babylonian soldiers that had defeated the army of Judah, it appeared to many that the story of the Jews had come to a dismal end.

The fall of Judah, the national state of the tribes of Judah and Benjamin, seemed to have been the last stage of Jewish destruction, following the sudden collapse of the other Jewish state, the great kingdom of Israel, 150 years earlier. Composed of the other ten tribes of Jacob and led by the mighty tribe of Ephraim, the kingdom of Israel was totally decimated in a war against the Assyrian king Sancheirev. That population of Israel was scattered throughout Asia Minor, eventually to disappear as an organized entity from the face of world and Jewish history, and to become the legendary group called "the ten lost tribes of Israel."[1] Now, after the new disaster of the fall of Jerusalem, only a handful of Jews remained in Judah and its capital, Jerusalem.

Riven by dissension and violent assassinations, they were powerless to maintain themselves against the Samaritans, Babylonians, Arabs and other tribes that now immigrated to Judah and inhabited their former kingdom. Many Jews, in disobedience to the prophet

---

1. Even though the ten tribes, as an organized political unit, disappeared from Jewish life by the time of the Second Commonwealth, there is considerable evidence that thousands of the ten tribes' *individual* descendants joined their brethren of Judah to help found and build the Second Commonwealth. (See *Tosafos, Gittin* 36b and *Arachin* 32a for support of this opinion. See also *Sefer HaGeulah* by Rabbi Moses ben Nachman [Ramban] [*Kisvei Ramban*, Rabbi C. Chavel, ed., Mosad Horav Kook, Jerusalem, 1963, Vol. I, p. 172] for the opinion that many of the Jews of Israel's ten tribes moved to Judah after the destruction of their kingdom, well before the destruction of the First Temple, and that their descendants accompanied their fellow Jews of the tribes of Judah and Benjamin into the Babylonian exile and were therefore represented among those Jews who returned from that exile to build the Second Commonwealth.)

Jeremiah, fled south to a second Egyptian exile. But there, too, they were relatively small in number and weak in communal organization. The majority of Jews were moved to Babylonia, where at first they served as slaves and prisoners, and later became upwardly mobile members of the rich and culturally strong Babylonian society. The Jewish world was in tatters, and the Jewish dream was shattered.

Up From Despair

HE DIFFERING DESPAIRING moods of the Jewish people at the beginning of the Babylonian exile are exemplified by two excerpts from the Bible. The first, Chapter 137 of Psalms, sorrowfully states: "By the waters of Babylon did we sit and weep as we recalled Zion... How shall we sing the song of God on foreign soil?" The psalm, reflective of the mindset of the Jews at the very beginning of the exile, while they were still under the trauma of the terrible defeat of Judah, nevertheless contains notes of vengeance and of eternal Jewish pride and faith. "If I forget thee, O Jerusalem, let my right hand fail ... Remember, O God, to the children of Edom, the day of the destruction of Jerusalem... Daughter of Babylon, despoiled, happy shall be he that repays you in kind for your cruelty to us."

This first mood of agony and anger was soon replaced by a second one of resignation and acceptance. The Jews acclimated themselves quickly to their new status of exile. They forgot their special role in history and moved to assimilate into the nation and society of their conquerors. In Chapter 20 of Ezekiel, the prophet reveals how the people of Israel, now in exile, feeling somehow rejected by their national God, desired to "be like the nations, like the families of the lands, to worship wood and stone." The Jewish people in the blackness of exile sought to deny or, at the very least, resign their unique role in the human story. But the Lord responded: "What enters your thoughts [to be allowed to assimilate and disappear], it shall not be...for with a strong hand and outstretched arm and with outpoured fury I shall rule over you."[2] Thus, early in the story of Jewish exile was the pattern for all later Jewish history established. Jews would attempt to assimilate and blend into the majority society, and

---

2. *Ezekiel* 20:32-33.

the Lord would always provide the circumstances that would eventually thwart them.

Focus on the Land of Israel

HE JEWS DID NOT have to wait long to witness the humbling of Babylon. The book of Daniel describes how the Persians and Medes overcame King Belshazar and Babylon, who were found wanting on the scales of God and disappeared from the world scene a scant few decades after conquering Jerusalem. Jews had already risen to high station in the Babylonian court and continued to occupy roles of importance under the succeeding Persian rule as well. Although there were those who actively campaigned for the right of return to Jerusalem and to rebuild the Temple, the exile appeared comfortable for most Jews. Yet the "strong and outstretched hand" soon manifested itself.

The Jews, feeling secure and accepted, were active participants in the coronation banquet of the new Persian emperor, Ahasuerus, and later, in spite of having a kinswoman as his queen, were nonetheless blindsided by a genocidal decree of complete destruction promulgated by the king's chief minister, Haman. Mordechai and Esther, as instruments of the Divine Will, upset Haman and his plans and saved the Jews from annihilation. The holiday of Purim, established to commemorate this deliverance from death, became not only the most joyous day of the Jewish year but also the symbol of the dangers and miracles of Jewish life and survival throughout Israel's long exile. The miraculous events helped inspire a refocusing of Jewish attention on a return to the homeland and especially to the holy city of Jerusalem.[3] Though a sizable number, perhaps a majority, of the world's Jews would continue in all future times to live in the Exile, the main events of Jewish history and Jewish life for the next five centuries, 350 B.C.E. to 150 C.E., would revolve around the Jews living in the Land of Israel and specifically in Jerusalem.

It is to tell the story of this period of the Second Commonwealth of Israel that the first part of this book is devoted.

---

3. Ramban, in his commentary to Talmud, *Shabbos* 88a, sees the story of Purim as God's reassertion of Israel's self-image as the Chosen People.

An International Faith

IT WOULD BE AN ERROR, however, to ignore the continually strong and vibrant influence the Jews living in the Exile had upon Jewish life in Israel during this half-millennium. In fact, it was over this period of time that a strong symbiotic relationship was created between the Jewish Commonwealth in Israel and the Jews of the Exile. It was during this period of time that Judaism became an international faith, spanning borders and locales. Haman's description of the Jews as a "singular people, scattered and dispersed"[4] throughout the known world of his day, remained an accurate one.

Jewish dispersion, in a paradoxical fashion, created Jewish solidarity and cohesion. Through the loyalty and support extended to the Jewish Commonwealth by the Jews worldwide, the status of the small and relatively weak entity in Israel was immeasurably magnified in the eyes of the non-Jewish world. Thus, Jerusalem was an international city in the ancient world, much as was Athens, Rome, Alexandria and Persopolis, even though it was never the seat of empire as were the others.

The world was fascinated by the Holy City, its people and faith. Jerusalem was always a magnet for tourists and visitors, both in its times of glory and in its periods of desolation and desertion. This phenomenon was encouraged by the presence of the Jews of the Exile, who always saw Jerusalem as their home and destiny. Thus, the story of the Jews in their homeland during the time of the Second Commonwealth must of necessity also be the story of the Jews in exile at that very same time.

The Centrality of the Oral Law

FINALLY, WE MUST RECOGNIZE the new emphasis necessitated by reactions to political situations on the fact that the Oral Law is the basis of Jewish life and society. We must recognize its continued acceptance, in spite of continuing controversy, as the central theme of the internal Jewish

---
4. *Esther* (3:8).

story of the Second Commonwealth and its aftermath. During biblical times, the presence of prophecy in Israel provided spiritual continuity from Moses and Sinai. The Oral Law, which alone guarantees biblical values and guidance in practical, everyday human life, was always an integral part of Jewish life. But it was during the period of the Second Commonwealth, with the passing of prophecy, that the Oral Law now became the only successor to the vision provided by that prophecy itself.

The prophets of Israel had performed a dual service. They were prophets, the transmitters of God's word. But they were also the conduits for the transmission of the traditions of the Oral Law[5]. When the era of prophecy came to an end with the death of Malachi, there were no more prophets to transmit direct, godly messages. But the prophets had trained successors as the conduit for the successful transmission of the traditions of the Oral Law to all later generations. The prophets in their prophecy roles were not serving as adjudicators of Jewish law[6]. But in their roles as the transmitters of the Oral Law, they served as the legal experts of Israel. It is this latter role that they passed on to the Men of the Great Assembly, who led Israel at the onset of the Second Commonwealth.

The further development of the Oral Law, its attendant wide public profile and the popular loyalty it enjoyed amongst the masses of Jewry now occupied the central issue and focus of Jewish spiritual life. There is no doubt that the intensified popular study and system of analysis by which the Oral Law became the single greatest unifying force in Jewry was mainly responsible for the survival of the Jewish people despite unrelenting tragedy, defeat and turmoil. Thus, this book, as were my others, will again be rich with the lives of rabbis, teachers and spiritual leaders. True, there will be kings, warriors, statesmen and other political leaders described as well, but mainly it will be the great rabbis of Israel, the teachers of the yeshivos, the holy men who had no personal agenda to pursue, who will be revealed as the true heroes of this period of Jewish history.

Their influence and guidance were not limited to their time, but remains alive today as the source of Jewish tenacity, scholarship and identity.

---

5. Mishnah, *Avos*, 1:1.
6. Talmud, *Shabbos* 104a.

Section I

The Beauty of Japheth and the Tents of Shem

1
Going Home
(400 B.C.E. - 330 B.C.E.)

THE FALL OF BABYLONIA to the newly emerging giant empire of Persia, which signaled a major change in world history, presaged a major change in Jewish history as well.

During the seventy years of exile that preceded the Persian triumph, the Jews grew to accept as normal their adjustment to their new home by the rivers of Babylon. The memory of their homeland, the Temple, and Jerusalem was still fresh in their minds, and as the seventy-year deadline declared by the prophets approached, the Jews waited for some sort of Divine signal that their exile was to end. They expected a miraculous development to occur — the hand of God to become clearly visible and lift them miraculously from Babylonia to Jerusalem, as it had once brought them forth from Egypt. But until the actual appearance of such a sign, they were content to build for themselves a new life in the valley of the Tigris and Euphrates. Earlier, the prophet Jeremiah had told them to "build homes and plant vineyards" in their new home, and the Jews complied while still waiting for the Divine appearance of redemption.

Babylonia's final fall and the resultant absorption of the Jews into Persian domination and society became the harbingers of this expected Divine signal. For the Persians immediately became involved with their "Jewish problem." The story of Purim and its description of the official attempt at Jewish genocide illustrates one aspect of Jewry's existence under Persian rule. However, the roles of Mordechai, Daniel and Nechemiah as powerful leaders and influential advisers in the Persian government highlight another facet of the selfsame Jewish life.

The influence of highly placed Jews in Persian society would provide the opportunity for the Jews' return to their homeland.

A Hostile Welcome

Cyrus

 GREAT PERSIAN KING, identified in the book of *Ezra*[1] as Cyrus,[2] arose and proclaimed: "Anyone among you from [God's] entire people — may his God be with him — let him go up to Jerusalem, which is in Judah; let him build the Temple of God, Lord of Israel — He is the God! — which is in Jerusalem."[3]

The return of the Jews to Jerusalem and Judah occurred gradually and in stages. The first wave of return, immediately after Cyrus' proclamation,[4] was small in numbers and in power. A second, larger group led by the aristocrat and leader Zerubavel,[5] composed of 42,360 adult males plus their wives and families and 7,337 servants, arrived soon thereafter in Jerusalem and began the actual work of rebuilding the city and the Temple. This group met determined opposition from the local peoples of the land who had supplanted the Jews after they were swept away into Babylonian captivity.

Opposition to the returning Jews also came from the small band of their correligionists who had remained in Israel during the time most of their brethren were in Babylonia. These disgruntled Jews,

---

1. *Ezra* 1:1.

2. Secular historians identify this Cyrus with the Persian emperor Cyrus the Great. Due to the difficulties in the exact dating of these events, alluded to in the preface, it is nearly impossible to identify with certainty the times and true identities of the Persian emperors mentioned in the Bible. For an attempt to decipher the mystery of the Persian emperors see "Who Was the Real Akhashverosh?" by Shelomoh Danziger, *The Jewish Observer*, Vol. 9 No.1, and *Jewish Action,* Vol. 51, No. 4, *Letters to the Editor.*

3. *Ezra* 1:3.

4. According to the traditional Jewish system of dating, this would have been in the year 371 B.C.E.

5. From the book of *Ezra,* Zerubavel emerges as a distinct personality — a leader of the Exile, a direct descendant of the royal house of David, apparently born in Babylon. However, an opinion in the Talmud (*Sanhedrin* 38a) identifies him as Nechemiah. Some rabbinical scholars suggest that the Talmud's reference is not to the famous Nechemiah but to a lesser-known person by that name (see *Daas Sofrim* on the book of *Nechemia* by Rabbi Chaim Rabinowitz), or that the famous Nechemiah was also called *Zerubavel,* which had become a title of honor.

mainly poverty-stricken and uneducated, resented the power and influence and apparent wealth of their newly arrived brothers.

The main opposition to the newly arrived Babylonian Jews came, however, from a group of people who, after the earlier destruction of the northern kingdom of Israel, had settled in the country and soon converted to Judaism in response to a plague of rampaging lions that decimated them.[6] Living in the area of the former capital of Israel, Shomron, they were called "Shomronim," or Samaritans.[7] Their animus toward the returning Jews was obvious and also violent. Aside from Samaritans, there also were various tribes of Arabs, Idumeans, Assyrians and Babylonians who had settled in the country and certainly were less than hospitable to the returning former masters of the land. All of these groups combined to oppose the attempt of the returning Jews to rebuild their nation, their capital, their Temple.

A section of the Wall of Jerusalem from the early 2nd Temple period

Rebuilding of the Temple is Halted

NEVERTHELESS, THE WORK of rebuilding the city's ruins and the Temple began. Accompanying Zerubavel as a leader of the new government was Yehoshua ben Yehotzadak, who was appointed by the prophet Zechariah as the High Priest of Israel and the custodian of the Temple, still under construction.[8]

Joining Zechariah in providing the necessary spiritual and idealistic guidance and encouragement to the harassed and sometimes downcast Jewish community were the last prophets of Israel, Chaggai and Malachi.[9] These three last prophets of Israel established the phys-

---

6. See *Pirkei D'Rabbi Eliezer*, Section 38.

7. In Talmudic times they were known by the appellation *Cuthim*.

8. See *Zechariah,* Chapter 3, for the prophetic vision involved in the appointment of Yehoshua.

9. While one opinion in the Talmud (*Megillah* 15a) considers Malachi a distinct prophet, others say "Malachi" (which translates "My messenger") was actually either Mordechai or Ezra. In any event, the Talmud (*Bava Basra* 14b) states definitively that Malachi was the last of the prophets, closing the era of prophecy.

The tomb of Cyrus

ical demarcation lines for the location of the altar, the Holy of Holies and the other sacred areas of the Temple. Under their instructions and guidance, the service of sacrifices resumed and the altar was consecrated and placed in use long before the actual Temple building itself was completed.

The work on the Temple proceeded slowly, hampered by a paucity of laborers and funds and an absence of tenacity on the part of the returning Jews. The neighboring Samaritans at first attempted to ally themselves with the Jews in the restoration of the Temple, but the Jews, suspicious of the true motives of the Samaritans, rebuffed them.

The Samaritans, smarting from their exclusion, then turned into bitter foes of the Jews and opposed the Temple-building project. They sent a delegation to King Cyrus demanding that he revoke the permission granted to rebuild the Temple. They raised the bugaboo of "dual loyalty," accusing the Jews of plotting against Persian rule in the Land of Israel and of shortchanging Cyrus on taxes owed.

Many officials of Cyrus' court were anti-Jewish, and the Samaritans' accusations fell on fertile ground. Cyrus succumbed to the pressures of his court and revoked his permission for the project. The work stopped forthwith, and the project seemed doomed to permanent abandon.

In the Wake of Purim

YRUS DIED SOON THEREAFTER and, in the ensuing chaos of succession, an army coup placed Ahasuerus on the throne of Persia. It was during his reign that the famous events of Purim occurred.[10] Ahasuerus' chief minister, Haman, attempted to annihilate all of the Jews in the Persian empire, and only the Divinely inspired, miraculously arranged

---
10. Jewish tradition places the events of Purim at c. 368 B.C.E., as mentioned above.

4 □ ECHOES OF GLORY

An illuminated Megillah from the 17th century

intervention of Esther and Mordechai averted the disaster.

The event left a traumatic scar on the Jewish psyche. Seemingly foiled in their attempt to rebuild their national home and Temple, terrorized by the close call of barely escaping Haman and his cohorts, the Jewish world, after the initial exhilaration of deliverance from Haman, slowly became a sad and depressed one. Many Jews despaired of their national and religious future. Increasing numbers, both in the Land of Israel and in Babylonia and Persia, assimilated and intermarried.

Ironically, in stark contrast to the negative attitude of such Jews was the positive attitude towards Judaism held by many non-Jews of

Depiction of scenes in the Purim story from the 3rd-century synagogue in Dura Europos, a city on the Euphrates. The synagogue was discovered in 1932 in an excellent state of preseveration.

THE BEAUTY OF JAPHETH AND THE TENTS OF SHEM

Going Home □ 5

the time. Beginning in the fourth century before the Common Era and continuing for the next millenium, a significant and constant number of non-Jews converted to Judaism and provided a necessary infusion of numbers, talent and devotion to Jewish society.[11] However, the Jewish world needed not only more Jews, but, just as importantly, a leader who would inspire and ennoble it, who would grant it vision and self-confidence and who would restore to it its diminishing heritage of Torah and destiny. Such a man now arose in Israel. His name was Ezra.

Ezra

ITTLE IS KNOWN TO US regarding Ezra's personal life.[12] He was a *kohen* — a member of the priestly family descended from Aaron. He was a *sofer,* a scribe, and a great scholar. In any event, Ezra's personal life would be subsumed totally in his gigantic public achievements. Jewish tradition accords him a place of honor equal to that of Moses[13] and Aaron.[14] He was one of those rare personalities who combined within themselves the ability to be both the religious and the temporal leader of Israel at the very same time. He possessed unbending will, skillful traits of diplomacy and government and a clear view of the realities and necessities of the Jewish situation in the Land of Israel.

Ezra also was the greatest Torah scholar of his time and the conduit to later generations of all the traditions of Torah and Israel. He foresaw that the survival of Israel, whether in the old-new homeland or in exile, was heavily dependent upon the Jews' understanding of

---

11. I will point out numerous times in later chapters of this book how, during the period of the Second Commonwealth and for a number of centuries thereafter, converts to Judaism and/or their descendants played vital leadership roles in the Jewish community and mightily contributed to the advancement of Torah study and observance of tradition amongst the Jewish people.

12. As noted above (note 9), some identify Ezra as the prophet Malachi, about whose life even less is known.

13. "The Torah could have been given to Israel through Ezra, if not that Moses preceded him" (Talmud, *Sanhedrin* 21b).

14. "Even if Aaron had been alive then, Ezra would have been greater than he in his time" (*Midrash Rabbah, Koheles* 1:4).

and loyalty to the Oral Law.[15]

With the end of the period of prophecy in Jewish life, the masses of Israel were no longer able to rely on the prophets for moral and traditional guidance. Ezra proclaimed that only by making the masses of Israel understand the continuing imperative of the Oral Law's supremacy in governing Jewish practice and values, even in the absence of prophecy, would the Jewish people retain their spiritual creativity and be able to contend effectively with the foreign cultures now swirling around them. By his teachings and public statements Ezra became the main historical catalyst in effectuating this appreciation of the ongoing supremacy of the Oral Law in post-exilic Jewish life.

The Second Temple

IN ABOUT 353 B.C.E., the Jews in Jerusalem, goaded into action by the challenge of the prophets to build the Temple even without royal permission,[16] renewed the interrupted work on the Temple. But in turn, the Samaritans and the other gentile tribes also renewed their activities opposing the building work, subverting it physically and politically. Nevertheless, the king of the Persians, Darius,[17] his regent and many of his courtiers, under the influence of Mordechai and other leading Jews,

---

15. The Oral Law (*Torah She'b'al Peh*) is the interpretation of the Bible, the explanation of the commandments and the actual rituals of Judaism that God transmitted to Moses at Sinai. Moses in turn taught this law to his generation and to Joshua, who transmitted it to later generations. This law was not written as a book or firmly codified, but rather remained as a vital and creative study that was taught, analyzed through debate and transmitted orally. However, at the end of the second century C.E., the process of transforming the Oral Law into a written code began with the editing of the Mishnah. This writing process continued for centuries, culminating in the final edition of the Talmud produced in Babylonia in the sixth century C.E. The Oral Law has always been the basic guide for traditional Jewish religious life. See the later chapters in this book describing the Mishnah and Talmud for a discussion as to how and why the Oral Law eventually became a written law.

16. See *Chaggai* 2:4.

17. Jewish tradition identifies this Darius as the son of Ahasuerus through Esther, which made him halachically Jewish. He was very young at the time and his regent, Artchashashta (Artaxerxes), controlled most of the power at court. Apparently, Artchashashta's favorable disposition toward the Jews was also due to both personal and political considerations. In any event, an official climate of benevolence towards the Jews in Jerusalem prevailed among the ruling circles of Persia at this time.

Nechemiah and Darius. Interestingly, the caption in the picture incorrectly identifies Nechemiah as Ezra.

were now much more favorably disposed towards the Jews than were their predecessors. The work therefore proceeded apace, and the Persian government even provided material aid for the project.

In about 350 B.C.E., the Temple building was completed and dedicated. Although the Second Temple was not originally as imposing physically or spiritually as the Temple of Solomon,[18] its completion was a major moment in Jewish history. The words of the prophets of Israel were fulfilled, and Jerusalem again became the center of the Jewish world.

Ezra had not joined the original group of Jews who returned to Jerusalem immediately after Cyrus' proclamation. He remained behind until after the Second Temple was completed. The primary disciple of Baruch ben Neriyah (who, in turn, had been the secretary and primary disciple of the prophet Jeremiah), Ezra did not leave Babylonia as long as Baruch was yet alive there.[19]

Ezra also worried about the fate of the Jewish community in Babylonia if all of its spiritual leaders would leave for Jerusalem. Who would safeguard the integrity of the Jewish community in Babylonia? He therefore "purified" the Babylonian Jewish community by sifting out all the lesser pedigreed elements and, ironically, bringing those elements with him when he finally arrived in Jerusalem.[20]

Through his efforts, Babylonian Jewry was left whole, strong and without problems of questionable Jewish identities and pedigrees. It therefore also retained a strong sense of self-worth and, throughout its long history, Babylonian Jewry felt itself to be the equal, if not the superior, of any other segment of world Jewry, including the Jewish state existing in the Land of Israel. Thus, Ezra's protective care and vision for Babylonian Jewry was vindicated, though sometimes the Babylonian Jewish Community overestimated its true importance in the Jewish world.

---

18. According to the Talmud (*Sotah* 48b) and other rabbinic sources, many of the miraculous and historic artifacts and qualities of the Temple of Solomon were not present in the Second Temple.
19. Talmud, *Megillah* 16b.
20. See Talmud, *Kiddushin* 69b and *Bava Basra* 15a.

Wall picture from a synagogue built in Babylonia about 245 C.E. Depicted are the Holy Temple, its implements, Aaron the Hight Priest, and sacrificial animals.

Building a New Community

HEN EZRA DID FINALLY EMIGRATE from Babylonia to Jerusalem, soon after the building of the Second Temple, he brought with him 1,496 chosen men, all fit for leadership roles, and their families. Ezra also persuaded, almost coerced, thirty-eight Levites, their families and their 220 Jewish servants with their families as well, to accompany him to Jerusalem. The Levites' presence was essential for the normal operation of the Temple services, and Ezra was angered by the refusal of the vast majority of the Levites to enthusiastically and voluntarily join the movement of returning to Zion and building the Second Commonwealth. He therefore curtailed some of their previous traditional privileges.[21]

Ezra had official fiat from the Persian authorities to take charge of the social and governmental affairs of the small Jewish community in the Land of Israel. He was not granted any police powers, nor did he have the necessary armed forces to protect the Jewish community from its surrounding enemies; but he did have tremendous force of personality and an undimmed sense of eternal mission. He sensed the opportunity for redemption that the return of Jews to

---

21. The most severe decree that Ezra issued regarding the Levites was the removal of their monopoly on receiving the *maaser* (tithe) on agricultural produce. During the time of the Second Temple, farmers were allowed to pay this tithe to *Kohanim* — the Levite priests descended from Aaron — if they so desired, and not exclusively to Levites, as was the case in First Temple times.

Jerusalem afforded, and he acted boldly to strengthen the fledgling Jewish entity in the Holy Land.

Ezra found Jewish social and religious life in Jerusalem in shambles. The markets of Jerusalem, open and operating on the Sabbath, weakened the Sabbath spirit of the holy city. The walls of the city were in ruins and the Jewish inhabitants were fair game for constant marauding raids by the inimical tribes that surrounded them. The knowledge and study of Torah was mainly ignored; not all Jewish males were circumcised; and intermarriage with non-Jewish women had become socially acceptable, apparently even reaching into the families of some of the religious leaders of the people.[22]

The Jewish community in Jerusalem, in spite of the new Temple standing in its midst, was on the verge of assimilation and self-destruction. The Jews did not feel Jewish pride. Even the Temple itself bore witness to their dependence on the good graces of the Persian king. The main eastern gate to the Temple, by royal Persian order, carried an engraving of the Persian city of Shushan over its arch, and was known throughout the time of the Second Temple as the Gate of Shushan.[23] The mood of the populace was apathetic and depressed. Yet, somehow, Ezra rallied the people to his banner and declared and enforced the supremacy of Torah in their public and private lives.[24]

His achievement of revitalizing Jewish life in Jerusalem in the years immediately following the building of the Second Temple was nothing short of miraculous. It ranks as one of the greatest individual accomplishments in all Jewish history.

Nechemiah

EZRA DID NOT REDRESS the situation in Jerusalem all by himself. His companion in leadership was a powerful and very wealthy nobleman, a Jewish courtier, intimate friend and cupbearer of the Persian king, Darius. His

---

22. See *Zechariah* (3:3) and the comments of Rashi and Targum on that verse, which indicate that the women involved in these instances were converts to Judaism and not really non-Jews. See also *Ezra* (10:18), where the verse describes these women as gentiles.

23. See Talmud, *Menachos* 98a, and the commentary of Rashi thereon.

24. See Talmud, *Bava Kamma* 82a, for ten major decrees in Jewish social and religious life instituted by Ezra.

name was Nechemiah.[25]

Attempting to enlist the king's permission and aid to reinforce the Jewish community in Jerusalem at the time of Ezra's arrival, Nechemiah was originally rebuffed by Darius. Nechemiah persisted, and eventually the king relented, granting him the right of police power. Even more importantly, Nechemiah was permitted to bring weapons and contingents of armed men with him when he arrived in Jerusalem in about 348 B.C.E. He entered the city secretly, bent on taking careful assessment of the situation and, together with Ezra, planned the program that would first provide physical security to the inhabitants of Jerusalem and then address the deteriorating spiritual and moral climate of the society.

With one hand on the sword and the other one on the brick trowel — literally — Nechemiah's men rebuilt the protective city walls of Jerusalem, repulsed the armed attacks of the Samaritans and others on the builders and restored a sense of order and security to everyday life in Jerusalem and Judah.

Darius

Nechemiah also took a firm stance within the Jewish community, eventually dominating all Jewish internal organization in the new nation. Such strong personality and firm leadership naturally earned Nechemiah less than universal approbation.[26] But he persevered and made a mighty difference in the story of the founding of the Second Commonwealth.

Persian Tolerance

HE ATTITUDE OF the Persian government towards the efforts of Ezra and Nechemiah to rebuild Jerusalem and the Jewish people was crucial. The policy of the Persian kings, from Cyrus to the last Darius, was generally one of religious tolerance and embracing of foreign cultures and beliefs. The approval of Haman's attempt to destroy the Jews was an aberration, in direct opposition to Persia's traditional policy of multicultural tolerance. This policy was enunciated in the book of *Esther,* where it was decreed that "each man shall rule in his own

---

25. See note 5, above.
26. See Talmud, *Sanhedrin* 103b.

home and speak the language of his people" (*Esther* 1:22).[27]

The Persians normally were not interested in building a "melting pot" empire. They saw themselves as rulers of a vast and universal empire that would politically and economically unite the world under their hegemony, yet allow individuals freedom of person and belief, and enable cultures to maintain their own societal norms. In this, they presaged many important ideas of the modern, democratic world in a fashion perhaps much more vital than their Grecian successors.

In order to retain control of each of its territories, the Persian empire's policy of tolerance and conciliation forced it to place its major reliance and trust in a strong priesthood in each territory, which represented the beliefs and culture of the local people, rather than in a strong territorial government, which might develop its own nationalistic goals and perhaps eventually rebel against Persian temporal rule. Thus was it in Egypt, where the Persians strengthened the local priesthood, and so would it be in Jerusalem: Persia supported Ezra and Nechemiah — who were primarily concerned with religious and cultural goals such as rebuilding the Temple — over the Samaritans and other tribes who, while easily assimilating into Persian culture, would nevertheless possibly retain dangerously strong nationalistic and territorial ambitions.

The Persian religion itself, in the time of Cyrus and Darius, was based upon the doctrine of Zoroaster, centered around the belief in a chief national god, Ahurmazda, who granted the Persians dominion "over this earth afar, over many peoples and tongues." This benign "master race" theory lay at the heart of Persian beliefs and attitudes.

Charitably, Ahurmazda accommodated other lesser deities, and the Persians imitated their god. They behaved humanely towards subject peoples, and their policy was to include local populations in their scheme of empire rather than to eliminate them.

All of the subjugated peoples of the Persian empire were liable for military service[28] and taxes upon their wealth, property and per-

---

27. Ironically, this reassertion of the traditional Persian policy of tolerance was made by Haman in the very document calling for the annihilation of the Jews.

28. The existence of a Jewish troop of soldiers in the service of the Persian king is recorded for us in the famous *Elephantine papyrii*. This collection of messages sent by Jewish soldiers stationed on the upper Nile River near the area of the current Aswan

son and, in turn, they could all rise to high positions in the empire's administration and army. Many also received grants of land and limited sovereignty from the Persian king.

The Persians had in their culture the concept of *noblesse oblige,* and thus, as did the British in later times, they saw in their imperial role the responsibility to promote effective administration, technology and civilization amongst backward peoples. The Persians constructed a great canal for sailing directly from Persian ports and the Indian Ocean to Africa and the Mediterranean, presaging again a modern idea, if not presaging the exact route, of the current Suez Canal.

As is natural in human affairs, the Persian society contained its fair share of xenophobia and religious fanaticism. However, after the events now commemorated on Purim, the Jews, though still inwardly wary and vaguely tense, outwardly did not feel themselves especially endangered under Persian rule, and there was no effort by the Jews in Judah and Jerusalem to free themselves from that rule. On the contrary, the Persian presence seemed to guarantee them free religious expression, the safety of the Temple in Jerusalem, and economic and social opportunities in building their new commonwealth.

The "Great Assembly"

EZRA ALSO ESTABLISHED a great governing authority that left an eternal imprint on Jewish life. He convened a "great assembly" of leading scholars and activists, including the prophets Chaggai, Zechariah and Malachi, and the scholars Mordechai, Yehoshua the High Priest, Nechemiah and even-

---

Dam includes requests from the soldiers to the priests of the Temple in Jerusalem to instruct them in ritual matters, to identify the correct calendar dates for the holy days, and to help strengthen them in their attempts to remain observant Jews. Numerous scholarly studies have been published over many decades regarding these fascinating ancient letters that have survived until our time and provide us a peek through the window of antiquity. The definitive work on this subject, in my opinion, is *Archives from Elephantine* by Bezalel Porten (Berkley, 1958). For an interesting short article on the matter, see "Of Ancient Mariners and Far-Flung Scribes" by Abraham Rabinovich, *Scopus Magazine*, Vol. 43 (1993-94), p. 24.

tually Shimon HaTzaddik (the Righteous).[29] These "Men of the Great Assembly" (*Anshay Knesses HaGedolah*) originally numbered 120[30] and were viewed as the unofficial government of Judah and of all Jews.

They promulgated societal laws, instituted ritual, established the basic order of prayer in Judaism, completed, sealed and canonized the Bible,[31] changed the script of basic Hebrew,[32] and — most importantly — served as the main conduit for the transmission of the Oral Law and the traditions of Sinai to the renascent nation. Many of the decisions of this group are recorded for us in the Talmud, where they are usually referred to as "ordinances of Ezra." Many of these ordinances still live in the collective memory, life-style and customs of the people of Israel today.

The Great Assembly's greatest contribution to the collective Jewish soul was the revitalizing of love of Torah within Israel. This love of Torah and its scholars and scholarship became the hallmark of Jewish life in the Second Commonwealth and thereafter. It created the climate that allowed for the later accomplishments of the Tannaim[33] and Amoraim[34] and for the creation of the Mishnah and Talmud. Only love of Torah — not merely knowledge of its contents, but unconditional and deep-felt commitment — could have sustained Israel in its long history of adversity. The Jewish

---

29. This great and holy man, who eventually served as the High Priest in the Temple, was "from the remnants of the Men of the Great Assembly." Most scholars interpret this phrase, which appears in the opening Mishnah of *Avos*, as meaning that Shimon was one of the last group of members of the 120 Men of the Great Assembly, which somehow disbanded at the time of Alexander the Great. However, Rabbi Reuven Margolies, in his seminal work *Yesod HaMishnah V'Arichasa* (Mosaad Harav Kook, Tel Aviv, 1956), suggests that there were never any replacements for the original 120 members and that therefore, due to continuing attrition over time, Shimon was the sole survivor of the original group of 120.

30. The present-day Israeli parliament, called *Knesset* (Assembly), chose to be comprised of 120 members, in imitation of the original Great *Knesset*.

31. Some of the books of the Bible were contested as to their canonization, notably the books of *Ezekiel* and *Koheles*. In any event, some well-known books, such as *Proverbs of Ben Sira*, attributed in medieval Jewish sources to a descendant of the prophet Jeremiah, were criticized and excluded. (*Sanhedrin* 100b discusses the work's dubious value.) However, *Proverbs of Ben Sira* remained very popular and well known amongst the Jews of Second Commonwealth times, and is even quoted in the Talmud a number of times. It is now found in its entirety in the Hebrew Apocrypha.

32. For a thorough and most scholarly review of the history of the different types of Hebrew alphabets, discussing which type was used in the original Torah of Moses, see *Torah Sheleimah*, edited by Rabbi Menachem M. Kasher, Vol. 29, Second Edition, Jerusalem, 1992 pp. 1-234.

debt to the Men of the Great Assembly therefore is really inestimable, for this group of sages, scholars and strong leaders provided the necessary moral and religious leadership for the Jewish story.

They realized that the phenomenon of prophecy, which had been the traditional means of emphasizing the morality and social justice of Jewish law, was ending. The Men of the Great Assembly were able to fully utilize the knowledge and authority of the legal rules of the Oral Law to provide the moral guiding force of Judaism.[35] It was this successful transmission of the source of Jewish moral force that guaranteed the development and survival of Jewish society. For civilizations are built and maintained not by might alone, but more importantly, by ideas and ideals.

The ideas and ideals implanted in the Jewish people by the Men of the Great Assembly have stood the test of time and circumstance. Unlike many other later idea-men in Western civilization, the Men of the Great Assembly have never become outdated and irrelevant. They remain instead a beacon of light whose decisions, ordinances and ideas are the basis of all thought and conduct in later Jewish life.

A manuscript of the first mishnah of Avos. This mishnah outlines the transmission of Torah from Moses to the Anshei Knesses HaGedolah

A Vital Partnership

THE ATTITUDE AND VALUE SYSTEM of the Men of the Great Assembly is succinctly recorded in the first chapter of *Avos* (*Ethics of the Fathers*) in the Mishnah. Their legacy to Israel was: "Be deliberate in judgment, create

---

33. The scholars of the Mishnah.
34. The scholars of the Gemara (Talmud).
35. Part of their method was, of course, propagating the words of the prophets themselves.

many, many students of Torah, and build a protective fence around the Torah." Fairness, strengthening public confidence in the rule of law and courts, universal education and emphasis on Torah scholarship, and the addition of protective rules and customs to guarantee the preservation of Torah observance were the tools to be employed in building the new Jewish world. These tools have remained efficient and valuable throughout all of Jewish life and history.

Nechemiah traveled back to Persia and then returned once more to the land of Judah. After another number of years, Nechemiah departed Judah to return to Darius' service in Persia, there to die far from his beloved Jerusalem.

Before Nechemiah departed, however, he and Ezra united to radically improve the spiritual lot of the Jews in the Holy Land. They forced the closure of the markets on the Sabbath, proclaimed the supremacy of Torah and tradition over all other factors in Jewish life, pushed to eliminate every vestige of paganism and pagan practices from Israel's midst, reintroduced the Hebrew language as the *lingua franca* of Israel, eliminating the Babylonian and Persian (though not Aramaic) tongues, and forced the dissolution of marriages with non-Jewish women throughout Judah.

In a great public ceremony in Jerusalem, they renewed the covenant of Israel and Torah first forged by Moses and Israel at Sinai. This covenant of Ezra and Nechemiah, known in its time as the *bris amanah*,[36] committed Israel to Torah study, Sabbath observance, moral behavior, commercial probity, and family integrity. All of this was accomplished against great opposition, even within the Jewish community itself.[37] But Ezra and Nechemiah never wavered.

Ezra and Nechemiah revitalized the spirit of the Jews, giving them the great gift of faith and spiritual purpose. This strengthened attitude of loyalty to Torah and Jewish life would remain the hallmark of most of the Jews living in the Land of Israel throughout the Second Temple period. It is impossible to imagine the people of Israel, Jewish survival and Torah life without recalling these two great men.

---

36. Literally, "covenant of trust."

37. Read the book of *Nechemiah* and you will be impressed by the ferocity and tenacity of Jewish opposition to Nechemiah and his policies.

2

Greece and Hellenism

(330 B.C.E.-150 B.C.E.)

AFTER THE PASSING OF EZRA, Nechemiah and Yehoshua the High Priest, the leadership of the Commonwealth of Judah devolved upon Shimon *HaTzaddik* (The Righteous). This great personality served in a dual position, that of High Priest and of the temporal leader of the Jews. He thus set a precedent, followed rigorously by the Hasmoneans two centuries later, of concentrating all leadership power in the hands of one person. This did not always yield sanguine results. However, in the hands of someone of the moral stature of Shimon *HaTzaddik,* this power of all-inclusive leadership was executed wisely, fairly and effectively.

During Shimon *HaTzaddik's* tenure, the population and economy of Judah grew greatly.[1] Prosperity and a sense of well-being flourished in the small Jewish nation, and the country seemed secure and tranquil under the benevolent and loose control of the Persian Empire. However, the future, even the immediate one, is rarely as it appears in the present, and great and profound changes were about to sweep the entire Mediterranean basin and Asia Minor, materially changing Jewish life and history as well. The changes were to come from the emerging empire of Greece.

---

1. The population of Jerusalem alone reached 120,000 during the reign of Shimon *HaTzaddik*. The overall population of all Judah at that time was estimated at 350,000. See Josephus in *Contra Apion* 1:197. Also see Paul Johnson, *A History of the Jews,* (Harper & Row), 1987 p. 97.

THE GREEK CITY-STATES

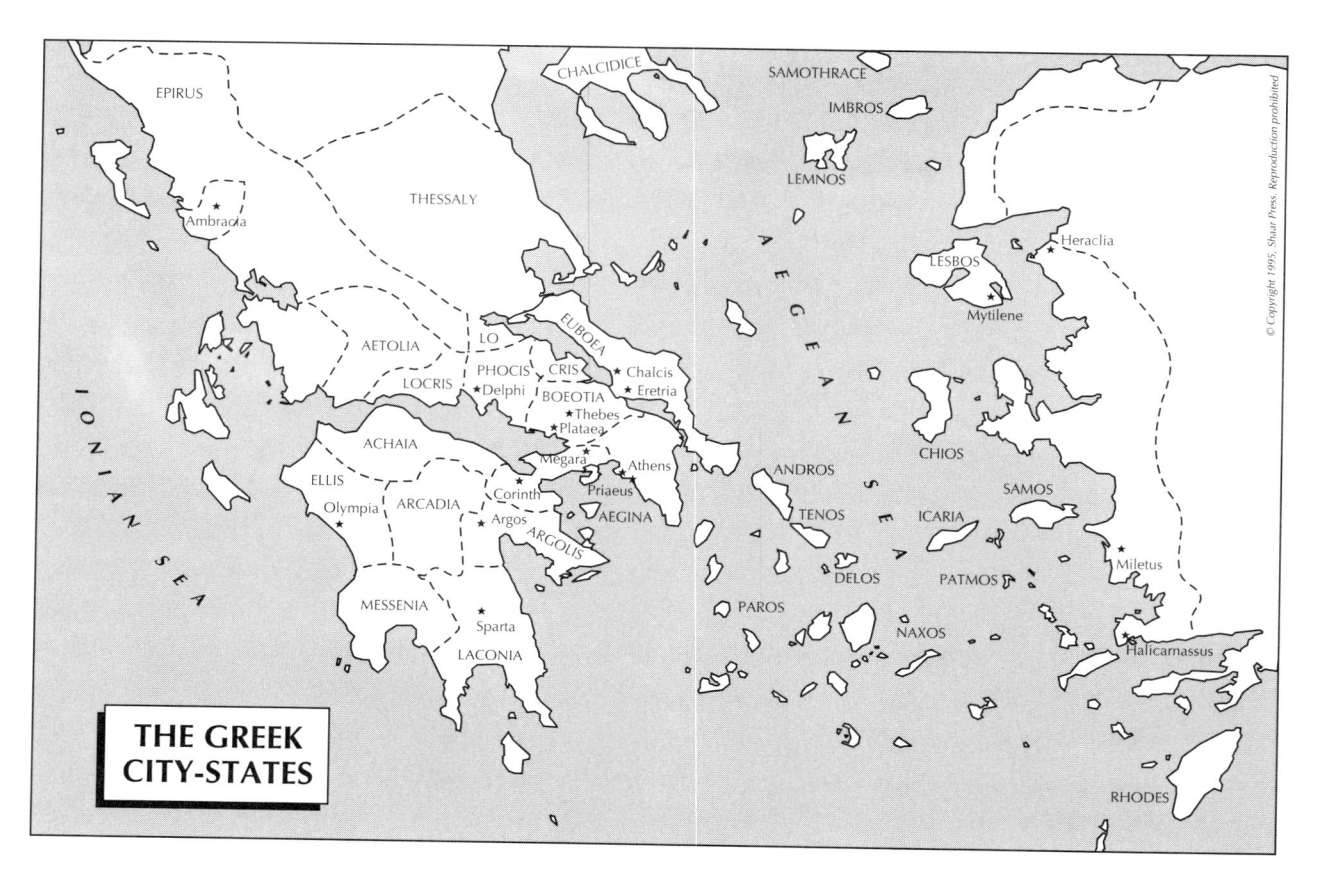

The Beginning of Greek Dominance

FOR MANY CENTURIES, Greece had remained a diffused and almost self-destructive entity. City-states (poleis), such as Thebes, Athens and Sparta, had emerged from the different Greek tribes and groups, and they were constantly at war with one another. Their early histories were replete with blood, barbarity and inhumanity. Yet, from their midst also emerged great advances in culture, technology and political thought.

The Greeks grew to be committed to the advancement of art, architecture, effective government, literature, drama and philosophy. They also established colonies throughout the ancient world, their new cities stretching from Sicily to Syria, and from Libya to the shores of the Black Sea. As would be the case in nineteenth- and twentieth-century imperialist civilization, one culture could somehow permit inhumanity and unspeakable barbarism to coexist with great advances in technology, science and the arts. In fact, one of the identifying features of Greek civilization would be this strange combination of terrible cruelty on one hand with exquisite beauty, creativity and talent on the other.

By the year 337 B.C.E. the constantly feuding Greek city-states began to coalesce under the strong rule of Philip of Macedon. By conquest, diplomacy and force of personality, Philip was successful in uniting Greek's small and weak city-states into a strong national entity and a powerful military presence. This prepared Philip to embark upon a more ambitious program. He now dreamt of empire and world dominion, of historic immortality and unlimited wealth, of overcoming the Persian Empire, the constant impediment to Greek expansion, and making Greece the center of the world. However, in 336 B.C.E.,[2] before any of his grandiose dreams could be realized, Philip was assassinated. He left an heir, a son who would eclipse him and be remembered in history as one of the most formidable conquerors and heroes of the ancient world. The name of this young man was Alexander. He would soon be referred to as "the Great."

Philip of Macedonia

Alexander the Great

ALEXANDER BECAME A MYTHOLOGIZED, larger-than-life figure. The legend of Alexander consists of many fanciful tales of a man combining superhuman courage with supernatural powers, and who experienced precisely accurate omens. Greek legend credited him with making the sea recede before him, taming wild animals by his gaze and words, holding back enormous weights and forces by his herculean strength, and being always able to divine and anticipate the plans and thoughts of his foes. The Talmud, always loath to ascribe supernatural powers to humans, nevertheless reports Alexander's remark that the likes of Shimon *HaTzaddik* appeared to him in dreams, predicting Greek victory before each battle.[3]

Alexander the Great

---

2. We are once again plagued by the problems in dating events of the ancient world. The date of Philip's death and Alexander's ascension to the throne of Macedon given here is in accord with most general history books of our time. According to this system of dating, Alexander was born c. 355 B.C.E. and died in 323 B.C.E. Thus, he would have visited Jerusalem c. 325-4 B.C.E. However, most traditional Jewish history books date his arrival in Jerusalem somewhat later and place his death anywhere between 318 and 313 B.C.E. It is a mystery that is not given to simple solution, and all dates given in this section relating to Alexander are subject to this modifying note.
3. Babylonian Talmud, *Yoma* 69a, *Tamid* 32b.

Tutored in his youth by the great philosopher Aristotle, who remained his private teacher and adviser, Alexander possessed intellectual curiosity and scholarly interests. However, his main goal in life was military conquest. He was a soldier and general for all his short life, constantly engaged in one military enterprise after another. Not surprisingly, he lived a life of dissolution and debauchery that contributed to his early death. He was an alcoholic, a womanizer and a man of violent mood shifts, capable of enormous kindness as well as unbelievable sadism. Yet, he was seen by all of his contemporaries as being "the Great."[4]

Grave of Shimon HaTzaddik

Division of the Greek Empire

IN 333 B.C.E. ALEXANDER AND HIS ARMY crossed into Asia Minor. There, according to legend, Alexander severed the knot that tied the yoke to the King of Gordium's chariot. By so doing, the legend goes, Alexander accepted the burden of the oracle's prediction that whoever did so would become the master of Asia. At Issus, later in the year, Alexander defeated Darius and his Persian army. Darius escaped to fight another day, while Alexander turned south to control Phoenicia, Syria, Judah and Egypt.

In 331 B.C.E Alexander once again met and defeated Darius and the Persian army at Gaugamela, and now ruled over the entire vast area of the Persian Empire. However, his restlessness and wanderlust drove him into new campaigns in Afghanastan, the Hindu Kush and the Punjab of India. By now, however, his troops had had enough of war and marching. They mutinied, forcing him to return

---

4. Significantly, however, the Jews in their writings and books never referred to Alexander as the "Great," but as the "Macedonian."

to Babylonia, where he died suddenly in Babylon.

At some time during his conquest of the Persian Empire, Alexander came to Jerusalem. As mentioned earlier, the Talmud relates that out of consideration for Shimon *HaTzaddik*, the High Priest and leader of Judah, Alexander spared Jerusalem and Judah from heavy-handed conquest. The Jewish commonwealth, however, did pledge allegiance to Alexander and agreed to pay permanent tribute and taxes to his coffers. In addition, as a sign of obeisance to Alexander, the Jews of Judah agreed to name after him all their sons born the following year. Thus did the name Alexander (Sender, Sandor) enter the list of "Jewish" names.

Alexander with Shimon HaTzaddik

Alexander, like most absolute monarchs, never faced his mortality. Thus, no realistic line of succession emerged during his lifetime. The reality of his youth further precluded his entertaining morbid thoughts of the inevitable. Thus, Alexander's unexpected death threw his empire into turmoil and war, with his kin and generals struggling for power and succession. No one person arose who had the talent, force of personality and stature of Alexander to rule the empire of the Greeks single-handedly. Thus, that empire broke into various warring factions.

By about the year 290 B.C.E., three major kingdoms had developed, each headed by one of Alexander's generals. These kingdoms would rule the Mediterranean world until their own eventual fall to Rome. The nucleus of Alexander's empire, Greece and Macedonia itself, was controlled by Antigonus Gonatas. Egypt and Libya, as well as some of the Greek islands and colonies in Asia Minor, became the kingdom of Ptolemy Soter. Finally, Syria, Babylonia and parts of Turkey were ruled by Seleucus. In the year 312 B.C.E., Seleucus and Ptolemy combined to defeat Antigonus and his son Demetrius in battle near Gaza in Judah, thereby thwarting their attempt for sole control of Alexander's empire. Seleucus then proceeded north to

Seleucus I

Ptolemy I

capture all of Babylonia and establish the Seleucid kingdom. Ptolemy retired south to consolidate his hold over Egypt, and he concentrated his government in the great new Greek city, Alexandria, named for its leader and hero. Within the next twenty years all the pieces of empire had sorted themselves out, and the three dynasties, Ptolemaic, Seleucid and Antigonid, were clearly established and demarcated. Nonetheless, these kingdoms remained antagonistic to each other, and competitiveness and war would long dominate their relations.

The year 312 B.C.E. became a significant one in Jewish life. That year was chosen to be *year one* in a new way of numbering the years of the Jewish calendar[5] — a system called *minyan shtaros* (*the dating of legal documents*). Used frequently in Jewish society during the Second Temple era and for generations thereafter, *minyan shtaros* existed side by side with the system of numbering years by starting from when the reigning monarch began his rule; later in Jewish history, it also paralleled the system of dating years from the time of Creation. In a sense, this new system of dating was the first harbinger of the growing influence the Greeks and their culture were beginning to have on Jewish life. *Minyan shtaros* came to remind the Jews that they could not live isolated from the general world. The Jews, as has been their wont, "judaized" the calendar of *minyan shtaros* and made it a natural part of Jewish life. However, they were always aware that it was a foreign import into their culture, and over the long exile of Israel they let it eventually fall into almost complete disuse.[6] Nevertheless, it marked the beginning of Hellenism as part of the Jewish story.

---

5. Secularists advance many theories to explain why 312 B.C.E. was chosen to be considered *year one* in a new Jewish dating system. However, the tradition of Israel is that this new system of dating was another form of Jewish appreciation extended to Alexander, in gratitude for his sparing the Temple and the city of Jerusalem around that time. The particular year 312 B.C.E. was chosen as *year one* because it coincided with the millennium of the Exodus from Egypt (1312 B.C.E.).

6. From its beginning over twenty-two centuries ago, the use of *minyan shtaros* by Jews was spotty. From 900 C.E. on, the use of *minyan shtaros* became almost unknown in Ashkenazic society. And though we do find marriage contracts (*kesubos*) amongst Sephardic Jews dated to the year of *minyan shtaros* even in the nineteenth century, today its use even by Sefardim is almost non-existent.

Division of the Commonwealth

THE COMMONWEALTH OF JUDAH lay squarely between the Ptolemaic kingdom of Egypt in the south and the Seleucid kingdom of Syria in the north. The land mass of the Holy Land was the commercial and strategic bridge between Africa and Asia Minor and thus was of vital importance to the two competing kingdoms. Domination of Judah and its highways would give the controlling empire great military and economic advantages. It is therefore not surprising that the competition between the Ptolemaic and Seleucid forces for supremacy in the ancient world would center on their struggle to rule over Jerusalem and Judah.[7] For the next 150 years (until about 165 B.C.E.), this struggle for dominance ravaged the Jewish state, with increasingly detrimental results. The Ptolemys and Seleucids each established their own Jewish groups in Judah who were allied with the goals and cultures of their imperial sponsors. The Jewish Commonwealth, from the time of Alexander's death till the successful revolt of the Hasmoneans in 165 B.C.E., was essentially a vassal state, alternating in its loyalty between Ptolemaic and Seleucid masters. It was also continually riven by disputes and even minor civil wars between the competing Jewish groups, ever interested in proving their devotion to their non-Jewish promoters.

The control over the affairs of the Jews of Judah exercised by the Men of the Great Assembly and Shimon *HaTzaddik* faded after the latter's death, and there now arose two parallel forms of Jewish government in Judah. One was the provisional government, led by Jews whose loyalty and goals were controlled by the agendas of Ptolemy and Seleucus. This power enforced governmental decrees, taxed the Jews and enrolled them as mercenaries in whichever king's army would be in favor at the time. The second government, religious and spiritual in nature and possessing no army, police or taxing authority, was composed of the disciples of the Men of the Great Assembly. They "governed" through education, religious behavior and example. This dichotomy of leadership over Jews living in Judah

---

7. A modern Israeli journalist characterized the State of Israel in the 1980's as being "a good little state in a big bad neighborhood." This description aptly fits the Jewish Commonwealth of Judah after the death of Alexander the Great as well.

THE SELEUCID AND PTOLEMAIC EMPIRES (240 B.C.E.)

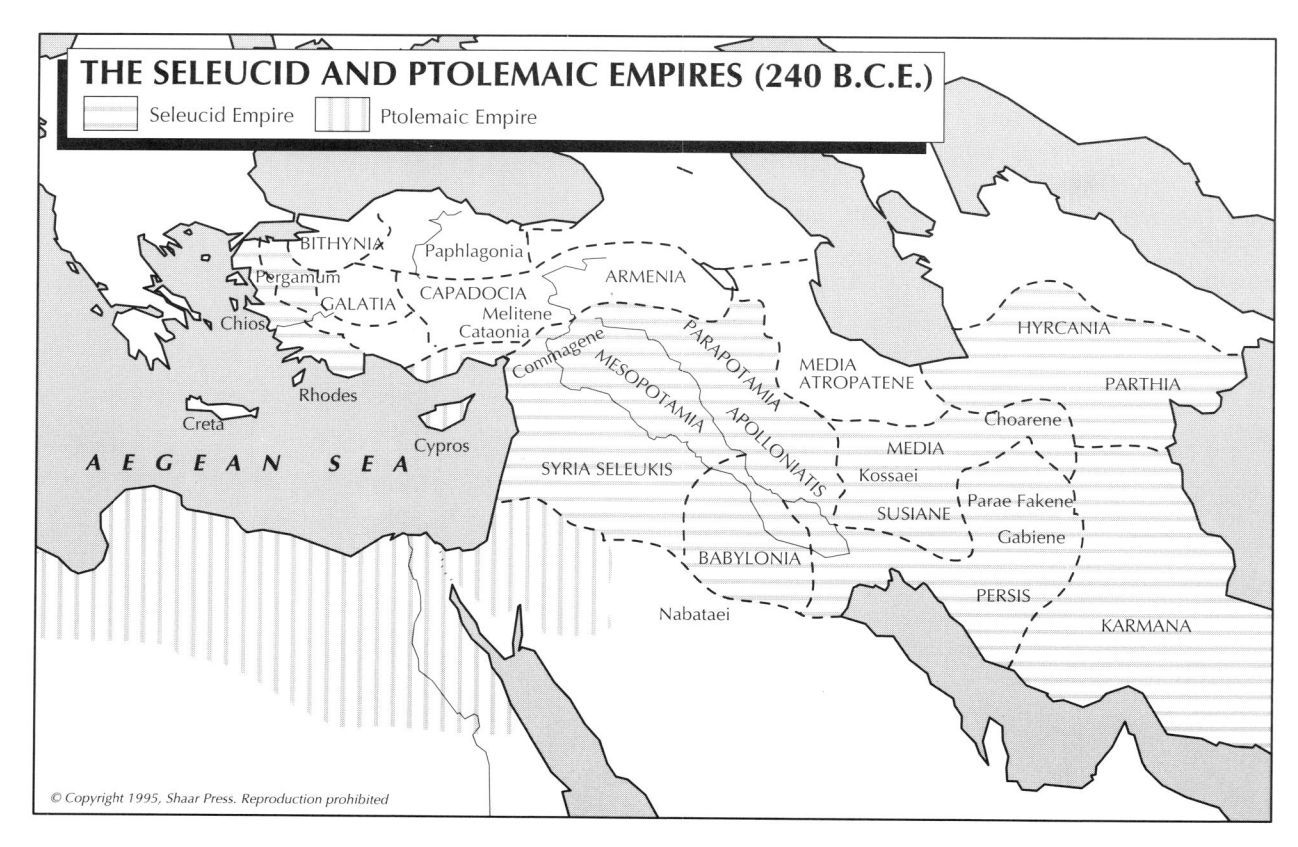

would continue throughout the period of the Second Temple, with only rare and short periods of unified leadership and purpose.

A Corrupting Alliance

THE PTOLEMAIC EMPIRE was dominant in Judah for most of the century following Alexander's death (323 B.C.E.). Ptolemy I (Soter) was a harsh taskmaster over Judah. He exiled many Jews to Egypt, especially to the city of Alexandria, where most of them were initially treated as slaves. Eventually these Jews were able to free themselves through ransom and royal fiat (under the rule of Ptolemy II [Philadelphus], a much gentler soul than his father), and there became famous for their skills as gold and silversmiths, leather and ceramic artisans, weavers and dyers, traders and merchants. Ptolemy I had also drafted thousands of Jews into his army and stationed them over the entire area of his considerable empire. Many of these Jewish soldiers remained in their new localities even after their army service ended, sowing the seeds of the broad Jewish exile that existed even in Greek and Roman times.

Under the rule of Ptolemy II, Jews in Judah became wealthy. They profited greatly from the transit trade between Alexandria and Damascus, and their agricultural produce was in great demand in Ptolemaic Egypt. Jews also became the tax and customs collectors for Ptolemy in Judah. Entire families of Jews became famous (or infamous) due to their tax services to Ptolemy.[8] The tax farmer or broker kept a percentage of the taxes collected as a fee for his work. There was therefore great incentive for ever-increasing rates of taxation. Tax collection unfortunately became synonymous with Jews throughout the Ptolemaic world. This prosperity in Judah led to the formation of a growing upper class whose loyalties lay with their Greek masters rather than with their Jewish brethren. This would inevitably lead to great strains within Jewish society, breeding future discord and violence. The families of the Temple's High Priests, especially, enriched themselves through their fawning service to the Ptolemys. The "ordinary" priests, as well as the masses of Israel and the great Torah scholars, were repelled by the spiritual, monetary and social corruption of the High Priesthood and its extortion of the Temple service. The corruption would eventually lead to this upper class becoming more Greek than Jewish, more pagan than godly.

Coin of Ptolemy I

Translation of the Seventy

PTOLEMY II (PHILADELPHUS), who reigned from 285-246 B.C.E., was a man of peace and culture. Rather than engaging in wars of expansion, he built libraries and schools. A bibliophile of note, Ptolemy II was interested in all cultures and many types of literature. He was therefore determined to translate the Hebrew Bible into Greek, and "invited" seventy Torah scholars to Alexandria to complete this project. The result was the "Translation of the Seventy" — the *Septuagint*. The

---

8. The most well-known Jewish family of tax collectors was that of Yosef ben Tovia. Its members were well known as *B'nei Tovia* and the family name became a pejorative term amongst Jews in Second Temple times. See *HaBais HaSheini B'Gadluso* by Joseph Klausner (Tel Aviv, 1930), p. 5. See also the next chapter in this book, "Twin Hellenism," for details of the careers of Yosef ben Tovia and his heirs.

translators were granted Divine aid in avoiding simplistic, literal translations that would distort the purely monotheistic message of the Torah.[9] Despite the supernatural quality invested in this great work of scholarship, the Rabbis generally disapproved of the project, and the eighth day of Teves, the day of the completion of the Septuagint, was marked on the Jewish calendar as "a day of darkness";[10] for the Septuagint not only taught the non-Jewish world Torah, it also taught the Jews Greek. The "beauty of Yefes," the Greek language, was now permanently enshrined in "the tents of Shem, the homes of the people of Israel."[11] Just as the agreement of the Jews to name their sons Alexander opened the door for Jews to use all other Greek names freely thereafter,[12] so too, the appearance of the Septuagint, authored by great scholars of Torah, allowed Greek to become an accepted language amongst Jews. This legitimization of the Greek language allowed Greek culture and values to enter the Jewish world, not surreptitiously, but rather through the front door. And thus entered the tremendous intellectual and social force of Hellenism.

Hellenism

WHAT WAS HELLENISM? It was a new view of man. Even though the Greeks were pagans, professing a belief in many fearsome and petty gods who toyed with the lives and futures of humans, in reality the Greeks were human-centered. They lived with an inner sense that man somehow was all-powerful and that the gods were basically disinterested in human behavior. The gods were there to be bribed, fooled and sometimes ignored, and clever humans would be able to live their lives without them. Moreover, many of the leading Greeks, such as Aristotle and even Alexander himself, no longer believed in the fantastic stories of the gods or even in their existence. Their worship

---

9. *Megillas Taanis.* See also Talmud, *Soferim* 1:7.
10. *Megillas Taanis.* See also Talmud, *Soferim* 1:7.
11. See *Genesis* 9:27.
12. The rapid spread of Greek names in Judah after Alexander's visit among Hellenistic Jews is seen by the use of names such as Jason, Menelaus and Hyrcanus. Greek names were evidently gaining acceptability, for the main disciple of Shimon *HaTzaddik* retained his Greek name, Antigonus, even after his conversion to Judaism.

was seen only as a unifying national force, while the existence of Zeus, *et al*, was not to be taken literally. (Aristotle believed in an imperfect monotheism and in a universe whose Creator really did not care what happened to individuals or even to humanity as a whole.) Thus, even if belief in the supremacy of the gods and their actual existence had begun to wane amongst the Greek intelligentsia, the service, sacrifices, temples and priests of Greek paganism always remained part of the matrix of Hellenism. This post-pagan view of the centrality of man (which would again dominate human thought in the nineteenth and twentieth centuries — the Modern Era) led to an explosion in the public exhibition of human talents. And the development and showcasing of those talents made Hellenism blindingly attractive to all non-Greeks in the third and second centuries B.C.E.

The Greeks valued literature, drama and poetry. The works of the great Greek poets and authors, such as Homer, Asclepiades, Callimachus, Theocritus, Apollonius and others are still valued by Western culture today. Sophocles, Aeschylus, Euripides, Aristophanes and Menander remain the fathers of modern drama, in tragedy and comedy.

The Greeks loved the sounds of words, the beauty of their juxtaposition and the refinement of imagination inherent in literature. Greek literature reflected Greek life in its accomplishments and failings. It remains our window into the psyche and soul of ancient Greece. The Greeks celebrated human behavior in all of its vagaries, including the most vulgar and debased. They described even their gods in purely human terms, many times most unflatteringly. Whereas the Jews attempted to raise man to godly and holy behavior, the Greeks brought their gods down to the level of the basest human actions and attitudes.[13] This literary attitude of denigrating the gods was one of the core attitudes of Hellenism, and it was one of its more insidious aspects as far as traditional Judaism was concerned, because Hellenistic Jews carried into Jewish life and society this attitude of cynicism, sniping criticism, stubborn disbelief in and

---

13. "Criticism [of the gods] had already begun in the sixth century (B.C.E.) with Xenophanes, who said with approval that 'Homer and Hesiod ascribed to the gods everything that among men is a shame and disgrace: theft, adultery, and deceiving one another.'" See *The Oxford History of Greece and the Hellenistic World* (New York, 1991), p. 325.

Ionic columns

continuing disrespect for the God of Israel and traditional Jewish practices and values.[14] They thereby sparked a continuing *kulturkampf* that lasted for centuries.

In Hellenism, there was no such thing as forbidden love or sexual taboos. It gloried in the wonder, attraction, passion, beauty and accomplishments of the human body. Nudity was common and accepted in the Greek world. The attitude responsible for glorifying the bare human body in sculpture and art also led to a glorification of sports, war and heroic physical exploits.

The curriculum of the "gymnasium," the primary school of Greek education, emphasized military and physical training, and so the curriculum's main product, Greek culture, always had a physical and militaristic bent to it. The Greek maxim "A sound mind in a sound body" was never as benign as it sounds to modern ears. Since Greece was a slave society, life was cheap and physical losers were not easily tolerated.[15]

Not surprisingly, circumcision was considered a mutilation of the "perfection" of the human body. For a Jew to be a true Hellenist, he would be required to undergo the painful correction of his circumcision. The body was holy and perfect, never to be tampered with. The Hellenists always worshipped at the temple of the human body.

The Spread of Greek Culture

HELLENISM BUILT BEAUTIFUL CITIES, with wonderful buildings and institutions to fill them. The aforementioned gymnasium, as well as the stadium, the theater, the odeum, the lyceum and the agora, were the main public places of the Greek city. The buildings showed a magnificence previously unknown in the ancient world. The Doric, Ionic and Corinthian architectural orders, with their stately columns and

---

14. Much of the deprecating and condescending attitude of secular Jewry in our time towards Jewish tradition and its practitioners mirrors the attitudes and behavior of the Hellenistic Jews of Grecian times.

15. The brutal Spartan custom of abandoning weak or deformed infants to die in the woods was also a piece of the Grecian matrix.

the exquisite use of marble and stone all combined to form the timeless beauty of classical Greek architecture. The ruins of the Acropolis at Athens, breathtaking even in destruction, and its marble friezes, currently housed in the British Museum in London, testify to the talent, ingenuity and skill of their Greek designers and builders.

Greek cities proliferated throughout the Greek empires. In Judah, the city of Gaza became a prototype for other, smaller Greek cities that began to appear there. These cities contained statues of Zeus, temples to Greek gods, theaters, stadiums and, of course, gymnasiums. They also became the centers of Hellenism within the Jewish society of Judah, and by their mere presence in Judah contributed to the growing trend of Hellenization in the country.

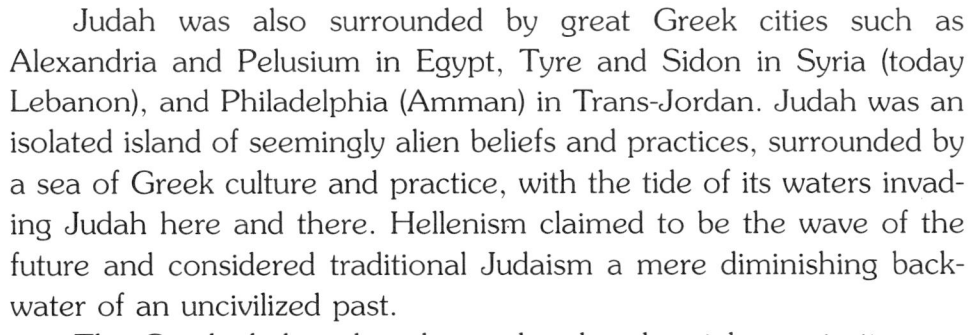

Corinthian columns

Judah was also surrounded by great Greek cities such as Alexandria and Pelusium in Egypt, Tyre and Sidon in Syria (today Lebanon), and Philadelphia (Amman) in Trans-Jordan. Judah was an isolated island of seemingly alien beliefs and practices, surrounded by a sea of Greek culture and practice, with the tide of its waters invading Judah here and there. Hellenism claimed to be the wave of the future and considered traditional Judaism a mere diminishing backwater of an uncivilized past.

The Greeks believed in their cultural and racial superiority over all non-Greeks ("barbarians"). The Greeks utilized this dignified but nevertheless pernicious master-race theory, similar to the belief of their Persian enemies, to justify their political and societal dominance over others.

Even though the notion that Greece is the mother of democratic government is popular and persistent, the truth is that Greek "democracy" was highly selective. The masses never had any voice in government and precious few personal rights. Greece was a slave society,[16] and human respect and compassion for unfortunates, the

---

16. Even though the society of Judah in the era of the Second Temple also permitted slavery, the prohibitions on the exploitation of slaves imposed on that society by the Torah led the Talmud to declare that "one who acquires a slave for one's service in reality has acquired a master over one's self." There is a great difference between a society that lives by a law that tolerates individuals acquiring slaves and then

poor and the disadvantaged was almost unknown. Charity, in a general and personal sense, formed no part of Greek culture, and the Torah's edicts regarding the necessity for charitable and generous behavior in public and private life stood in sharp contrast to the cold practices of Hellenistic life.

Hellenism was a monarchical, autocratic system of government. The kings and rulers of the Greek colonies and dominions were all-powerful. They ruled sometimes wisely, sometimes foolishly, sometimes sadistically, many times by pure whim. But they always ruled solely and absolutely. Because of this absolute power and its attendant aggressive tendencies, all of the Greek rulers after Ptolemy II were constantly engaged in wars, most of which were unnecessary, unproductive and ultimately inconsequential. Nonetheless, war, violence, pillage and mercenary armies became a feature of Hellenistic life, dimming the false sheen of its cultural veneer.[17]

Doric columns

The only way the Greeks allowed strangers to enter their world as their seeming equals was by the public adoption of the ideas and practices of Hellenism. Most of the peoples of the ancient world succumbed and became Hellenized. In Judah the Greeks would meet strong resistance to their culture, and this resistance would be mainly structured in religious terms.

The Development of Philosophy

THE MAJOR INTELLECTUAL thrust of Hellenism lay in its development of the discipline of philosophy. After Aristotle, philosophy was customarily divided into three parts: logic, physics and ethics.[18] Philosophy before

---

strictly governs that master-slave relationship (ancient Judah) and a society that bases its economic and social welfare on unlimited slave labor (ancient Greece, and later ancient Rome). The attitude towards the inherent sanctity of each individual human being and human life generally is one of the main differences between these two societies.

17. The pithy advice of Rabbi Yehudah HaLevi, the twelfth-century poet laureate of the Jewish people, was "Be not seduced by Greek wisdom and knowledge, for it is all flowers but bears no fruit."

18. See *Oxford History of Greece and the Hellenistic World*, p. 426.

Aristotle had also encompassed the knowledge of the natural sciences, such as astronomy, mathematics, anatomy, biology and botany, as well as metaphysics. However, by the time of Plato's death in 347 B.C.E., metaphysics began to separate itself from the realm of philosophers to become "science," and eventually became the almost exclusive pursuit of other scholars. The study of science moved from Athens to Alexandria and flourished there under the patronage of the Ptolemys, whereas the development of the remaining branches of philosophy — logic and ethics — remained centered in their Athenian birthplace.

Aristotle finalized this division between logic and ethics on one hand and physics on the other by his concentration on ethics. Yet, since physics was much more of a speculative science in the ancient world, with little stress given to empiric proofs and strict mathematical calculations and formulae, it sometimes still fitted neatly into the contemplative, esoteric and ingenious world of philosophic thought. Aristotle therefore still posited astronomical and physical theories regarding the universe, its creation and its continuing physical nature and laws. But he made it clear that "the pursuit of scientific knowledge ceased to be the defining mark of the philosopher. Rather, a man's philosophy was something that he lived by, and a philosopher's task was to discover the 'best life,' to teach it, and to live it."[19] Thus, the attainment of an "ethical" life became the highest goal of Hellenistic philosophy, and how to define that "ethical" life became the stuff of the major philosophic debates among the Hellenists.

Aristotle

Three Schools of Thought

THIS DEBATE WAS CONDUCTED under the rules of "logic" that the Greek philosophers, mainly Socrates, Plato and Aristotle, had developed and polished over centuries of philosophic thought, dialogue and contemplation.[20] Eventually a man of Hellenistic philosophy would be characterized (or stereotyped) as an Epicurean, a Stoic or an Academic. All of these schools of philosophy were successors to

---
19. *Ibid.,* p. 421.
20. Discussion, debate and oral and written disputation were the basic methods of refining philosophic thought in ancient Greece.

Aristotelean thought and would eventually mark the intellectual limits of Hellenistic philosophic inquiry.

In vast oversimplification, some elements of these schools are as follows: In Epicurus' philosophy [*hedonism*], all our knowledge is grounded ultimately (and exclusively) on experience and perception [*empiricism*].[21] The Stoic school rejected hedonism and longed for a life of "virtue" and self-discipline, if not self-denial. Rejecting the pure empiricism of Epicurus' system of logic, Stoicism also valued reasoning, deduction, intuition and imagination as acceptable aids to arriving at truths.[22] The Academics were followers of the school of Plato. Their highest goal was self-knowledge; they believed that somehow a world of self-knowing people would also be a world of harmony and human progress, and that such knowledge is not dependent upon any sort of empiric proof for its value and truth. Virtue and truth "can be grasped only by people who have thought and reasoned, and is not accessible to those who wrangle blindly about their experience without reflecting on it."[23] Therefore, virtue and truth can never be the property of the masses of humanity — only of the elite.[24] Great debates continued and continue over what Plato really meant in his works, but there is no doubt as to the lasting influence of the Academics in the Hellenistic world and thereafter.

Socrates

---

21. *Oxford History of Greece and the Hellenistic World*, p. 423. The term *apikorus*, used pejoratively by the Talmud and in later times by traditional Jewry to describe Jewish heretics, deviationists and non-believers, is a direct derivative of the name of this school of Greek philosophy. A world view of life solely devoted to bodily pleasures and never allowing for Divine revelation of truths is certainly anathema to Jewish tradition, life-style and thought.

22. The pessimism, utter fatalism, near complete negation of the body, and exclusive reliance on man's reasoning for the discovery of virtue and good placed Stoicism beyond the pale of traditional Jewish society.

23. *Oxford History of Greece and the Hellenistic World*, p. 289.

24. Plato's positing of the exclusive nature of knowledge, making it attainable only to the few, his failure to recognize the evil that lies in all human beings, no matter how intellectually great, and the denial that any supernatural forces or revelations are possible — all of which are components inherent in Plato's debunking of all Greek mythology — placed Plato's ideas on a collision course with traditional Jewish thought and beliefs as well.

The Philisophic Challenge

THESE DEBATES REGARDING philosophic ideas and truths would rage in the Hellenistic, and later Roman and Christian, worlds for centuries. What the Jewish response should be to Aristotle and the Hellenistic philosophers — or if there is such a thing as a Jewish response to them — would also be argued by Jews for almost two millennia. For the Jewish world could not easily avoid confronting the assault of Greek philosophy on its cherished beliefs. Many Jews would unfortunately succumb to that assault. Others would simply ignore the challenge of ideas and take refuge in their unshakable faith in Torah. Still others would attempt to deflect this assault of Greek thought by reinterpreting it and somehow reconciling, with varying success, the beliefs of Israel with the logic and forms of Greek philosophy. This intellectual struggle within and without Judaism would consume the time and ingenuity of countless great men.

Out of all of the attacks of Hellenism on established traditional Jewish life, the philosophic challenge would prove to be the most serious, vital and long-lasting. It would survive the death of Hellenism, the destruction of Rome and the establishment of Christianity. Philosophy would continue as the dominant force in world civilization for millennia. Only in the modern era, when the world generally has turned its back on Plato, Aristotle and their schools and disciples,[25] has the debate regarding the legitimacy of philosophy as a part of Judaism abated, to be replaced by a much more rancorous and terrifying dispute regarding the verity and relevance of the faith and practices of Judaism itself in the modern world.

The Ravages of Hellenism

TO SUM UP, THE SUCCESS of Hellenism in the ancient world was its ability to infiltrate, undermine and eventually replace most of the previously dominant Mediterranean cultures. In the Jewish world, and particularly

---
25. The modern world has exchanged Socrates' motto, "Know thyself," for the current wisdom, "Feel good."

Statue of a Greek runner

in the Jewish state, Hellenism represented a challenge to all the basic precepts of Judaism. Although the more advanced Greek philosophers, such as Aristotle, certainly did not believe the Greek gods to be real or even relevant, Hellenism still denied monotheism. It portrayed fate, when dealing with man, as being random, cruel and capricious, leaving no room for the Jewish concept of a personal, concerned and just Creator. It preached hedonism and asceticism at one and the same time, fostering extreme behavior, with no life-style considered aberrant.

Where Judaism saw sanctity in all forms of human actions and declared the supremacy of discipline and morals over instinct and desire, Hellenism saw only pleasure or, alternatively, abstinence, isolation and despair. Life had no meaning beyond its immediate and limited horizon. Man could never be freed from the nonsensical and essentially evil behavior of the gods or, if you wish, of nature or fate. Therefore, beauty, physical courage, and constant adventure were considered the only sensible values in life. Nudity was to be encouraged and accepted, for man was in the body, while modesty of dress and speech was mocked and despised. The cruelty of the gods was to be imitated by their pawn and victim, man. The strong had the right — nay, even the duty — to impose their will on the weak.[26] Morality was relative and equivocal, not bound to absolute standards. Conquest, empire, riches and slaves were the goals of government. Life was fast and cheap. Technology, material gain and personal, physical gratification were the measures of human existence.

Traditional Judaism was horrified by the onslaught of such an alien force, especially since it was cloaked in the gorgeous attraction of Hellenistic culture. Yet initially, Hellenism was successful in making deep inroads into Jewish life and society.

---

26. This was a cardinal belief of Adolf Hitler as expressed in his book, *Mein Kampf*.

3
Twin Hellenism — Ptolemaic And Seleucid

BY THE TIME PTOLEMY II ascended to the throne in 285 B.C.E., Judah had been completely incorporated into the Ptolemaic Greek empire. Ptolemy II, who, as we read earlier, sponsored the Septuagint, did not desire political control alone. He envisioned the spread of Greek culture and the ideas of Hellenism throughout the Mediterranean basin — especially in the Land of Israel. "Greek" cities were founded in Judah; Greek became the spoken language of the Jewish socioeconomic upper class; and Greek manners, styles and values came to dominate a large section of the Jewish society in Judah.

The upper class, the wealthy, the leaders of the priesthood and the more cosmopolitan element of the Jews all cast their lot and future with Ptolemaic Greek culture and with the political rule of the Ptolemys. These Jews declared themselves to be "Hellenized,"[1] and, as with so many newly converted idealists, they were not satisfied with merely following their own new-found star personally. They were determined to change the entire Jewish society, even by force, if necessary, into a Hellenistic one. They viewed Alexandria as the center of their world and hoped to convert Jerusalem into Alexandria's image.

---
1. Traditional Jews in later times, being less enamored of Greek culture, called these Hellenistic Jews *Misyavnim,* a pejorative term showing contempt for those who "make themselves Greek."

The Jews of Alexandria

IF THE HELLENISTS WERE determined to make Jerusalem Greek, there was a strong counter-movement to make Alexandria more Jewish. It is true that the Alexandrian Jews were suffused with Greek culture and a strong sense of philosophic speculation and artistic appreciation.[2] However, they also remained proud of their heritage, loyal to the interests of Jerusalem and defenders of Jews from their enemies everywhere. Already during the declining years of the First Temple, a substantial Jewish community had formed in Egypt. There is ample evidence of a surrogate Jewish Temple and altar built in Elephantine, in southern Egypt, which serviced the Jewish population of Egypt from 604 B.C.E. until 410 B.C.E.[3] The Talmud[4] describes the magnificent Jewish buildings in Alexandria in a later era, including an impressive synagogue that held a vast throng of worshipers. The city of Alexandria also hosted in its suburbs a magnificent and functioning replica of the Temple in Jerusalem, called the Temple of Chonyo.[5] It was even larger and more ornate than the real Temple in Jerusalem.[6]

The contest between Hellenism and Judaism would occur in various arenas. The Jews of Alexandria apparently were able to reconcile the irreconcilable and live as major participants in Alexandrian life for

---

2. Philo of Alexandria, a Hellenized yet observant Jew, was a famous Jewish philosopher who lived in the first century of the Common Era. He epitomized the essential Alexandrian Jew — urbane, scholarly, assimilated into the general society, yet somehow proudly Jewish and a defender of his faith and brethren.

3. See *Hadrachah B'Limud Toldos Yisrael,* by Chaim D. Rabinowitz, Jerusalem, 1979, pp. 54-55. Also see note 23 to the chapter "Going Home," above.

4. *Succah,* 51b.

5. For the conflicting stories regarding the beginning of this Temple in Alexandria, see the Talmud, *Menachos* 109b. The Talmud there reports that Chonyo, bitter over being rejected as successor to his father's position of High Priest, left Jerusalem and founded the Alexandrian Temple. There are those who identify the Alexandrian Chonyo, a great-grandson of Shimon *HaTzaddik,* as the founder of the Alexandrian Temple. However, the Talmud and Jewish tradition, which do not obfuscate facts even when great and holy families are involved, apparently identify Chonyo as the son, not the great-grandson, of Shimon *HaTzaddik.* The Temple of Chonyo was destroyed by the Romans in 73 C.E., three years after the destruction of the Temple in Jerusalem.

6. Herod's beautification of the Jerusalem Temple would not take place until centuries later.

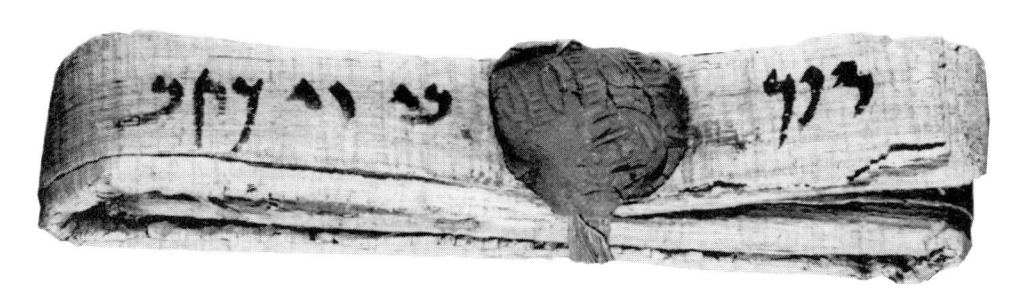

Papyrus deed from Elephantine

many centuries.[7] No such reconciliation was possible in Judah and Jerusalem. Jewish life and disputes, as well as the Jews themselves, always were much more intense in the Holy Land than elsewhere.[8] There, the struggle between the Hellenists and the rabbis would continue unabated, unreconciled and violent for centuries.

Parallel Governments

WHEN SHIMON HATZADDIK died in 273 B.C.E., he was succeeded as High Priest by his brother, Elazar. However Elazar did not inherit the entire mantle of his brother. As mentioned in the preceding chapter, Shimon had been not only the High Priest, but also the tax franchiser, the President of the Sanhedrin (*Nasi*) and the official head of that great court (*Av Beis Din*). Elazar, although High Priest, retained in addition only the political role of tax franchiser. Since he lacked the scholarship and moral standing of his brother, the members of the Sanhedrin appointed as their head not Elazar but Antigonus of Socho, the main disciple of Shimon. Thus there began the system of parallel governments in Judah, mentioned in the previous chapter, a system which would continue throughout the life of the Second Commonwealth. The High Priest, and later the king, represented governmental power. The Nasi and Av Beis Din were the religious, spiritual and moral leaders of the people. Many times the two systems had the same goals and values and were mutually supportive; many times they were in complete opposition to each other. This dichotomy often led to violence and sometimes even civil war in Judah. Jewish public life in the Second Commonwealth was a rocky one.

---

7. Jews remained major participants in Alexandrian life until the decline and temporary destruction of that city in the fourth century of the Common Era.
8. A situation which pertains in present-day Israel as well.

The Saducees

DURING THE REIGNS OF ELAZAR in Judah and Ptolemy II in Egypt, perhaps because of the strong Hellenistic influences current then in Judah (this was when the Septuagint was published), two important students of Antigonus of Socho attempted to introduce a new form of belief and practice into Jewish life.[9] These two disciples of Antigonus, Zadok and Bysos, preached a form of Judaism devoid of belief in the divinity of the Oral Law, the traditions of Sinai as transmitted through the generations. Their followers, never insignificant in number and always powerful in wealth and influence, were called Zadokim (Saducees) and Bysosim (Boethusians). Eventually these groups would rise to power and control in Judah, though their beliefs and policies never mustered majority support among the populace.

The Saducees were always more acceptable in the eyes of the Hellenist Jews than their rabbinic foes. This alliance of the Hellenists and the Saducees against traditional Judaism guaranteed constant turmoil in Jewish life throughout the time of the Second Temple and even thereafter. However, the main struggle now was not between the Saducees and the rabbis, but between the Hellenists and the main body of the Jewish public.

Tax Collection

IN 245 B.C.E., Ptolemy III was just beginning his reign. At that time, the new High Priest of Judah was Chonyo II.[10] Following in the footsteps of his predecessor Elazar, Chonyo was not only High Priest but tax franchiser as well. For unknown reasons,[11] Chonyo refused to forward the tax col-

---

9. See Rashi on *Avos* 1:3 for an account of the incident that precipitated their breaking ranks with traditional Judaism.

10. It is not conclusively clear whether this is the same Chonyo as the one who founded the Temple in Alexandria. It is therefore also unclear whether he is the son, grandson or great-grandson of Shimon *HaTzaddik*. See note 5, above.

11. Josephus attributes Chonyo's behavior to intrinsic personal greed and avarice. Others are of the opinion that Chonyo chose this method as a declaration of independence from Ptolemaic rule, feeling that Ptolemy III was a weak and irresolute ruler. Still

lections from Judah to the emperor in Alexandria. There is no greater form of rebellion against an emperor than withholding tax monies collected ostensibly on his behalf. Ptolemy III reacted violently and threatened to invade Judah and level Jerusalem in retribution. The Jews of Jerusalem were in no position to offer effective resistance to Ptolemy III's strong army and thus, in panic and fear, convened to decide upon a method of escape from their precarious situation. Chonyo offered to resign, but the other leaders felt that this act of contrition would not in itself prevent Ptolemy from wreaking his vengeance upon them. At this critical juncture, Yosef ben Tovia, a nephew of Chonyo, volunteered to go to Egypt and attempt to mollify Ptolemy.

This mission, fraught with danger and intrigue, perfectly fitted the personality of Yosef. He was a talented and charismatic person who succeeded in charming Ptolemy, calming him down regarding the threat of any Jewish rebellion in Judah, and assuring him that the taxes he desired would be collected and forwarded to him. However, Yosef failed to withstand the temptation of personal gain at the expense of the public good. Yosef, through his assurances, insinuated himself into the role of the official tax franchiser of the king, replacing his uncle, Chonyo. He made grandiose promises of delivering a greatly increased amount of taxes, even guaranteeing Ptolemy a minimum base amount of tax money, no matter what the actual collections would be. In return, he was given permission to raise the taxes on the people of Judah to cover his "expenses" and was promised a hefty commission fee as well on the taxes actually collected. Thus, in 243 B.C.E., was born the prototypical Jewish tax collector, serving a foreign master, oftentimes to the detriment of his people and the shame of his own good name. He would be a fairly permanent and usually despicable fixture in Jewish life throughout ancient and medieval history.

Division of Power

ANTIGONUS' POSITIONS AS NASI and Av Beis Din were also divided upon his death between two of his leading disciples, Yose ben Yoezer[12] and Yose ben Yochanan. Thus, the four positions of power in Jewish life — High

---

others feel that Chonyo was urged to withhold taxes by the Seleucid king of Syria, who promised to come to his aid against Ptolemy III.

12. He would later be martyred by the Greeks for teaching Torah publicly.

Priest, tax franchiser, Nasi and Av Beis Din — were now in the hands of four different people. This situation of diffused power contributed to ongoing disputes within the Jewish power structure, a problem that would plague and eventually overwhelm the society of the Second Commonwealth. Also at this time different opinions began to evolve regarding the actual halachic practices ordained by the Oral Law of Sinai.[13] Thus, with Yose ben Yoezer and Yose ben Yochanan emerged the period of the *zugos* (*pairs*), as well as the continuing reality of differing halachic opinions, and the opinions themselves all became part of the transmission of the Oral Law.

For the next two centuries, until the advent of Herod, the *zugos* were the teachers of Israel, the guardians of tradition and the moral leaders of the people. The Sanhedrin emerged now not only as the supreme court of justice but even more importantly as the main yeshivah academy of Judah. Each new generation of religious leadership would be drawn from the young scholars who sat at the feet of the members of the Sanhedrin. Thus, the positions of Nasi and Av Beis Din evolved from formal judicial roles to primary educational roles, and ones of greater influence.

The Persistence of Hellenism

THE MAJOR COUNTERFORCE the people of the Torah had to face at the time was that presented by the prevailing Greek culture. Though the political rule of the Ptolemys over Judah was rather benign, the unrelenting pressure of Ptolemaic Hellenism ravaged Jewish society. Since this brand of Hellenism was always presented with a smiling, non-coercive face, the traditional rabbinic leaders found it difficult to unmask before their people the true pernicious and dangerous nature of Hellenism and Ptolemaic rule. Thus, Alexandria and all it stood for threatened to eclipse Jerusalem and its ideals in the eyes of the Jews of Judah. But Providence intervened, as It always does, to force the Jewish people to reassess their situation.

---

13. The first recorded halachic dispute in post-biblical times and literature is that between Yose ben Yoezer and Yose ben Yochanan regarding the placing of one's hands on a sacrificial animal on a holiday. The dispute regarding this issue was not definitively settled until almost two centuries had passed. See Mishna, *Chaggigah,* Chapter Two.

The Ptolemys saw themselves as the peak of all Greek culture and accomplishment. They controlled Judah by taxation, by continually building new "Greek" cities in the area and by infiltration into Jewish life through the language and customs of Hellenism. Ptolemy IV (221-205 B.C.E.), one of the more arrogant of the dynasty, attempted to defile the Temple in Jerusalem, but upon entering those hallowed precincts he fell unconscious. Upon recovering, he harbored great hatred of the Jews and Jerusalem; but he could not effectuate his vengeance, for his attention was soon distracted by the Seleucid kingdom of Syria.

Antiochus III

THE SELEUCID EMPIRE, centered in Syria, suffered from an inferiority complex vis-a-vis its Ptolemaic competitor. The Hellenism of the Seleucids was much less glittering than that of the Ptolemys. And the Seleucids were much more heavy-handed in their treatment of vassal states. The Seleucids

Ptolemaic Dynasty*

	From Creation	B.C.E
Ptolemy I Soter	3438-3476	323-285
Ptolemy II Philadelphus	3476-3515	285-246
Ptolemy III Euergetes	3515-3540	246-221
Ptolemy IV Philopator	3540-3556	221-205
Ptolemy V	3556-3581	205-180
Ptolemy VI Philometor	3581-3616	180-145
(Ptolemy VI and VII co-rulers)	(3591-3597)	(170-164)
Ptolemy VII Physcon	3616-3645	145-116
Ptolemy VIII Lathyrus	3645-3654	116-107
Ptolemy IX Alexander (brother of Ptolemy VIII)	3654-3673	107-88
Ptolemy VIII Lathyrus (regained throne)	3673-3680	88-81
Ptolemy X Alexander (son of Ptolemy IX)	3681	80
Ptolemy XI Auletes (son of Ptolemy VIII)	3681-3703; 3706-3710	80-58; 55-51
Ptolemy XII	3710-3714	51-47
Ptolemy XIII (brother of Ptolemy XII)	3714-3717	47-44

*Unless otherwise indicated, each king is the son of his predecessor.

Seleucid Dynasty*		
	From Creation	B.C.E.
Seleucus I Nicator	3449-3480	312-281
Antiochus I Soter	3480-3499	281-262
Antiochus II Theos	3499-3515	262-246
Seleucus II Calinicus	3515-3535	246-226
Seleucus III Soter	3535-3538	226-223
Antiochus III the Great (Son of Seleucus II)	3538-3574	223-187
Seleucus IV Philopater	3574-3586	187-175
Antiochus IV Epiphanes (son of Antiochus III)	3586-3598	175-163
Antiochus V Eupator	3598-3600	163-161
Demetrius I Soter (son of Seleucus IV)	3600-3609	161-152
Alexander Balas (impostor) 3609-3614	3609-3614	152-147
Demetrius II Nicator (son of Demetrius II)	3614-c. 3621	147-140
Antiochus VI Dionysius (son of Alexander) [Throne in contention]	3615-3619	146-142
Diodotus-Tryphon (usurper)	3619-3624	142-137
Antiochus VII Sidetes (son of Demetrius I)	3621-3632	140-129
Demetrius II Nicator (regained throne)	3632-3635	129-126
Antiochus VIII Gryphus	3636-3665	125-96
Antiochus IX Cyzicenus (son of Antiochus VII)	3648-3666	113-95
Demetrius III Eucerus (son of Antiochus VIII)	3665-3673	96-88

*Unless otherwise indicated, each king is the son of his predecessor.

never convinced anyone; they coerced them. And the Seleucids coveted the wealth, the cities and the territory of the Ptolemys, especially the area of Judah.

When Ptolemy IV died in 205 B.C.E., he was succeeded by his very young son, Ptolemy V. The immature and inept young king was unable to control his army or empire effectively and appeared vulnerable in the hungry eyes of the Seleucids. The king of the Seleucid Empire, Antiochus III (223-187 B.C.E.), invaded Judah in 199 B.C.E., and in a series of battles and feints outmaneuvered Ptolemy's army and forced its withdrawal from Judah. By 198 B.C.E. Judah had passed from the Ptolemaic Empire to the Seleucid Empire.

Antiochus was a fierce warrior who had great expansionist ideas for Seleucid rule. He called himself Antiochus the Great, attempting to wrap himself in Alexander's mantle. But in the year 190 B.C.E. he ran afoul of the new bully making its appearance in the Mediterranean area — Rome — and was soundly defeated. Forced continually to pay Rome great tribute, Antiochus, like all rulers ever after, searched for new taxes to meet his voracious monetary needs. Though originally very generous to his new Jewish vassals, Antiochus' troubles eventually forced him to raise new taxes from Judah. However, before the situation became truly onerous, Antiochus died and was succeeded by his son, Seleucus IV (187-175 B.C.E.).

Antiochus III

An Attempt to Rob the Temple

SELEUCUS IV ALSO FOUND HIMSELF under enormous monetary pressures. The Hellenist Jews in Jerusalem, alarmed by the new, ugly face of rapacious Seleucid Hellenism, attempted to ingratiate themselves with the new king. Sparked by a slight to one of the leading Hellenists in Jerusalem by the High Priest, Chonyo III,[14] they informed Seleucus that the Temple in Jerusalem contained untold treasures that should be appropriated by the Seleucid Empire. Seleucus jumped at the bait and ordered one of his ministers, Heliodorus, to travel to Jerusalem and confiscate this vast wealth.

Chonyo III opposed the Hellenists and their plans. He was joined in this opposition by Yehoshua ben Perachyah, the Nasi, and Nitai HaArbeli, the Av Beis Din. However, the tax franchisers, the descendants of Yosef ben Tovia, supported the efforts of the Hellenists to despoil the Temple, thereby hoping for an even greater commission fee to reward their acts of extortion.

Heliodorus attempted to rob the Temple but, like Ptolemy IV before him, he was stricken unconscious at its entrance. Heliodorus was properly chastened and returned to Syria with a report to Seleucus about the foolishness of defiling the Temple of the God of Israel. However, the Jewish Hellenists, disbelievers and self-haters to the

---

14. Chonyo III the High Priest (c. 176 B.C.E.) was the grandson of the High Priest Chonyo II. After Chonyo II had died, the High Priest was his son, Shimon. When Shimon died, his son Chonyo III succeeded him.

Antiochus IV *Antiochus V* *Antiochus VII*

end, petitioned Seleucus to send another emissary to despoil the Temple. Chonyo III intervened, begging Seleucus to let well enough alone. But before any decision could be made, the hand of Providence again appeared, and Seleucus was assassinated. The loyal Jews of Jerusalem breathed more easily, but, unbeknownst to them, they were about to be faced with an even graver crisis.

Seleucus was succeeded by his brother, Antiochus IV, called Epiphanes (the illustrious) to his face, and Epimanes (the madman) behind his back. He would be the Antiochus who would forever live in infamy in the story of Chanukah.

4
Economic and Social Life in Judah in Second Temple Times

NAPOLEON'S QUIP that an army moves on its stomach certainly applies to societies and nations as well. Second Commonwealth Judah was no exception.[1] The economic circumstances of Judah's life, its prosperity and economic vitality, greatly influenced its spiritual, social, military and governmental framework. I therefore pause in the story of war, political machination and rivalry of ideas and personalities — the pivotal centers of Second Commonwealth history — to review some of the more mundane economic and social conditions of Judah in Second Temple times.

The Basis of the Economy

WHEN EZRA AND NECHEMIAH led the return to Zion, they found there a country apparently devoid of economic opportunity. The land was desolate and untilled, and the few arable fields that existed were controlled by Samaritans, other foreigners and a few absentee Jewish landlords. Nechemiah declared a moratorium on debts, broke up the large landholdings of the absentee landlords and distributed plots of land to the Jews returning from Babylonian exile.

---
1. The words of the Rabbis, "Without flour there is no Torah," (Mishnah, *Avos*, 3:17) indicate their realistic approach to the life and survival of the Jewish people and state.

This laid the basis for a primarily agrarian economy, and this type of small-farmer-based agriculturally productive economic system characterized life in Second Commonwealth Judah for most of its existence.

Nechemiah created an economic system not of serfs and lords, but rather of small farmers, middle-class merchants and wholesalers, and a small priestly aristocracy. There was therefore in Judah a large core of economically independent, self-sufficient, middle-class people who were not intimidated by any attempts at establishing a ruling aristocracy or even dictatorial rule. Therefore, from the time of Ezra until the time of Herod, the country's rulers were essentially responsive to the will of the masses and attempted to protect these hard-working, productive, independent people from possible exploitation by the Jewish aristocracy, as later represented by the Saducees, as well as from the foreign domination of the Greeks and Romans in all its variant forms.

It was among these farmers and small merchants that the Pharisees had their base of support. Their loyalty to Torah and Jewish tradition, their respect and love for the Torah scholars of Israel, was part of their makeup, and it was the support of this middle class that expanded the influence and study of Torah throughout Judah.

The influence of Torah values also helped strengthen the economy in the times after Ezra and Nechemiah. Industry, thrift, a sense of accomplishment and satisfaction, an avoidance of unnecessary luxuries and ostentation,[2] all marked the Jewish society.

Many Jews at that time developed a cattle-and-sheep-raising industry.[3] The necessity for these animals in the Temple service provided a basic and continual market. Animals were also imported into the country from Transjordan and Syria to augment the local flocks and herds. Milk and dairy products were abundant, and some fine and expensive cheeses were marketed throughout Judah and

---

2. The words of the rabbis in the Mishnah (Avos, 4:1), that wealth is to be defined in terms of self-sufficiency and satisfaction with one's situation, are wholly consistent with the society of the Second Commonwealth, certainly until the time of Herod.

3. Nonetheless, these occupations were not held in high esteem by the rabbis of the time. From the Talmud it is obvious that shepherds especially were held to be the "used car salesmen" of that era. However, from Moses to David to Rabbi Akiva, some of the greatest leaders of Israel were drawn from the ranks of shepherds.

especially in the Jerusalem area.[4] There was a special wool market located in Jerusalem.[5] Jews were specialists in spinning the wool as well as in dyeing it.[6] Flax grew in great quantities in Judah, and from it linen — some of it very fine and of superior quality — was manufactured, processed and much of it exported.

In these items, as in much else, Judah was completely self-sufficient, and in fact a net exporter in trade with other regions. Large quantities of wool also led to the manufacture of cloth and textiles, much of which was exported, and even under the reign of the Ptolemys and the Seleucids, the wealth and prosperity of Judah continued. In fact, it was this continuing prosperity that fanned the avarice of these foreign rulers and allowed them to tax the country heavily.

Jews were forced to pay head tax, salt tax, luxury goods tax, real estate tax, animal tax, and agricultural produce tax, in addition to other fees and transfer taxes. Nevertheless, the Jews were able to survive and even prosper under such an onerous burden, due to their healthy economic infrastructure, their thrift and their personal efficiency and work ethic.

The Tyropean Valley leading northward toward the Beis HaMikdash and the Fortress of Antonia; from the Holyland Hotel model of Jerusalem at the time of the Second Temple.

---

4. There is scholarly opinion that the Tyropean Valley, running alongside the west face of the Temple Mount, was so named due to the cheese makers and marketers located there. Tyropean was a derivative from the Greek word for cheese. Joseph Klausner, *Habayis Hasheni B'Galuso*, (Tel Aviv), 1930, p. 48.

5. Talmud, *Eruvin*, 101a.

6. Dyeing cloth remained a Jewish trade throughout ancient and medieval times, both in the Levant and in Europe.

Agriculture

ALTHOUGH MANY FIELDS were watered by elaborate canal irrigation systems,[7] most were dependent upon the relatively short and fickle rainy season for nourishment.[8] Because of this uncertain state of water supply, prayers for rain and fast days to gain Divine favor for abundant rainfall were regular features of Jewish life in the Second Temple era and continue to be so today.[9]

The basic grains of the country were wheat, spelt, rye and oats, with much barley being raised for the consumption of the lower economic class, for animal feed and for export. Rice originally had to be imported into Judah but gradually became a local crop in Second

---

7. These fields, watered "through human agency" were called *bais hashelachin*.

8. These fields were called *bais haBaal*, fields watered automatically by the "owner" — by G-d Himself. See Mishnah, Bava Basra, (3:1), for a contrast between the legal aspects of these two types of fields.

9. Prayers for rain and/or dew are part of the regular daily prayer services of Jews. Special prayers for rain and dew are recited on *Shemini Atzeres,* at the conclusion of the *Succos* holiday, and Pesach, respectively. An entire tractate of the Talmud, *Taanis,* deals with prayers and fast days regarding rain and drought. Far from its home, in distant exiles, Jews have continued to pray regularly and fervently for abundant rain to always fall in the land of their residence as well as in the Holy Land, even when that country was practically empty of Jews.

Part of an ancient water supply system: the aqueduct at Caesarea

48 ☐ ECHOES OF GLORY

Grain mill at Sepphoris

An oven at Katzrin

Temple times. Yields on the fields of grain averaged between five and ten times the seed planted,[10] with the Galilee being more fertile than Judah to the south.

Except in times of severe drought, Judah was a net food exporter, and the cities of Alexandria in Egypt, and Tyre and Sidon in

---
10. Klausner, pp. 43-44.

Tools of the agricultural trade from the Second Temple period. Top to Bottom: Wheat mill, wine press, wine pit.

50 ☐ ECHOES OF GLORY

Lebanon, were the main markets for its grains and fruits. Large amounts of grain were stored by the government as a guarantee against future famine and to help stabilize the product's price structure, especially in regard to the export market. In the ancient world, as in medieval times, bread was truly the staff of life, and therefore, self-sufficiency in grain production brought Judah the reputation of being a prosperous country, with all of the blessings and disadvantages that accompany such a reputation.

Judah was also known for its wine. Among the famous wines of Judah were those of the areas of Sharon, Carmel[11] and Ashkelon. These wines were exported and well known throughout the Mediterranean world. The great variety of wines recorded in the Talmud[12] give further evidence of the abundance of different types of grapes and vineyard localities in the Jewish state. Vinegar, as a by-product of wine, was also readily available, as were raisins.

The importance of wine as a ritual drink for the Sabbath and holidays, as well as its use as the basic drink at daily meals, made the wine industry necessary and prosperous. The prohibition against the use of non-Jewish wine, which was strengthened at the time of the Hasmonean war against the Greeks, *ipso facto* guaranteed a strong local market for Jewish wine in Judah, free of competition from Italian or Greek imports. In contrast, the wines of Judah were exported as far as Greece and Rome, where they were appreciated because of their unique taste and fine color. The tradition that wine from the Holy Land was special was carried into the Middle Ages by Christian monks who produced such wine and exported it to Europe.[13] Because of the prosperity of the Jewish wine industry, many people were employed in the growing of the grapes, in harvesting and crushing them, and in producing the wine itself.

---

11. See Talmud, *Nidah,* 21a.
12. See Talmud, *Menachos,* 86b and 87a, for example.
13. The wines produced at the Abbey D'Latrun in modern day Israel and exported to France (talk about sending coals to Newcastle!) are a current example of this ancient practice.

A Talmud-era olive press

Produce

OLIVE OIL WAS ALSO a strong cash crop and export product for which Judah was renowned. It was produced in differing grades[14] and served many consumer needs. It was used as food, as fuel, as a cleansing agent, as a depilatory and as a cosmetic, as well as for various medicinal purposes. Olive oil, in the ancient world, was the most complete and versatile of agricultural products. Its wide variety of uses contributed to the constantly strong demand for it; and, like wine, its use in the Temple service guaranteed its importance in the eyes of the population of Judah.

Vast groves of olive trees existed in Judah, with the choicest oil coming from the Galilee.[15] The Mount of Olives[16] is one of the famous mountains overlooking the Temple Mount. Olive presses existed everywhere and were staples of every agricultural home.

Olive oil was a very strong export product, more so even than

---

14. See *Menachos* 86a for details of the differing grades of olive oil available in Judah in Second Temple times.

15. See Mishnah, *Peah,* (7:1,2) for oils that came from the Galilee.

16. In the time of the Second Temple this mountain was called the Mount of [the Anointing] Oil.

52 ☐ ECHOES OF GLORY

The Mount of Olives

wine, and olive oil from Judah was to be found throughout Egypt, Lebanon and Syria. Only with the destruction of thousands of olive trees during the century of the Roman wars in Judah did the export of olive oil from Judah decline.

The memory of the Temple's use of Judean olive oil was preserved in the long Jewish exile through the use of olive oil as the preferred fuel for the lights of the Chanuka *menorah*. The production of olive oil was less labor-intensive than that of wine, but nevertheless, because of the widespread existence of olive presses everywhere throughout the country, olive oil — in all its grades and varieties — was the product that a large segment of the population of Judah was constantly engaged in preparing and marketing.

The country was also rich in dates, figs, pomegranates and other fruits. Date honey was the basic honey used in the country, far surpassing in popularity its competitor, bee honey.

Date "wine" was a favorite alcoholic beverage, and it served as the beer of its time. Compressed dates, both fresh and dried, were part of the regular diet of the Jews in Judah and were also exported. The dates of Jericho and the Jordan Valley were especially favored because of their sweetness and size.

The dates of Judah were in demand in Rome[17] and other places

---
17. See Talmud Yerushalmi, *Maaser Sheni,* chapter 4, section 1.

in the Mediterranean world, and the date, together with the fig and the grape, became a "Jewish" symbol in the artwork of the time. Figs, both fresh and dried, were also exported, though not in the same volume as the dates.

Balsam (balm, stacte), myrrh, and other spices were highly prized, both for their fragrance and medicinal powers. The balsam from Jericho was famed throughout the world and, according to Pliny the Elder, the Roman historian, it was more expensive than gold itself and held to be almost priceless.[18] It was grown in the area of the Dead Sea, especially around Ein-Gedi.

Other Resources

THE SEA OF GALILEE and the Mediterranean spawned Jewish fishermen. All types of fresh- and salt-water fish were consumed in Judah, with fish juice and salted, cured, dried fish being very popular.

Fish was originally imported from the Lebanese port cities of Tyre and Sidon,[19] but after the Hasmonean conquest of the Mediterranean coast, Judah no longer needed to import fish. Fish and its by-products were so plentiful that they became a staple of the diet of the Jews in Judah.

The Dead Sea also supplied export materials in terms of sulfur, pitch and other minerals mined from its waters and surrounding land. Chemicals for cosmetics also came from that area of Judah, as well as from the bark of the caper tree that was ubiquitous throughout the land.

The country was rich in stone, and there were quarries everywhere. However, there were few metal mines in Judah proper, and apparently only some small mines in the Negev, mainly in the territory of the Idumeans, were productive. Much of the iron came from Lebanon and Transjordan, a distinct disadvantage in times of war, while truly fine stone and marble came from Greece and Italy. Most of the buildings in the country were of stone or stucco construction, with many fine houses and palaces located in Jerusalem. Thus, there was a veneer of prosperity that unfortunately masked the underlying social and political problems of Judah in the time of the Second Temple.

---

18. Quoted by Klausner, p.47.
19. See Nechemia, Chapter 13, verse 16.

The Trades

THE AGRICULTURAL SEGMENT of the economy of Judah during Hasmonean and later Second Temple times was paralleled by another part of the economy driven by labor — small shopkeepers and tradesmen of all varieties. Many of the great spiritual leaders, rabbis and even the members of the Sanhedrin supported themselves from the work of their hands and/or enterprise.

Every possible trade and profession was present in Judah. Many of its manufactured products, especially weapons, jewelry, papyrus, ink and written scrolls, were exported to Greece, Egypt and Rome. Most of the artisans came from certain select families whose sons apprenticed themselves to their fathers or to other artisans for expert training. The service of the Temple required many particular skills and artisans, and those engaged in supplying and servicing the Temple found their occupations most lucrative, and hence they zealously guarded their concession.[20]

As in any society, there were disparate ranges of income, but on the whole, the fiercely independent individual Judean of that time attempted to be self-sufficient, and even members of the lower class rarely resorted to begging or brigandage to alleviate their economic plight. Nevertheless, there did exist in the society "professional" poor who depended upon the contributions of others for their succor. The rabbis viewed these people as providing an opportunity for charitable works, though they did attempt to expose the undeserving ones among them. Unfortunately, there also was a small, loosely organized but pernicious class of Jewish robbers, outlaws and criminals, and they would play a decisive role in the Jewish war against Rome that led to the destruction of the Temple in 70 C.E.

One is struck by the relatively stable economy and social relationships among the Jews in Second Temple Judah. However, the divisiveness of the people was never far from the surface. In the last century of the Second Temple, although the prosperity of the country grew, so did the internal strife that would eventually destroy the Jewish state.

---

20. See Talmud, *Yoma* 38a, for a list of some of these occupations and the families that monopolized them.

Slavery

THE ECONOMIC BASE of much of the ancient classical world was slavery. Slaves were considered the main booty of war, and an active and ever-expanding slave trade accompanied the growth of the Greek world and later the Roman Empire. Slaves were not only taken from the captured warriors of the enemy's army, but were also imported into the Mediterranean basin from Central Africa, the Balkans,[21] Gaul (France), Germany, Persia and Asia Minor.

The Torah[22] made specific provision for the existence of slavery in society, with separate categories and rules for males and females as well as for Jews and non-Jews. However, the rules regarding the care and treatment of slaves, as explained by the Oral Law of Torah, made slavery economically unattractive, if not morally reprehensible, and a great burden on the home and psyche of the slave's master. The Talmud succinctly summed up the situation by stating: "One who acquires a slave for oneself in reality acquires a master over oneself."[23]

The rabbis had a dim view of the institution of slavery, seeing it as creating a cancer of immorality,[24] slothfulness,[25] unreliability,[26] and pernicious theft[27] that weakened society. The Talmud relates descriptions of noble slaves who were more family members than home laborers,[28] but such refined people and idyllic situations were apparently rare.

---

21. Since many Balkan people, mainly of the Slavic tribes, were slaves of the Romans, the Jews began to call them "Canaanites," which was a Jewish euphemism for slave. Hence, in the halachic literature of the Middle Ages, all Slavs, Poles and Russians are referred to as "Canaanites."

22. See *Exodus*, Chapter 21.

23. Talmud, *Kiddushin* 20a.

24. Mishna, *Avos*, Chapter 2 section 7.

25. Talmud, *Kiddushin* 49b.

26. Talmud, *Bava Metzi* 86b.

27. Yalkut, *Bereishis, Vayeshev* section 145.

28. Talmud, *Berachos* 16b, relates the almost familial relationship between Rabban Gamliel (of Yavneh) and his scholarly slave, Tevi.

It may be an over-generalization, but it can be said that one of the major differences between Greek and Roman society on one hand and Jewish society on the other was that the former was built upon the labor and talents of slaves, whereas the latter was always a society of free and fiercely independent people.

Population Centers

ALTHOUGH IT IS NEARLY IMPOSSIBLE to determine the population of Judah with exactitude, it is clear from many sources[29] that the country was densely populated. Jerusalem certainly was a city of hundreds of thousands, and Shomron (Sebastia), Caesarea, Hebron, Jaffa, Yavneh, Lod, Tiberias, Bais Guvrin and Tzipori were all significant population centers.

Possessing a large population base allowed Judah to create the necessary internal markets for its local goods and services and also to provide a pool of labor and consumption for foreign raw materials and finished products. It also provided the government with manpower to maintain significant standing armies.

Jerusalem's economy centered about the Temple, its needs and the tourism it engendered. Jaffa was the main port of the country, the lifeline of commerce and Judah's window to the world. The Galilean cities were the centers of agricultural commerce and provided vast storage facilities for the grain and other produce of the fields and orchards of their hinterland. Tiberias was a fishing center, while Caesarea and Shomron (Sebastia) were heavily populated by non-Jews, which gave those cities a more rakish and cosmopolitan reputation.

From all accounts, Judah contained many millions of Jews, and its population was larger in Herod's time than it had been in First Temple-era Judah and Israel combined. Throughout the time of the Second Temple, the economy of Judah expanded, and the population base of the country continued to grow. This blessing of prosperity and population could have made Second Temple Jewish life idyllic had it

---

29. Talmud Yerushalmi, *Megillah* 1:1; Josephus, *Wars of the Jews,* 7:3:2; Cassius Dio, XIX.

not been for the violence, jealousy and hatred which so affected that society, and especially its political leaders.

A strong economy is a great national asset. However, without equally strong moral leadership and social behavior, no society is able to survive indefinitely simply because of its economy. Judah was to prove no exception to this exacting rule of human history.

5
Chanukah and the Hasmoneans

A WITCHES' BREW OF TRAGIC EVENTS combined to bring the smoldering cultural dispute between the Hellenists (Jewish and non-Jewish) and their rabbinic Jewish foes into open physical war.

Antiochus, who believed himself to be the true reincarnation of Alexander the Great, initiated the fray. He had himself declared a god, his likeness to be worshipped publicly, and, as his madness began to take hold, simultaneously attempted to gain world dominion by force. Antiochus was particularly interested in completely dominating Judah, which the Seleucids had already wrested from the Ptolemys some time earlier. He intended to use Judah as the base, the jump-off point, for conquest of Egypt and the destruction of his archenemies, the Ptolemys. To do so, he first had to pacify Judah and its stubborn Jewish population, which silently remained loyal to the Ptolemys and would not under any circumstance accept a human being as a god. Antiochus enlisted the Jewish Hellenists in his cause. As is often the case in Jewish history, Jewish traitors were able to do far more damage to their people than were non-Jewish oppressors. The vehicle for the Hellenists' attempt at domination and victory would be the office of the High Priest.

The Greek Notion of Sports

IN 174 B.C.E. Chonyo,[1] the High Priest of the Temple in Jerusalem and a devout Jew, was deposed by Antiochus. Accepting a large bribe from Chonyo's Hellenized brother, Jason, Antiochus appointed this wretch as the new

---
1. Some scholars identify this Chonyo as the one who built the temple in Alexandria, and they explain that somehow he later returned to Jerusalem, to become High Priest there as well. However, others say he was possibly that Chonyo's great-grandson.

High Priest. Jason promised to provide large tribute to the coffers of Antiochus and committed himself to the realization of the king's goal of complete Hellenization of the people of Judah. By royal decree, he erected near the Temple Mount in Jerusalem a large school (*gymnasium*) devoted to Greek education and athletics. He also encouraged widespread participation in sports and the glorification of the human body.

Modern Jews often find it difficult to appreciate the traditional Jewish objection to organized sports activities, and especially the constant and vocal opposition to such activities by the rabbis of antiquity, an attitude perhaps somewhat mitigated, at least in the United States, in the modern era of organized, commercialized professional team sports.[2] But sports in the Greek world were an individual rather than a team effort, many times leading to arrogant self-aggrandizement and competitive violence. Greek sports always meant nudity, and oftentimes decadent behavior. And the arenas of sports training and actual competition were always lined with statues and altars to the various gods of the Greek pantheon, with sacrifices to these gods preceding all athletic contests, much as singing the national anthem introduces sports events in our society. Thus, sports were identified with the paganism and licentiousness of Greek society and became anathema to the traditional Jewish life-style.

Jason's Decline

JASON INFLUENCED MANY of the priests of the Temple to disregard strict observance of Temple ritual and to encourage the Jewish populace to adopt Greek sports, ways and values completely, including the pre-game sacrifices to Greek gods. Jason also saw to institutionalizing in Judah the public worship of Greek gods. But, as is often the case, the initial reformer was viewed as being too moderate by the enthusiastic second wave of reformers. The extreme Hellenist Jews accused Jason of failing to be Greek enough, and much of his support in the Hellenistic community of Judah dissipated.

---

2. See Avraham Kariv's essay on sports printed in his *Me'shilushim V'ad Heina*. It ends, "ישחקו הנערים כאות נפשם אבל לאו דוקא לפנינו, Let the youth play as is their wont, but not necessarily in front of us."

In 171 B.C.E. Jason himself was removed from office by Antiochus and replaced by a bigger crook, bribe-giver and self-hating Jew, Menelaus. Menelaus, once himself an emissary of Jason to Antiochus, had turned around to use his position to undermine Jason and have himself appointed High Priest.[3] In order to pay the huge bribe he had promised Antiochus, Menelaus and his brother Lysimachus sold off many of the golden vessels of the Temple. Those who protested this brazen act of rapacious blasphemy were severely punished. Chonyo, the legitimate High Priest earlier deposed by Jason and a bitter and outspoken critic of Menelaus' treachery, was for this reason now murdered by assassins sent by Menelaus.

Although this might have been an opening for Jason to reclaim his old ill-gained position, believing silence to be the better part of valor, he made no public protest then and bided his time, waiting for the inevitable fall of Menelaus and Lysimachus.

Jason's tomb in Jerusalem, restored from ruins found on the site.

Menelaus and Lysimachus

MENELAUS AND HIS BROTHER Lysimachus were aware of the growing opposition to them and their policies among the people of Jerusalem. The rabbis openly preached their opposition to Hellenism and thus against Menelaus as well. As the situation worsened, Lysimachus panicked and ordered his army to subdue his rabbinic foes. The people of Jerusalem arose in revolt against Menelaus and Lysimachus, defeated their forces and were successful even in killing Lysimachus. Emissaries were sent to Antiochus demanding the removal of Menelaus, but the wily High Priest used bribery, flattery and falsehoods to convince Antiochus of his loyalty and importance to the emperor. Many of Menelaus' rabbinic foes were then put to death and open civil war was now a foregone conclusion.

---

3. The fact that Menelaus was not even a *Kohen,* a descendant of the priestly family of Aaron, did not seem to inhibit Antiochus from appointing him to the post of High Priest or Menelaus from seeking and accepting that appointment.

Civil War

IN 169 B.C.E. Antiochus realized his dream of conquering Egypt and disgracing the Ptolemys. However, his triumph was very short-lived; for the newly emerging superpower of the age, Rome, objected strenuously to this land-grab and forced Antiochus to withdraw from Egypt by threatening him with war.

Roman foreign policy at this time resembled that of England in the eighteenth and nineteenth centuries regarding continental Europe. Rome would not allow any single power to become dominant in any area of the Mediterranean basin, just as England later felt its vital interests threatened if any European power were to be dominant on the continent. Antiochus' diplomatic defeat fooled the Jews in Jerusalem into thinking that they could safely rebel against Menelaus.[4]

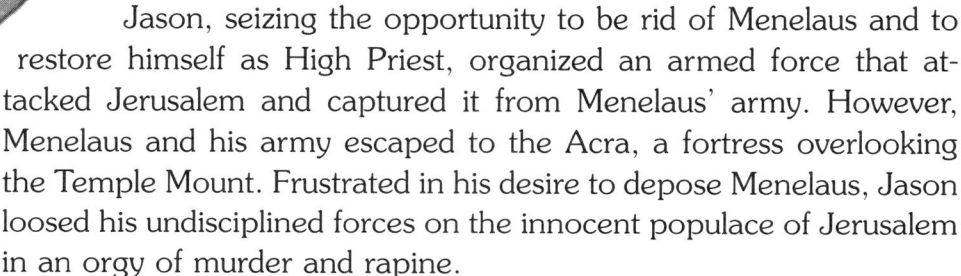

Antiochus IV

Jason, seizing the opportunity to be rid of Menelaus and to restore himself as High Priest, organized an armed force that attacked Jerusalem and captured it from Menelaus' army. However, Menelaus and his army escaped to the Acra, a fortress overlooking the Temple Mount. Frustrated in his desire to depose Menelaus, Jason loosed his undisciplined forces on the innocent populace of Jerusalem in an orgy of murder and rapine.

Antiochus, reeling from the debacle of his failed Egyptian campaign, turned to deal with the unrest in Jerusalem. He saw the struggle between Menelaus and Jason as, in effect, a rebellion against him. Invading Judah and capturing Jerusalem, the troops of Antiochus massacred thousands of innocent Jews.[5] Jason fled the city, never to return to Jerusalem, dying as a fugitive attempting to escape the sword of Antiochus.

Antiochus now began his attempt to eradicate Judaism, if not the Jews. He entered the Temple in Jerusalem, pillaged the vessels and gold of the Temple, and forcibly reinstalled Menelaus as High Priest. However, Antiochus was not wholly convinced of Menelaus' loyalty and devotion to his program of de-Judaizing the

---

4. There were rampant rumors in Jerusalem that Antiochus himself had been killed in the Egyptian campaign, thus fueling the plan of rebellion against his rule.

5. Josephus puts the number killed at upwards of 40,000.

Jews.[6] In 167 B.C.E. Antiochus dispatched his general, Apollonius, together with a large army, to Jerusalem. Another massacre of innocent Jews ensued, and the Acra fortress now was placed under permanent Syrian control and garrisoned by a large Syrian force. The Syrians breached the Temple walls in thirteen places and forbade the Jews to repair them. Greek temples and altars were now constructed throughout Judah. The decree was passed that pigs must be the usual animals to be sacrificed, even as part of the service in the Holy Temple in Jerusalem! Circumcision was banned, along with the celebration of the Jewish festivals and New Moon, observance of the Jewish Sabbath and of the Jewish dietary and ritual purity laws, and study of the Torah. All books of the Bible and the holy scrolls themselves were to be confiscated and burned. In short, any Jewish behavior was forbidden upon pain of death.

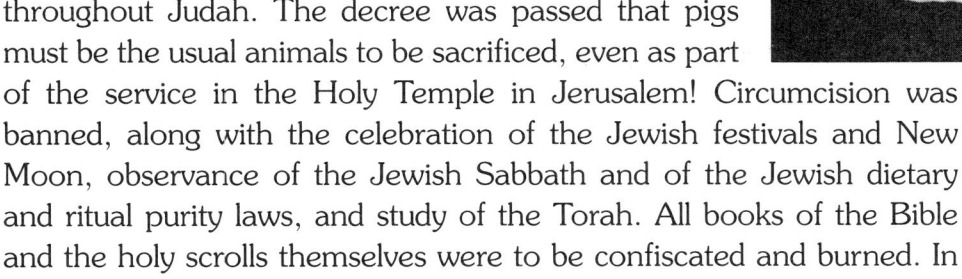

Menorah from Talmudic times

Persecution

MENELAUS SET OUT to do Antiochus' dirty work with a vengeance. In short order, an idol was actually erected on the Temple's altar and on it, daily, Menelaus' renegade priests indeed sacrificed pigs to the bewildering variety of Greek gods listed by Antiochus. Women who allowed their sons to be circumcised were killed with their sons tied around their necks. The scholars of Israel were hounded, hunted down and killed. Jews who refused to eat pork or sacrifice hogs were tortured to death.

The Jews resisted passively but tenaciously and refused to be cowed by the brutality of Antiochus and his Jewish henchmen. Legendary martyrs entered Jewish history and the Jewish collective memory and soul.[7] The reign of terror against Jews and their religious practices continued unrelentingly for a number of years. Many Jews

---

6. Alas, such is always the fate of apostate Jews toiling for foreign masters. They can never lose their Jewishness. Menelaus was the precursor of the likes of Lazar Kaganovich, Stalin's brother-in-law and a leading member of the Politburo until his downfall.

7. The story of the execution of Chana and her seven sons may have entered Jewish martyrology at this time, though it is not clear that that atrocity actually occurred during this era.

lost their lives rather than succumb to Menelaus and Antiochus; their heroic tenacity kept Judaism alive despite overwhelming odds. Others gave in to the tremendous pressure of the Hellenists, out of despair or out of eventual conviction. The future of Judaism in Judah and the Diaspora hung in the balance, with the Hellenists and Antiochus apparently holding the upper hand. But at this point the future of Judaism, and world civilization itself, was changed by the heroic actions of a handful of Jews who were able to reverse this catastrophic situation.

Chanah and her seven sons, from a 15th-century manuscript

Mattisyahu and His Sons

EVEN THE SMALLEST HAMLET in Judah was not safe from the oppression of the Hellenists. The altars to Zeus and other pagan deities were erected in every village in Judah, and Jews of every area were forced to participate in the sacrificial services.

In the small village of Modi'in[8] there lived the family of Mattisyahu ben Yochanan, members of a priestly unit (*Kohanim*) attached to the High Priesthood in the Temple in Jerusalem. Mattisyahu himself was already aged and physically weak in 166 B.C.E. Nevertheless, when the Greek army attempted to activate the pagan worship service in the main square of Modi'in and found a Jew who would accommodate them, Mattisyahu led his five sons and other townspeople in revolt, killing the traitor and the Syrian-Greek soldiers surrounding the altar.

This act was the spark that lit the long-smoldering fire of Jewish revolt against Antiochus, Menelaus and Hellenism. Echoing the words of Moses shouted at an earlier moment of national crisis,[9] Mattisyahu proclaimed, "Whoever is for God — let him come to me!" Mattisyahu and his sons, Shimon, Yochanan, Yehudah (Judah), Elazar and Yonasan, rallied an army of 6,000 to their cause and retreated to the

---

8. Ancient Modi'in is about twelve miles northwest of Jerusalem. Modern Modi'in is located about twenty miles west of Jerusalem.
9. *Exodus 32:26.*

desert of Judah, from where they conducted a successful guerilla war against the more numerous and better-armed Syrian Greeks. By the time Mattisyahu died in 165 B.C.E., the war against the Syrian Greeks and their Hellenist Jewish allies was in full force, with the army of the traditional Jews led by Yehudah, who was known as *Maccabee*.[10]

Praying at the graves of the Hasmoneans

Yehudah HaMaccabee

MATTISYAHU WAS THE PATRIARCHAL FIGURE, the hoary hero of the rebellion. He was the one who gave it spiritual justification and religious fervor. Yehudah, however, was the pragmatic leader, the warrior general whose skill, courage and tactics translated the religious hope of freedom into victory on the battlefield. After Mattisyahu's death, it was Yehudah's raw valor that rallied the Jewish forces and steeled them for the long ordeal ahead. Philip and Apollonius, the two main generals of Antiochus in Judah, attempted to annihilate the Hasmonean forces but instead suffered serious setbacks at Nablus and Beis Choron. Antiochus sent a third general, Seron, with a far larger army, to Beis Choron; but this force was also defeated by Yehudah.

Antiochus, enraged by the ineptitude of his generals, wildly swore to crush the Jews and lay waste to their country. However, he himself had great problems at home. His treasury was drained by his lavish personal spending, campaigns of conquest, the upkeep of his large standing army and the necessity of paying tribute to Rome. Therefore, before turning to Judah, he first invaded Persia to collect

---

10. Jewish tradition maintains that the name is formed by the acronym of the first letters of the verse in *Exodus* 15:11, *"Mi Camocha Ba'eilim Y'(Hashem),* — Who is like You amongst the powers, Hashem!" However, the word *maccabee* may really be Greek in origin and could be loosely translated as "the hammer."

Mattisyahu slaying a Hellenist, as depicted on the wall of the 3rd-century synagogue in Dura Europos

real or imagined tribute owed him. Bogged down in this thankless task, Antiochus appointed his blood relative, Lysias, to serve in his absence as head of the government of Syria and guardian of his young son, the heir to the throne, Antiochus V Eupator. The future of the war against Judah now was in Lysias' bloody hands.

The Miracle of Chanukah

LYSIAS APPOINTED THREE of the most able generals of Syria — Ptolemy Dorimenes, Nikanor and Gorgias — to crush the Hasmonean rebellion. An enormous Syrian army, numbering almost 50,000 men, marched into

Latrun — 19th-century view from the medieval fortress

Judah and encamped near the town of Emmaus.[11] Yehudah marshalled his forces at Mitzpah, the biblical site of the home and grave of the prophet Samuel, twelve miles east of Emmaus. With guile and courage, Yehudah outmaneuvered the far larger Syrian army, forced it to divide and then destroyed its various components, killing many thousands and forcing the survivors to flee north to Syria. Lysias evidently despaired of subjugating Judah.

There was now no large Syrian force remaining in Judah, and Yehudah and the Hasmonean army turned in joy and awe to the task of liberating Jerusalem and purifying the Holy Temple. The accomplishment of this historic task is the basis of the miracle and festival of Chanukah.

Yehudah HaMaccabee

The Jewish army retook Jerusalem, destroyed the pagan idols on the Temple Mount, purified the Temple and its vessels, drove out the hated Hellenist Jewish collaborators, and lit the candelabra in the Temple, which miraculously remained lit for eight days with only one day's fuel in its cups. Even though the military and political victories of the Hasmoneans were, historically speaking, short-lived, the glow of the holy fire they lit in the Temple in 165 B.C.E. still shines in the Jewish world today.

Significance of the Miracle

CHANUKAH IS NOT MERELY a commemoration of a victory of arms. Neither is it the symbol of religious freedom that much of modern Jewry, in its heartbreaking ignorance of its tradition, believes it to be. It is rather a clear restatement of an essential truth: that Torah demands of the Jewish people, individually and nationally, continuing sacrifice and unwavering commitment, and that when these are

19th-century silver dreidel

---

11. Today's monastery, tank museum and police station at Latrun is located near ancient Emmaus.

Chanukah menorah: "The eternal lights of Chanukah have never diminished for 21 centuries"

present in Jewish society, spiritual and even supernatural help will always guarantee Jewish survival.

The ritual of Chanukah observance throughout the ages, though not ignoring the military victory and heroism of the Hasmoneans, places its main emphasis on the rekindling of the Temple candelabra and the miracle of the small one-day pitcher of olive oil that fueled the holy candelabra for eight days. The symbol of the candelabra of the Temple and of the eternal light shining therefrom has become the symbol of the people and the Torah of Israel.[12] It is because of this emphasis on spiritual triumph and the victory of belief in Torah ritual and values that Chanukah is timeless and eternal. If it were only the commemoration of military might, Chanukah long ago would have disappeared, a hollow anniversary day, much as a celebration of the First Battle of Bull Run by the American South would be today.

Yehudah and the Hasmoneans used the respite granted them by the withdrawal of the Syrian armies to strengthen their fortifications and consolidate their control over the area surrounding Jerusalem. The walls of the Temple and of Jerusalem itself were repaired and in many places rebuilt.

The Hasmonean Kingdom

In 164 B.C.E. Yehudah sent forces north to Galilee and east to Trans-Jordan to help defend Jewish settlements besieged by non-Jewish tribes. The Hasmoneans again met with military success, but the small numbers of Jews actually living in those outlying areas of Israel precluded permanent

---

12. In our time the State of Israel has borrowed the menorah to symbolize its role, albeit in a secular form, as a "light unto the nations," and to convey the expectation of sacrifice on its behalf.

68 □ ECHOES OF GLORY

Jewish occupation. Yehudah therefore evacuated those Jews to the Jerusalem enclave in Judah, thereby strengthening the Jewish presence in the environs of the Holy City. The Hasmonean army also attacked

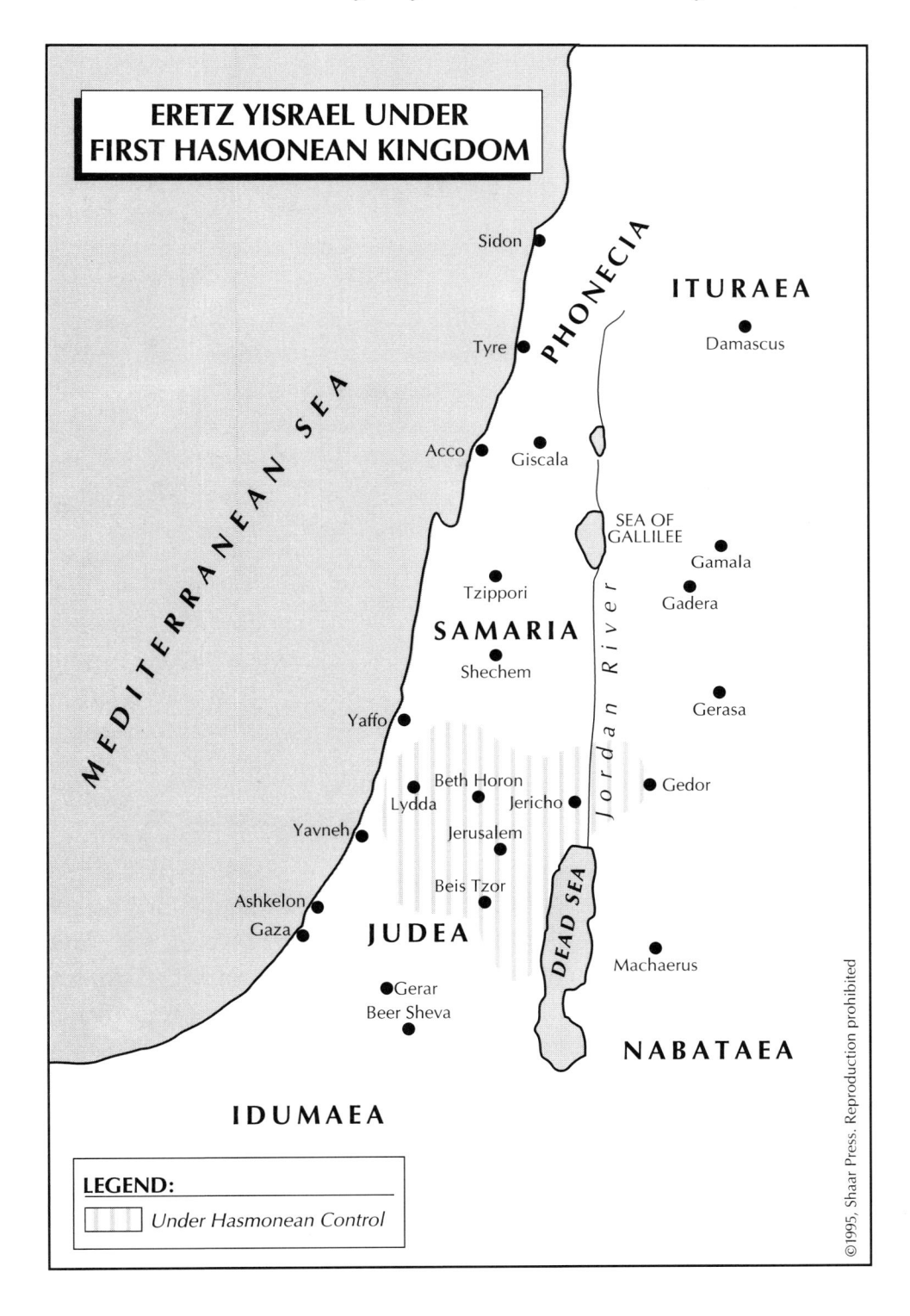

ERETZ YISRAEL UNDER FIRST HASMONEAN KINGDOM

- Sidon
- Tyre
- Acco
- Giscala
- Damascus
- Tzippori
- Shechem
- Gamala
- Gadera
- Gerasa
- Yaffo
- Beth Horon
- Lydda
- Jericho
- Gedor
- Yavneh
- Jerusalem
- Beis Tzor
- Ashkelon
- Gaza
- Machaerus
- Gerar
- Beer Sheva

MEDITERRANEAN SEA • PHONECIA • ITURAEA • SEA OF GALLILEE • Jordan River • SAMARIA • DEAD SEA • JUDEA • NABATAEA • IDUMAEA

LEGEND:
▌ Under Hasmonean Control

©1995, Shaar Press. Reproduction prohibited

and conquered the Idumeans (Edomites),[13] restored the city of Hebron to Jewish control and regained possession and use of the port of Jaffa.

By 163 B.C.E. the Hasmonean kingdom, centered in Jerusalem, was viable in terms of territory, reaching the Mediterranean on the west and the Negev desert in the south. (See Map.) There was a sense of euphoria in Judah, and Jews, for the first time since the building of the Second Temple, hoped for actual governmental independence and true political self-determination. But this heady optimism was premature, for the Syrian Greeks still had not reconciled themselves to the permanent loss of Judah. The Hasmonean family and kingdom would have yet to pay a steep price in blood and terror before establishing its kingdom.

Lysias and Philip

IN 164 B.C.E. the wicked Antiochus died, far from home on a wasted campaign in Persia. His young son, Antiochus V Eupator, was crowned king, under the regency of Lysias. However, unbeknownst to Lysias, Antiochus, while in Persia, had appointed a close advisor, Philip, as co-regent. As expected in such an unwieldy situation, Philip and Lysias agreed to disagree and launched a bitter dispute over control of the young king and the Syrian kingdom.

Lysias saw that an opportunity for victory over Philip lay in conducting a successful military campaign against Jerusalem and thereby gaining wide popular acclaim and support. Towards that end, Lysias rallied the Hellenist Jews throughout Judah, especially those holed up in the Acra fortress near the Temple Mount in Jerusalem, to open warfare against the Hasmoneans. Lysias himself again raised a large army[14] and

---

13. The Idumeans were a fierce, warlike tribe that had long plagued the Jewish population of Judah. They were descended from the biblical Edomites, the family of Esau, Jacob's brother. At the time of Nebuchadnezar, they joined the Babylonians in destroying Jerusalem and despoiling its Jewish inhabitants and were always inimical to their Jewish neighbors. Nevertheless, at the insistence of the Hasmonean rulers, the Idumeans eventually underwent a forced, pro-forma conversion to Judaism. As we will see in later chapters, this policy was frowned on by the rabbis, and in the persons of Antipater and Herod these "converts" would return to haunt the Hasmoneans and the Jewish commonwealth.

14. The *Book of the Maccabees* estimates the Syrian army at 100,000 infantry, 20,000 horsemen and numerous elephant units.

marched against Jerusalem. Sweeping aside the weak Jewish garrisons at Beis Tzur and Beis Zechariah, the Syrian army stood at the walls of Jerusalem. The siege of the city was bitter and costly to both sides, with the Hasmonean army forced to fight the external Syrian enemy and the internal Hellenistic Jewish enemy at one and the same time.

Before the siege could be decided, however, Lysias received news that his rival, Philip, was attempting a coup in Syria and would crown himself as emperor. Lysias immediately struck a truce with Yehudah HaMaccabee, granting the Jews full religious and some political autonomy, and nullifying the horrendous decrees of Antiochus Epiphanes; but at the same time he tore down many of the defensive walls and fortresses of Jerusalem. He then hurried back to Syria, executed Philip and established himself as ruler. However, his power was short-lived, for Antiochus V Eupator was assassinated in 161 B.C.E., and with his death came the end of Lysias' rule as well.

Yehudah Defeats the Syrians

THE NEW EMPEROR of Syria was Demetrius, a member of the royal Seleucid family, who had been held as a hostage of Rome until 161 B.C.E. Attempting to consolidate his power after the deaths of his rivals, Lysias and Antiochus V Eupator, Demetrius also turned to a campaign against Judah and Jerusalem. Again aided and abetted by the renegade Jewish Hellenists, who were led this time by an apostate pretender to the High Priesthood named Alcimus, the Syrian army invaded Judah, rescinded the decree of autonomy granted by Lysias to Yehudah HaMaccabee, and reinstated Syrian rule over the countryside. Once again Yehudah responded to the threat and mobilized the Hasmonean army for battle.

Demetrius

The Syrians were led by their famous general Nikanor, who had already tasted defeat at the hands of Yehudah several years earlier. At Beis Choron, north of Jerusalem, the battle was joined. Yehudah and the Hasmonean army, though greatly outnumbered, prevailed upon the battlefield, killing Nikanor and eventually destroying his entire army. The victory was so stunning and complete that the rabbis de-

Hasmonean hideouts in the Judean hills

clared its anniversary, 13 Adar, a special day of thanksgiving to God and rejoicing for Israel.[15]

Yehudah was well aware, though, that the threat from Syria had not yet passed. He searched for a policy that would safeguard the victories of Chanukah. In his zeal to save the freedom of the Jewish commonwealth, however, he neglected the counsel of the rabbis and made a grievous, far-reaching error.[16]

Yehudah entered into a treaty with Rome, in which Rome allegedly guaranteed to intervene on Judah's behalf against any further Syrian aggression. It was a case of inviting the bear into the home in order protect it from the lion. The problem is that after the lion is frightened away, how does one get the bear to leave as well? This will be discussed later.

In 160 B.C.E. Demetrius, unafraid of distant Rome, sent yet another army to subdue Jerusalem. This time the Hasmonean army wavered in the face of overwhelming Syrian strength. The battle at Elasah, west of Jerusalem, was undecided until the moment Yehudah himself fell, mortally wounded. The death of the great Jewish warrior demoralized the Hasmonean camp, and the Syrians and their Jewish Hellenist collaborators returned to power in Judah and Jerusalem.

Five years after the great miracle of Chanukah had lit the lamp of Jewish freedom and Torah life in Jerusalem, that fire was in danger of being snuffed out by the Syrians and Hellenists. It was a dark hour and an intense crisis in the struggle for Jewish survival.

---

15. See Talmud Yerushalmi, *Taanis*, Chapter 2, Section 12.
16. See the commentary of Ramban on *Bereshis* 32:4 for an incisive view of the strategic and spiritual pitfalls caused by Yehudah's well-intentioned but disastrous plan.

6

The Hasmonean Dynasty

(161 B.C.E.- 37 B.C.E.)

AFTER THE DEATH OF Yehudah HaMaccabee, the mantle of Jewish leadership passed to his surviving brothers, Yochanan, Yonasan and Shimon.[1] The political and military situation had so deteriorated after Yehudah Maccabee's death that the Hasmonean forces were forced to abandon Jerusalem and attempt to reorganize themselves in the desert of Judea, hard by the Dead Sea. The Syrian general, Bacchides, attempted to overwhelm the remaining Hasmonean forces in their new bivouac. The Jews were already weakened by the fact that Yochanan, the elder Hasmonean brother, was killed in 161 B.C.E. by marauding Bedouin tribesmen. However, Yonasan and Shimon, together with the remaining Hasmonean forces, fiercely resisted Bacchides, inflicting major casualties on his army and forcing him to give up the pursuit of their weakened forces. Bacchides retreated to Jerusalem, where he installed the apostate Jew, Alcimus, as High Priest. However, Alcimus died of a stroke in 159 B.C.E., and Bacchides, exhausted by his Judean adventure, returned that year with his army to Syria.

The violent standoff between the Jewish Hellenists and the Hasmoneans debilitated both sides, and for two years that struggle also abated. But in 157 B.C.E. the contest was renewed when the Hellenists petitioned King Demetrius I of Syria to return Bacchides and his army to Judah and there to end the Hasmoneans, once and for all. Demetrius foolishly acceded to their demand, and Bacchides once again began the pursuit of Yonasan and Shimon and their

---
1. Elazar, the fifth Hasmonean brother, had been killed during a previous battle with the Syrians.

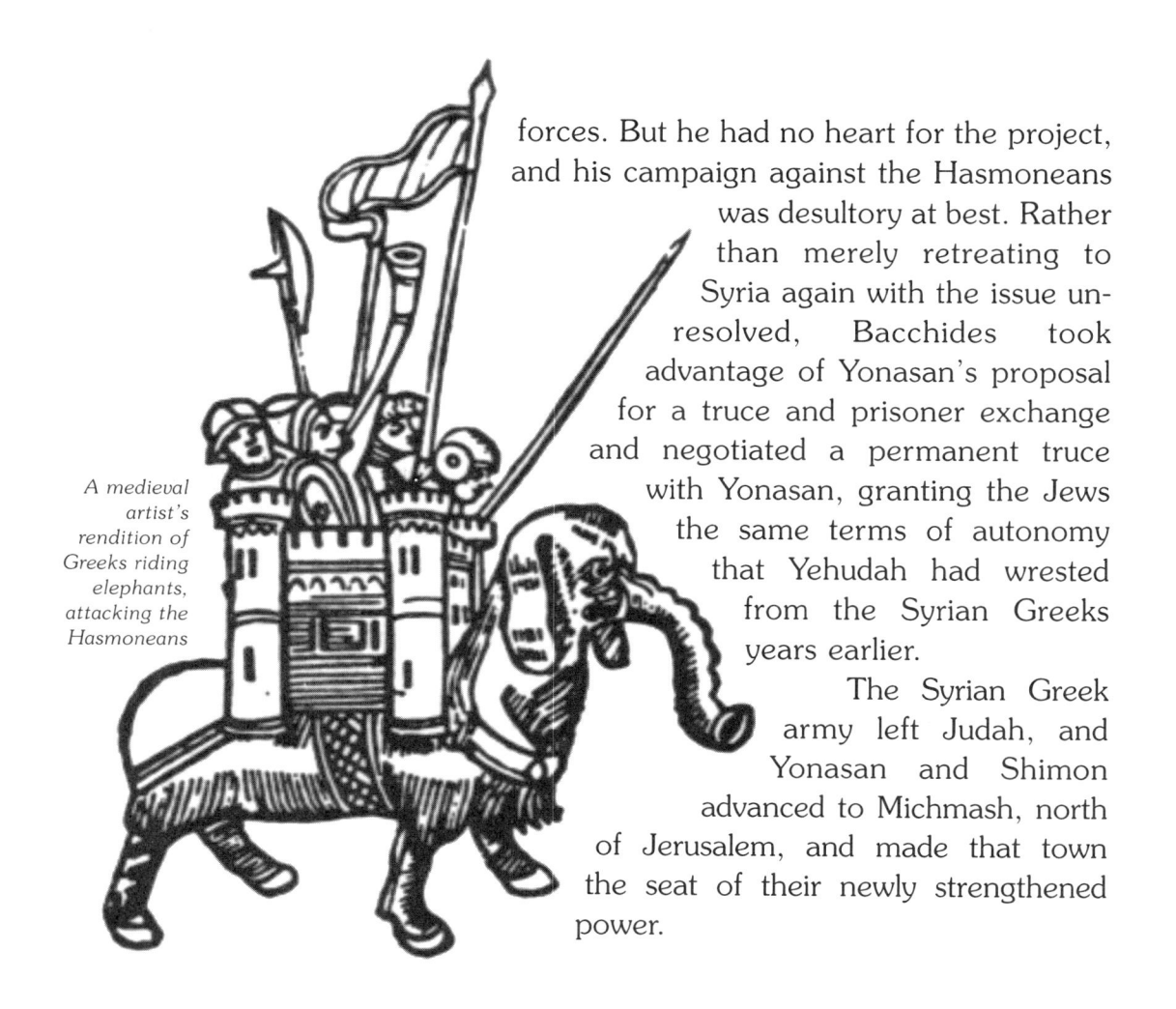

forces. But he had no heart for the project, and his campaign against the Hasmoneans was desultory at best. Rather than merely retreating to Syria again with the issue unresolved, Bacchides took advantage of Yonasan's proposal for a truce and prisoner exchange and negotiated a permanent truce with Yonasan, granting the Jews the same terms of autonomy that Yehudah had wrested from the Syrian Greeks years earlier.

The Syrian Greek army left Judah, and Yonasan and Shimon advanced to Michmash, north of Jerusalem, and made that town the seat of their newly strengthened power.

A medieval artist's rendition of Greeks riding elephants, attacking the Hasmoneans

A Clouded Destiny

THERE WAS ALWAYS a dark cloud of tragedy hanging over the family of the Hasmoneans. This great, heroic family of Jewish destiny always paid in blood for its efforts and miscues. In its more than a century of ruling Judah, unremitting strife, divisiveness and violence would dog the steps of the Hasmoneans. Why? Jewish thinkers[2] in all later ages searched for the key to understanding this disturbing pattern. But, as in much of Jewish history, clear and logical answers to paradoxical questions such as this one remain scarce. The story of Yonasan is an example of such a vexing tragedy.

---

2. We have already noted, in the last footnote to the previous chapter, that Rabbi Moshe ben Nachman (Ramban), in his commentary on the Bible, deals extensively with explaining the causes behind the fate of the Hasmoneans.

Alexander Balas

THE CONSTANT THREAT of Syrian reconquest prevented the Hasmoneans, under the leadership of Yonasan, from asserting their dominion over Jerusalem and the Temple. The paralyzing stalemate between the Hellenists and the Hasmoneans brought a spirit of apathy to the people of Jerusalem and Judah.

The rabbis attempted to strengthen the spiritual basis of Jewish life and rally the people to the cause of Torah and tradition. However, the strong political and social power base of the Hellenists thwarted many of the initiatives for a stronger Torah life created by the rabbis. It was obvious that without a dominant political and governmental structure friendly to the ideals of tradition and Jewish observance (i.e., the Hasmoneans), Jewish survival itself was jeopardized.

Alexandar Balas

The opportunity for renewed Hasmonean dominion presented itself in 153 B.C.E., as the product of a Byzantine plot regarding the leadership of Syria.[3] A pretender to the throne of Syria, Alexander Balas, rose to challenge the rule of Demetrius. Alexander Balas claimed to be the son of Antiochus IV and thus the legitimate heir to the throne of the Seleucids. Indeed, he bore a remarkable physical resemblance to Antiochus IV, though to knowledgeable people he was obviously an impostor. The foreign enemies of Syria[4] combined to support Alexander Balas' spurious claim. He made Acre his center of power and threatened to invade Syria proper and depose Demetrius.

In reaction to his growing isolation and danger, Demetrius reached forth to Yonasan, offering him rule over a fully autonomous Judah in return for his support against Alexander Balas. While not officially accepting the offer, Yonasan shrewdly and forcefully acted upon it.

---

3. The influence of indirect and seemingly unrelated events on the story of the Jewish people is part of the pattern of that story. The hidden hand of Providence directs, while man storms and schemes.
4. Led by Ptolemaic Egypt.

Yonasan's Rise

YONASON AND THE HASMONEAN GROUP left Michmash and moved to Jerusalem. The Syrian army garrisoned in Jerusalem was withdrawn and returned to Syria to help bolster Demetrius' defense against Alexander Balas. Yonasan immediately acted to refortify the city's strong points and repair all of the breaches in the outer walls of Jerusalem.

Yonasan was a very astute diplomat and a shrewd judge of the egos of the contestants for the Syrian throne. He therefore sent emissaries to establish a relationship with Alexander Balas, while delicately continuing to nurture his association with Demetrius. Alexander Balas, feeling himself dominant in the struggle for the Seleucid Empire, appointed Yonasan as leader of Judah and empowered him to serve as the High Priest in the Temple. Yonasan's accession to the High Priesthood ended the rule of the family of Zadok in that position. Under Yonasan, the land of Judah and the city of Jerusalem finally breathed free from Syrian domination. Thus, twelve years after the miracle of Chanukah, the victory of the Hasmoneans finally was confirmed by the events of history.

Yonasan threw in his lot with Alexander Balas, becoming a valuable ally of his. The Hellenists complained to Alexander Balas about Yonasan's rule, but were severely rebuffed by him. Thus Judah, though still nominally under Syrian control, became, for all practical purposes, an independent state, after almost two centuries of Greek domination.

Changes of Power

ALEXANDER BALAS WAS SUCCESSFUL in his campaign against Demetrius, eventually defeating and subsequently executing him. But Alexander Balas proved to be a cruel despot, foolish in politics and diplomacy and dissolute in his personal life. His father-in-law Ptolemy, the Egyptian king, eventually turned against Alexander and supported a new usurper to the Seleucid throne, Demetrius II, a son of the Demetrius killed by Alexander Balas. Demetrius II not only succeeded in driving

Alexander from the throne but also married the queen, the daughter of Ptolemy of Egypt. Alexander Balas himself was assassinated in exile in 145 B.C.E.

Yonasan, sensing the inherent weakness and instability of the Seleucid kingdom, negotiated a new agreement with Demetrius II which gave Judah dominion over an additional three areas of Samaria and Galilee, as well as substantially reducing the tribute payment of Judah to Syria. The Judean state was now growing in size, power and influence. Yonasan was committed to further growth and expansion.

Demetrius II proved to be no more able or popular than his father or Alexander Balas had been. Soon a new usurper to the Seleucid throne arose. His name was Tryphon, a former official of Alexander Balas. Installing himself as regent for the infant son of Alexander Balas, Tryphon became the true center of power in Syria.

Once again Yonasan exploited the insecurity of the new Seleucid rulers and obtained from Tryphon decrees confirming all of the advantageous arrangements granted the Hasmoneans by Demetrius I, Alexander Balas and Demetrius II. Yonasan also furthered his goal of conquering all of the Land of Israel by then occupying the southern coast of Israel, including the mainly Greek cities of Ashkelon[5] and Gaza, as well as the remainder of the Galilee. Thus, Yonasan was now within reach of the Hasmonean goal of restoring all of the Land of Israel to Jewish rule for the first time in the life of the Second Commonwealth. But, as was the case with many great leaders of Israel from Moses onward, Yonasan would not live to see the fulfillment of his dream, now seemingly so close at hand.

Tryphon's Treachery

THE CONTINUING TURMOIL in Syria had, as mentioned, brought a new leader, Tryphon, to power in the Seleucid world. But this turmoil also destabilized Hasmonean power. The Jews were never certain which, if any, of the Seleucid leaders to trust or negotiate with. They

---
5. Ashkelon would soon revert back to an independent Greek enclave, no longer under the rule of the Hasmoneans.

tired of the seemingly endless war with Syria and longed for a Syrian leader strong and good enough to fashion a lasting peace agreement with them.

The Hasmoneans hoped that Tryphon would be such a leader. They were mistaken, for Tryphon, feigning friendship and peace towards Judah, actually began raising a large army, intending to invade and conquer the Jewish state. Overconfident and underestimating Yonasan's resolve, Tryphon marched across the northern Jordan River and reached Beis She'an, south of Tiberias. There he was met and stymied by the Hasmonean army.

Tryphon immediately declared his intention of establishing a permanent peace with Judah and invited Yonasan to confer with him regarding the terms of the treaty. The place of the meeting was set at Acre, then under Tryphon's control. Naively, Yonasan accepted Tryphon's assurance of safe conduct and peaceful intent. When arriving in Acre, the Hasmonean king was immediately arrested and held hostage for an outlandish ransom. Though Yonasan's brother Shimon, the last surviving Hasmonean brother agreed to pay the ransom, Tryphon nevertheless killed Yonasan and sent only his remains to Shimon in return for the paid ransom. This despicable act of cruel treachery guaranteed the continuation of the Hasmonean war against Syria.

Shimon's Victory

SHIMON FOUGHT A SKILLED MILITARY and political war against Tryphon. Heavy winter snows, rare for Judah, impeded the progress of Tryphon's army, and, harassed incessantly by the Hasmonean army, the Syrians were finally forced to withdraw from Judaean soil.

Shimon entered into an alliance with Demetrius II, the rival and enemy of Tryphon, who was now rising to power in Syria. The new circumstances of Syria had forced a change in its traditional enmity towards Judah and Judaism. The small Jewish commonwealth was now freed completely from taxes and tribute to Syria, and the last of the Hasmonean brothers, Shimon, was able to achieve that which had eluded all of the others — true independence and sovereignty for Judah. Shimon declared himself "nasi" (prince, president, leader)[6] and minted Hebrew coins to commemorate the new independent state of Judah. Yonasan's capture of Jaffa was effectively consolidated by Shimon. The road to Jerusalem from the coast was completely secured, and the fortress of Acra in Jerusalem, the stronghold of the Hellenists and the Syrians, was occupied by the Hasmoneans.

In a last-gasp effort to turn back time and its consequences, Antiochus VII, the successor to Demetrius II, attempted one more battle of conquest against Judah. Shimon defeated the Syrians decisively near the town of Yavneh in 137 B.C.E., and a new era of peace, prosperity and spiritual and physical renewal began in Judah.

A Tragic Breakdown

HISTORY AND LIFE TEACH that self-inflicted wounds are the most dangerous and mortal of all blows. The Hasmonean dynasty would eventually do to itself and to Judah what the hated Greeks and Syrians could not do. The independence of the Jewish state and its remarkable opportunity for physical and spiritual growth and tranquility would go largely unexploited due to human frailty and internecine dynastic dispute. An instability would now work its way into Jewish life, both public and private, that would eventually sap the vitality of the population and allow Judah to become conquered and subjugated once more. The climate of disputes that erupted regarding temporal power and control would spill over into the religious world of Jewry as well. Hatred of other Jews became an accepted social norm, and this vitriol would eventually poison Jewish society and lead to the destruction of the Jewish state and the Temple.[7] The successes of Shimon would begin to wither almost immediately as family friction, sibling jealousies, and foolish and irresponsible behavior took control of events.

---

6. Shimon hesitated to call himself "king" due to the fact that he was a *Kohen* (priest) and not descended from the tribe of Judah and the family of David, to whom Jewish royalty was entrusted. His descendants would not harbor any such hesitations.

7. See Talmud, *Yoma* 9b.

The Extermination of a Family

SHIMON'S SONS, Yochanan Hyrcanus, Yehudah, and Mattisyahu, and their brother-in-law Ptolemy ben Chovov, the husband of Shimon's oldest daughter, all jockeyed for positions of power even while Shimon still ruled.

While the sons of Shimon remained at least publicly loyal and respectful to their father's rule, Ptolemy was made of much crueler and evil stuff. As a wedding gift to his new son-in-law, Shimon had granted Ptolemy rule over Jericho.[8] The young groom was disappointed by his wedding gift and instead dreamed of being the sole ruler over all of Judah.

He entered into secret negotiations with Antiochus VII, still smarting from his defeat by Shimon at Yavneh, and attempted to guarantee his role as the future leader of Judah by promising cooperation in Antiochus' new campaign to reconquer Judah. Antiochus committed himself to invading Judah and taking Jerusalem, while Ptolemy undertook to assassinate his father-in-law and brothers-in-law. Shimon, unaware of the cabal and treachery surrounding him, innocently accepted Ptolemy's invitation to attend an elaborate family banquet at Ptolemy's Jericho palace.

Yehudah and Mattisyahu, sons of Shimon, accompanied their father to Jericho. There, they and their father were hacked to death by the mercenary guards of Ptolemy. Thus did the last of the original Hasmoneans meet the same violent end that overtook all of his brothers, completing the inexplicable family tragedy. Shimon's wife, the mother-in-law of Ptolemy, was taken hostage and held in Ptolemy's fortress.

Yochanan Hyrcanus, who did not accompany his father to Jericho, was nevertheless also marked for death by Ptolemy's agents. He, however, discovered the plot and killed the plotters before they could strike. In 135 B.C.E., he proclaimed himself as the successor to his father, Shimon. The new *"nasi"* of Judah immediately arrived in Jerusalem, there to consolidate his hold on the government of Judah.[9]

---

8. Ah, Jericho, even then! Jericho apparently appeared to be an expendable territory, not necessarily part of a real Jewish state.
9. *First Book of Maccabees,* Chapter 16, sentences 11-24.

Ruins of the palace at Jericho

The saga of the Hasmoneans and that of the commonwealth of Judah now entered a new era.

Yochanan Hyrcanus immediately embarked upon the first of the many unfortunate and regular civil wars that would stain Hasmonean rule. He raised a large force and proceeded to lay siege to Ptolemy and his forces, who had taken refuge in the fortress of Jericho. Ptolemy, faced with capture or starvation, played his hostage card.

He exhibited Yochanan's mother daily from the parapets of the fortress, mocking and insulting the family of Shimon. There were days when the poor woman underwent public beating on the orders of Ptolemy, in sight and earshot of her son Yochanan. Nevertheless, she entreated her son not to succumb to blackmail and to continue the siege. But other factors intervened to thwart Yochanan's campaign. Antiochus VII, true to his evil bargain, moved on Jerusalem, and Yochanan Hyrcanus was forced to raise the siege of Jericho and hurriedly redeploy his forces to protect the capital of Judah. Ptolemy, in a final fit of vindictive cruelty, now killed his mother-in-law and fled across the Jordan, never to be heard from again in Jewish life.

Coin minted by Yochanan Hyrkanus

THE BEAUTY OF JAPHETH AND THE TENTS OF SHEM *The Hasmonean Dynasty* □ 81

Jewish Independence Regained

YOCHANAN HYRCANUS WAS hard-pressed to repulse the invasion of Antiochus VII. In a year-long war (135-134 B.C.E.) that exhausted the Jewish army, no decisive result was attained. Yochanan was forced to agree to a humiliating armistice. Under its terms, much of the defensive wall of Jerusalem was again razed, Jewish hostages were taken as guarantees for the payment of continuing taxes to Syria, while an initial, one-time, punitive tax payment of five hundred talents of silver was extracted from Yochanan's treasury. But Providence intervened again on behalf of a Hasmonean leader, for in 129 B.C.E. riots and mutinies swept Syria. Antiochus VII, flushed from a successful campaign against Parthia,[10] was surprised and deposed by his enemies. Chaos now reigned throughout Syria, and with it, the centuries-long attempt by Syria to control Judah finally came to a failed end.

Yochanan swiftly took advantage of the changed situation in Syria and rebuilt the wall of Jerusalem, negotiated the return of the Jewish hostages held previously by Antiochus VII and discontinued the payment of tribute to Syria. Yochanan thus regained the level of Jewish national independence first achieved by his father, Shimon, years earlier. The Hasmonean dynasty was now on the verge of attaining diplomatic and popular success and territorial security. Yochanan Hyrcanus prepared to change roles from defender of a small, beleaguered country to conqueror of the neighboring lands surrounding Judah.

Enlarging Judah's Borders

THE AREA OF JUDAH was limited since its founding by Ezra to the vicinity of Jerusalem and the land south and east of it.[11] Under previous Hasmonean rule, some areas of the Mediterranean coast, basically from Ashkelon to Jaffa, were also annexed to Judah, as were pieces of Galilee.

---

10. Paradoxically, many Jewish soldiers fought in the army of Antiochus VII. The Jewish presence in his army was apparently of such consequence that Antiochus VII avoided hostilities on Saturday, the Jewish Sabbath, and on the festival of Shavuos as well, in order to appease his Jewish soldiers.

11. There were numerous Jewish settlements in the Galilee from the time of Ezra

ERETZ YISRAEL UNDER YOCHANAN HYRCANUS

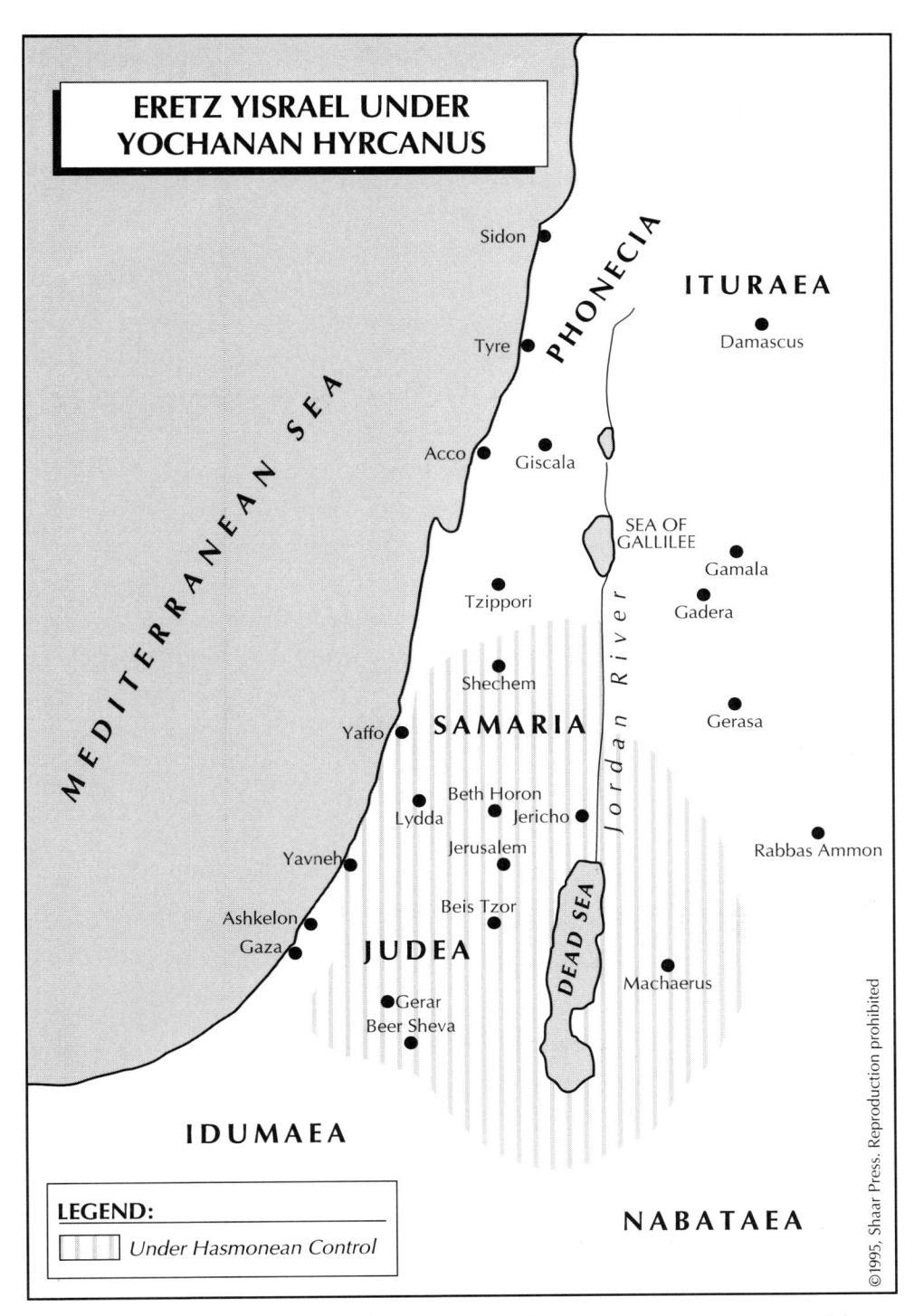

Yochanan Hyrcanus longed to restore the Jewish commonwealth to its biblical borders. He moved his army, commanded now by his two

---

onward, but these areas were primarily viewed as Jewish enclaves on foreign territory rather than part of the Jewish commonwealth.

sons, Yehudah Aristobulus and Antigonus, north of Jerusalem, capturing the Samaritan stronghold of Shomron and destroying the Samaritan temple on Mount Grizim, near Shechem (Nablus). He also moved his forces east of the Jordan River, conquering large sections of Transjordan and expanding the Hasmonean rule over those lands. He then turned his attention to the southern part of the Land of Israel. He struck at the Idumeans in their Negev home, and after conquering them, forced them to convert to Judaism. This fatal error on his part brought upon him the opposition of the rabbis, always opposed to forced and insincere converts to Judaism. But in the flush of his continuing successes the matter was glossed over, only to rise and destroy Yochanan's successors two generations later. The Idumeans provided fierce warriors and wily diplomats to the service of the Hasmonean king, who came to rely upon them more and more during his reign.

Consolidating his gains, Yochanan Hyrcanus conquered the Lower Galilee and the Valley of Jezreel, and the Hasmonean empire now stretched nearly to the promised biblical borders of Israel, from Dan to Beersheba and from Transjordan and the Golan to the Mediterranean. Yochanan also strongly fortified Jerusalem, rebuilding its walls and reinforcing the ramparts around the Temple Mount. Yochanan Hyrcanus thus became one of the great warrior kings in Jewish history, and under his rule the Jewish commonwealth was strong, prosperous and seemingly secure for the first time since the Jewish return from Babylonia over two centuries earlier.

Dissent from Within

HOWEVER, AS WE NOTED, Jews seemingly suffer good fortune poorly. The last years of the reign of Yochanan Hyrcanus were clouded with communal and religious dissension within the Jewish society. The discredited Hellenists disappeared from the scene, but new forces rose to take up their cause and disrupt Jewish traditional life. The old aristocracy of the priesthood, who were originally shunted aside by the Hasmoneans and their allies among the *Kohanim* (priests of the family of Aaron), joined forces with the Sadducees in opposition to the Hasmoneans and their rabbinic Pharisee allies.

The Sadducees now openly denied the validity of the Oral Law and refused to accept upon themselves the decrees, interpretations, attitudes and authority of the leading Pharisee rabbis. The Sadducees held the lower economic class of Jews in contempt and mocked their loyalty to Jewish tradition and custom. They interpreted the Torah according to their own spirit and whim, at times prohibiting that which traditional Judaism allows[12] and at other times behaving far more leniently.[13] Though not pagan, as were the Hellenists, the Sadducees nevertheless inherited the Hellenists' disdain for Torah, tradition, and other, less "sophisticated" Jews. They encouraged a life of hedonism and the pursuit of luxury and pleasure, to the exclusion of the traditional Jewish life-style and value system. In their haughtiness and pseudo-sophistication they separated themselves from the Jewish masses, and in their inability to appreciate and believe in the Oral Law they created a frozen, inflexible and uncaring Judaism which eventually came to stand for foreign values and which deteriorated into empty pompous ceremonies, Temple culture and Greek and Roman affectations.

15th-century cholent pot

Efforts of the Pharisees

DURING THE REGIME OF Yochanan Hyrcanus, the Pharisees were led by the second generation of the *Zugos* (the "Pairs"), who were the leaders of the Sanhedrin and of the Pharisees, and thus of traditional Jewry. They were Yehoshua ben Perachya and Nitai HaArbeli. They instituted universal Jewish education, strengthened the yeshivos and

---

12. For example, the Sadducees permitted no hot food on the Sabbath. In response to this, the rabbis ordained that hot food must be part of the Sabbath day menu, a custom observed until today throughout the Jewish world in the form of variations on the venerable pot stew dish, *cholent*. In a more cruel vein, the Sadducees interpreted "an eye for an eye" literally and were always quick to enforce the death penalty for legal infractions. The Pharisees, on the other hand, interpreted "an eye for an eye" in accordance with the Oral Law as being only a matter of monetary damages and rarely justified the actual use of the death penalty.

13. Adoption of different calendar rules, elimination of certain Temple libations and offerings and a general laxity in ritual observance were some of the characteristics of Sadducee life.

Torah schools, raised many disciples and encouraged the growing pride in the emerging Jewish empire. They urged the creation of a society based upon respected teachers, loyal friends, charitable judgment of others, condemnation of evil and evildoers, and a tenaciously optimistic view of life.[14] However, they were troubled by Yochanan Hyrcanus' reaction to his successes. For even though he supported the program of the Pharisees for the majority of his reign, he began to truly believe in himself, not only in matters of diplomacy and war, but in matters of religious interpretation and innovation as well, and he came under the influence of the Sadducees toward the end of his life.

Some of his religious ordinances and recommendations were accepted by the rabbis, but some were not. As noted earlier, the rabbis also criticized the forced conversion of the Idumeans by Yochanan Hyrcanus. Yochanan, like many a leader, did not suffer such criticism well. He felt that his great accomplishments on behalf of the Jewish people and state should grant him universal and unquestioning approbation amongst Jews. He resented the Pharisees' complaints about his meddling in religious affairs. The rabbis also were troubled by the fact that a warrior, and therefore a killer, served as the High Priest of Israel, and Yochanan was well aware of the undercurrent of opinion amongst the Pharisees that he resign the office of High Priest. This demand was never formally made to him, as it would later be made to his son, Alexander Yannai.

A Troubled End

THE LEADERS OF THE Hasmonean ruling class began to feel themselves closer to the society of the Sadducees than to the Pharisees. Power corrupts and success misleads. The Sadducees shrewdly exploited Yochanan Hyrcanus' differences with the Pharisees.

The new aristocracy of the Hasmoneans slowly joined forces with the remnants of the old priestly aristocracy, forgetting that their triumph over the Hellenists would now be undone by this unfortunate alliance with the spiritual heirs of their enemies. Yochanan himself changed

---
14. See Mishnah, *Avos*, Chapter 1, Mishna 6 and 7.

sides and became a Sadducee.[15] He now vented his wrath against his Pharisee critics, exiling many of them and even killing some. The people sided with their rabbinic teachers against the unwarranted oppression of their ruler, and when Yochanan Hyrcanus died in 104 B.C.E., after a lifelong struggle on behalf of his people and their country, he was in large measure unmourned by that people. His long reign of thirty-one years ended in a cloud of civil strife and tragic error.

One of the last acts of Yochanan was to enter into a formal alliance with the new great world power, Rome. He was able to wrest favorable terms from Rome regarding the export of grain from Judah to Rome, and the port city of Jaffa became a major commercial port. Rome would now continue to be a major factor in the life of Judah for the next four centuries, eventually dominating and finally destroying the small Jewish state. But at the time, Yochanan's alliance with Rome was viewed as a diplomatic coup. The Jews shortsightedly celebrated a tactical victory, which in reality was a strategic defeat. When Yochanan died, the country he had governed was much greater in size, wealth, prestige and security than it had been when he succeeded his father, Shimon, to the leadership of Judah. However, the rift between the Sadducees and the Pharisees, and its attendant violence and hatred, boded evil for the future of the Hasmonean state.

The Essenes

ASIDE FROM THE EMERGENCE of the Pharisees and Sadducees, another group developed in the Jewish society of the Hasmonean era. This group was an extremist break-off from the Pharisees and were known as Essenes.[16] Small in number but of strong social influence because of their seemingly blameless personal moral lives, the Essenes established small communes in the Judean desert[17] where they lived lives of

---

15. See Talmud, *Berachos* 29a: "Believe not in yourself, even until the day of your death, for Yochanan the High Priest served in the holy Temple for eighty years, and at the end of his life became a Sadducee."

16. The word may be a Greek corruption of the Aramaic word *chassya*, corresponding to the Hebrew word *chassid*, meaning "pious ones."

17. The famous "Dead Sea Scrolls," found at Qumran in the Judean desert, are thought to be of Essene origin.

A portion of Habakkuk from the Dead Sea Scrolls

Caves at Qumran believed to have been used by the Essenes

asceticism and self-denial.

The Torah of Israel is one of balance and normalcy. It abhors extremism and unnecessary mortification of the flesh. "Its ways are ways of pleasantness and all of its paths lead to peace."[18] Thus, in a short period of time the Essenes removed themselves completely from the orbit of Jewish life. In their communes they owned no private property, shared all worldly goods, remained mostly celibate (thus guaranteeing their eventual demise as a group), immersed themselves many times daily in purifying waters, practiced vegetarianism, spoke few words, if any at all, shunned all technological advances, cursed the rise of cities, and spent their days copying and studying the holy books of the Bible and their own interpretations. Each of these ideas and practices, in moderation and limited by traditional halachic perspective, had positive qualities. But taken together, in a world view of apocalypse, isolation from society and

---

18. *Proverbs* 3:17.

extremism of religious behavior, this Essene program was one of destruction and extinction. It is upon the Essene community that the early Christians would rely in a later century for many of their theological ideas and supporters.

The Essenes never became a part of mainstream Judaism, and with the later rise of Christianity in the world, they would disappear completely from Jewish society.

Yehudah Aristobulus

THE DEATH OF YOCHANAN HYRCANUS brought his son, Yehudah Aristobulus I, to the Hasmonean throne. This headstrong and power-hungry man proclaimed himself as king,[19] no longer satisfied with the euphemistic title of "nasi" (prince or leader) used by his grandfather and father during their reigns. This naturally brought upon him the ire of the rabbis, who continued to maintain that the official throne of Judah belonged to the descendants of David and the tribe of Judah, and not to the priestly (kohanim) Hasmoneans descended from the tribe of Levi. In return, Yehudah Aristobulus I persecuted the rabbis and their Pharisee followers. He ruthlessly exiled many of them, and hundreds of Pharisees were painfully and violently executed. Yehudah Aristobulus I was insecure in his power and soon exhibited fatal symptoms of royal paranoia.

Apparently Yochanan had wished his wife, Yehudah Aristobulus' mother, to serve as ruler, or at least as regent, upon his death. However, Yehudah immediately turned against his own family, imprisoning his mother and a number of his brothers and eliminating their base of support in the Hasmonean court. Yehudah entered into a power-sharing partnership with his brother, Antigonus, who was a beloved favorite of Yehudah. In fact, Antigonus was the only member of his family whom he favored. Antigonus became the head of the Hasmonean army and led a successful campaign to annex the remainder of the Upper Galilee to the Jewish state. Following his father's policy of forced conversions to Judaism, Antigonus coerced the non-Jewish residents of the Upper Galilee to adopt the Jewish

---

19. In spite of calling himself king, the coins minted in Judah during the year-long reign of Yehudah Aristobulus I proclaim him only as *nasi*. It may be that the coins were minted at the beginning of his rule, before he accepted monarchy.

religion.[20] This policy of forced conversions intensified the opposition of the rabbis and Pharisees to the government of Yehudah Aristobulus I.

Opposition to the Hasmoneans

YEHUDAH ARISTOBULUS WAS ENAMORED of Hellenism, though he was not an open Hellenist. His personal distaste for the Pharisees and the rabbinic leaders of traditional Jewry contributed to his joining the camp of the bitter foes of his family. Greek ways, names, words[21] and values became ever more acceptable in Jewish society, especially among the upper and ruling classes, because of his encouragement.

He was convinced that the survival of independent Jewish political life, and in fact the Jewish state itself, depended upon close association with Rome and the adoption of the societal norms of Greco-Roman civilization. This attitude signaled a landmark departure by the Hasmonean royalty from the policies of their forebears and of traditional Jewry.

The balance of the Hasmonean dynasty (about sixty more years) would now be marked by increasing civil violence and popular rebellion against their government. The masses of Israel, originally grateful to and worshipful of the Hasmoneans, rose in opposition to the new dictators who revived the dormant virus of Hellenism. It would be a very rough ride henceforth for the Jewish state in the era of the

---

20. There is some scholarly opinion that these Upper Galilee converts were in fact descendants of Jews of the Ten Tribes who had lived there in the era of the First Temple. Apparently, according to this theory, these one-time Jews had drifted away into paganism over the centuries and forgot their Jewish roots.

21. Yosef Klausner, in his book *HaBayis HaSheni B'Gadluso* (Tel Aviv, 1930), is of the opinion that the Greek word *Sanhedrin*, describing the legislature/high court of Judah, entered the Jewish vocabulary in the year of the reign of Yehudah Aristobulus I. His theory is that the institution until then, during the reign of the early Hasmonean leaders, was called *Chever haYehudim* (The Council/Alliance of the Jews). Even during the reign of Yehudah Aristobulus I, the coins minted described him as the head of the *Chever haYehudim*, whereas the term *Sanhedrin* only became popular during the reign of Alexander Yannai, Yehudah Aristobulus' brother and immediate successor. The definition of the term *Chever haYehudim* and whether it was the original Hebrew term for the religious high court of Israel remains yet a matter of scholarly conjecture.

Second Temple. But first, personal intrigues would intervene in the Hasmonean story and bring the dynasty to near disaster.

Two Brothers Die

THE VICTORY OF ANTIGONUS brought him fame, popularity and also jealous enmity. Many in the Hasmonean court bore him no love and, playing on the ever-increasing paranoia of Yehudah Aristobulus, a plot to destroy Antigonus was hatched and executed. Innocently violating Yehudah Aristobulus' rule of forbidding anyone to appear at the court in military gear and armed,[22] Antigonus was killed by zealous soldiers guarding the king. Yehudah Aristobulus was crushed emotionally and physically by the tragedy of his brother's death at the hands of his own soldiers. Having ruled for only one year, Yehudah Aristobulus died in 103 B.C.E., childless and unloved, his brothers and mother still chained in his prison.

Shlomis Alexandra

YEHUDAH ARISTOBULUS, though apparently unbeknownst to him, had the good fortune of marrying one of the great women of Jewish history. His wife, Shlomis Alexandra,[23] was a sister of Shimon ben Shetach, the new leader of the Pharisees, who, together with Yehudah ben Tabai, formed the third generation of the *Zugos* ("Pairs"), the religious guides and leaders of Judaism. Although married to an opponent of the Pharisees, Shlomis remained loyal in her heart to her brother and the tradition of Israel that he represented. When her husband died, she briefly assumed power as queen. She released all of Yehudah's family from prison and canceled the program of persecution against the Pharisees.

---

22. The plotters arranged for a royal messenger to instruct Antigonus falsely to come immediately to the king's palace although he was armed, insisting that this was the specific wish of Yehudah. The royal palace guards, who were unaware of the cabal, felt themselves bound by the existing ordinance.

23. She was also known as Salome and as Queen Shlomzion. One of the main thoroughfares in modern Jerusalem is named Shlomzion Hamalkah after her.

Table of Zugos (Pairs)

Generation	Nasi / President of the Sanhedrin	Av Beis Din / Dean of the Sanhedrin	Years in office
1	Yose ben Yoezer	Yose ben Yochanan	c. 210 - 138 B.C.E.
2	Yehoshua ben Perachya	Nittai HaArbeli	c. 138 - 83 B.C.E.
3	Yehudah ben Tabbai	Shimon ben Shetach	c. 83 - 58 B.C.E.
4	Shemaya	Avtalyon	58-35 B.C.E.
5	Hillel	Shammai	32-0 B.C.E.

Yehudah's oldest brother, Alexander Yannai[24] (Janeus), exercised his duty of yibum (levirate marriage) and became Shlomis' husband as well as the new Hasmonean king of Judah. Under the strong influence of his new wife, Alexander Yannai relaxed all of the remaining decrees against the Pharisees and publicly took a pro-Pharisee stance. He conferred with his brother-in-law, Shimon ben Shetach, on state matters, and apparently the potential for a new era of growth and harmony had dawned on the Hasmoneans and Judah. But this was more of a mirage than reality.

Alexander Yannai

ALEXANDER YANNAI WAS the most powerful and the most complex of all the Hasmonean rulers. He was ruthless, cunning, paranoid and utterly without fear or conscience. He was determined to make Judah the leading military force in the Middle East and to extend its dominion over the widest possible area. His agenda was conquest and war. Alexander did not really have the wholehearted support of the Jewish people for his wars of conquest and aggrandizement, and he therefore had to rely more and more on mercenaries and foreign soldiers and officers. Slowly, the Idumeans became more entrenched in the Hasmonean military, a fact which would lead to the demise of the Hasmonean dynasty itself. Foreign, non-Jewish soldiers had no sympathy for the

---

24. The name Yannai, a very popular one in Second Temple times, is apparently a derivative nickname of Yonasan.

people or Land of Israel and would easily obey orders, persecuting those Jews who incurred Alexander Yannai's displeasure. Alexander's rule over Judah came to rely more upon the sword and the whip than upon respect and patriotism. His twenty-seven-year reign (103-76 B.C.E.) over Judah would be one of violence, blood and civil war. But he would also bring the Hasmonean empire to the apex of its power, influence and territory.

Alexander's initial goal was to capture all of the Mediterranean cities and ports of the Land of Israel. As mentioned above, Alexander's grandfather, Shimon, had completed the capture of the main port city of Jaffa, thus providing Judah with an outlet to the sea. However, nestled along the Mediterranean were an additional seven coastal enclaves, some of them thriving ports, which remained under Greek control. Alexander's objective was to control the entire sea coast of the Land of Israel, from Rafiach in the south to Acre in the north.

The Greek cities of the coast appealed to Ptolemy VIII Lathyrus, king of Cyprus and pretender to the throne of Egypt (then occupied by his mother, Cleopatra, and another of her sons), for help in their struggle against Alexander Yannai. Ptolemy dispatched a substantial army, which fought Alexander to a standstill. Cleopatra, wary that Ptolemy's success in Judah would provide him with a springboard for invading Egypt, entered into an alliance with Alexander Yannai against her own son, Ptolemy. Their alliance succeeded in defeating Ptolemy and ousting him from the coast of the Land of Israel. Alexander Yannai then subjugated all of the cities of the coast and established Judah as a major center of commercial shipping[25] in the Mediterranean area.

This first campaign of Alexander, which came so close to disaster and ended so triumphantly, was the opening act in a lifelong drama of war and conquest which would restore to Judah the borders of Israel achieved during the biblical era of David and Solomon.

Alexander Yannai also conquered much territory east of the Jordan River. All of the ten Greek cities east of the Jordan — the Decapolis — fell to Alexander's forces. From the Bashan and Golan

Coins minted by Alexander Yannai, note the anchor on the second coin from the top

---

25. On the coins minted by Alexander Yannai during his reign, there appeared an anchor. This was a symbol of the growing importance of seafaring to Judah.

ERETZ YISRAEL UNDER ALEXANDER YANNAI

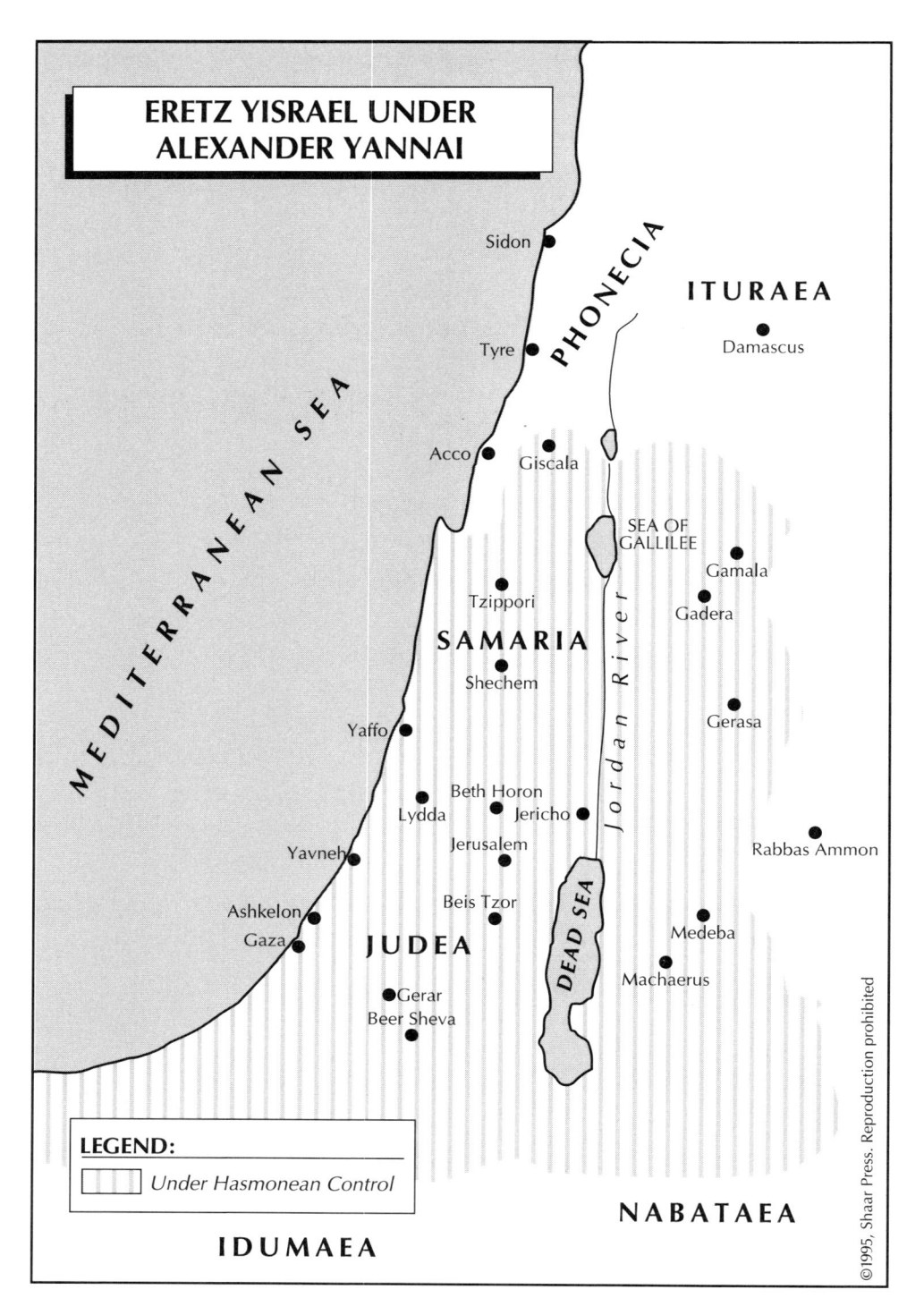

Map shows locations including: Sidon, Tyre, Acco, Giscala, Tzippori, Shechem, Yaffo, Beth Horon, Lydda, Jericho, Jerusalem, Yavneh, Beis Tzor, Ashkelon, Gaza, Gerar, Beer Sheva, Damascus, Sea of Galilee, Gamala, Gadera, Gerasa, Rabbas Ammon, Medeba, Machaerus. Regions: PHONECIA, ITURAEA, SAMARIA, JUDEA, IDUMAEA, NABATAEA. Features: Mediterranean Sea, Jordan River, Dead Sea.

LEGEND: Under Hasmonean Control

©1995, Shaar Press. Reproduction prohibited

in the north to the eastern shores of the Dead Sea in the south, Hasmonean rule was accepted. All of the Greek enclaves in Judah proper were also conquered by Alexander, with many of their inhabitants converting to Judaism, willingly or otherwise.

ECHOES OF GLORY

Alexander Yannai and the Pharisees

ALEXANDER'S MILITARY SUCCESSES brought him wide recognition and respect in the general non-Jewish world. But the rabbis and Pharisees in Judah saw in him a violent, blood-letting[26] egotist, who converted others to Judaism by force, maintained a cruel and alien mercenary army that heavily drained the economic resources of Judah, and continued to serve as both king and High Priest against the will of the religious leaders of the people.[27] Alexander Yannai, stung by the criticism of the rabbis, now openly adopted the ways of the Sadducees, viewing the Pharisees, and especially their leader, his own brother-in-law, Shimon ben Shetach,[28] as mortal enemies. Alexander rooted out the Pharisees from positions of importance in his government and in the Sanhedrin and replaced them with the leaders of the Sadducees and the corrupt priestly aristocracy. The king arrested a large number of the Pharisees, torturing, crucifying and otherwise executing many of them. Shimon ben Shetach and other leaders of the Pharisees who escaped Alexander's dragnet fled the country or went deeper underground. In

---

26. Though this is not the place for a detailed exposition of the traditional rabbinic attitude towards war, some explanation of the matter is necessary to help us understand the fierce opposition of the Pharisees to the rule of Alexander Yannai. The rabbis realized that though there may be a just war, a necessary war, a victorious war, there never is a cheap, painless war. The historian W. Bruce Lincoln, in his book *Passage Through Armageddon* (New York, 1986, p. 188), states the concept succinctly: "...these wandering folk (the war refugees of World War I) were ever-present grim reminders that many suffered and few benefited when rulers and statesmen unsheathed the swords of nations." The rabbis were no pacifists. They supported the original Hasmonean war of independence against the Syrian Greeks. But wars of conquest and self-aggrandizement were another matter. They found no comfort in Alexander's policy of expansion at the expense of so much pain, tragedy and blood. The attitude of the rabbis towards permanent solutions of national problems is reflected in the words of the prophet Zechariah: "Not by might nor by force, but rather by My spirit, says the Lord of Hosts."

27. See Talmud, *Kiddushin* 66a, for the description of Alexander Yannai's confrontation with the Pharisees over his serving as both king and High Priest.

28. See Talmud Yerushalmi, *Nazir*, Chapter 5, section 3, for the story of why Alexander felt he was unjustly treated and exploited by Shimon ben Shetach. The incident records a dispute regarding a large donation the king granted to enable three hundred Nazarites to purchase the sacrificial animals they needed in order to be released from their vows. He felt he was tricked into contributing a larger portion than he thought he had agreed to. From that moment onward there was bad blood between the brothers-in-law, not only on an ideological basis but on a personal one as well.

spite of all of his foreign and military successes, Alexander Yannai had brought the Jewish state to the brink of civil war.

A School System

THE PHARISEES, under the leadership of Shimon ben Shetach, mounted a two-pronged attack on Alexander Yannai and the Sadducees. Not only did they openly criticize his rule and policies, but more importantly, they moved to solidify Torah knowledge and traditional Jewish values, based upon the Oral Law, among the masses of Israel. The great teacher of Israel, Yehoshua ben Gamla, established a sweeping, broad innovation in public life — a general public school system that provided Torah education for every Jewish child in the land.[29] Shimon ben Shetach, by diplomacy, persuasion, tact and Providential aid, was able to remove many of the Sadducee members of the Sanhedrin and replace with rabbinic scholars loyal to the Oral Law and Jewish tradition. Thus, even though the Sadducees and Alexander Yannai appeared to be in control of the country and its policies, the Pharisees had in reality co-opted much of their power in society through their educational system and their influence on the Sanhedrin.

Frustrated by the success of the Pharisees in rooting themselves within the masses of Israel, and allowing his paranoia to completely overwhelm his rationality, Alexander Yannai reacted to the growing Pharisee power in rage and violence. He became openly provocative in his behavior towards the Pharisees and their sensitivities. Soon he would wildly throw the match into this tinderbox.

Sacrilege in the Temple

ONE OF THE MAJOR RITUAL ISSUES contested between the Pharisees and Sadducees was the requirement for a water libation offering on the Altar of the Temple during the festival of Succos. This requirement, since it was

---

29. Shimon ben Shetach himself established a public school system, on a small basis, in Jerusalem in about the year 97 B.C.E. Yehoshua ben Gamla's efforts to create an all-encompassing school system throughout Judah were not fully completed until about the year 65 B.C.E.

Waters of the Silwan

not specifically spelled out in the words of the Torah, became a prime example of the exegesis method of the Oral Law and was celebrated with great joy and pomp in the Temple and in the environs of Jerusalem during the Succos holiday. It became the symbol of the authenticity of the Pharisaic interpretation of the Torah and of Jewish ritual and life. The Sadducees, complaining that the water libation offering was not in accord with their belief in only the written Torah, denigrated the event and mocked it. But the masses of Israel sided with the Pharisees, and the celebration of this event, from the mo-

An 18th-century depiction of Simchas Beis Hashoeva

ment of the drawing of the water from the pool of Shiloach (Silwan) to the actual libation and pouring of the water on the Temple altar, was the occasion for the greatest expression of public joy in Jewish life.[30] Therefore, when Alexander Yannai, serving as the High Priest in the Temple on the festival of Succos in the year 95 B.C.E., recklessly, insolently and provocatively took the water libation and poured it on his feet instead of on the Temple altar, he in effect declared war on the Pharisees and the Oral Law of Israel.

The shocked throng in the Temple, recoiling from this act of sacrilege, turned violent. The assembled congregation, who were holding citrons (*esrogim*) in their hands in commemoration of the ritual of Succos, threw these *esrogim* at Alexander Yannai, almost stoning him to death.

In panic and anger, Alexander called in his mercenary guards, who promptly massacred thousands of Jews standing in the courtyard of the Temple. The floor of the Temple ran red and thick with the blood of innocent Jews, killed at the order of Alexander Yannai. Such an outrage could not be forgiven, and civil war and armed rebellion against the king now became a sickening reality.

Civil War

FOR ALMOST FIVE YEARS, until the year 90 B.C.E., the mindless violence always associated with a civil war remained at a minimum. Sporadic attacks against the government and the Sadducees were met by brutal punishments on the part of Alexander Yannai. Torture, maiming and mutilation, and even the horrific death of crucifixion, were regularly used by the Hasmonean king against his own Jewish people. This studied brutality initially maintained a veneer of order in a country whose population seethed in anger against its king and his authority. However, when Alexander Yannai's unnecessary war of conquest and aggrandizement against Arabia ended in retreat and defeat in the year 90 B.C.E., the Pharisees, sensing an opportunity to capitalize

---

30. During the celebration, all of Jerusalem was lit by the light of festive bonfires, and there was a great deal of merriment, joy and dancing. The Talmud (*Succah* 51a) states that "he who did not attend a *Simchas Beis haShoeva* (the Hebrew term for the celebration of this water libation offering) never saw a joyous celebration in his life."

on the king's defeat and loss of prestige, rose against his rule in open civil war.

This civil war lasted for almost six years, until 85 B.C.E., and over 50,000 Jews died in this terrible family struggle. As the forces of Alexander began relentlessly to gain control of the situation, desperate and radical elements, overcome by the prospect of defeat in their years-long struggle to overthrow Alexander Yannai and blinded by his implacable hatred of all things sacred,[31] committed an act of national self-destruction. They appealed to the Syrian king Demetrius III (Eucerus) to invade Judah and depose Alexander Yannai! Demetrius promptly complied and, together with a large Jewish force of warriors that he incorporated into his army, entered into battle against the old Hasmonean enemy of the Syrians.

Alexander Yannai's End

AT THE BRINK OF WAR with their own brethren, the Jewish soldiers in the army of Demetrius instinctively recoiled at the prospect of killing fellow Jews. They refused to obey the battle orders of Demetrius' generals, and large numbers of them deserted the Syrian forces and went over to fight on the side of Alexander Yannai. Demetrius, recognizing the changed odds of battle and the likelihood of abject defeat, broke off the combat and retreated to Syria.

Alexander Yannai now had the opportunity to conciliate his pharisaic foes. However, blinded by his hatred, bitter experiences and progressing paranoia, Alexander Yannai brutally instituted a reign of terror and persecution against the Pharisees. He executed hundreds of them — men, women, children and infants — in one day, inflicting upon them barbaric and fiendish deaths, to which he himself was a witness. The Pharisees, exhausted by the years of blood and strife, no longer responded in violence, preferring to wait for time and God's will to remove Alexander.

---

31. As Alexander Yannai's forces gained the upper hand against the Pharisees in this bitter civil war, Alexander offered to negotiate an armistice and settlement of the conflict. He asked the Pharisees to communicate to him what concessions would be necessary on his part in order to end the bloodshed. The bitter answer came back: "Our only request is your death!"

After the situation in Judah quieted, Alexander resumed his wars of conquest which continued until his death, choosing life in an army tent, far removed from Jerusalem and the people of Israel, whose love and loyalty he was unable to earn. He could never create for himself a more tranquil existence.

As his end neared, Alexander Yannai instructed his wife, Shlomis, the future regent of Judah, to make peace with the Pharisees and to separate the High Priesthood from the monarchy, as per their wishes. He even moderated his view regarding the Pharisees, saying: "Fear not the Pharisees [though they conducted a civil war against the government], nor even the Sadducees, but only fear the hypocrites [political opportunists who cloak themselves in falsely pious behavior but who are personally morally corrupt], who disguise themselves as Pharisees. They commit deeds as evil as those of Zimri and somehow expect a reward as great as that of Pinchas."[32] Alexander Yannai, alone and sad, died in his army tent while besieging the city of Regev in Transjordan in the year 76 B.C.E. Thus ended the life and reign of the most turbulent of the Hasmonean kings.

A Period of Healing

THE ADVENT OF SHLOMIS ALEXANDRA to the throne of Judah marked the start of an era of healing and respite in the troubled Jewish society. Shlomis installed her brother, Shimon ben Shetach, the head of the Pharisees, as her chief government minister. Yehudah ben Tabai, exiled to Egypt during the persecution of the Pharisees by Alexander Yannai, returned to become the President (*Nasi*) of the Sanhedrin, with Shimon ben Shetach serving as Chief Judge (*Av Beis Din*). The Pharisees were careful not to intensify any civil war potential with the Sadducees, though Shlomis did convict and execute those Sadducee conspirators who advised Alexander Yannai to kill eight hundred Pharisee hostages ruthlessly in one of the worst atrocities of the civil war. The government extended great effort in establishing and encouraging a Torah school system, and it restored the Temple

---

32. Talmud (*Sotah* 22b). Zimri was the renegade chief of the Shimeonites who publicly cohabitated with a princess of Midian, and Pinchas was the zealous hero who, by executing them, received divine reward (*Numbers* 25:6-15).

priesthood and administration to the control of the Pharisees. For ten years, till her death in 66 B.C.E., Shlomis ruled wisely, cautiously and minimally. The Pharisees reinvigorated the Jewish people spiritually, while at the same time, peace, prosperity and security existed throughout Judah. But this was a short respite of goodness in a long story of sadness in the era of the Second Temple.

Shlomis Loses Power

SHIMON BEN SHETACH died in 68 B.C.E., and his death left a void in the leadership of the government of Shlomis Alexandra. She was now an aging queen, the mother of quarrelsome sons already contesting the distribution of their inheritance, and Shimon's death left her without the benefit of her most trusted and loyal counselor. Her two sons, Hyrcanus and Aristobulus, were of differing natures and temperaments. Hyrcanus, the older son, served as High Priest during the regency of his mother and was close to the Pharisees, personally and ideologically. He was a person of serenity, soft-spoken and considerate. His younger brother Aristobulus was ambitious, jealous, angry, volatile and violent. His mother distrusted Aristobulus, aware of his personal shortcomings, and never appointed him to serve in any position of power and influence. He chafed at her bit, resented his exclusion from importance and conspired to gain power and control.

The Sadducees sensed that Aristobulus could become a tool of theirs and sought to befriend and compliment him, gaining his confidence and cooperation. Aristobulus saw his future with the Sadducees and now used all of his brute personality to place him and them in power. He badgered, threatened and cajoled his sick, dying mother to turn over major Hasmonean fortresses to the forces of the Sadducees. He threatened that he would form an alliance with Aretas, the leader of the Arabs and an old and bitter Hasmonean foe. Afraid of new wars, feeling motherly compassion on her deathbed, and sapped of the energy to forcefully deny her son's power grab, Shlomis succumbed to Aristobulus' demand and transferred the requested fortresses to his Sadducee allies. The fortunes of treasure stored in those fortresses were now confiscated by Aristobulus and the

Sadducees and were used to hire a large army of mercenaries to back Aristobulus' attempt at wresting power.

The Pharisees were justifiably concerned over this dangerous turn of events and petitioned the queen to overcome Aristobulus and the Sadducees forcibly. Shlomis, literally with her last breath and unable to act on her own, authorized the leaders of the Pharisees to proceed as they saw fit. In 66 B.C.E. she died, and interred with her was the last great hope for the survival of the Hasmonean dynasty and the security of the Temple and the Second Commonwealth.

Section II

Edom Ascendant

7
Rome the Colossus

THE WORLD HAS SEEN many empires come and go, but there has been only one Rome. No empire in the story of civilization has in its time dominated as high a proportion of the world's population, fashioned so much of civilization in its image, left such large architectural and archaeological footprints and provided so lasting a matrix of what imperial rule could be.

Rome was able to absorb into itself myriad cultures, some very sophisticated and advanced,[1] and remake them in its own form. The military might, tactics, weaponry and strategy of the Roman legions and their generals have influenced the gruesome science and teaching of war until our own time. Roman law, engineering, planning, art, literature, oratory and politics remain the underpinnings of much of the world's society today. Rome was not only the most powerful nation in the ancient classical world, it was practically the one and only power, and it remained so for six centuries.[2] In a great measure, for all of that time, Rome was the world itself.

Romulus and Remus with a she-wolf (Lupa Romana), the symbols of the founding of Rome

It is not my purpose here to give a detailed history of the Roman empire. However, for the six centuries that Rome dominated the world, its rule consistently intertwined with Jewish life and survival, both in Judah and in the developing Diaspora, and therefore some knowledge of the story of Rome and its emperors is a prerequisite for understanding the Jewish story of the time. Rome and Jerusalem were fierce and unforgiving competitors, and the events and trials of each always influenced the other. For many

---
1. Such as Greece and Ptolemaic Egypt.
2. C. 200 B.C.E. till c. 400 C.E.

centuries, therefore, their stories remained inseparable one from the other.

Julius Caesar

Top: Cicero
Bottom: Julius Caesar

ALTHOUGH IN THE FIRST CENTURY before the Common Era Rome styled itself a republic, it was far from our definition of that form of government. The Roman Senate appointed consuls as the executive heads of the government, who many times proved to be tyrannical and dictatorial. One of the greatest consuls of the time was the famed philosopher and orator, Cicero.[3] He was preceded in office by the dictator Sulla, appointed in 82 B.C.E., and the duet of Crassus and Pompey in 70 B.C.E. It was in the same year that Pompey was absent from Rome (63 B.C.E.), conquering the Middle East and capturing Jerusalem, that Cicero became consul. Pompey returned to Rome and bided his time, and in 60 B.C.E. his political machinations forced Cicero from office. Thus, the triumvirate consulate of Julius Caesar, Pompey and Crassus was formed. To help cement this unwieldy alliance, Pompey married Julia, the daughter of Julius Caesar, in 59 B.C.E. However, in 54 B.C.E. Julia died childless, and the bonds between Pompey and Julius Caesar were severed. The eventual competition between Pompey and Caesar soon deteriorated into open civil war, and it came to be that in 49 B.C.E. Julius Caesar became the sole ruler of Rome,[4] forcing Pompey to flee to the Middle East.[5] Caesar pursued Pompey, defeated his army at the Battle of Pharsalus in 48 B.C.E. and had Pompey murdered.

Julius Caesar was now dictator of Rome, its sole ruler and power; in short — its Caesar. However, the comment of his contemporary, Hillel, "As you have drowned others, so shall you be drowned," soon applied to him. He was assassinated in 44 B.C.E. by Brutus and Cassius. Rome was again plunged into civil war.

A new triumvirate was then formed, composed of Mark Antony, Lepidus, and Caesar's godson, Octavian, later known as Augustus.

---

3. 106 B.C.E.-43 B.C.E.
4. The famous "crossing of the Rubicon" heralded Caesar's bid for exclusive power.
5. Among Pompey's eastern allies was Herod, described elsewhere in this book.

L-R: Pompey, Mark Antony, Augustus

These men energetically pursued the forces of Brutus and Cassius and triumphed over them at the Battle of Phillipi in 42 B.C.E., whereupon Brutus and Cassius committed suicide.

Mark Antony was attracted to the Middle East and became a patron and protector of Herod. However, in 32 B.C.E. he and Octavian, their individual drives for exclusive power now insatiable, openly fought for control of Rome. In 31 B.C.E. at the Battle of Actium, Octavian triumphed over Mark Antony.

Herod, although he had been Antony's protegé and ally, nevertheless was able to convince Octavian to allow him to continue as the ruler of Judah. Antony committed suicide in 30 B.C.E., and Octavian became the Caesar of Rome, now calling himself Augustus. He would reign as Caesar until 14 C.E.

Herod and his descendants were favored and protected by Augustus, who much preferred having them rule over the strategic territory of Judah to having an independent Jewish commonwealth inimical to Roman rule and values.

The long rule of Augustus consolidated power in the hands of the Roman Caesar, expanded Rome's dominion over the farthest corners of the then-civilized (and even uncivilized) world, and impressed upon all the permanence of Roman world dominion. But all dictatorships, no matter how strong and eternal they appear from the outside, are eventually corroded and weakened from the inside. Rome, masking its own internal divisions and doubts, now became a heavy-handed master, thereby guaranteeing continuing internal struggle and rebellion in the next generation.

A Conflict of Approaches

THE JEWS WERE A DIFFICULT PUZZLE for the Romans to solve. As mentioned earlier,[6] Rome was a slave state, while Judah was basically not. Rome was pagan, tolerant of many gods and of differing and exotic forms of ritual worship. Jewish society was monotheistic, exclusive in its religious outlook, intolerant of all forms of paganism and its immoral excesses. Rome wished to conquer and dominate the world. Judah wished to be left alone. Rome was all statues and gladiators, wars and triumphs, idols and pomp. It was theaters and circuses, gruesome public tortures and executions, color, food, and noise. Judah was relatively drab and abstract, bemused, sophisticated[7] and restrained, with scholars as its heroes and leaders.

The Romans, who prided themselves on their tolerance of all other pagan religions and gods, were first baffled, then frustrated and finally infuriated by Judaism and the Jews. The open contempt exhibited by many Jews towards Rome, its gods and values, brought about a reaction

Roman theater and arena, Aurelus, France

---

6. See the earlier chapter, "Economic and Social Life in Second Temple Times."

7. One of the oft-repeated Roman criticisms was that the Jews were "atheists," since they worshipped an invisible God and allowed no physical representation of Him to be erected. In the ancient world, an incorporeal, invisible, omniscient, omnipotent, universal Creator was a concept that eluded the minds of most men, even the great philosophers of the time.

108 ◻ ECHOES OF GLORY

of veiled enmity and then open hatred from Rome towards the Jews. Rome and Jerusalem were on a collision course from the time of Pompey's conquests in 63 B.C.E. And although Rome won the early rounds of the struggle, it would be Jerusalem that would eventually triumph.

Tiberius

THE DEATH OF AUGUSTUS brought to rule his adopted son, Tiberius.[8] He ruled for 23 years (14-37 C.E.). During his reign, the empire built by Augustus remained outwardly stable. However, bitter intrigues and bloody fights marked the inner workings of power. Tiberius "was dour and introspective, poisoned by unhappy private experience, with more than a touch of melancholia and insecurity."[9] Tiberius' adopted son (who actually had been his nephew) and heir apparent, Germanicus, died in 19 C.E. Drusus, the biological son of Tiberius, died four years later in 23 C.E. Both died under suspicious circumstances, with rumors flying through Rome that they had been poisoned by the agents of Sejanus, the commander of the Praetorian Guard, and Livia, Tiberius' evil and scheming mother.

A cameo honoring Tiberius' victories

Tiberius, weary of tragedy and tired of governing, retired into seclusion on the island of Capri. The actual reins of government were now in the hands of Sejanus. But Sejanus' abuse of power became so great that eventually word reached Tiberius of the debacle of government in Rome. In 31 C.E. Tiberius ordered the execution of Sejanus.

---

8. Tiberius' mother, Livia, was a later wife of Augustus. She was a strong, conniving and completely unscrupulous woman, who eventually forced her husband Augustus to adopt Tiberius as a son and later appoint him as his successor, even while Augustus still lived. Legend has her poisoning all of the natural descendants of Augustus in order to assure Tiberius' accession to power.

9. *The Oxford History of the Roman World,* ed. John Boardman, et al (New York 1968), p. 168.

The final years of Tiberius "were years of gloom, intrigue and uncertainty, over which loomed the cynical and suspicious shadow of a lonely old man encompassed by astrologers on the island of Capri."[10] Tiberius died in 37 C.E., generally unmourned, and without having prepared a suitable successor as emperor.

Caligula

Caligula

THERE NOW CAME TO POWER as Caesar a mentally unbalanced, sadistic, brazenly immoral and frightening person, Gaius (Caligula),[11] a grandson of Tiberius. "His brief reign has an air of melodramatic unreality: mental and emotional instability, vicious cruelty, incest, ridiculous indecision and waywardness... fantasies of divinity which...bred unrest among the Jews."[12]

Roman emperors from Julius Caesar on had begun to fancy themselves as being superhuman.[13] From this fantasy, it was not far for them to go to place themselves in the pantheon of pagan gods. Since the Roman belief was that a god — no matter how evil his or her behavior — was immune from any punishment or pain in the hereafter, the paradox arose in Roman life that the more evil the emperor, the more likely he was to have himself declared a god in order to protect himself from the punishment he richly deserved for his behavior on earth.

Some of the emperors, such as Tiberius, were cynical enough to have themselves declared gods while having no faith in gods or any sort of hereafter. However, Gaius, in his madness, truly believed himself a god and demanded the worship due one. The Romans and other pagans in the empire were able at least to pay lip service to Gaius' divinity, especially when faced with the alternative of the torture chamber and/or crucifixion. Not so the Jews, to whom any

---

10. Ibid., p. 169.

11. Though he is known to the world as Caligula, this was only a nickname given to him in his youth because of his predilection for wearing certain pairs of slippers. What a benign name for such a monster!

12. Ibid., p. 170.

13. Legends as to Julius Caesar's supernatural qualities, experiences and accomplishments abounded. One of them claimed he was born of a virgin. Another reported that he was impervious to fire.

110 ☐ ECHOES OF GLORY

representation of a divine being in a human form and body — whether that being claimed to be divine or not — was anathema.[14] Thus the Jews, both in Judah and in the other parts of the Roman Empire, were restless and even openly rebellious against Roman rule and forms during the short four-year reign of Gaius. This open defiance of the emperor would set the stage for the ongoing bloody rebellions of the Jews against Roman rule for the next two centuries.

Claudius

GAIUS' MADNESS REACHED ITS PEAK when he installed his horse as a member of the Roman Senate, and the poor beast actually was forced to attend some of the sessions. The Praetorian Guard, tired and frightened of the emperor's madness, mutinied, slaughtering Gaius and his family. The Roman Senate and the Praetorian Guard together placed Gaius' uncle, Claudius, on the emperor's throne.

Claudius, a semi-cripple and stammerer, was regarded as weak, pliable and dull-witted by many of his contemporaries. However, he proved their assessment wrong and overall was an effective and strong ruler, although his reign was subjected to severe criticism by contemporaries and later historians. He mollified the Jews, conquered southern Britain, expanded the rights of freedmen and citizens, made the Roman economy richer and brought good men into high public office, even though many of them were not of aristocratic origin. However, his private life was a shambles, and he was a terrible husband and father. Claudius died in 54 C.E., possibly poisoned by his family and/or political opponents.

Claudius

Upon the death of Claudius, yet another unstable and cruel person, Nero, Claudius's stepson, became emperor. He would rule till 68 C.E. and play a key role in bringing on the great Jewish revolt, which culminated in the destruction of the Temple in Jerusalem in 70 C.E.

---

14. The inability of early Christianity to appreciate this basic tenet of Judaism led to much strife and provoked otherwise avoidable battles and bloodshed.

Nero

NERO BECAME EMPEROR while yet an adolescent. Youth and power make for a heady brew. There were many rivals for the favors and ear of Nero. Messallina, Nero's mother, attempted to dominate him and meddled in all of his personal and political affairs. Nero soon tired of her interfering ways and in 59 C.E. arranged for her murder.[15] Seneca, Nero's tutor and a respected Roman statesman, together with Burrus, the prefect of the Praetorian Guard, now had access to the mind and will of the emperor. They lent stability and moderation to Nero's reign. However, the death of Burrus and the retirement of Seneca in 62 ushered in a new and more turbulent time.

Nero now surrounded himself with sycophants and criminals. His new Praetorian prefect, Tigellinus, was one of the most unsavory characters in all of Roman history. He maintained a malevolent influence over Nero, who all on his own was already possessed of a degenerate character. Nero was dissolute, extravagant, immoral, violent and capricious. His military campaigns in Britain and Armenia were unsuccessful and actually lost territory for the empire. His pillaging of the Roman treasury reached such a degree as to force a devaluation of Roman currency through debasement of the basic Roman coinage.[16] Nero's instability led to a feeling of restiveness and uncertainty throughout the empire.

In 64 C.E. a great fire ravaged the city of Rome.[17] After the embers cooled, Nero embarked on a great urban reconstruction program. The centerpiece of this effort was his own new palace, *Domus Aurea* (*Golden House*). An enormously grandiose building,[18]

---

15. Murder, as an instrument of policy or as a means of settling family problems, was an acceptable practice throughout Roman history, especially amongst the aristocracy and military leaders. It is no wonder that the rabbis recoiled at the policies and behavior of Roman government and the values of Roman civilization.

16. For the effect of this currency devaluation on Jewish life in certain *halachic* (legal) circumstances, see Talmud, *Kiddushin* 12a.

17. The legend of Negro "fiddling" on his violin while Rome burned has become indelibly etched into the collective memory of European civilization.

18. "Even today, ravaged by the passage of time, the decoration of the *Golden House* makes a stunning impact on the visitor, just as it did nearly five centuries ago when

it was ruinously expensive to build. Rome was rife with rumors that Nero himself had ordered the disastrous conflagration in order to clear land for the site of his new palace.

As mutterings against Nero's rule became louder, Nero searched for a scapegoat to quiet the populace. Under the rule of Nero in his last years of power, the Jewish population of Rome was subject to random violence and open discrimination. However, the main victims of Nero's persecutions were the growing number of Christians living in Rome. They were executed, tortured and maimed as part of government policy. Nero forbade any conversions of pagans to either Judaism or Christianity on pain of death.[19]

In 65 C.E. Nero discovered a plot to remove him from power. He had many suspects — real and imagined — executed, among them his own mentor, Seneca. Alone, insecure, half-mad, Nero embarked upon a reign of terror that destabilized his very government. In 68 C.E., a rebellion led by Servius Galba, the commander of Roman forces in Spain, so unnerved Nero that he committed suicide. His death ushered in the "year of the four emperors," and only with the ascension to the throne in 69 C.E. of Vespasian, the conqueror of Judah, was stability restored to the Roman government.

For almost five centuries, the Jewish people and the Roman Empire would be locked in a macabre tandem, each one dueling, influencing and attempting to overwhelm the other. Rome, the colossus of the ancient world, would be transformed by its encounter with Judaism, and would eventually succumb to the new faith of Christianity. The seemingly eternally impervious colossus would eventually collapse from its own cruelties and internal weaknesses.

Raphael and Giovanni di Udine, according to Vasari, were both seized with astonishment at the freshness, beauty, and excellent manner of these works" (*The Oxford History of the Roman World*, p. 429).

19. For an example of Nero and his attitude towards Roman converts to Judaism, see Talmud, *Gittin* 56a.

8
Aristobulus, Hyrcanus and Antipater

THE HASMONEAN FAMILY may not as yet have realized it, but it was rapidly approaching the end of its rule over Judah. The year 68 B.C.E. marked the outbreak of hostilities between the two sons of Alexander Yannai, Aristobulus and Hyrcanus. The shameful civil war conducted by two brothers in pursuit of personal power sealed the loss of Jewish independence. The Jewish state would manage to limp along as a national entity for longer than another century, but the war of succession between Aristobulus and Hyrcanus marked the waning of Hasmonean power and any true Jewish national autonomy in Judah.

Aristobulus continued to enjoy the support of the Sadducees, who were growing in numbers, power and influence. This party already controlled the High Priesthood and had much support among the wealthy, aristocratic priests (*kohanim*) living in Jerusalem. And even though most of the Sanhedrin consisted of Pharisees loyal to the Oral Law and tradition, the Sadducees managed to become a major force in the Sanhedrin. Thus, Aristobulus had powerful allies in his quest for the throne.

The masses of the people remained opposed to the Sadducees, and hence to Aristobulus as well; but Aristobulus, cunning, unscrupulous, aggressive and insatiably ambitious as he was, pursued his campaign for power and rule uncompromisingly and ruthlessly.

Hyrcanus, in turn, remained governed by his much gentler demeanor and disposition. Soft-spoken, compassionate to a fault, abhorring violence and war, Hyrcanus was not on his own a person to conduct civil war successfully against a brother, no matter how vicious and evil that brother may have been. But his spine was stiffened by an Idumean general named Antipater.[1] An able administrator, a fierce warrior, and a cunning schemer, Antipater befriended the weak Hyrcanus and saw the civil war between the Hasmonean brothers as a vehicle by which to rise in rule over Judah. Antipater was "blessed" with the necessary traits for successful cabals — patience, tenacity, guile and the absence of all moral and humanitarian compunctions. He would use them all, and then some, in his rise to power.

Brother Against Brother

ARISTOBULUS ENGAGED the forces of Hyrcanus outside Jericho in autumn of 68 B.C.E. and emerged victorious. Hyrcanus, true to his nature, reconciled himself to his defeat and publicly renounced all claims to the throne and to political power. Thus retired from public life, Hyrcanus seemingly posed no further threat to Aristobulus, who rapidly moved to consolidate under himself all governmental power in Judah. But Antipater continued to incite Hyrcanus against his brother.

A soft nature, which is usually an admirable trait, in Hyrcanus' case proved his undoing. At Antipater's urging he entered into secret negotiations with Aretas, king of the Arab tribes and longtime foe of the Hasmoneans, to join him in a war to depose Aristobulus. As bait for this sorry adventure, Hyrcanus promised Aretas to restore to Arab rule those parts of Transjordan previously conquered by Alexander Yannai and annexed to Judah.

Aretas supplied Hyrcanus with a large army, and Hyrcanus moved against Jerusalem. His supporters in Jerusalem opened the city gates for him and his forces. Aristobulus was forced to retreat within the fortifications of the Temple Mount and destroyed the linking bridge to the city proper. The siege of the Temple Mount proceeded with ferocity, cruelty and hatred. Any possible reconciliation between the brothers was rendered impossible by the atrocities committed by each side. There is no fight equal to a family fight in terms of bitterness and

---

[1]. Antipater had been appointed a governor for the Jewish king, Alexander Yannai, over a large part of southern Judah and southwest Transjordan. This area was populated in the main by the Idumeans, who had been forcibly converted to Judaism by the Hasmonean kings (see chapter 6).

The Fortress of Antonia, from the model at the Holyland Hotel

unforgiving attitude. The civil war between these Hasmonean brothers remains one of the sorriest chapters in Jewish history.

The Rabbis Withdraw from Politics

THE RABBIS AND MORAL LEADERS stood aghast at the dissolution of the Hasmonean unity. They viewed the war between the brothers as a purely personal dispute, having no ideological or social purpose, and thus they turned away in disgust from both sides.[2]

The rise of the Sadducees to power, the chaos in society caused by the Hasmonean civil war, and the appearance of Antipater and his malevolent family as a force in the life of Judah caused the rabbis great concern. The heads of the Pharisees at the time of this civil war were Shemaya and Avtalyon,[3] the fourth set of the *Zugos* (*pairs of*

---

2. The attitude of the rabbis is best summed up in the story of the famous miracle worker of Judah, Choni *HaMe'agal,* who was arrested by Hyrcanus, brought before the walls of the Temple and asked to curse Aristobulus and his forces. In a paraphrase of "a curse upon both of your houses," Choni refused to do so.

3. These two great leaders of Israel were converts to Judaism or the children of such converts. They were descended from the royal family of Sancherib, the king of Assyria, who conquered and dispersed the ten northern tribes of Israel and captured Shomron. (See Talmud, *Gittin* 57b.) The phenomenon of converts, or those descended directly from converts, assuming roles of leadership in the Jewish spiritual world recurs often in the centuries that immediately preceded and followed the destruction of the Second Temple. Ravad I (see *Herald of Destiny* [Brooklyn, N.Y.: Shaar Press, 1993], p. 16) stated that

Talmudic scholars who headed the central academies of Torah learning and authority). Their attitude toward the civil war and the government of Judah at that time is succinctly summed up in their advice to refrain from public comments about the government and to maintain a very low profile in all public and governmental matters.[4]

Although the rabbis withdrew from direct participation in political life, they pursued ever more strongly their agenda of spreading Torah education to the masses and advocating the rule of Jewish traditional values and morals in everyday life. Thus, long after Aristobulus, Hyrcanus, Antipater and Herod disappeared from the scene, consigned to arcane history books, Shemaya and Avtalyon and their main disciple, Hillel, remained vital and influential in Jewish life, always remembered and permanently heroic.

A Pig on the Temple Mount

AS THE SIEGE OF the Temple Mount continued, food supplies on the Mount itself, and in other parts of Jerusalem as well, began to decline. The demands of large amounts of livestock for the ongoing daily Temple service quickly exhausted the supply of the Temple stockyards.

Despite their role of besieging the Temple, the Jews forming Hyrcanus' forces were themselves loyal to the Temple service and the God of Israel,[5] and helped supply the necessary animals for the daily public offerings, sending them up by basket pulleys over the Temple wall. When the siege did not proceed as expeditiously and easily as anticipated, a suggestion was made to Hyrcanus to stop supplying the proper animals for the Temple service. The logic ran as follows: By enabling Aristobulus to preserve the Temple service, Hyrcanus was allowing him to earn enough credit to receive heavenly aid in

---

the flood of talented converts into Judaism at this crucial time in Jewish history was a Divine "blood transfusion" into the Jewish body politic, enabling it to survive the terrible tests of the time.

4. See Mishnah, *Avos* 1:10,11.

5. The illogical phenomenon of brothers praying to the same God and observing the same rituals and faith, while at the very same moment attempting to kill each other, has always been one of the more puzzling traits of human nature. From the biblical story of Cain and Abel through our very time, such civil wars and familial violence have dogged man's attempt to civilize himself.

withstanding the siege. Therefore, Hyrcanus should discontinue providing Aristobulus with the sacrificial objects. This diabolical reasoning was accepted by Hyrcanus, who then ordered that a pig be sent up in the pulley-basket!

The paws of the pig touched the walls of the holy Temple Mount, and all of the Land of Israel shook from the reverberations of the sacrilege.[6] The degradation of the Hasmoneans' behavior had reached its worst. Because of this, the end of an independent Judah was now at hand.

Pompey's Intervention

IN 63 B.C.E., WHILE THE Hasmonean civil war was in full force, the Roman Empire began its conquest of the Middle East. Pompey commanded the Roman legions that subjugated all the nations of the area, as well as most of Asia Minor. An ambitious, wily and cruel person, Pompey knew no bounds in his avarice. Corrupt and insatiable, he was always open to bribes and offers. The two Hasmonean brothers, exhausted and stalemated by their long and bitter struggle and fearing Rome's uninvited intervention, attempted to preempt Pompey's probable invasion of Judah by referring their dispute to his adjudication.

Each of the brothers offered Pompey large bribes to decide in his particular favor. Aristobulus' bribe was larger, and thus Pompey's original decision was to order Hyrcanus and Aretas, the Nabatean Arab king who was Hyrcanus' ally, to lift their siege of the Temple Mount and recognize Aristobulus' claim to govern. Ever persistent and single-minded, Antipater, Hyrcanus' erstwhile supporter, appealed to Pompey to reconsider the matter.

Pompey called both sides before him for a hearing. Forgetting Aristobulus' large bribe, which he had already pocketed, Pompey now bowed to the argument of Antipater that while alive, Shlomis Alexandra, the queen mother of the two feuding brothers, had really preferred Hyrcanus over Aristobulus to succeed her. In truth, Pompey

---

6. See Talmud, *Sotah* 49b and *Menachos* 64b, and Josephus. This incident is also recorded in the Talmud in *Bava Kamma* 82b, but there it is intimated that it was Hyrcanus who was inside the Temple Mount and Aristobulus who sent up the pig from outside the walls.

chose Hyrcanus not because he wanted to fulfill the wishes of the deceased queen of Judah, but because he correctly surmised that Hyrcanus was a weak person and would be an ineffective ruler, thus granting Rome de facto control over Judah without a war.

Hyrcanus declared himself king and High Priest, and Aristobulus, bowing to Pompey's orders, surrendered all the country's fortresses. It becomes clear that at this point it was Pompey — who now destroyed most of these fortresses — and not Hyrcanus who actually reigned supreme in Judah.

Second Siege of the Temple

WHEN POMPEY'S LEGIONS finally marched upon Jerusalem, Aristobulus made one more attempt to preserve the city's independence from Rome. But he internally lost heart upon seeing Pompey's army at the city walls and personally withdrew from the fray. On top of this, Hyrcanus, still foolishly thinking his brother Aristobulus a greater enemy than Pompey, ordered the gates of Jerusalem opened before that Roman general. Nevertheless, Aristobulus' forces, even without the enthusiasm and leadership of their leader, continued their defense of the Temple Mount against Pompey and Hyrcanus.

This second siege of the Temple lasted for over two months, with the Roman catapults and battering rams finally prevailing. Aristobulus and his family were captured and sent to Rome, to be degraded in the Roman processional triumph.[7] On the Temple Mount, the Romans perpetrated a great massacre of the defending Jews. Thousands were slaughtered outright and thousands of others tortured to death. But despite the murderous attacks upon the *Kohanim,* resulting in 12,000 deaths, the Temple itself was not destroyed, nor was the Temple service itself much interrupted!

In spite of the Roman behavior, Hyrcanus gladly assumed the role of High Priest and nominal king as well. But in reality, Antipater wielded the main political power, always forcing the weak Hyrcanus to follow his will. And Hyrcanus' kingdom itself was a much reduced

---

7. Aristobulus' son Alexander managed to escape from the Romans and would return to Judah in an attempt to expel Rome from the country. The details of this ill-fated venture will be given later in this section.

one. Pompey removed Transjordan, Gaza, Jaffa, Ashdod, Yavneh and other cities from Jewish government and assigned them to Roman rule. He also decreed that much of the remaining land be divided and given to his soldiers as reward for their prowess in battle. The Hasmonean kingdom was thus reduced to the area around Jerusalem, parts of Edom in the south and Galilee in the north, and a narrow corridor in the south of Transjordan towards Aqaba. However, even this area of Jewish sovereignty was not exclusive, being subject to the control of the Roman proconsul in Damascus.

Pompey's Regime

POMPEY RETURNED HOME to Rome in triumph and glory. He paraded Aristobulus and his family before the Roman mob but, in an uncharacteristic act of mercy, spared their lives. Aristobulus would therefore be heard from again. Pompey, Julius Caesar, Cassius, Brutus, Octavius and others would struggle for control of Rome over the next decades. This turmoil strongly affected the land of Judah as well, and the Hasmoneans alternated between hope and despair of regaining their true independence as each twist of events unfolded.[8]

Pompey had installed a harsh regime over Judah and Jerusalem. Many of the walls and fortresses of Jerusalem were leveled and near-confiscatory taxes were imposed on the Jews in Judah, especially upon those living in Jerusalem.[9] The Jews squirmed under the new hardships, but since their religious freedom and national government survived (albeit in a weakened and crippled state), they somehow made peace with the new situation imposed upon them by Pompey.

In the year 57 B.C.E., six years after Pompey's conquest of Jerusalem, the Roman general Gabinius was appointed proconsul of Damascus, thus becoming the *de facto* ruler of Judah. He went beyond Pompey's already harsh decrees, and in turn abolished the

---

8. See the later chapter "Rome the Colossus" for a review of these struggles for power among the Roman generals and consuls.

9. Though no clear record of such a policy exists, it seems to me that this high tax on Jews living in Jerusalem was part of a broader Roman policy to make Jerusalem a non-Jewish city and to remove its standing as the capital of the Jewish state and people. Such a policy can be discerned as well in the attitude of much of the non-Jewish world towards Jewish control over Jerusalem in the last decade of the twentieth century.

Sanhedrin and its central authority, subdivided small Judah into five smaller and almost insignificant sections, drove the Jews from the coastal cities and repopulated those cities with non-Jews, increased the already high taxes due Rome, rebuilt the Greek cities destroyed by the Hasmoneans, and attempted to install a non-Jewish majority population in Judah. The Jews, furious at this turn of events, now began to arm for war against Rome, just as their great-grandparents had done against Greece and Syria.

Alexander's Escapes

ALEXANDER, THE SON OF ARISTOBULUS, escaped Rome and returned to Judah. He soon organized a large Jewish army and declared war against the Romans, using the few remaining fortresses not leveled by Pompey as a base of operation. However, by the end of the year 57 B.C.E., the Romans crushed the Jewish forces and once again captured Alexander and sent him to Rome in chains.

Mount Tabor

A better escape artist than a military leader, Alexander somehow once again extricated himself from Roman captivity and returned home to Judah. There he again rallied another large force of Jews to fight Rome and restore true Jewish independence in the country.

His uncle Hyrcanus, under the malevolent influence of Antipater, refused to help the Jewish revolt and remained in collaboration with the Roman forces in the country. In 49 B.C.E. Gabinius defeated the forces of Alexander near Mount Tabor.[10]

---

10. This was the spot where the prophetess Devora and the general Barak defeated the Canaanite army of Sisera and Yavin in biblical times (*Judges*, Chapter 4).

ERETZ YISRAEL UNDER ROMAN OCCUPATION

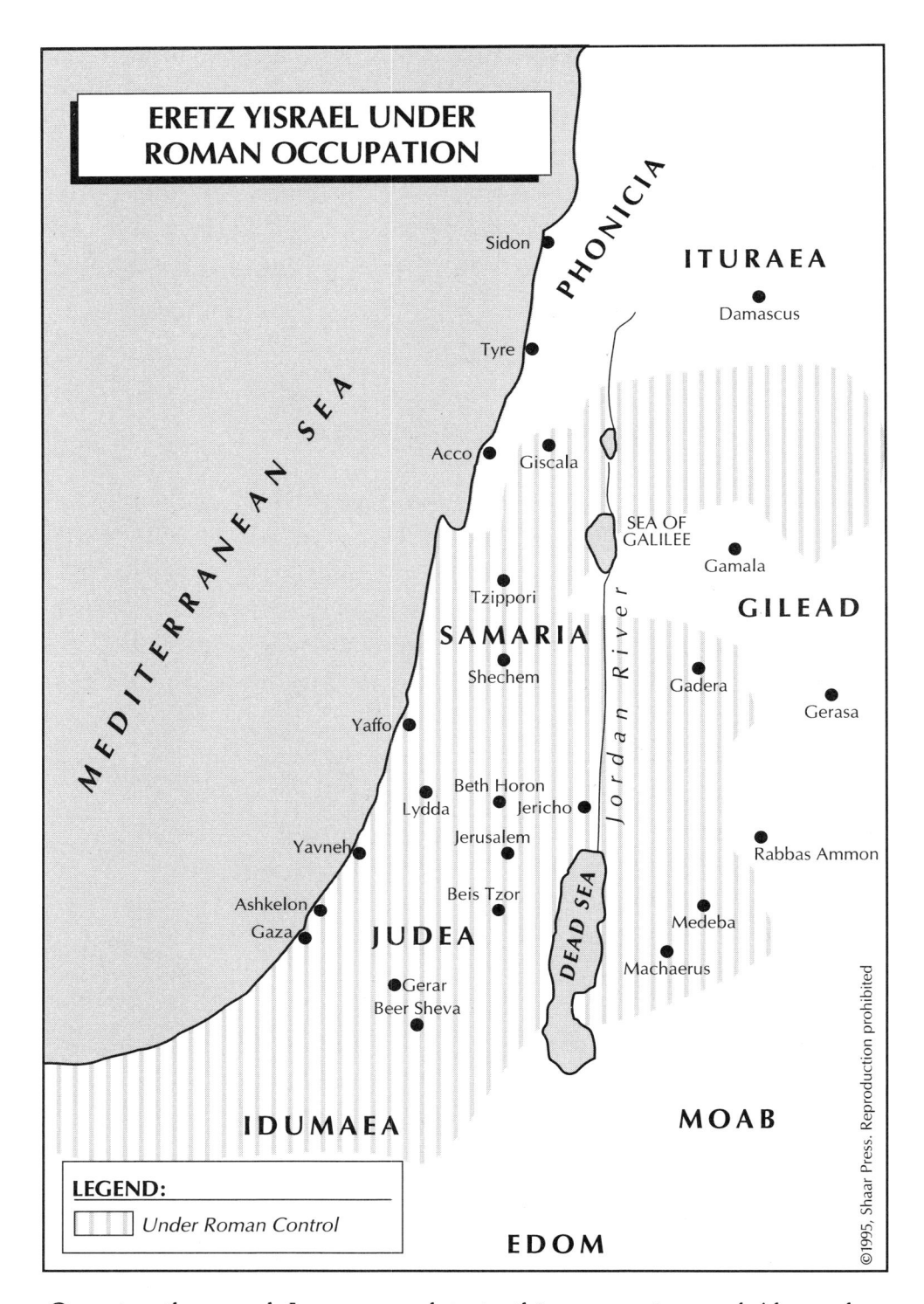

LEGEND:
Under Roman Control

Over ten thousand Jews were slain in this encounter, and Alexander, captured for the third time by the Romans, was summarily executed. But the Jewish attempt to overthrow Roman rule over Judah still continued for the next two centuries.

Disbanding of the Sanhedrin

AFTER GABINIUS HAD BANISHED the Sanhedrin from its seat within the Temple Mount in Jerusalem,[11] Antipater interceded with him to have the powers of the Sanhedrin transferred to Hyrcanus, as High Priest. Any powers granted to Hyrcanus would in effect be exercised by Antipater, his *grise eminence*. Gabinius sensed this truth and saw in Antipater a willing ally of Rome who would make Roman governing of Judah easier and less costly. Thus, an unholy alliance of Hyrcanus, Antipater, Gabinius (who was responsible to Pompey) and the Sadducees now ruled Judah.

New religious and judicial councils were established in Jerusalem, Gezer, Tzippori (Safed), Jericho and Chamas (Transjordan), all under the control of Antipater and the Sadducees, meant to substitute as the central authority in place of the disbanded Sanhedrin. The rabbis responded to this dire challenge by campaigning among the people encouraging them to remain steadfast in their devotion to Torah and the Oral Law and to ignore to whatever extent possible the government, the new religious councils and the Idumean/Roman/Jewish oppressors.[12]

Shemaya and Avtalyon led the struggle for Jewish survival and continuity, and their persistence and devotion eventually won the day. Their disciples became the leaders of Israel of then and now, and in the darkest days of cruel foreign rule they kept the Jewish spirit independent and vital.

Caesar and Pompey

IN 49 B.C.E., while the Jews in Judah were under the yoke of Gabinius, a power struggle that led to civil war dominated the affairs of the Roman Empire.

Julius Caesar, the most famous of the Roman gen-

---

11. Gabinius divided the members of the Sanhedrin into many groups and scattered them throughout Judah. Thus, the Sanhedrin itself was no longer a strong force in Jewish life. See Talmud, *Sotah* 48a, for its description of the sadness in Jewish life caused by the evil decree ending the power of the Sanhedrin.

12. The genius of the rabbis in adopting such a policy of ignoring instead of violently opposing hostile government, both Jewish and non-Jewish, has been amply established in Jewish history down to our very own time.

erals and a member of the ruling body of Rome, made open war against Pompey and quickly seized control of Rome and the western part of the empire. He now was determined to pursue Pompey, who still dominated the eastern portion of the empire, and destroy him and his power base.

In the turmoil occasioned by this civil war, Aristobulus escaped from Rome with the blessings of Julius Caesar, and attempted to reach Judah and free it from Pompey's domination. Julius Caesar, ever the strategist and tactician, not only supported Aristobulus in this bold move, but even committed two of his legions to Aristobulus' command in order to destroy Pompey.[13] But Pompey, sensing the danger, had his agents poison Aristobulus before he could reach Judah, and thus this new attempt at restoring independent Hasmonean rule in Judah died stillborn.

Julius Caesar defeated the forces of Pompey at the battle of Pharsalus in Greece in 48 B.C.E. Attempting to achieve final victory over his Roman enemies, Caesar invaded Egypt and captured Alexandria. However, due to a rare tactical blunder, he soon found himself and his army besieged in Alexandria by Pompey's army and its Ptolemaic allies. Sorely in need of friends, Julius Caesar looked about for any help that would extricate him from his dangerous situation.

Antipater cunningly convinced Hyrcanus, the Jewish king and High Priest, officially an ally of Pompey, to switch sides and come to the aid of Julius Caesar. Antipater was convinced, and correctly so, that eventually Julius Caesar would prevail over Pompey, and he wanted to be on the winning side when the spoils of the civil war were divided. Thus, Hyrcanus committed over three thousand Jewish soldiers to an expeditionary force that invaded Egypt and helped raise the siege of Alexandria. In addition, Hyrcanus urged the Jews of Egypt, an influential group in the Egyptian population, to support Julius Caesar and abandon Pompey. Thus, when the Roman civil war ended in Julius Caesar's complete victory, Hyrcanus and Antipater felt themselves entitled to imperial favor. They would need it.

---

13. Undoubtedly planning to have those very same two legions take control of Judah for him after Aristobulus would eject Pompey from the country. It is always interesting to see how clear and plentiful is hindsight, and how short in supply is foresight!

Antipater's Ascension

THE INTERNAL STRUGGLE between the offspring of Alexander Yannai for power in Judah did not end with the deaths of Aristobulus and his son Alexander.

Antigonus, the second son of Aristobulus, was also released from captivity in Rome by Julius Caesar at the beginning of the civil war, when Julius Caesar was attempting to have Aristobulus drive Pompey out of Judah. Now that the war had ended in Julius Caesar's triumph, Antigonus came forward to press his claim as the rightful king and High Priest of Judah. He invoked the memory and rights of his dead father, Aristobulus, who, he claimed, had died in service to Julius Caesar while attempting to reach Judah to fight Pompey's forces. Naturally, his claim was hotly contested by Hyrcanus and Antipater, who pointedly reminded Julius Caesar of their actual help when he was besieged in Alexandria.

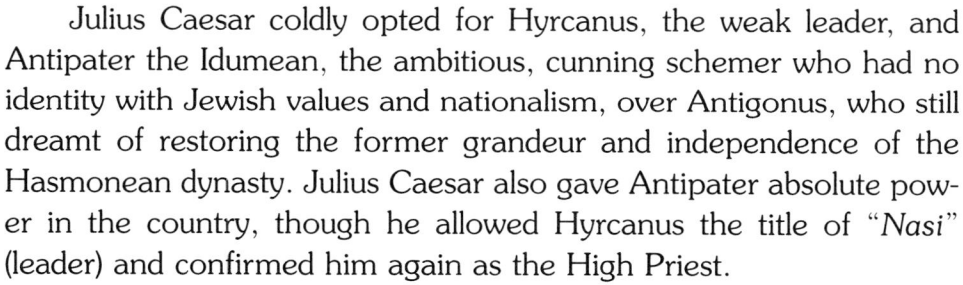

A coin minted by Antipater

Julius Caesar coldly opted for Hyrcanus, the weak leader, and Antipater the Idumean, the ambitious, cunning schemer who had no identity with Jewish values and nationalism, over Antigonus, who still dreamt of restoring the former grandeur and independence of the Hasmonean dynasty. Julius Caesar also gave Antipater absolute power in the country, though he allowed Hyrcanus the title of *"Nasi"* (leader) and confirmed him again as the High Priest.

Antipater, now openly the ruler of Judah, prepared to do the bidding of his Roman masters, no matter what. Julius Caesar, as an act of grace to Antipater, revoked the harsh decrees and burdensome taxation imposed on the Jews and Jerusalem by Pompey and Gabinius. He also allowed the walls and fortifications of Jerusalem to be rebuilt and restored Jaffa and a number of other coastal cities to Jewish rule. Thus, the beginning of Antipater's rule was marked by solid accomplishments on behalf of Judah.

Herod

WHATEVER ANTIPATER WAS, his son Herod was more so. The oldest son of Antipater, he was Roman-educated and possessed of a terribly mercurial and volatile personality. He was vindictive to a fault, never forgetting an

Herod

insult or slight, whether real or imagined. He was a paranoid egomaniac, violent, brutal and sadistic. He was also a fierce warrior, seemingly oblivious to personal danger, an able administrator and a charismatic leader. He was driven by insatiable ambition and was never burdened by any scruples whatsoever.

In 46 B.C.E. Herod's father, Antipater, appointed him governor of Galilee, the northern part of Israel. Herod immediately smelled an incipient revolt by the Galileans against Rome and his own rule. The fact that Galilee was, and would remain for the next centuries, the center of opposition to any foreign domination of the Jews contributed to Herod's suspicions. In a preemptive strike, he arrested and executed a large number of Galileans whom he accused of sedition. These killings were brutal,[14] illegal, and without any trial or pretense of law or justice being served.

Herod's behavior shocked the country. Even Hyrcanus initially felt that Herod had to be brought to justice for these murders. And so, at the insistence of the rabbis and the people, Hyrcanus convened a special court, composed of many of the leading scholars of the generation, to try Herod for his crimes.

Herod's Trial

IT WAS NOT CLEAR whether Herod would appear before this tribunal to be judged. His father advised him to flee until the matter blew over. But it was not in the nature of Herod to flee from his problems or enemies. His solution to difficulties was always to confront them with guile, force and violence, and thus eliminate them, no matter what the human or moral cost. Herod thus appeared for the court trial, but he dressed himself not as a penitent but in royal purple garb, bringing with him a large and menacing retinue of armed guards.

Herod's guards, demeanor and actions intimidated the court, so that many of the judges refused to participate actively in the proceedings. However, the great sage and strong personality, Shammai,[15]

---

14. Herod's sadism was so legendary that the mere mention of his name made people quake in fear. He not only killed and tortured and maimed, but he loved every moment spent committing these atrocities.

15. See more about him in the later discussion of Hillel in this section.

Herod's palace at Masada:
L: The mosaic floor at the bathhouse entrance
R: Herod's living quarters

nevertheless rallied the court against Herod's brazen defiance, and the court steeled itself to find Herod guilty of murder and to sentence him to execution. However, here the weakness of Hyrcanus again asserted itself to the detriment of the Jews and history. He could not see himself, as head of the court, allowing the death of the son of his friend Antipater. Instead, Hyrcanus recessed the trial for the day, preventing the verdict from being pronounced until the next morning. That night, Hyrcanus personally arranged Herod's escape to Damascus, and he provided for his protection under the Roman proconsul stationed there.

In Damascus, Herod somehow had himself immediately appointed by the Romans as a military governor in southern Lebanon. There he raised a large army and set out to raze Jerusalem and avenge himself on those who had exhibited the temerity to judge him. However, even his father, Antipater, opposed this reckless course of action against the rabbis and ordered his son to return to Lebanon with his forces.

Herod grudgingly retreated, but he continued to nurture his grudge against Hyrcanus,[16] the members of the court and even his own father for years. Only in blood would the affront be revenged.

---

16. Even though Hyrcanus had saved Herod from execution by the court, Herod never forgave Hyrcanus for convening the court to try him for murder in the first place.

Antipater's Wiles

HEROD, IN HIS EGOMANIA, fashioned himself as Herod "The Great" long before he actually rose to absolute power over Judah. His ambitions were limitless, his scruples nonexistent, and his dreams warped and dark. Yet he stamped himself and his accomplishments on the Land of Israel in such an indelible way that his presence there is felt until today.[17]

It was Herod who ended the reign of the Hasmoneans and destroyed their family, completely subjugated Judah to the rule of Rome and paved the way for the destruction of the Temple and the Jewish state. However, all of this was not yet clearly discernible in 45 B.C.E., when Herod was military governor of southern Lebanon.

The political situation in Judah was inextricably bound to the continuing power struggles in Rome itself; Julius Caesar had been the great benefactor of Antipater and Herod, and it was under Caesar's aegis that real control of Judah slipped from the hands of the Hasmoneans and into the claws of the Idumean father and son. Thus, the assassination of Julius Caesar in 44 B.C.E. sent tremors of anxiety through the allies of Antipater and Herod and raised the hopes of the Jews who opposed their tyranny.

Antipater was, as always, the wily master of intrigue and unscrupulous opportunism. Forgetting the dead Caesar, he immediately began to pander to Cassius, one of Caesar's assassins, who escaped to Syria in order to raise funds and rally forces for his attempt to succeed his fallen victim. In return for Antipater's support,[18] Cassius reappointed him, Herod and Phasael (another son of Antipater) as tax collectors over Judah, with broad police and governmental powers.

Herodian columns at Machpelah

---

17. The Western Wall, the building over the Cave of the Patriarchs, Herodium, Masada and some of the remains of ancient Caesarea are all of Herodian origin and construction.

18. In the process, Antipater helped Cassius conquer four cities in Judah, sold many of the inhabitants as slaves, and thereby realized a substantial fortune, which Cassius used to outfit his army for the coming battle for control of Rome.

The Idumean tax collectors went to their task with a vengeance. Jews unable or unwilling to pay the extortionist tributes were sold into slavery and sometimes tortured to death before the eyes of their horrified families and neighbors. Understandably, the enmity of the Jews toward Antipater and his sons grew and deepened. Even Hyrcanus, fearing for his own life and family, turned against Antipater.

Antipater was finally poisoned to death, undoubtedly by Jewish hands, in 43 B.C.E. However, Herod and Phasael immediately moved to assert their power in Judah and cruelly prevented any successful move to depose them.

Herodian stones of the Western Wall:
L: Note holes used to carry the stones
R: Note whiteness of newly uncovered stones

Herod's Persistence

THE ROMAN CIVIL WAR for the succession to Julius Caesar's power climaxed in 42 B.C.E. That year, at the Battle of Philippi, the triumvirate of Mark Antony, Octavian and Lepidus defeated the forces of Brutus and Cassius, thus apparently ending the legitimacy of Herod's power base in Judah.

Herod, like his father before him, was always able to tack with the changing winds blowing from Rome, and he persuaded Mark Antony, the new Roman ruler of the Middle East, to appoint him again as the Roman tax collector for Judah. The Jews of Judah sent numerous delegations to Antony to demand Herod's removal from the country, but to no avail.[19]

Mark Antony remained Herod's patron throughout his reign, but the Jews did not despair of ridding themselves of the Idumean monster.

---

19. Many of the members of these Jewish delegations were imprisoned by Antony, and some were even executed.

In 40 B.C.E., the Parthian army defeated the Roman legions, and Rome's grip on Judah loosened. Antigonus, the Hasmonean nephew of the High Priest Hyrcanus, proclaimed himself ruler of Judah and, with Parthian support, successfully besieged and occupied Jerusalem. Herod surrendered but somehow escaped imprisonment and punishment and fled to Egypt. Phasael, Herod's brother, committed suicide. Hyrcanus, who was viewed as a collaborator and traitor by Antigonus and most of Judah's population,[20] was removed from the office of High Priest and replaced by King Antigonus himself.[21] Judah rejoiced at having restored the Hasmoneans to power and in having rid themselves of the despised Herod.

Herod's palace — the Phasael Tower, named after Herod's brother. The minaret was added at a later time.

But the euphoria would prove to be premature.

Herod traveled from Egypt to Rome to plead his case before the Roman Senate. At the urging of Mark Antony, the Senate wilted and proclaimed Herod as the legitimate king of Judah, though not committing any Roman legions to enforce their proclamation. Herod then came to Syria, where he raised a large army and set forth to conquer Judah and Jerusalem on his own.

For the next three years (40-37 B.C.E.) a bloody war ensued between Herod's forces and those of Antigonus the Hasmonean. Finally, in 37 B.C.E., Herod crushed the Hasmonean army, entered and occupied Jerusalem, and slaughtered thousands of the Hasmonean supporters. Antigonus was beheaded, and Herod achieved his goal of sole autocratic rulership over Judah.

---

20. The final act of treacherous weakness by Hyrcanus vis-á-vis Herod, which sealed Hyracnus' lasting doleful reputation among the Jews, was his arranging the marriage of his granddaughter Miriam (Mariamne), a Hasmonean princess, to the hated Herod. This "royal" marriage granted Herod a thread of legitimacy in his otherwise spurious claim to be the true king of Judah.

21. In order to prevent Hyrcanus from ever again assuming the role of High Priest, Antigonus ordered Hyrcanus' nose and ears to be mutilated, thus rendering him halachically unfit to serve as a priest in the Temple. Cruelty was not limited to the person of Herod alone.

ECHOES OF GLORY

Herod's palace in Jerusalem, from the Holyland model

A reign of terror swept Judah, with Herod wreaking terrible vengeance upon his opponents (again, both real and imagined). Herod had the unhappy trait of never remembering a friend and never forgetting an enemy. Most of the members of the Sanhedrin were executed, with only the great Shammai being spared and allowed to continue his activities in public life. Herod would rule Judah for more than thirty-two years until his death in 4 B.C.E. His rule marked the end of true Jewish independence in Judah and set the stage for the eventual destruction of the country and the Temple by the Romans.

Hillel

IN THE MIDST OF the oppressive darkness Herod spread over Jewish life, a shining personality emerged, whose radiant goodness lights human civilization even today. Hillel *HaBavli* ("the Babylonian") emerged from his humble anonymity and personal economic poverty[22] to become the *Nasi* (head of the Sanhedrin) as well as the conscience and religious leader of Jewry.[23]

Hillel is one of the greatest heroes of all Jewish history. Kind, patient, wise, innovative, far-seeing, he was an intellectual giant whose persona was defined by his holy spirit. Slow to anger, warm and ac-

---
22. See Talmud, *Yoma* 35b.
23. See Talmud, *Pesachim* 66a, for a description of the circumstances leading to Hillel's succeeding the *B'nei Beseira* and becoming the leader of the Jewish people.

cepting,[24] Hillel took strong initiatives to negate the influences of Herod's cruelties and aping of Roman ways. But he did so indirectly and not through confrontation.

He strengthened Torah learning among the masses of Israel, revitalized the tradition and supremacy of the Oral Law,[25] ordained timely and necessary applications of *halachah*[26] and reinvigorated the flagging spirit of the people groaning under the tyrannical yoke of Herod. Hillel was the embodiment of the words of the prophet Zechariah, who said, "Not by might nor by force, but rather by My spirit, says the Lord of Hosts."[27] In fact, in Hillel we are able to discern clearly the main personal quality that characterized all the great men of the Mishnah and Talmud — serenity of spirit. No matter how hectic and difficult the times, no matter how sad and vexing personal life is, a godly person is serene in the face of both triumph and adversity. The prototype for such serenity is Hillel.

A Prozbul document

---

24. See Talmud, *Shabbos* 31a.

25. "In the beginning (of Second Temple times) the Torah was under threat of becoming forgotten by Israel, until Ezra came from Babylonia and reestablished it (in the Land of Israel). The Torah again was under threat of becoming forgotten by Israel (at the end of the reign of the Hasmoneans). Then came Hillel *HaBavli* and reestablished it once more" (Talmud, *Succah* 20a).

26. See Talmud, *Gittin* 34b, for a discussion of Hillel's establishment of *prozbul* as a legitimate method of preventing the biblical cancellation of personal loan obligations in the Sabbatical (*Shemittah*) year. There is a vast literature available in Jewish scholarship regarding the legalisms and public policy involved in *prozbul* and other forms of rabbinic decrees instituted by Hillel and his successors, "in order to keep the world in good repair." Those interested in knowing more about this fascinating aspect of halachic vitality are urged to follow the dictum of Hillel himself — "Go forth yourself and study the rest."

A New Focus

BUT HILLEL DID MORE than provide leadership for his generation. He is the architect of the basic Jewish mechanism which allowed for Jewish national survival under foreign[28] and often relentlessly hostile rule. Hillel, together with Shammai, the Sanhedrin under them, and their yeshivah colleagues, built a Jewish life so rich in spiritual and social content that it allowed Jews to ignore and discount the government and ruler that nominally dominated them.

To the average Jew in Judah in 30 B.C.E., Hillel was more important than Herod, just as in nineteenth-century Eastern European Jewish life, rabbis, Chassidic masters and Jewish culture were more significant to the Jew of the *shtetl* or the urban ghetto than was the Czar and his government. Beginning in Judah at the onset of the first millennia of the Common Era and stretching in time until our very day, the government that ruled over the Jewish people, whether in the Holy Land or the Diaspora, was to very many Jews largely irrelevant to the development of their own Jewish life, culture, values and life-style.

Naturally, when the government became overly oppressive and violent it could not be ignored, and its actions inescapably shaped inner Jewish life itself. But from the time of Herod onward, Jews ignored the policies and caprices of government whenever possible[29] and lived their lives to the beat of a deep, inner rhythm which was represented by the personality, example, decrees and serenity of faith of Hillel.

The Houses of Hillel and Shammai

UNTIL THE TIME OF HILLEL, there were few, if any, disputes in matters of Jewish law and tradition. The power of the Sanhedrin, coupled with the loyalty of the populace to the great teachings of the Pharisees, enabled all questions to be solved and policies to be clearly and unanimously enunciated. But the

---

27. *Zechariah 4:6.*
28. Even Jewish "foreign" rule.
29. From my blessed personal experience of being able to live part of the year in Jerusalem, I can personally testify that this attitude is still quite strong among many Jews living under Israeli government rule today!

The Hasmonean Dynasty

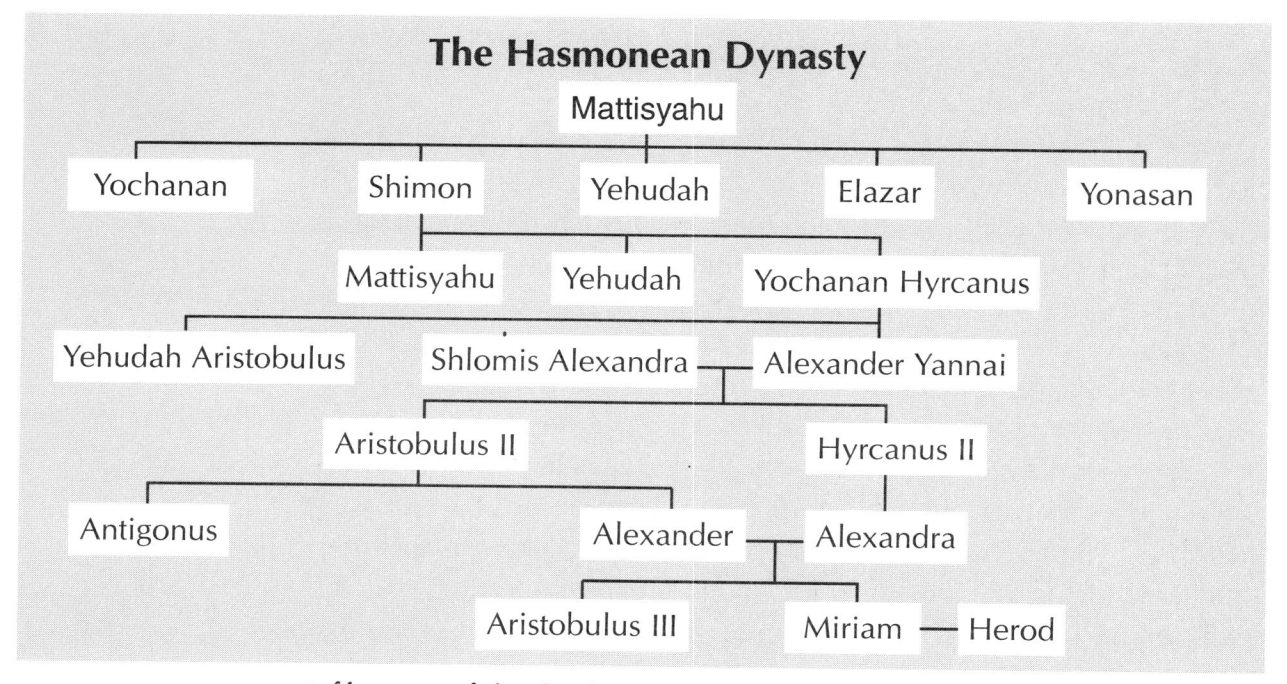

- Mattisyahu
  - Yochanan
  - Shimon
    - Mattisyahu
    - Yehudah
    - Yochanan Hyrcanus
      - Yehudah Aristobulus
      - Shlomis Alexandra — Alexander Yannai
        - Aristobulus II
          - Antigonus
          - Alexander — Alexandra
            - Aristobulus III
            - Miriam — Herod
        - Hyrcanus II
          - Alexandra
  - Yehudah
  - Elazar
  - Yonasan

infiltration of the Sanhedrin by the Sadducees, the shameful behavior of the last Hasmonean kings and princes, and the corruption of many of the leading priestly families created a climate where disputes regarding matters of Jewish law and tradition also began to arise. The memory of clear decisions in Jewish law began to fade.

Hillel and Shammai disputed only a small number of Torah legal issues. Their disciples in later generations, forming the House of Hillel and the House of Shammai, already disputed hundreds of matters due to the changing circumstances and increased difficulties of the time. These circumstances caused a weakening in the teacher-student transmission of the Torah heritage, forcing the disciples of Hillel and Shammai to engage in continued debate. In future generations, legal and halachic issues would continue to be debated, analyzed, disputed and reconciled. The principles elucidated during the course of these discussions became the basis for the opinions and decisions of the Mishnah and Talmud, and remain the subject of Torah study until today. However, the loss of clarity in legal decision led to many problems that would later arise in Jewish life.[30]

In their personal lives, the members of the two schools of

---

30. Rabbi Menachem HaMeiri, the great fourteenth-century Talmudic scholar, in his introduction to the Mishnah, *Avos*, characterizes the beginning of halachic disputations at the time of Hillel and Shammai as being the time "when darkness descended on the (Torah) world."

Herod's palace — showing L-R: Hippicus, Mariamne and Phasael Towers, from the Holyland model

Shammai and Hillel remained on good terms throughout the centuries, but their scholarly disagreements were often pointed, abrasive and irreconcilable. In the vast majority of cases, the final Talmudic decision followed the opinions advocated by the school of Hillel, although the opinions and personalities of the school of Shammai were yet most influential throughout the first and second centuries of the Common Era.

Further Atrocities of Herod

IN THE MIDST OF Herod's reign of terror in Judah, soon to be described, Hillel's attitude towards the tyrant is reflected in his statement[31] upon seeing a skull floating in the water: "...Because you drowned others, you have been drowned, and those that drowned you will in their turn also be drowned." Herod would pursue a program of relentless persecution and terror against the disciples of Hillel and Shammai.[32] Paranoid, sadistic, impulsive, insecure, jealous and violent, Herod systematically destroyed the Hasmoneans, the rest of his own family, Jewish independence and eventually himself.

At the onset of Herod's rule in 36 B.C.E., he forced a marriage with the Hasmonean princess, Miriam (Mariamne), the granddaughter of Hyrcanus, the now-aged, deposed and maimed High Priest.

---
31. Mishnah, *Avos* 2:6.
32. Nevertheless, so great was the standing of Hillel and his compatriot Shammai amongst the people that even Herod desisted from harming them and their families.

EDOM ASCENDANT — *Aristobulus, Hyrcanus, and Antipater* □ 135

Miriam's brother Aristobulus III, handsome, headstrong and popular amongst the people as an Hasmonean descendant, was allowed by Herod to become the High Priest. However, the young man proved to be too reckless, flaunting his public popularity in the face of Herod, who was well aware of his own lack of popularity. Herod solved the problem in his characteristic fashion. He invited his young brother-in-law to the winter palace in Jericho for a swim and there had his guards drown him in the pool.

Herod's bereaved mother-in-law, Alexandra, the mother of Aristobulus III, lodged murder charges against Herod with Mark Antony. Antony, as usual, acquitted Herod of any wrongdoing.[33] Herod would eventually avenge himself on Alexandra for her act of defiance. But Herod's open dependence upon Mark Antony would now bring upon himself his greatest crisis.

Family Murders

IN THE YEAR 31 B.C.E. Antony and Octavian struggled against each other for control of Rome. Octavian defeated Antony that year in the battle of Actium and became the sole leader of Rome, eventually calling himself Augustus Caesar.

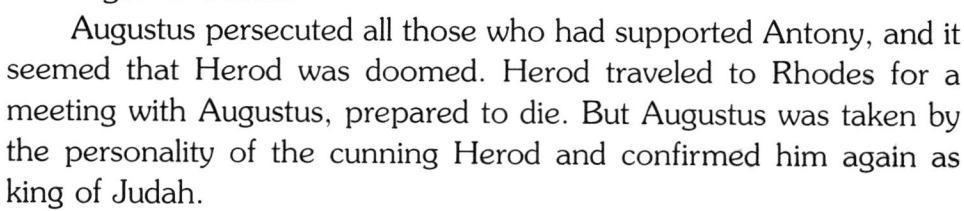

Augustus persecuted all those who had supported Antony, and it seemed that Herod was doomed. Herod traveled to Rhodes for a meeting with Augustus, prepared to die. But Augustus was taken by the personality of the cunning Herod and confirmed him again as king of Judah.

Herod celebrated his good fortune by having his now-aged grandfather-in-law, Hyrcanus, executed, somehow feeling that this feeble, old, weak person constituted a threat to his rule. The Hasmonean family was now in danger of becoming extinct.

Herod's wife and queen, Miriam, openly showed her disdain towards the man to whom she had unfortunately been "sold," the murderer of her grandfather. Herod was madly in love with Miriam and yet at the same time was insanely jealous and suspicious because of her open coolness towards him. Rumors of Miriam's hatred of

Augustus

---
33. A large bribe from Herod helped Antony appreciate Herod's innocence.

ERETZ YISRAEL UNDER HEROD'S RULE

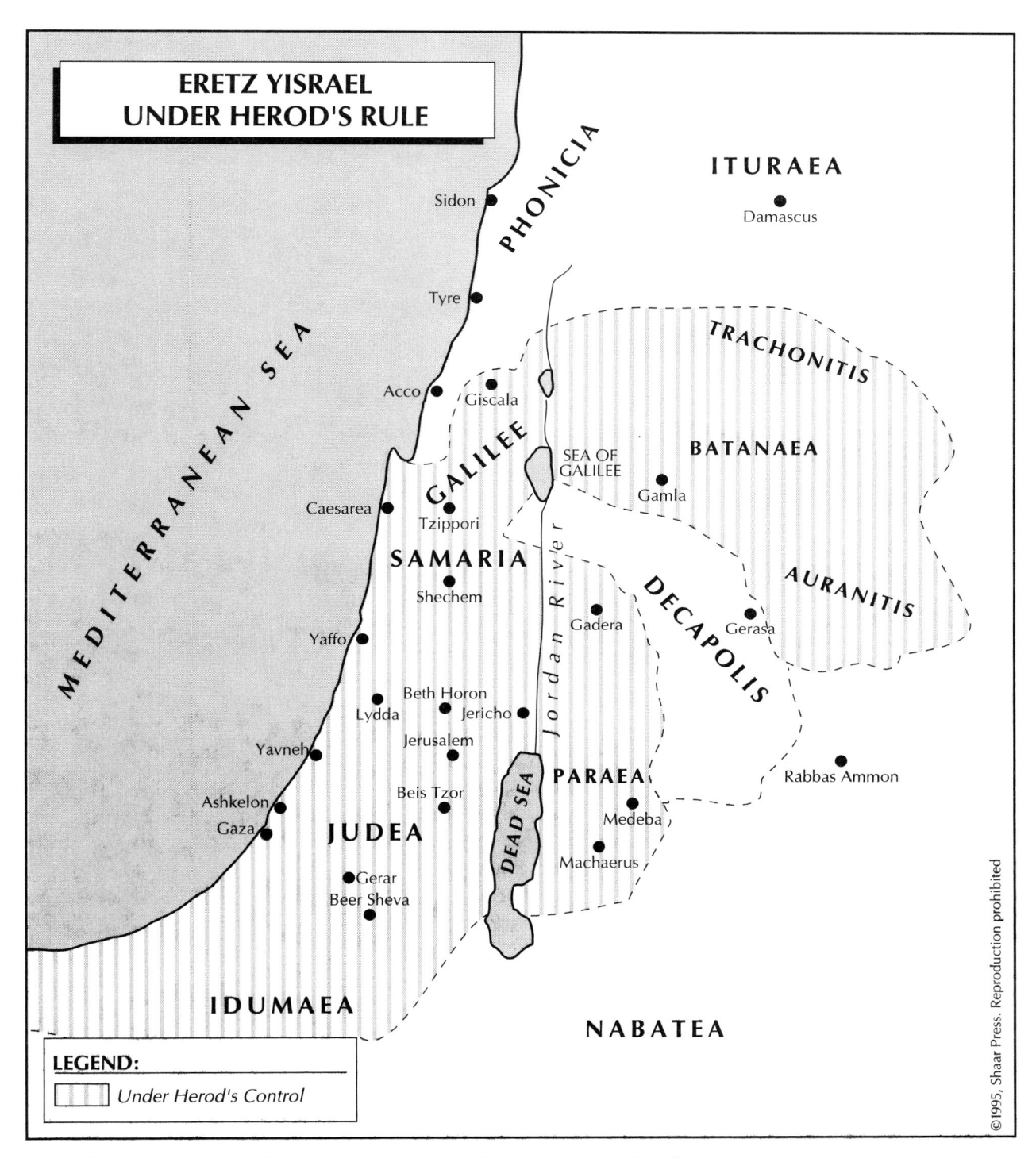

Map showing territories under Herod's control, including Judea, Samaria, Galilee, Paraea, Idumaea, Batanaea, Auranitis, Trachonitis, and surrounding regions (Phoenicia, Ituraea, Decapolis, Nabatea). Notable cities marked include Sidon, Tyre, Acco, Giscala, Caesarea, Tzippori, Shechem, Yaffo, Lydda, Beth Horon, Jericho, Jerusalem, Yavneh, Beis Tzor, Ashkelon, Gaza, Gerar, Beer Sheva, Damascus, Gamla, Gadera, Gerasa, Rabbas Ammon, Medeba, and Machaerus.

Legend: Under Herod's Control

©1995, Shaar Press. Reproduction prohibited

Herod swirled about the court, and Herod, in a rage of jealous paranoia, arrested her and put her on trial for treason. She was convicted[34]

---

34. As with all later tyrants, acquittals in state trials during the reign of Herod were almost nonexistent.

and put to death. After her execution, Herod, crazed with grief and remorse, killed all of the hapless judges who had been so quick to succumb to his will and pervert justice. Herod now fell into a deep depression, and the government of Judah was paralyzed by his absence.

Miriam's mother, Alexandra, attempted to mount a revolt against the incapacitated Herod and rid Judah of that terrible tyrant. The plot was discovered by Herod's agents, and Alexandra was also killed by Herod.

The last Hasmonean, a young princess, upon hearing that Herod intended to marry her and make her queen, committed suicide, and with her death no further descendants of the Hasmoneans were possible.[35] From that time forward, anyone who claimed to be a Hasmonean was thereby deemed by Jewish law to be descended from a non-Jewish slave, i.e., from non-Jewish mates of Herod.[36]

Herod was not yet finished with murdering his own. He had two sons by his beloved wife, Miriam, who were yet alive, and when they grew to maturity he made public his wish to bequeath to them his empire. However, another son of Herod, Antipater, born of an Idumean woman, poisoned his father's mind against the sons of Miriam.

Antipater spread malicious rumors that Miriam's two sons were planning their father's assassination. Herod, always paranoid enough to believe the worst no matter how outlandish the accusation, had his two sons tortured to death before his very eyes.[37] Antipater, in turn, also came under suspicion of plotting against his father, and he too was executed by Herod.

Three other sons of Herod somehow managed to outlive their mad father. All were from non-Jewish mothers and had little or no understanding of the people they would attempt to rule. The three, Archelaus, Antipas and Philipus (also known as Herod Philip), would divide Herod's empire among themselves at his death. Meanwhile, Agrippa, the grandson of Herod and Miriam (through one of the sons of Herod that the madman tortured and martyred), was spirited away to Rome, there to be raised in the style and schooling of the Roman aristocracy. He would eventually return to Judah and become the last "Jewish" ruler of the country before its destruction by the Romans.

Coin minted by Herod Philip

Agrippa

---

35. Talmud, *Bava Basra* 3b.
36. Ibid.
37. The probable date of these murders is 7 B.C.E.

Herod's Temple

WHILE HEROD KEPT ON KILLING, he also kept on building. His megalomania reflected itself in the construction of some of the major edifices of his time. The remnants of the great palaces, castles and fortresses at Herodian, Masada, Caesarea, Hebron and Antipatris all testify to Herod's lavish program of construction and public works.

Herod's major building project was the reconstruction of the Temple in Jerusalem. After taking down the original structure, he built a new, magnificent edifice, enlarging the courtyard and Temple Mount in the process, in only three years, all the while allowing the Temple services to continue to function. The Talmud states that "one who was not privileged to see Herod's Temple never saw a truly magnificent building."[38] The floor was of carrara marble, and its blue tinge gave the impression of a moving sea of water. Gold, silver, tapestries and balconies abounded, and the entire Temple compound was hailed as one of the architectural wonders of a classical world that included the Parthenon, the Pont du Gard and the Roman Colosseum.[39]

Entrance to the Temple, after its renovation by Herod, from the Holyland model

In its own time it became a tremendous tourist attraction, with special areas and sections of the Temple compound set aside for the

---

38. *Bava Basra* 4a.
39. Herod contaminated the Temple compound by placing an enormous golden eagle — the symbol of Rome — over the main arch of the Temple's southern entrance promenade. Jewish zealots attempted to remove and destroy the eagle, claiming its presence to be sacrilegious and a dishonor to the Temple. Herod reacted to this opposition in a predictably brutal fashion, killing thousands of people to avenge this insult to Rome and himself. Thus, even while raising the Temple to its utmost physical glory, Herod at the same time succeeded in alienating a large section of the Jewish people from faith in the holiness and services of the Temple itself. For the final eighty years of the Second Temple, the corruption of the priesthood and the introduction of Roman ways and values in the Temple compound subdued the enthusiasm of the Jewish people for its magnificent central Temple building.

The Pont-Du-Gard, Nimes, France

use of non-Jews. Yet, in less than a century, the Temple would be razed to the ground, with only a small section of the western outer retaining wall of the courtyard surviving till today. Nevertheless, it is through the massive stones of this piece of wall that even Herod has been able to remain immortal through millennia.

Hillel's Legacy

HEROD WAS NOT THE ONLY great builder of the time. Hillel and Shammai were also unsurpassed constructors. But whereas Herod built physical, tangible monuments, Hillel and Shammai and their disciples built the spiritual infrastructure that would protect and preserve the people of Israel for all time. By the time of his death in about 10 C.E., Hillel had laid the foundation for the work of the scholars of the Mishnah, who successfully translated the principles of the Oral Law into writing. Thus, the Oral Law, whose transmission was endangered by Roman persecution, was able to remain the foundation and backbone of Jewish life to this day.

A sign from the Temple, written in Greek, forbidding entry by non-Jews beyond the sign

Herod was not the true leader of the people of Israel; Hillel was. The government and country of Judah would eventually fail and fall. The people of Israel, blessed with their Torah and traditions, their unique life-style of morality and probity, and their great God-given vision of universal human brotherhood and faith, would survive and even prosper under all circumstances. Hillel enabled the Jewish people to grasp the difference between national entity and spiritual peoplehood. By protecting and enhancing the latter, Hillel guaranteed the Jewish ability to survive the loss of the former.

9
The End of the Second Commonwealth

HEROD DIED IN 4 B.C.E., unloved and unmourned. His son Archelaus immediately claimed the throne of Judah for himself. To win over the population, Archelaus made a number of cosmetic concessions to the traditions and wishes of his Jewish subjects. He indicated that he would remove the corrupt and insincere High Priest appointed and maintained by Herod, and promised to replace him with someone more morally fit for the role; and he gave vague assurances of granting amnesty to the political prisoners who filled Herod's jails. But time proved that his own base character would not allow him actually to practice such wisdom and compassion.

Like his father before him, Archelaus was vain, violent, insecure and cruel beyond description. He determined that Judah would be ruled only by the lash and the sword. He made this painfully clear on the first Pesach after his ascent to power. In order to intimidate the Jews, Archelaus ordered his foreign mercenary soldiers to slay over three thousand Jews in the Temple, on the pretext that they were gathering there for purposes of rebellion. And so, when Archelaus left for Rome immediately after that Pesach, expecting to be confirmed there as king by the emperor Augustus, he found an imposing delegation of Roman and Judean Jews in the emperor's court lobbying against his appointment. These Jews asked that Judah and Jerusalem be governed directly by the Romans, rather than by the Herodian family.

Even as the matter of Archelaus' appointment hung in the balance, his cruelty did not abate. On the holiday of Shavuos, just seven weeks after Pesach, Archelaus once again massacred thousands of

Coins minted by Archelaus

Jewish worshipers on the Temple grounds. Jewish delegations from Judah again implored Augustus to reject Archelaus as king. Augustus, troubled by his own family problems and not wanting Rome to become too deeply enmeshed in the fractious affairs of the Jews, refused their request and allowed Archelaus to remain in power, although he never did officially grant him the title of king.

A Respite from Cruelty

THE OPEN ENMITY of the Jews toward Archelaus caused him to become even more vicious and violent. His nine-year reign was one long, bloody disaster. Finally the Romans themselves, appalled by the destructive bent of Archelaus, removed him from power in the year 6 C.E. and exiled him to distant Gaul. Augustus now placed Judah under the jurisdiction of the Roman proconsul in Damascus, with the actual administration of government in Judah being conducted by a Roman procurator headquartered in Caesarea.

The procurators, in the main greedy and corrupt people as well, nevertheless constituted a marked improvement over Herod and Archelaus. They never pretended to be Jewish or to have Jewish interests at heart, and therefore they meddled little in internal religious Jewish life. Now, the Sanhedrin returned to open and active operation, and the disciples of Hillel and Shammai became the acknowledged leaders of the Jewish people.

The Roman procurators were basically interested only in extorting great personal wealth for themselves and keeping the country politically quiet. Painful and shameful as this policy was, it nonetheless enabled the Jews to retain a great deal of religious, social and organizational autonomy, and thus the final decade of Augustus' rule passed, mainly with peace reigning over Judah. Hillel's son Shimon was the head of the Sanhedrin, and his wisdom and sterling character made him the de facto leader of the Jews.

Corruption in the High Priesthood

HOWEVER, NOT ALL OF THE JEWS were satisfied with the status quo. Two extreme parties arose among the Jews. One was a rebirth of the old Sadduccee party, and the other was the party of the Zealots (*Kanaim* in Hebrew).

The new Sadducees objected to the power of the Pharisee-dominated Sanhedrin and wished to "Romanize" the Jews, much as their ancestors had attempted to Hellenize the Jews two centuries earlier. The power base of the Sadduccees was formed by the aristocracy, the wealthy landowners and the Temple Priests. The Sadduccees conspired with the avaricious Roman procurators to gain control over the allocation of priestly functions and positions in the Temple.[1]

Once again, the very office of High Priest showed itself especially susceptible to corruption. Great bribes were paid to the Roman procurators to gain this office, and High Priests came and went at a dizzying pace, many times serving even less than a year in the post.[2] The complete abandonment of Jewish tradition and values by the Sadduccees in the years preceding the destruction of the Temple demoralized much of the Jewish population of Judah and brought about a climate of divisiveness and polarization in Jewish life.

Even among the Pharisees, differences of opinion and varying nuances of observance were no longer easily tolerated, and people became reluctant to accommodate differences of opinion and practice.[3] Suspicions that others had fallen prey to Saducean heresies[4] allowed for the acceptance of zealotry within traditional Jewish life, contributing to the spirit of unfounded and uncalled-for communal hatred in Jewish society. This climate of suspicion and hatred was the death knell of the Second Commonwealth. Thus, the Sadduccees were

---

1. See Talmud, *Pesachim* 57a, for the caustic comments of the rabbis regarding the power-grabbing, monopoly-holding, corrupt practices of many of the leading priestly families. Also see Talmud Yerushalmi, *Yoma* 1:1.

2. Jewish tradition implies that not even one of the later High Priests of the Second Temple survived in office for more than a year.

3. See the introduction to *Haameik Davar, Bereishis,* by Rabbi Naftali Tzvi Yehudah Berlin, the great leader of the Volozhin Yeshivah in the nineteenth century, for his pungent comments regarding the unreasoning intolerance and hatred of brothers that was present at the end of Second Temple times.

4. Ibid.

ruinous to Jewish national existence, not only through their own actions and policies, but — with results which were even more insidious — through the reaction to them that poisoned general Jewish society.

The Zealots

THE SECOND EXTREMIST GROUP, the party of the Zealots, consisted of Jews who despaired of Jewish life and survival under Roman domination. They yearned for true national independence and freedom from the yoke of Roman proconsuls and puppet Judean kings, and they soon turned to violence to achieve their goals. According to Josephus, the Zealots became active in about 6 C.E. under the leadership of Judah of Galilee. Their descent into violence coincided with a general breakdown of law and social convention at the end of the Second Temple era.

Groups of armed Jews, little more than brigands and robbers, extorted wealth from whomever they could. Because of their predilection for the use of a short dagger — *sicarii* — as their favorite weapon, these criminals came to be known as *Sicarii*.[5] In an unholy and ultimately tragic alliance, many of the *Sicarii* joined with the Zealots and became the leading fighters against Rome. However, these murderers also killed or maimed any Jews who stood in their way, and thus the war they eventually fought against Rome would also be accompanied by a bloody civil war among the Jews themselves.

There was no person or group who could control the Zealots/*Sicarii* combination, and by the year 30, the country of Judah was near chaos. Blood and violence ruled the roads and the streets, and the call of the Sanhedrin and the rabbis for peace, forbearance under Roman rule and moderation of radical policies was overwhelmed by the nationalism, misguided patriotism, greed and self-righteous fanaticism of the Zealots/*Sicarii* and their followers. They viewed the Pharisees and their rabbinic leaders as weak, if not traitorous, Jews. Murder among Jews became so common in Judah that in the year 30 C.E. the Sanhedrin despaired of the situation and no longer heard capital cases.[6] There were strong forebodings that

---
5. The word *sicarii* is Latin. The Talmud, in an Aramaic adaptation of the term, calls these brigands *Sicricon*.
6. Talmud, *Shabbos* 15a.

Tomb of R' Yochanan ben Zakkai

the end of the Jewish state was near and that the existence of the Temple itself was in jeopardy.[7]

To further complicate this tragic and muddled situation, there arose, in growing numbers, sects that preached the imminent coming of the Messiah. Most of these groups were offshoots of the Essenes, whose extremist behavior earned them the disfavor of the rabbis. The largest and most influential of these Essene-spawned sects developed into Christianity, eventually breaking away completely from the Jewish society in which it had been formed.

Christianity will be discussed in more detail in a later chapter, but suffice it for now to say that such a strongly messianic and apocalyptic force as Christianity only served to further unhinge Jewish society in the last decades of the Second Temple's existence. Indeed, the political and military turmoil of Judah's decline would be matched by a general spiritual chaos among many Jews of the time. Only the faith, strong leadership and spiritual serenity of the disciples of Hillel — mainly his son Shimon, his grandson Rabban Gamliel the Elder, and the great Rabban Yochanan ben Zakkai[8] — enabled the Jewish people to emerge from the coming disaster unbroken and somehow resilient.

Pontius Pilate

WHEN AUGUSTUS DIED in 14 C.E., his successor, Tiberius, appointed Valerius Gratus as procurator of Judah. Greedy to a fault, he instituted a system of graft and payoffs that encompassed every religious and political post of power in the country. The Jews complained bitterly to the

---

7. The holy Rabbi Tzadok began a forty-year fast in the year 30 C.E. in fear of the anticipated destruction of the Temple. See Talmud, *Gittin* 56b, and the commentary of Rashi there. Also see Talmud, *Yoma* 39b, for a description of the disturbing physical changes on the Temple Mount and grounds which indicated its impending destruction.

8. According to the Talmud, he was "the least" of Hillel's eighty major disciples. This, in spite of the fact that he had mastered in their entirety the vast unwritten libraries of the Oral Law.

Roman proconsul in Damascus, and in time Valerius was eased out of his position. However, he was succeeded by an even more corrupt and rapacious man, Pontius Pilate.

Pontius assumed control of Judah in 25 C.E. and remained in power for ten years. Under his rule the country was in constant turmoil, with the Roman occupiers guilty of systematic extortion and atrocities. When Pontius brazenly attempted to loot the treasury of the Temple, armed clashes between the Romans and the Jews took place.

As the country teetered on the brink of war, Rabban Gamliel *HaZaken* (the Elder), Hillel's grandson and the head of the Sanhedrin, travelled to Damascus to plead with Vitellius, the Roman proconsul, to have Pontius removed from office. Vitellius agreed, and Pontius was soon recalled to Rome. But the situation in Judah would nevertheless now reach the final stage of great national crisis.

The reader will recall that the despicable Herod, after murdering the rest of the Hasmoneans, had wedded the sole survivor, Miriam. Herod begot Aristobulus, who in turn fathered Herod Agrippa. Fatherly feelings being among the least of Herod's traits, he executed his son Aristobulus in one of his insanely paranoid moments, when Agrippa was but three years old. When the orphaned boy was six

Inscription in Caesarea by Pontius Pilate in honor of Tiberius Caesar

Coins minted by Pontius Pilate

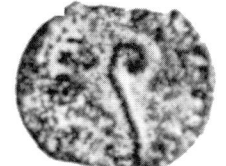

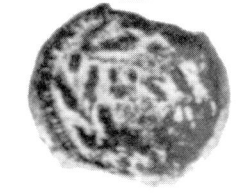

Tomb of Hillel HaZaken

EDOM ASCENDANT *The End of the Second Commonwealth* □ 147

years old, he was sent as a hostage to Rome, where he was raised as a member of Roman aristocracy. Two of his schoolmates, Gaius and Claudius, were to become emperors of Rome.

Gaius and Agrippa

GAIUS BECAME EMPEROR in the year 37 and appointed his old school friend Agrippa ruler of Transjordan. Eventually the entire Galilee was incorporated under his rule.

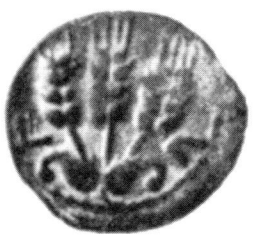

Agrippa grew to be a complex person. Roman to the core, he nonetheless proudly identified himself with Judaism and the Jewish people. Though relatively uneducated in Jewish knowledge and traditions, he never worshipped pagan gods and took great pains to refrain from eating pork or other obviously forbidden foods. The Jews also accepted him. His descent from the last Hasmonean princess and his obvious affinity for Judaism endeared him to the Jewish nation. Furthermore, his strong and successful efforts to broaden Jewish autonomy under Roman rule and his success in improving the economic and social welfare of the Jews under his domain earned him increasing affection among those Jews otherwise strongly suspicious and antagonistic toward Roman-appointed rulers. Again the status quo temporarily became encouraging as far as Roman-Jewish relations were concerned.

Gaius' increasingly visible and violent insanity, however, shattered this dream of Roman-Jewish cooperation. In the year 40, Gaius (who had recently proclaimed himself as a god) decided to have an image of himself erected in the Temple. He assigned the task to the Roman proconsul in Damascus, Petronius, under whose jurisdiction Judah and the Temple still lay. Petronius, well aware that this would be a *causus belli,* stalled. However, Gaius increased his pressure on him, and the statue was finally prepared for installation in the Temple. Agrippa, aware of the desperate consequences of such an act, intervened with his old friend and schoolmate, and in a lucid moment, as a personal gesture of accommodation to Agrippa, Gaius retracted his order. Soon after, in the year 41, Gaius was assassinated, and Agrippa's other old friend and classmate, Claudius, ascended to the imperial throne of Rome.

Coins minted by Agrippa I

Claudius

CLAUDIUS IMMEDIATELY EXPANDED Agrippa's kingdom to include Judah and Jerusalem, making all the Jews living within the biblical borders of the Land of Israel united once again under one rule, as in Hasmonean times. Agrippa's popularity amongst his Jewish subjects soared. He was held in such high esteem that the masses of Israel were willing to forget his Herodian descent and treat him as a full-fledged Jew.[9]

During the reign of Agrippa, Judah and its citizens felt themselves independent and serene. Though all taxes to Rome were paid and the other obligations to Rome were scrupulously fulfilled by Agrippa's government, the Jews did not complain overtly of Roman rule, for they saw Agrippa as their ruler and not Claudius. Agrippa became so emboldened by his Jewish popularity that he fortified Jerusalem, building a third outer wall to complement the earlier Herodian fortifications.

However, the blissful situation did not last long. The Romans took dim notice of Agrippa's pro-Jewish activity, and Claudius ordered him to stop the project before the third outer wall was completed. Not satisfied with this step, many Roman enemies, resenting Judah's renaissance, lay in ambush for Agrippa's life. In the year 44, while on a visit to the Greco-Roman city of Caesarea, Agrippa was poisoned and died. With him also died the hoped-for survival of Judah and the Temple.

Agrippa's death was mourned not only by the Jews of Judah but by Claudius as well. Agrippa had been a good friend and loyal ally. In fact, the emperor would have appointed Agrippa's seventeen-year-old son, also named Agrippa, as successor to his father and the leader of Judah, except that the boy's young years "cautioned" against such a move. Claudius therefore "temporarily" restored the rule of Judah to the Roman procurators. This type of rule, more than anything else, led to the great Jewish revolt and war against Rome that ended disastrously for the Jews. A succession of seven venal, corrupt and cruel procurators[10] created a situation of turmoil and desperation in Judah which culminated in the eruption of the Jewish

---

9. See Talmud, *Sotah* 41a-b.
10. Fadus, Tiberius Alexander, Cumanus, Felix, Festus, Albinus and Florus.

war against Rome in the year 66. The steps which led to the revolt may be detailed as follows.

The Path to Revolt

IN THE YEAR 48, when Agrippa II became twenty-one years old, Claudius finally appointed him as ruler over some provinces in Transjordan and over the Temple in Jerusalem.[11] However, he never appointed him ruler over Judah, which remained under the heel of the Roman procurators.

Intrinsically, this decision sat well with the Jews. Agrippa II did not have his father's feelings of commitment and empathy toward the Jewish people; and although he did intervene a number of times on behalf of the Jews against the provocations of the Samaritans and Romans,[12] he generally was indifferent to the plight of the Jews under Roman rule and reckoned mainly with the wishes of the Roman rulers. But the actual choice of the procurator of Judah was tragic. In the year 52, Claudius granted this position to an insecure, particularly insensitive and cruel person named Felix, who soon earned the enmity of the masses of Jews in Judah. As a result, the forces of the Zealots, who had continually preached open war against Roman rule, increased dramatically.

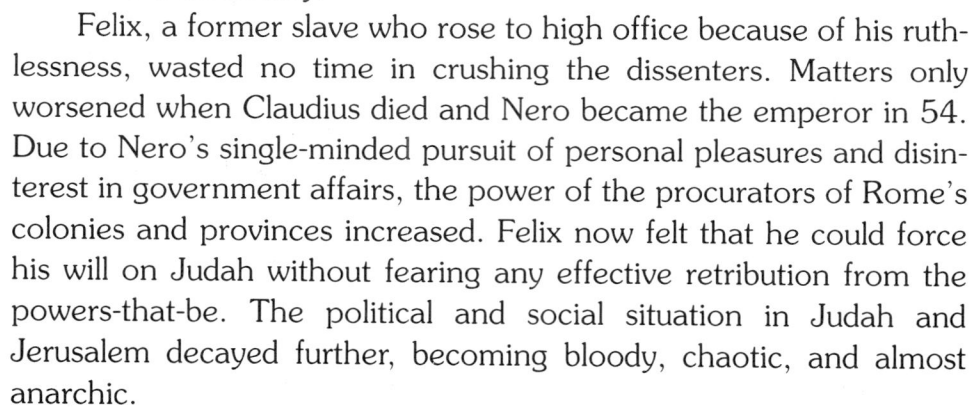

Felix, a former slave who rose to high office because of his ruthlessness, wasted no time in crushing the dissenters. Matters only worsened when Claudius died and Nero became the emperor in 54. Due to Nero's single-minded pursuit of personal pleasures and disinterest in government affairs, the power of the procurators of Rome's colonies and provinces increased. Felix now felt that he could force his will on Judah without fearing any effective retribution from the powers-that-be. The political and social situation in Judah and Jerusalem decayed further, becoming bloody, chaotic, and almost anarchic.

The Jewish community was rent by schism and violent dissent. Aside from the divisive religious groupings of Pharisees, Sadducees, Essenes and emerging Christians, there were also warring political factions who stopped at nothing in an attempt to gain their ends.

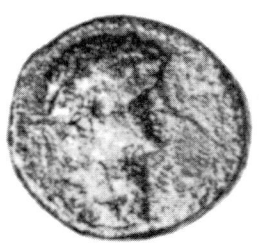

Coins minted by Agrippa II

---

11. He was successful in having Claudius remove Cumanus, one of the worst Roman procurators of Judah, from power.

150 ☐ ECHOES OF GLORY

THE DIVISION OF JERUSALEM

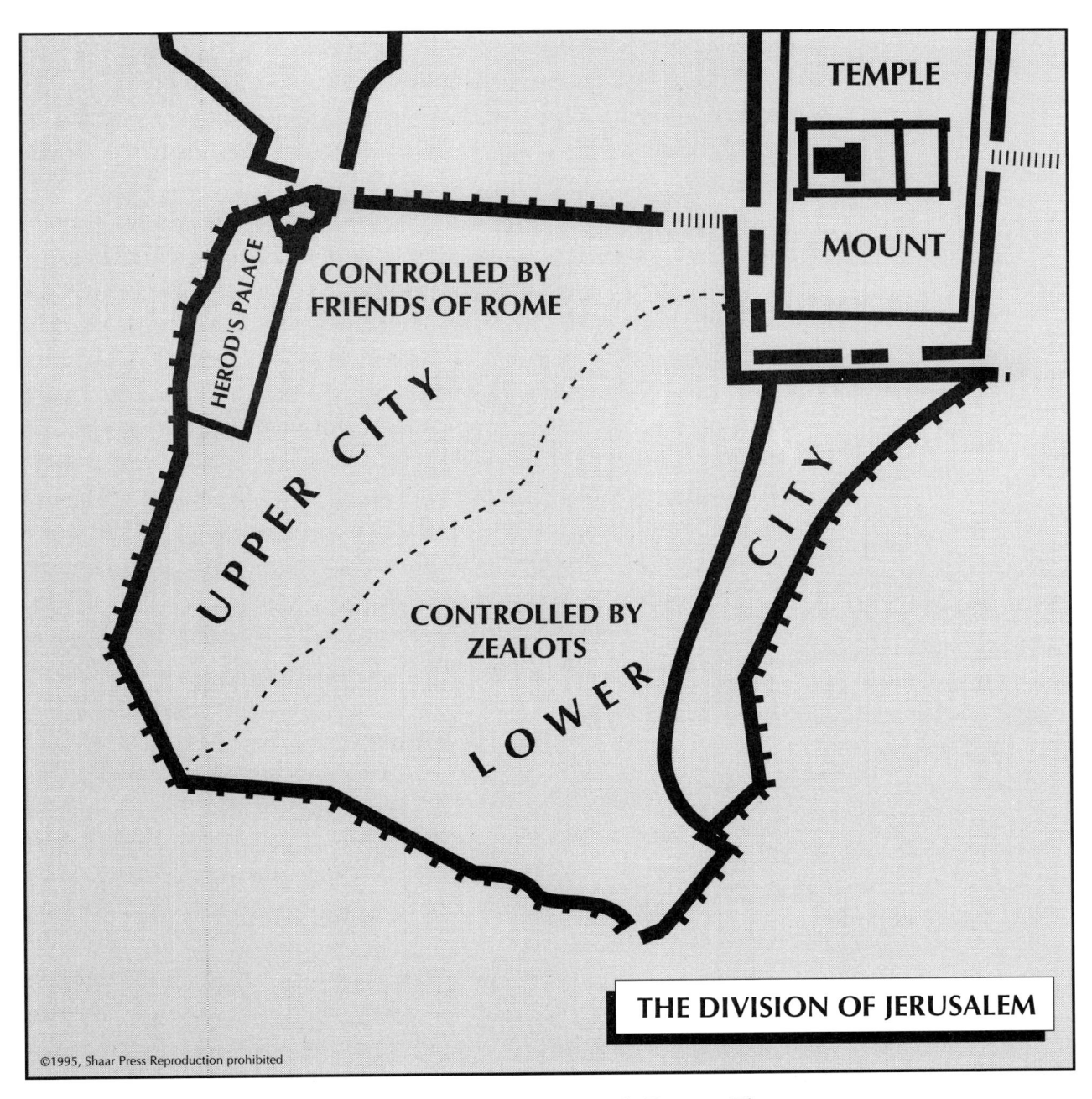

(Map showing Herod's Palace, Upper City "Controlled by Friends of Rome," Lower City "Controlled by Zealots," and Temple Mount.)

The Zealots, we know, advocated open war with Rome. The aristocrats and wealthier class, who had most to lose in a war against Rome, formed a rival group, Friends of Rome, that openly advocated submission to Roman rule and a gradual acculturation of Judah into a miniature Rome.

Most Jews were neither Friends of Rome nor Zealots. They wanted only the maximum freedom possible under Roman rule, stopping short at the prospect of open war, which they correctly felt would be suicidal. However, moderates by nature are not decisive enough to control events in a volatile state and time. In such times the radical groupings almost always gain power, since they are never plagued by self-doubt and always have simple, doctrinaire solutions to the daunting problems of society.

The Zealots slowly grew in strength and influence, aided, as mentioned above, by the continuing unnecessary and foolish cruelties and excesses of the Roman procurators. But the Zealot group itself was splintering into ever more violent fringe factions. The *Sicarii,* as mentioned above, were a group of criminals who, under the guise of national patriotism, perpetrated acts of extortion, murder and armed robbery against Jew and Roman alike. Another splinter group, the *Biryonim,* formed the most violent faction of the Zealots, committing atrocious acts of violence indiscriminately, all in the name of Jewish freedom. The Roman procurator Felix himself employed *Sicarii* and renegade *Biryonim* to do his dirty work, including the assassination of the High Priest Yonason in the year 60.

Life in Jerusalem was in shambles, and the entire Jewish situation in Judah spun out of control.

Florus

IN THE YEAR 61 Felix was replaced by another corrupt and unscrupulous procurator, Albinus. He in turn was succeeded by an even worse character, whose cruelty and avarice would finally spark the great Jewish rebellion against Roman rule.

In 64, Gessius Florus was appointed by Nero as procurator of Judah. Florus purposely provoked the Jews into acts of violence against Rome, hoping that in retaliation the Roman government would destroy Judah completely and expel the Jews from Jerusalem. This malevolent strategy worked exactly as he hoped.

Florus prevailed upon Nero to remove the right of citizenship from the Jews of Caesarea, making them completely subservient to the Greco-Roman population of that city. Riots ensued, with many Jews killed and some synagogues desecrated. Florus naturally refused to intervene, and when the Jews defended themselves and removed the scrolls of the Torah from their synagogues in Caesarea for safe hiding, he ruthlessly ordered the Roman legions to punish the Jews.

Florus pursued the same policy of persecution against the Jews of Jerusalem. When Jewish youngsters mocked him during one of his public appearances in Jerusalem, Florus let his Roman legions run amok. Over 3,600 Jews were slaughtered in one day.[13] Florus arrested certain elders in Jerusalem and had them publicly flogged and then crucified. When the Roman legions began to advance toward the Temple Mount, armed Jewish resistance flared. Razing all the corridors and connections between the Temple and the northwestern Fortress of Antonia occupied by the Roman garrison, the Jewish defenders isolated and besieged the Roman soldiers. This battle in Jerusalem, which occurred in the year 66, marked the beginning of the great Jewish war against Rome.

Florus fled Jerusalem for the safety of Caesarea. The Pharisees, fearful that Rome would see the incidents in Jerusalem as a full-fledged uprising, sent a delegation to Florus' superior, Gallus, the Roman proconsul in Damascus. There the delegation proclaimed Jewish acceptance of Roman rule, but denounced Florus' behavior and demanded his removal from office.

Gallus sent a personal delegate to Jerusalem to investigate the matter on the spot. He was joined by Agrippa II, who unexpectedly returned to Jerusalem from a stay in Egypt. Agrippa II portrayed himself as a peacemaker between the Romans and the Jews. Under his influence, the Jews began to reconstruct the halls joining the Fortress of Antonia and the Temple compound. The Jews also collected the taxes due to Rome for that year and sent them off in a timely fashion. However, when Agrippa II refused to back the demands of the Jews to have Florus replaced, he lost all credibility in Jewish eyes. Mobs of Jews gathered in the streets, shouting threats against Florus and Agrippa II. Agrippa II also fled Jerusalem for Caesarea, in fear and shame, harboring a great deal of resentment against Jewish Jerusalem.

Inner Strife

NOW THE JEWS LEFT in Jerusalem began to fight — with one another. As a statement of defiance against Agrippa II, who had been nominally in charge of the Temple, and against Rome, Agrippa's patron, the Jews of Jerusalem

---

13. Josephus, *The Wars of the Jews,* Chapter 14, Section 2.

drove the Sadducean priests from the Temple. Against the wishes of most of the leading rabbis associated with the House of Hillel, the new, more extremist and fanatical priests refused to allow into the Temple offerings and sacrifices donated by non-Jews. This was a break with centuries-old custom and was a direct insult to the Roman emperor, who regularly sent gifts and offerings to Jerusalem for Temple use.[14]

The Sadducees and Friends of Rome exploited the radical policies of the new priests and complained to Nero that the new Temple policy was meant to foment a complete break with the Roman world and an outright war against Rome. The Sadducees contacted Agrippa II, still smarting from his humiliation by the Jewish mobs in Jerusalem, and he dispatched an armed force of three thousand mercenaries to capture Jerusalem and drive the Zealots from the Temple. These forces of Agrippa made contact with the small Roman garrison concentrated in the Fortress of Antonia, and together, these forces attempted to drive the Zealots from the city. Their effort ended in abject failure.

An inscription reading "Ben Yair" found amoung the ruins of Masada

On the eighth day of Av in the year 66, the fighting began in Jerusalem and raged for a full month. The Zealots were supported by a band of renegade *Sicarii,* led by Menachem of Galilee. The army of Agrippa II and its Roman allies were slowly driven out of the Upper City and finally took refuge in Herod's Palace, at the extreme northwest corner of the city. Agrippa's soldiers and the Roman garrison surrendered after being promised safe conduct out of Jerusalem. However, Menachem and his outlaws slew the unarmed Roman soldiers, thus guaranteeing that the Jews could themselves expect the same treatment from later Roman armies they would have to face.

In the ongoing internecine warfare between the Zealots themselves, Menachem was killed, and his relative, Elazar ben Yair, led the *Sicarii* out of Jerusalem to the mountain fortress of Masada, near the Dead Sea. Elazar ben Ananias, the son of a former High Priest, now became the head of the Zealots, who controlled Jerusalem. The Jews of Jerusalem declared themselves independent of Roman rule.

---

14. The famous incident of Kamtza and Bar Kamtza described in the Talmud, *Gittin* 55b-56a, should be viewed in the perspective of this new policy of Jewish religious zealotry in Temple affairs. It is clear from the Talmudic account that the sages would have offered the emperor's sacrifice, and that in order to avoid potential bloodshed, most of the sages wanted to offer it even though it had been blemished by a provocateur. Nevertheless, the zealots prevailed; the offering was rejected, with disastrous results.

Mikveh at Masada

Though Rabban Shimon ben Gamliel the Elder was officially a member of the governing council of the newly independent Jewish mini-state, the attitude of the Pharisees towards the conduct of a war of independence against Rome was very cool. The rabbis and sages of Israel were very hesitant to pursue the fight, knowing that failure would doom the Temple and drive Israel into a prolonged and harsh exile.

A Fatal Triumph

THE SUCCESS OF THE JEWS in driving Rome from Jerusalem sent shock waves throughout the Roman Empire. It also unleashed a wave of bloody pogroms against Jews, especially in Caesarea, Alexandria and Damascus. Thousands of Jews were slaughtered in these riots, and thousands more were sold into the slave markets of Rome. This reaction only intensified the anti-Roman feelings of the Zealots in Jerusalem, and many of the more moderate Pharisees now hardened their position and came to support the Zealot leaders in their struggle against Rome.

It was a terrible time to be a Jew in the Roman world. Gallus, the Roman proconsul in Damascus, massed an army to recapture Jerusalem. Agrippa II joined Gallus and placed his mercenaries at

Gallus' disposal. However, the Roman forces were decisively defeated by the Zealots at Beis Choron, outside of Jerusalem, the site of the Hasmonean victory centuries earlier. Over six thousand Romans were slain, and Gallus retreated, in panic and shame, back to Damascus. The triumphant Jews minted coins[15] in honor of their great victory and armed themselves for the inevitable struggle against the greater legions that Rome would send against them.

Rome could not sit idly by and allow an independent Jerusalem to exist. It was a matter not only of imperial pride, but more importantly a matter of a dangerous precedent being set against Roman hegemony over the world. If Jerusalem could be independent of Rome, then why not Athens, Alexandria, Damascus, Gaul and Spain? Self-centeredly, the Zealots of Jerusalem saw themselves as engaged merely in an isolated struggle for national independence; they felt they were simply attempting to be free of Rome and left alone, with no grand scheme to end the Roman Empire. Fatally, they did not realize that, strategically speaking, Rome would be forced to exert its entire might against the Jews and crush them. It would be either Rome or Jerusalem.

The rabbis and sages of Israel were well aware of the true strategic nature of the matter. They held that the revolt in Jerusalem and the subsequent Roman war was suicidal to Jewish statehood.[16] But they were powerless in the face of the continuing violence of the extremist Jewish nationalist factions and their criminal allies.

With perfect hindsight, one can see that the Zealots' victory over Agrippa II and Gallus actually doomed Jerusalem to destruction. For had Gallus triumphed, even though in human terms the Jews would have been punished awfully, Jerusalem would not have been leveled, the Temple would not have been burned to the ground and the Jewish population of Judah would not have been sold into slavery and scattered throughout the world. Many have been the times that Providence has used apparent victory as the vehicle to initiate a more final, crushing defeat.

The Roman war against Judah and Jerusalem must also be seen against the backdrop of the increasingly virulent anti-Semitism then

---

15. Minting coins was always an expression of newly won independence.

16. This is only one of many historical incidents where the strategic view of the rabbis and Torah scholars of Israel was sharper and more accurate than the view of the nation's generals, political leaders and government experts.

growing throughout the Roman Empire. This hatred of Jews was a feeling inherited from the Greeks, who had come to despise the Jews even before being defeated by the Hasmoneans; the clash of cultures that had come forth from the meeting of Hellas and Judah only became more intense after that defeat.

The Greeks resented the Jews' exclusivity, were insulted by their unwillingness to participate in state religious functions and rejected what they perceived as Jewish aggressiveness in spreading Hebrew ideals in a pagan world.[17] Back in the year 133 B.C.E., the Seleucid ruler, Antiochus Sidetes, had justified the idea of completely annihilating the Jews by stating that the Jews were the only people who refused to associate with the rest of humanity and become part of the whole.[18]

Anti-Semitic literature proliferated among the Greeks and was soon accepted by Roman society as well. Jews were accused of every imaginable crime and of being disloyal to the state. In Rome, the advent of emperor worship during the era of the Caesars led to direct religious confrontation with the Jews and exacerbated the charge of disloyalty. Jewish dietary and purity laws were mocked, circumcision was attacked as being barbaric and the Sabbath was denigrated throughout the Roman Empire, usually at the instigation of Greek intellectuals and office-holders. Thus the Roman legions, and their non-Roman components as well, viewed the Jews with enmity and scorn without ever having laid eyes upon them. When the Jews fought these legions viciously and many times successfully, their hatred of the Jews became unreasoning and pathological.

Josephus Flavius

THE ROMAN GOVERNMENT dispatched to Judah four legions[19] of crack troops under one of its most experienced, battle-hardened, wily commanders, Vespasian. In the year 67, Vespasian began his campaign to end the Jewish state. His strategy was to leave Jerusalem for the last, first con-

---

17. One particular situation that irked the Greek intelligentsia was the popularity and dissemination of the Septuagint among Jews and non-Jews in cities such as Alexandria.
18. Paul Johnson, *A History of the Jews,* p. 134.
19. They were legions V, X, XII and XV. X Legion was one of the more elite Roman fighting forces and was commanded by Vespasian's son, Titus.

centrating his efforts on securing the coastline and capturing the main Jewish fortresses outside the city. Once so isolated, Jerusalem would fall by siege and starvation. Agrippa II still sided with the Romans and added his army to Vespasian's forces. Vespasian landed his army at Acre and made plans to subdue the Galilee and the northern seacoast. The bitter war that would destroy the Jewish state was now in full swing.

As commander of the Jewish forces in the Galilee, the government in Jerusalem sent an improbable soldier whose later influence in the Jewish and general world far outshone his generalship. His name was Josephus Flavius.[20] A Sadducee in his youth, he accepted the modernity and values of Roman culture. He was also very opportunistic, ambitious and self-confident. Using these qualities, he solicited military appointment over Galilee from the Zealot-dominated government in Jerusalem. Arriving in Galilee, he found a Jewish community badly split over the merits of the war.

A group of *Sicarii*, under the command of Yochanan of Gush Chalav (John Gischala), openly opposed Josephus. Josephus used cash payments to tame them to his will. He exploited all local Jewish divisions to gain further power for himself, and he was finally able to gain administrative dominion over the area. However, eventually Josephus was accused by the moderates of being too warlike against the Romans, and by the Zealots and *Sicarii* of being a traitor in disguise to the Jewish cause. Yochanan of Gush Chalav demanded that the Jerusalem government recall Josephus from the Galilee. Rabban Shimon ben Gamliel the Elder agreed and sent an emissary to remove Josephus. Josephus merely laughed at the order and sent the emissary packing. Commanding an army of 65,000 men,[21] Josephus felt confident and strong. He was sadly mistaken.

The truth was that even though the Zealots were prepared to take on Rome, the people of the Galilee were not. The largest city of the Galilee, Sepphoris (Tzippori),[22] sent a delegation to Acre to ask the Romans to spare the city upon its surrender. In fact, the delegation asked the Romans for protection from their fellow Jews — the

---

20. His Hebrew name was Yosef ben Mattisyahu HaKohen, and he was a member of the famous Ben Gurion clan of Temple priests.

21. This figure is Josephus'. Most historians believe it to be improbable and highly exaggerated.

22. Not far from the site of the present-day Acco-Nazareth road.

Zealots. In turn, they committed themselves to refraining from opposing the Roman legions' march through the Galilee. The Romans, however, were less than benevolent in their treatment of the Galilean Jews. Although Sepphoris itself was spared, dozens of surrounding villages and hundreds of farms were destroyed, with great loss of life and thousands of people sold into slavery.

These Roman excesses stiffened Jewish resistance, but Josephus' forces were nevertheless defeated in an open battle with the Romans, north of Sepphoris. Josephus himself escaped to Tiberias, and from there he arrived with new forces at the Herodian fortress of Yodefat (Jotapata), northwest of Sepphoris. In the spring of 67 Vespasian laid siege to this seemingly impregnable fortress.[23] For forty-seven days the bloody battle raged, with both sides suffering large casualties. But Vespasian, ever the bulldog, persisted in his attacks and would not withdraw. Josephus, realizing that eventually the fortress would fall and preferring to be a live turncoat rather than a dead hero, surrendered to Vespasian, while most of his Zealot commanders committed suicide. Vespasian soon realized his captive's value as a Jewish "expert" and adviser, and employed Josephus as a propagandist and communicator to the Jews. Josephus correctly assessed the hopelessness of the Jewish war against Rome and pleaded with the Jews to lay down their arms before their whole country was destroyed. But the Zealots labeled Josephus a traitor, and the masses of Jews placed little stock in his soothing words.

Vespasian's Campaigns

DURING THE SUMMER and autumn of 67, Vespasian marched through the Galilee, suppressing all Jewish resistance. Tiberias surrendered without a fight. However, the fortress of Gamla in the Golan Heights resisted bitterly until the Romans prevailed, and the city was razed. The fortress of Meged near the Sea of Galilee, after resisting to the end, was also put to the torch.

---

23. Built on the slopes of Mount Atzmon, the fortress was unapproachable on three sides due to deep ravines that ringed the area. However, on the fourth side, Roman engineering, as it would later do at Masada, enabled the enemy to mount an effective siege and undermine the defensive walls of the fortress.

Gamla

The main remaining pocket of resistance in the Galilee was Gush Chalav, where Yochanan and his *Sicarii* were centered. Vespasian besieged the city, but the defenders held off the attacking Roman legions, launching suicide squad attacks to repel them and pouring burning oil on the Roman soldiers encamped below the walls.[24] Yochanan, realizing that Gush Chalav was an eventual death trap, organized an escape party of his most trusted and talented *Sicarii,* and somehow led them out of Gush Chalav. They reached Jerusalem, there to fight the Romans again. After the fall of Gush Chalav, Vespasian declared the Galilee pacified and turned to secure his flank and supply bases on the seacoast.

By now, the Zealots in Jerusalem had taken to quarreling with each other. The outlying Jewish communities in Judah were isolated, operating without leadership, direction or inspiration. Vespasian moved south along the coast, securing Caesarea and Jaffa. He then moved inland, capturing the fortresses of Antipatris, Thamma, Lydda (Lod), Yavneh, Emmaus, Beis Guvrin, Maabarta and Jericho. By the

---

24. The Jews' use of burning oil as a weapon against the Roman army would be analogous to the use of poison gas by any of the combatants in World War II. It simply was not acceptable even in war. The Romans retaliated by crucifying hundreds of already-captured Jewish soldiers. The cruelty on both sides in the Judean War was unprecedented even in the ancient world. The first use of a new and terrible weapon always may produce tactical advantage. Whether that use is strategically wise, however, is another matter. Indiscriminate bombing of cities and civilian populations was a new terror weapon introduced by Germany at the start of World War II. However, it guaranteed retaliation in kind and provoked the eventual destruction of every major German city by Allied bombing. History always leaves us with tantalizing questions of tactics versus strategy.

end of the year 68, the people of Jerusalem were isolated from the rest of Judah's Jewish population. Many thousands of Jewish and Roman lives had already been lost in Vespasian's campaigning. But Vespasian could now feel that he had Jerusalem within his grasp, and that he would soon conquer the city that represented Judaism and the Jewish people.

A coin minted by Nero

The Year of the Four Emperors

NERO DIED[25] IN 68, and turmoil swirled about in Rome in choosing his successor. The year 69 is famous in Roman history as "The Year of the Four Emperors." Four great military leaders of Rome[26] contested for the imperial wreath. Vespasian, one of the contenders, temporarily discontinued his campaign against Jerusalem and rested outside its walls, cocking his ear to news from Rome instead.

First, Servius Sulpicious Galba, at the age of seventy-one, declared himself head of Rome, and the Senate approved. However, he was weak in administration, without outstanding military credentials, and naive in his choice of subordinates. This being the case, one of his generals, Marcus Salvius Otho, heading the Roman legions on the Rhine and the Danube, rebelled and proclaimed himself emperor and had Galba murdered. In turn, Aulus Vitellius, another general who was commanding legions in upper Germany and Gaul, warred with Otho and defeated his armies, forcing Otho to take his own life. Vitellius now became the self-proclaimed emperor of Rome, but he treated Rome as a conqueror, not as a ruler. Vespasian's brother Sabinus, soon to be killed himself in the rioting, conspired to foment rebellion against Vitellius.

War, confusion, intrigue and fear stalked Rome. The empire was in danger of disintegrating. Now German legions invaded Rome and massacred many of its citizens, including the overreaching Vitellius. The Senate and Roman aristocracy, together with the remaining generals, searched for a stable, strong leader who would restore order to

---

25. Nero's final years are described in greater detail in the chapter "Rome the Colossus."
26. These kinsmen of Herod had become ever stronger and more militant in the decades of the rule of Herod and his descendants.

the city and the empire. The battle-hardened, able and popular Vespasian was the man chosen by them to save Rome and rebuild its shattered empire.

Vespasian did not let the developments in Rome distract him from his war in the Middle East. As mentioned, he marked time there, awaiting the call from Rome. He moved against Jerusalem in the year 69 and quickly surrounded the city with the vaunted Roman siege machines.

Roman catapult

Three Factions in Jerusalem

THE JEWS HAD USED the respite given them by Vespasian's delay while awaiting news from Rome to engage in fierce struggles among themselves.

The Zealots were overcome with internal dissension, and eventually the more extreme factions took power. They were determined to go down with the ship and to force everyone on board to go down with them. The appearance of Yochanan of Gush Chalav in Jerusalem together with his *Sicarii* strengthened the hands of the more radical nationalists. Yochanan boldly promised a Jewish victory over the Romans, even though more reasonable people realized the hopelessness of the situation. The Zealots, the *Sicarii,* and the *Biryonim,* all began to extort wealth from the more moderate elements in Jerusalem, ostensibly to promote the war effort. This patriotic practice soon degenerated into outright thievery and murder. When the situation finally spun out of control, Rabban Shimon ben Gamliel the Elder withdrew from the government, unable to countenance the lawlessness of the Zealots or to influence them to moderate their behavior.

The Sadducees and the Friends of Rome, together with many moderate Pharisees, did form an army and gained control of most of the city, but the Temple Mount remained in the hands of the Zealots. Yochanan of Gush Chalav now took command of the Temple Mount's Zealot forces. The first phase of the Jewish civil war ended with the moderates controlling the city, the extremists holding the Temple and the Romans surrounding the city. During this entire period of internal strife, the daily Temple services continued without interruption. All sides were confident of Divine intervention exclusively on their behalf.

The moderates attempted to remove the extremists' control of the Temple Mount and destroy the forces of Yochanan of Gush Chalav. In fear of being wiped out, Yochanan made a shameful alliance with the Idumeans, promising them great plunder in return for their aid. To allow the Idumean forces into the city, the Zealots exploited a breach in the Roman siege lines and overcame the Jewish sentries, loyal to the moderates, posted at the city's southern gates. The moderate forces were thus caught in a pincers, the Zealots attacking them from the Temple Mount to the north and east, and the Idumeans charging upon them from their rear to the south and west. The moderates were slaughtered, and the Idumeans pillaged and looted for days, with thousands of innocent Jews losing their lives in the senseless massacre. Thereafter, the Idumeans quickly withdrew from Jerusalem, never really having any intention of being drawn into defending Jerusalem against the besieging Roman legions. The Zealots, however, continued their reign of terror within the city and slew many more Jews, justifying their actions with claims that the victims were sympathizers or even collaborators with Rome.

In desperation, the remaining opponents of the radical Zealots called upon Shimon bar Giora,[27] a personal and sworn enemy of Yochanan of Gush Chalav, to save them. Although he himself was a Zealot, his hatred for Yochanan of Gush Chalav was overwhelming enough to convince him to join the moderates.[28] Shimon and his troops infiltrated Jerusalem and fought a number of pitched battles against the forces of Yochanan. Yochanan and his men again retreated to the Temple Mount, where they hunkered down behind the massive fortifications.

Shimon bar Giora took control of the Lower City,[29] and the more moderate Zealots and the remnants of the Friends of Rome concentrated themselves in the Upper City,[30] near Herod's palace, under the

---

27. This conversion was purely prophylactic, for at heart Shimon remained a radical Zealot with a flair for dramatic, though self-destructive, behavior.
28. All three leaders of the defenders of Jerusalem, Shimon bar Giora, Yochanan of Gush Chalav and Elazar ben Shimon, cordially despised one another.
29. The Lower City was south and west of the Temple. It was a lower-class neighborhood with small shops and narrow streets.
30. The Upper City was immediately adjacent to and west of the Temple. The nobles, priests and wealthier class lived in this section of the city.

command of Elazar ben Shimon.[31] Thus these three warring factions, bent upon killing each other, constituted the armed Jewish forces defending Jerusalem from Rome.

A Meeting with Vespasian

THE ZEALOTS, IN ALL OF their different forms, were rightly suspicious that many of the Jews in Jerusalem were willing to come to terms with Rome and stop the bloody and unequal struggle. They therefore resorted to acts of suicidal desperation to force the Jewish population to fight to the end. For years, vast warehouses of food had been prepared to help the Jews withstand a siege. Shimon bar Giora and his men set fire to these great storehouses, so that the people would have no choice but to fight or starve. Such irrational behavior forced the leader of the Pharisees, Rabban Yochanan ben Zakkai,[32] to take a great gamble. Despairing of saving Jerusalem, he attempted to salvage the greater prize, the people of Israel, from extinction.

Related to one of the leaders of the *Biryonim,* Rabban Yochanan was able, through this relationship, to have himself smuggled out of Jerusalem in a coffin under the guise of a corpse taken out for burial. Arriving inside the Roman siege lines, he was taken before Vespasian for interrogation. Rabban Yochanan predicted to the general that he would shortly become emperor. This prediction was immediately fulfilled when messengers arrived to inform Vespasian that the legions and Senate of Rome had declared in his favor in the struggle for the imperial throne.

In his ecstasy, Vespasian granted Rabban Yochanan some favors. Among them was that the Torah center at Yavneh would be spared and protected, and that those scholars who wished to repair there to join Rabban Yochanan ben Zakkai would be given safe conduct

---

31. Elazar ben Shimon had been removed as head of the Zealots by Yochanan of Gush Chalav.

32. The titular head of the Pharisees now was Rabban Gamliel II, the son of Rabban Shimon ben Gamliel the Elder. However, because of the danger to the family of Hillel from the Romans and the Zealots, Rabban Gamliel II assumed a low public profile, and Rabban Yochanan ben Zakkai, a member of an aristocratic priestly family and a disciple rather than a descendant of Hillel, became the leader.

through the Roman lines.[33] By this seemingly insignificant gesture, the conqueror of Jerusalem indirectly became the providential agent for the salvation of the Jewish people.

Yavneh, the symbol of Torah study and devotion in all of the various identities it would acquire over the centuries, would now replace Jerusalem as the center of Jewish life. The Jewish people would survive and remain true to itself and its eternal mission even without country or national independence. Jerusalem, in its physical ruin, would now become primarily a spiritual place, its reality nurtured only by the scholars of Yavneh.

Yavneh

RABBAN YOCHANAN BEN ZAKKAI took the historic gamble that Israel could survive without Jerusalem but not without Yavneh. Vespasian, a man who dealt exclusively in physical space and territory, did not appreciate the daring nature of the request of Rabban Yochanan ben Zakkai, a man who dealt in time and spirit. Vespasian never imagined that Yavneh would become a far greater threat to the Roman world than Jerusalem had ever been. The great Torah school at Yavneh, which set the stage for the creation of the Mishnah and Talmud, was impervious to destruction by legions and siege machines. Ideas and intellect, commitments of spirit and faith are not susceptible to catapults and spears. Rabban Yochanan ben Zakkai, by choosing Yavneh over Jerusalem, won the strategic encounter with Rome.

With the surviving great scholars of Israel[34] gathered about him, Rabban Yochanan ben Zakkai set out to rebuild the shattered Jewish

---

33. Other favors granted by Vespasian included medical treatment for the sainted Rabbi Tzadok, physically incapacitated because of his forty-year fast, and a guarantee of amnesty for the family of Rabban Gamliel II.

34. Among the scholars of Yavneh were Rabbi Chanina S'gan HaKohanim, Rabbi Shimon Ish HaMitzpeh, Nachum HaModi, Rabbi Chanina ben Antigonus, Rabbi Elazar ben Yaakov I, Rabban Gamliel II, the brothers Rabbis Yehudah, Shimon and Yehoshua, all of the family of Bnei Beseira, Shmuel HaKattan, Rabbi Dosa ben Hyrkanus, Rabbi Tzadok, Rabbi Papius, Rabbi Zechariah ben Kavutal, and the five major disciples of Rabban Yochanan ben Zakkai: Rabbi Eliezer ben Hyrkanus, Rabbi Yehoshua ben Chananyah, Rabbi Yose HaKohen, Rabbi Shimon ben Nesanel and Rabbi Elazar ben Arach.

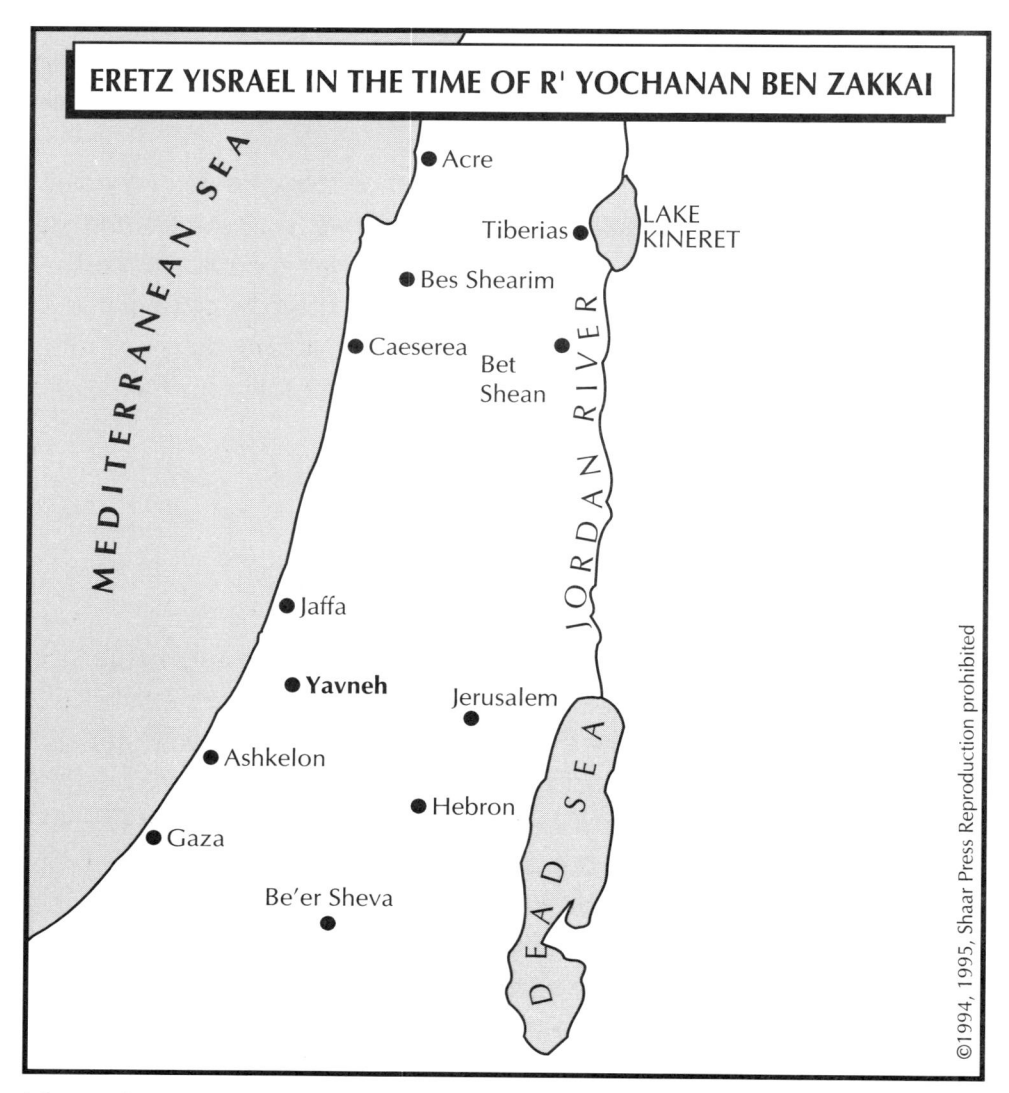

ERETZ YISRAEL IN THE TIME OF R' YOCHANAN BEN ZAKKAI

life in the country. Thus, some months before the destruction of the Temple and Jerusalem, not only did the great yeshivah at Yavneh open operation immediately, but the Sanhedrin reorganized itself and also became operational in Yavneh.

Rabban Gamliel II, in spite of Vespasian's promise of amnesty, kept a very low profile in the early years of Yavneh. He was still a very young man at that time, and he willingly deferred his position to Rabban Yochanan ben Zakkai, who remained the open leader of the scholars and decision-makers of Yavneh until his death. Rabban Gamliel's father, Rabban Shimon ben Gamliel the Elder, who was the *Nasi*, the titular head of the Sanhedrin, had been slain in the Roman siege of Jerusalem, and Rabban Gamliel was to be appointed his successor, but the appointment was delayed until Yavneh was firmly established under the leadership of Rabban Yochanan ben Zakkai. Once appointed as *Nasi*, Rabban Gamliel II became known as Rabban Gamliel of Yavneh, to differentiate him from his grandfather, who became known as Rabban Gamliel the Elder.

The news of the expected fall of Jerusalem was greeted in Yavneh by mourning and grief,[35] but also by renewed determination to rebuild Jewish life and the people of Israel even without a Temple, national independence, or the city of Jerusalem.

Titus Attacks Jerusalem

WHILE YAVNEH WAS BEING FORMED, Jerusalem was being destroyed. Vespasian left Jerusalem's siege lines, first for Egypt and then for Rome, where he was acclaimed the fourth emperor of the year 69. Vespasian's rule, however, was stable, lasting a decade and ending with his death in 79. Before leaving the Jerusalem battlefront, Vespasian appointed his son Titus, the commander of the Tenth Legion, as the new general commander of the war against the Jews.

Titus, pug-nosed and pugnacious to a fault, was a fierce warrior who tolerated no niceties in battle. He immediately moved against the city, sensing that hunger and internal divisions amongst the Jews had weakened the defenders irreparably. The Roman main camp was west of the city walls, midway between the New City (the northern section of Jerusalem) and the Upper City (in reality, the middle of Jerusalem). The Roman attack began immediately after the Pesach holiday in the year 70 with a fierce bombardment of missiles of stone, iron and fire, launched by catapults which sent them on a trajectory, enabling them to reach all of the populated neighborhoods of the city. Jerusalem began to burn.

Titus on a bronze coin minted by Agrippa

The Roman attack concentrated on the northern walls of the city. After a month of battering from the Roman siege machines, the outer third wall north of the city gave way. The defenders fought bravely and tenaciously, but by June the second defensive wall was also breached. The Romans scaled the final wall and entered the New City section of Jerusalem. Hand-to-hand fighting ensued, but the

---

35. See *Avos d'Rabbi Nosson,* Chapter 4.

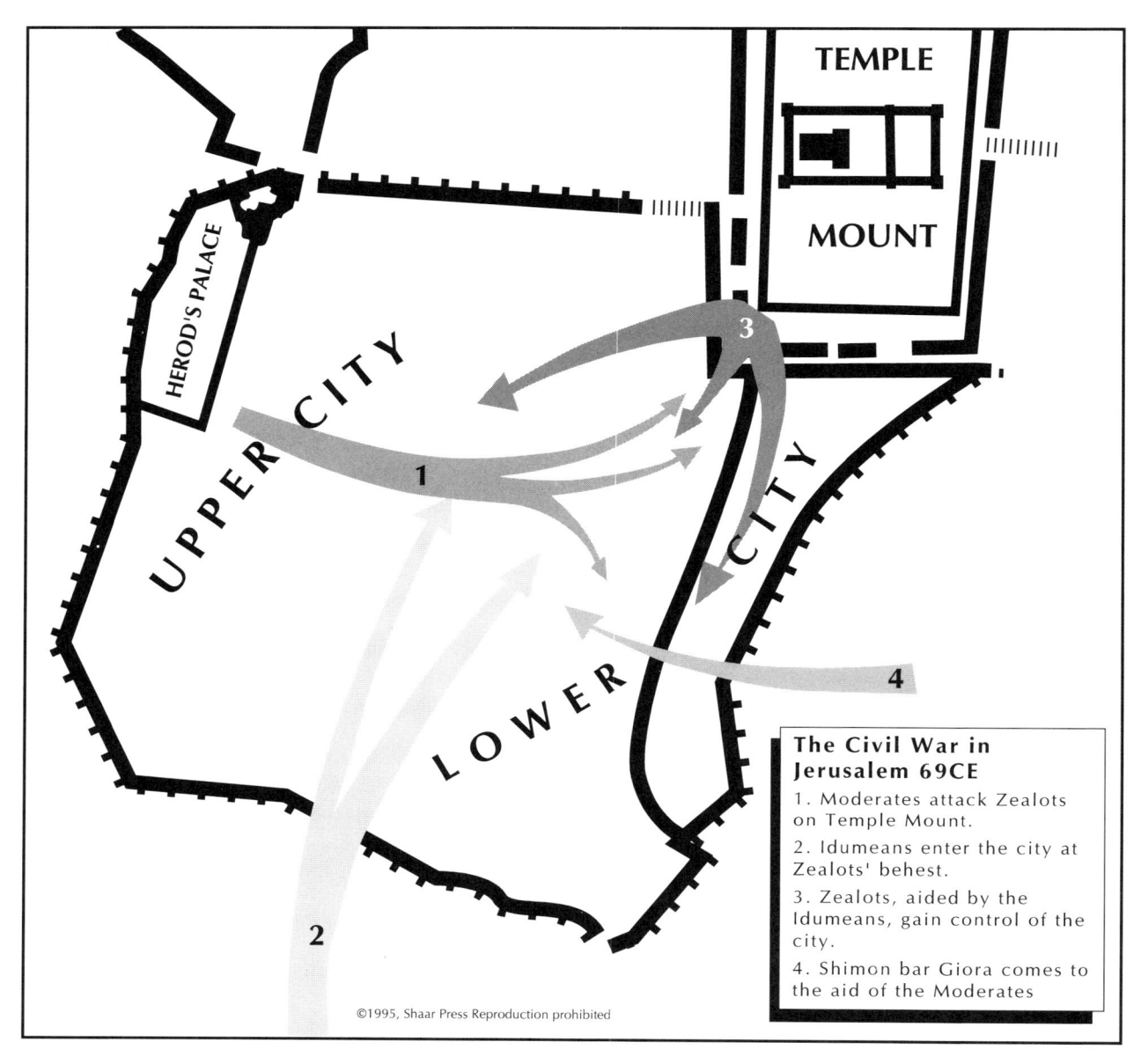

The Civil War in Jerusalem 69CE
1. Moderates attack Zealots on Temple Mount.
2. Idumeans enter the city at Zealots' behest.
3. Zealots, aided by the Idumeans, gain control of the city.
4. Shimon bar Giora comes to the aid of the Moderates

Romans prevailed, burning and pillaging as they advanced. No house in the New City survived the Roman attack, and that part of the city was completely leveled.

Yochanan of Gush Chalav retreated with his forces to the Temple Mount, there to make his last stand, while Shimon bar Giora took command of the Jewish forces defending the Upper City. The Lower City was also defended by Zealot forces, but it would not have to bear the major brunt of the final Roman onslaught. Titus sent Josephus to the Jewish lines of defense to convince the Jewish forces to surrender and save the city and Temple from destruction. But Josephus, viewed by most Jews as a traitor, could hardly serve as a credible negotiator. Stones and epithets were hurled at him, and he barely made it back alive to the Roman lines. Titus now vowed war to the end and promised only death and destruction to the defenders of Jerusalem.

The two major Jewish strongholds that protected the Upper City and the Temple Mount were Herod's Palace and the Antonia Fortress. Titus' attempts to overcome them by force at the end of June failed. He then tightened the siege noose around the city, preventing any food or reinforcements from reaching the encircled Jews. The ravages of famine were visible throughout Jerusalem, with hunger and disease claiming thousands of lives. Jewish smugglers caught by the Romans were crucified before the horrified eyes of the Jewish defenders on the walls. Titus denuded the area around Jerusalem of trees and used the lumber to build assault ramps leading to the Antonia Fortress.

Weakened by the ravages of hunger,[36] the defenders were unable to thwart the Roman assault teams. In July, on the fifth of Tammuz, the Antonia Fortress fell, and Titus ordered it razed to the ground. On the seventeenth of Tammuz, after twelve days of ferocious battle, the walls of the Temple Mount were themselves breached. On that day, the sacrificial ritual in the Temple ceased. For the next three weeks, the Jews and Romans dueled for control of the Temple.

Tishah b'Av

ON THE NINTH OF AV, in August 70,[37] the Romans broke into the Temple. Roman soldiers threw firebrands into the Temple building, and the supposedly fireproof building of marble, granite and stone began to burn.[38]

---

36. The famine was partially self-inflicted because of the burning of the food warehouses by the Zealots themselves, as described above.

37. Many traditional Jewish writers place the destruction of the Temple not in the year 70, but in the year 68. There are many reasons advanced by both sides of the disagreement regarding the date of the destruction of the Temple. In my tape cassette history series, I myself had once advocated 68 as the correct year. After some research I have reconsidered the matter, and I am now convinced that the year 70 is the year of the burning of the Second Temple. Rabbi Hersh Goldwurm arrived at the same opinion (*History of the Jewish People,* Mesorah Publications, 1982, p. 213).

38. Josephus claimed that Titus had given strict orders to spare the Temple building. But God decreed that the Divine anger be spent on the lumber and stones of the building, while the Jewish people would somehow be spared destruction and total annihilation.

Masada

It burned for the next thirty hours, well into the afternoon of the tenth of Av. In the smoke of the Temple, the Jewish national existence in the Land of Israel was snuffed out, not to be restored for almost nineteen centuries. The Roman soldiers gathered whatever wealth and ritual artifacts they could from the burning Temple, some of which the soldiers would divide among themselves as the booty of war, and some of which they would cart off to Rome to be paraded in Titus' triumphal procession. The Romans whooped with joy at their victory, while the Jews wept and once again set aside the ninth of Av as the day of universal Jewish lamentation. Yavneh would now have to serve in place of the Temple, and as a capital, nation and homeland. "The Judean state as a political entity was gone. All that remained was the spirit and the religion of the Judeans: Judaism."[39]

The Romans completed the mop-up of the country. Flavius Silva, Titus' successor as commander of the Roman Tenth Legion, laid siege to the *Sicarii* fortress of Masada. In 72, Elazar ben Yair, the commander of Masada, and his troops chose suicide over fighting to the death or surrender, and almost one thousand Jews — men, women and children — took their own lives and left this seemingly impregnable fortress to the Romans. A major fortress on the east coast of

---

39. Solomon Zeitlin, *The Rise and Fall of the Judean State,* Philadelphia: Jewish Publication Society, 1978, Vol. III, p. 151.

Detail from Arch of Titus in Rome showing the Jews in captivity, carrying Temple articles

the Sea of Galilee was another point of combat. There the Jews put up fierce resistance till the end. The Roman casualties were so heavy that the morale of the attacking legion broke. Only the direct orders of the emperor Vespasian forced them to return to the offensive and achieve ultimate victory. Every Jewish defender there was killed.

By the year 73 the country was pacified, and Rome reigned supreme in the Land of Israel. Shimon bar Giora and Yochanan of Gush Chalav had been taken to Rome in chains and paraded before the howling, hooting Roman mob as part of Titus' triumph in the year 71. Shimon was publicly executed, and Yochanan died not long after in a fetid Roman prison. The great Arch of Titus was erected in Rome to commemorate the fall of Jerusalem and the Temple. The Romans minted coins and stamped them with the words *Judea Capta* ("Judah is captured") to mark the defeat of the Jews. They sold hundreds of thousands of Jews into slavery, and so many Jewish slaves were available, flooding the market, that in many instances there were no buyers at any price.[40]

But the end of the Jewish state in no way signified the end of the Jewish people. Its God and His Torah would continue to sustain it throughout later history.

Coins minted by Vespasian inscribed "Judea Capta" celebrating his victory over Jerusalem

---

40. Fulfilling the dire biblical prediction recorded in *Deuteronomy* (28:68).

Section III

Response to Exile

10
Yavneh and Its Wise Men

AFTER THE FALL OF JERUSALEM, Rabban Yochanan ben Zakkai and his colleagues immediately began the task of rebuilding the Jewish people. They were faced with the daunting and somewhat paradoxical tasks of building a vibrant Jewish society no longer centered on the Temple, Jerusalem or a national home, and yet perpetuating within that new Jewish life an undying memory of, loyalty and commitment to that very same Temple, Jerusalem and national home. It is the genius of Rabban Yochanan ben Zakkai that produced both desired results and thereby created the means of Jewish survival — spiritual, physical, social and national — that remained valid for the next nineteen centuries.

A series of public ordinances (*takanos*) was enacted and became part of Jewish life and ritual. These ordinances were "in memory of the Temple." Some of them replicated in the synagogue what had been Temple ritual,[1] while some of them purposely differentiated between Temple behavior and the new situation of a Templeless Israel.[2] Rabban Yochanan ben Zakkai, by force of his enormous personality, was successful in having these ordinances accepted among the Jews without the disputes and struggles that would mark later attempts to adjust custom and ritual. However, Rabban Yochanan ben Zakkai was clearly aware that ordinances alone could not preserve Jewish life. Institutions of public leadership and education were the key to survival, and he proceeded to establish them as well.

---
1. See Talmud, *Rosh HaShanah* 29b-30b.
2. Ibid.

The Sanhedrin

THE KEY INSTITUTION in Jewish life in the two centuries after the destruction of the Temple was the Sanhedrin. This body of scholars was no longer so much a supreme judicial court as a spiritual and even temporal governing body for the Jews, those remaining in Judah and those in the Diaspora as well. A great investment of effort and will would be exerted to make the Sanhedrin and its leaders, the *Nasi* and the *Av Beis Din*, supreme in all decisive matters of Jewish life. Although Rabban Gamliel II was always the titular head of the Sanhedrin in Yavneh, it was Rabban Yochanan ben Zakkai who undertook the actual tasks of leadership and direction at the onset of the Yavneh Sanhedrin. As was stated, Rabban Gamliel II, still wary of the Romans, had little or no public persona in the first years of Yavneh.[3] It was only after it became clear that the Romans did not intend to persecute the family of Hillel — even after a significant increase in the number of sages gathering at Yavneh — that Rabban Yochanan ben Zakkai dared to publicly install Rabban Gamliel II as *Nasi*.[4]

The institution of Rabban Gamliel was a high priority of Rabban Yochanan ben Zakkai, for he was zealous to preserve the prerogative of the descendants of the House of Hillel as the rulers of Israel. Not only was it a matter of their royal lineage and personal greatness but, even more importantly for the time, reestablishing the Hillelean dynasty would create a sense of stability and continuity for a people who had just lost their Temple and national independence. Thus, Rabban Yochanan ben Zakkai resumed his pre-Temple-destruction role as the

---

3. The Talmud in *Taanis* 29a relates that immediately after the leveling of Jerusalem by Terentius Rufus in c. 75 C.E. a warrant for the arrest and execution of Rabban Gamliel II was issued, but one of the Roman officers intervened to inform him secretly of his impending arrest and thus saved him. To escape public exposure, Rabban Gamliel immediately left the Yavneh yeshivah and went into hiding for a number of years. Terentius Rufus should not to be confused with Tineius Rufus who was the persecutor of Rabbi Akiva almost seventy years later — see Yitzchak Isaac HaLevy, *Doros HaRishonim*, I,5 [appearing in current editions of the work as Volume III], pp.76-78.

4. Nevertheless, Rabban Gamliel II as *Nasi* did lead a turbulent life much beset by controversy. The attention he attracted placed him in constant jeopardy of conflict with the Roman authorities, and a great deal of his life was spent under the threat of Roman arrest, with the periods of relative calm and security in his life brief and far between.

Av Beis Din, secondary in power to the *Nasi.* However, Rabban Yochanan ben Zakkai's abilities and personality never allowed him during the period of Yavneh to be of secondary influence.

Preserving the Oral Law

ANOTHER MAJOR PROJECT of Yavneh was to create a medium through which the Torah, especially the Oral Law of Israel, would be maintained, preserved and expanded in its outreach to the Jewish people. The *Mishnah Rishonah* (*First,* or *Early Mishnah*) was a compilation of notes and decisions concerning the Sinaitic Oral Law, preserved from the time of the Men of the Great Assembly. It grew gradually from generation to generation, but it was not as yet a major compendium of law and certainly not in the form of an official, edited, written work of legal authority. After the destruction of the Temple, the men of Yavneh added to this evolving legal work eyewitness accounts of the Temple buildings, courtyards and precincts, details of the sacrifices and offerings of the Temple services and a review of many of the laws of purity that pertained during the Temple times. Foremost among the scholars of Yavneh in this endeavor, second only to Rabban Yochanan ben Zakkai himself, were Rabbi Shimon Ish HaMitzpeh[5] and Rabbi Elazar ben Yaakov.[6] Since the passage of time was bound to dim the memory of the Jewish people regarding the order, services,

---

5. Rabbi Shimon Ish HaMitzpeh was of very advanced age when the center in Yavneh was created, being yet a colleague of Rabban Gamliel the Elder, the grandfather of Rabban Gamliel II of Yavneh. He was the original editor of the Mishnah's tractate *Tamid* (which details the Temple services and sacrifices) and, according to one opinion in the Talmud, was also the original editor of tractate *Yoma* of the Mishnah (which deals mainly with the ritual services of the High Priest in the Temple on the day of Yom Kippur). See Talmud, *Yoma* 14b; *Yerushalmi Yoma* 2:2; HaLevy, Volume IV (now Volume III), p. 82; A.M. Naftul, *HaTalmud V'Yotzrov* (Tel Aviv), 1976, Vol. I, p. 34.

6. The Talmud (*Yebamos* 49b) states, "The teachings of Rabbi Elazar ben Yaakov [the Elder] are few, but pure in content." He is the founding editor of tractate *Middos,* the volume of the Mishnah that actually deals with the descriptions and dimensions of the Temple buildings and area. See Talmud, *Yoma* 16a; Yerushalmi, *Chagigah,* Chapter 3, section 1; Mishnah, *Middos,* chapter 5, section 4. He should not be confused with the second Rabbi Elazar ben Yaakov, a disciple of Rabbi Akiva, who lived in the middle of the second century, seventy years after this Rabbi Elazar ben Yaakov (the Elder) was active in Yavneh.

ritual and glory of the Temple, the men of Yavneh felt compelled to preserve this heritage for the ages while contemporaries of the Temple operations still lived and vividly remembered them. This work of Yavneh, combined with the earlier texts of the *Mishnah Rishonah,* served to lay the foundation for the later great works of Rabbi Meir first and finally Rabbi Yehudah HaNasi, which in succeeding generations became the written Mishnah itself.

A Smaller Community

AFTER THE DESTRUCTION and leveling of Jerusalem and the fall of Masada in 73, the Romans gradually shifted from military occupation of Judah to civilian administration. The attitude of the Jewish population ranged from open hostility, to begrudging acceptance, to servile cooperation regarding the Roman rulers of Judah.

The ravages of the long and bloody war against Rome had materially reduced the Jewish population of Judah.[7] The Jewish population throughout the rest of the Roman Empire also declined significantly. At the beginning of the Common Era, historians estimate that the Jewish population in the Roman Empire numbered at least 10,000,000. Two centuries later, fully two thirds of this number were either dead, assimilated into Roman society or, in increasing numbers, Christian.[8] The decline in Jewish fortunes in the first century of the Common Era brought with it a concomitant decline in Jewish numbers.

Life in the Roman exile differed from the earlier one in Babylonia, following the First Temple's destruction, which had been a relatively benign experience (except for the Purim crisis). This time the Jews were not concentrated in one country, but were scattered throughout the Roman Empire. Roman domination, culture and mores were much more dangerous to Jewish physical and spiritual survival than Babylonian or Samaritan society ever had been. The great rabbis at Yavneh recognized this and formulated a solution that would outlive Rome and all later inimical cultures.

---

7. The Roman historian Tacitus lists the Jewish casualties of the war from 66-73 as numbering approximately 1,200,000!

8. See the later chapter, "The Rise of Christianity," for details regarding this trend.

The Synagogue

THUS, IT WAS AT YAVNEH that the institutionalization of prayer not only as a personal expression of spiritual communication but as the official replacement for the now-discontinued Temple service and sacrifices[9] occurred. The ancient prayer service formulated and founded by the Men of the Great Assembly was renewed, strengthened and expanded.

The rabbis of Yavneh created as the major concentration of prayer, aside from the biblically obligatory recitation of the *Shema* ("Hear, O Israel, the Lord our God, the Lord is One"), the *Amidah*,[10] the prayer recited while standing with feet together facing the Temple Mount. Public daily prayer became a requirement in Jewish society. This necessity naturally created and institutionalized the house of

---

9. As per the words of *Hosea* (14:3): "And may our lips discharge our obligation of sacrifices of bulls."

10. More popularly known as the *Shemoneh Esrei*, the "Eighteen Blessings" that comprise the Amidah service. The later chapter on Christianity will explain how and why the eighteen blessings became nineteen.

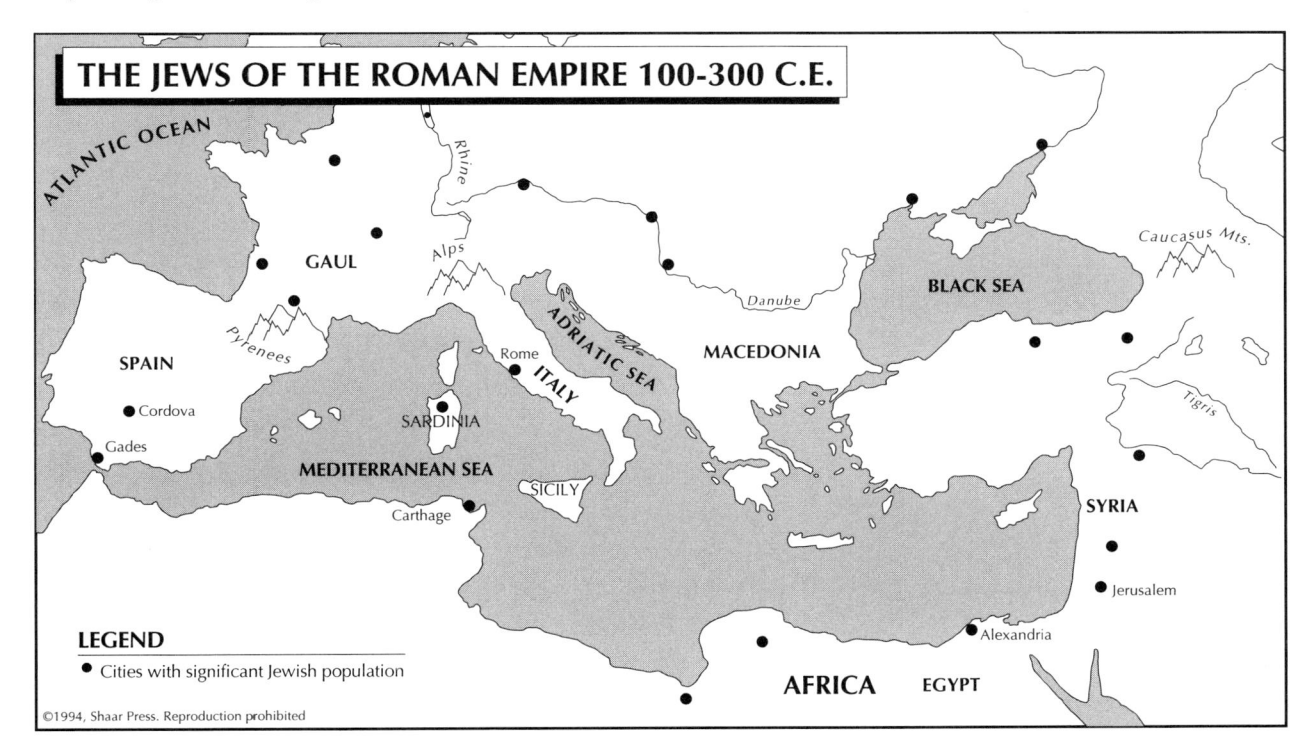

THE JEWS OF THE ROMAN EMPIRE 100-300 C.E.

LEGEND
• Cities with significant Jewish population

©1994, Shaar Press. Reproduction prohibited

Synagogue floor at Bet Shean

prayer within Jewish society.[11] The synagogue now became the "miniature Temple" and increasingly served as the central organ of Jewish communal life.

Much of the spirit and ritual of Temple service was reflected in the prayer services and the synagogue. The physical features of the synagogue such as the women's gallery, the central *bima* (stage), the holy ark containing the Torah scrolls, the curtain hung before that holy ark — all were reminiscent of the glories of the Temple in Jerusalem.

Yavneh's emphasis on public daily prayer and the establishment of synagogues made Jerusalem and its Temple a living factor in Jewish life, so that the physical destruction of the Temple and Jerusalem did not dim their importance in the minds and hearts of Jews throughout millennia. Yavneh, by strengthening and creating forms for the spiritual in Jewish life, guaranteed the physical survival of the Jews and their eternal attachment to the Land of Israel.

---

11. Solomon Zeitlin, in *The Rise and Fall of the Judean State* (Vol. III, pp. 445-6), states, "...the synagogue as a house of worship was not instituted until after the destruction of the Temple." This statement may be an exaggeration, but it is beyond doubt that the emphasis on the synagogue and its centrality in Jewish life stems from the period of Yavneh.

Ruins of the synagogue at Gamla

Five Disciples

ALL THIS SAID, the rabbis of Yavneh should not be seen as a monolithic group. The major policy and legal issues of the time were complex and weighty, and there was much inner discussion among the rabbis, accompanied by protracted and sharp debate. Ultimately, Rabban Yochanan ben Zakkai's opinion usually carried the day, but he did abstain regarding some issues.[12]

After the departure of Rabban Yochanan ben Zakkai from Yavneh, the many different crosscurrents of policy and personages came to the fore publicly. Rabban Yochanan ben Zakkai raised five main disciples, most of whom would fulfill crucial roles in Jewish leadership at the beginning of the second century. These five scholars were Rabbis Eliezer ben Hyrcanus, Yehoshua ben Chananyah, Yosi HaKohen, Shimon ben Nesanel and Elazar ben Arach.[13] These great men carried forth their great mentor's traditions and policies for preserving the cohesiveness and nature of the Jewish people, particularly those

Tomb of R' Eliezer ben Hyrcanus

---

12. See *Tosefta, Kelim* 2:7.
13. Mishnah, *Avos* 2:8.

RESPONSE TO EXILE　　　　　　　　　　*Yavneh and Its Wise Men* □ 181

still living in the Land of Israel. This sometimes brought them into open conflict with Rabban Yochanan ben Zakkai's successor, Rabban Gamliel II, and made the next period of Yavneh a very turbulent one.[14]

Titus and Domitian

IN THE YEAR 79, Vespasian died and was succeeded as emperor by his son Titus, the conqueror of Jerusalem. The Talmud[15] portrays the life of Titus as one of pain and agony after his campaign against the Jews and Jerusalem. Roman history records for us that he was the emperor for only two years, until 81, and that during his short reign two great disasters shook the city of Rome.[16] It was also during his reign that the great Roman Colosseum, that enormous monument to man's cruelty and inhumanity, was completed and opened. Surviving until today are two architectural remnants of the rule of Titus, the Colosseum and the Arch of Titus, the latter marking his victory in the war against the Jews. Titus died suddenly, probably murdered by his brother Domitian, who succeeded him as emperor.

Domitian was a cruel and vindictive person. While Titus was still alive and on the throne of Rome, the rabbis of Yavneh feared that their old enemy would attempt to eradicate the Jewish people from Judah. They sent a high-level delegation to Rome to plead the cause of the Judean Jews directly. This delegation was composed of Rabban Gamliel II,[18] Rabbi Eliezer ben Hyrcanus and Rabbi Yehoshua ben Chananyah.[19]

---

14. Rabbi Elazar ben Arach did not stay in Yavneh after the death of Rabban Yochanan. Under the influence of his wife, he moved away to Emmaus, a comfortable seaside resort town on the Mediterranean coast of Syria. Subsequently, his scholarship and Torah leadership diminished, because he did not have the company and stimulation of outstanding Torah scholars (*Avos d'Rabbi Nosson* 14-6). We will elaborate below upon the reign of Rabban Gamliel II.

15. *Gittin,* 56b.

16. The great volcano Vesuvius erupted in the year 79, burying Pompeii and Herculaneum. In the year 80, a great fire destroyed much of Rome, including the Capitoline Temple. Titus lived to see that fire begets fire.

18. The appearance of Rabban Gamliel II in Rome as a member of this delegation was a supremely courageous and almost brazen act. The Roman authorities in Judah were agitating for his arrest and execution, forcing him to take a very limited, low-keyed role in Yavneh. Yet here he is in Rome, bearding the lion in its own den!

19. Their mission is mentioned in Yerushalmi, *Sanhedrin,* Chapter 7, section 13.

The main purpose of the Jewish mission was to lighten the crushing economic burden placed upon the Judean Jews and to enable those Jews to have greater control over their internal affairs. This was especially imperative regarding the practice of their religion, without coercion to observe pagan forms or to discontinue rituals the Romans found somehow offensive.[20] The rabbis' main weapon in their mission was pure moral persuasion, something which was not always a valued commodity in Rome. They arrived in Rome just prior to Titus' murder and therefore soon found themselves forced to negotiate with Domitian, whose reputation for cruelty was far more fearsome than his brother's.

While in Rome, the rabbis discovered that a decree was about to be promulgated that would threaten Jewish life not only in Judah but throughout the Roman world. By miraculous bureaucratic intervention, that decree never was formally adopted.[21] Nevertheless, the rabbinic delegation left Rome shaken, with the realization that Domitian and the Roman court were implacable foes of the God and people of Israel, and that the situation of the Jews in Judah was likely to deteriorate in the near future.

Domitian would rule for fifteen years, until his own assassination in 96. Under Domitian, the consolidation of the great conquests and wealth of Rome continued. Organizing Rome's finances now became a priority, with the necessity for realistic budgets and fiscal planning replacing the whims and caprices of the earlier emperors. This new

Top: The Arch of Titus in Rome
Bottom: The Roman Colosseum

---

20. Circumcision, *tefillin,* and ritual purity in family life were Jewish practices that the Romans found particularly irksome.

21. See *Midrash Rabbah, Devarim, V'Eschanan,* Chapter 2, section 15, for particular details of this event.

RESPONSE TO EXILE

Yavneh and Its Wise Men □ 183

interest in a sound currency and stable government economy brought a more orderly, though no less onerous, policy of taxation to the Jews of Judah, and thus allowed for the redevelopment of a more stable economic base in Judah as well, something which was vital to the success of the policies of the rabbis of Yavneh. However, like his father and brother before him, Domitian disdained even paying lip service to the republican forms of government and to the Senate aristocracy and ruled as an autocrat. This arrogance would eventually cost him his throne and his life.[22]

The Leadership in Yavneh

RABBAN YOCHANAN BEN ZAKKAI left Yavneh a few years after its establishment[23] and moved to the nearby village, Bror Chayil. His absence from Yavneh allowed Rabban Gamliel II to begin to play a stronger role of leadership in Yavneh, eventually resuming his full exercise of the powers of the *Nasi*, thus becoming head of the Sanhedrin and the yeshivah at Yavneh. Rabban Yochanan's main students, following the lead of their master and sensing growing Roman pressure against Yavneh, also left Yavneh during its first decade of existence, establishing their own judicial courts and centers of learning, thereby spreading the study of Torah throughout the Jewish population in the Land of Israel.[24]

When Rabban Yochanan ben Zakkai died,[25] his students began to return to Yavneh, once again taking leading roles in the administration of its institutions of leadership. However, their return to active participation in the affairs of Yavneh later would bring them into tension and even open conflict with Rabban Gamliel II. Much of the tension felt at Yavneh was a direct result of the worsening atmosphere that existed in Judah because of increasing Roman enmity towards the Jews generally and towards Yavneh particularly. Fifteen years after Vespasian had granted Rabban Yochanan ben Zakkai's insignificant request for "Yavneh and its wise men," the Roman authorities began to sense that Vespasian had struck a bad bargain. They saw a revitalized Jewish

---

22. See *The Oxford History of the Roman World,* p. 181.
23. Probably around the year 76.
24. See Talmud, *Sanhedrin* 32b.
25. Probably around 79.

PLACES THE SANHEDRIN SAT

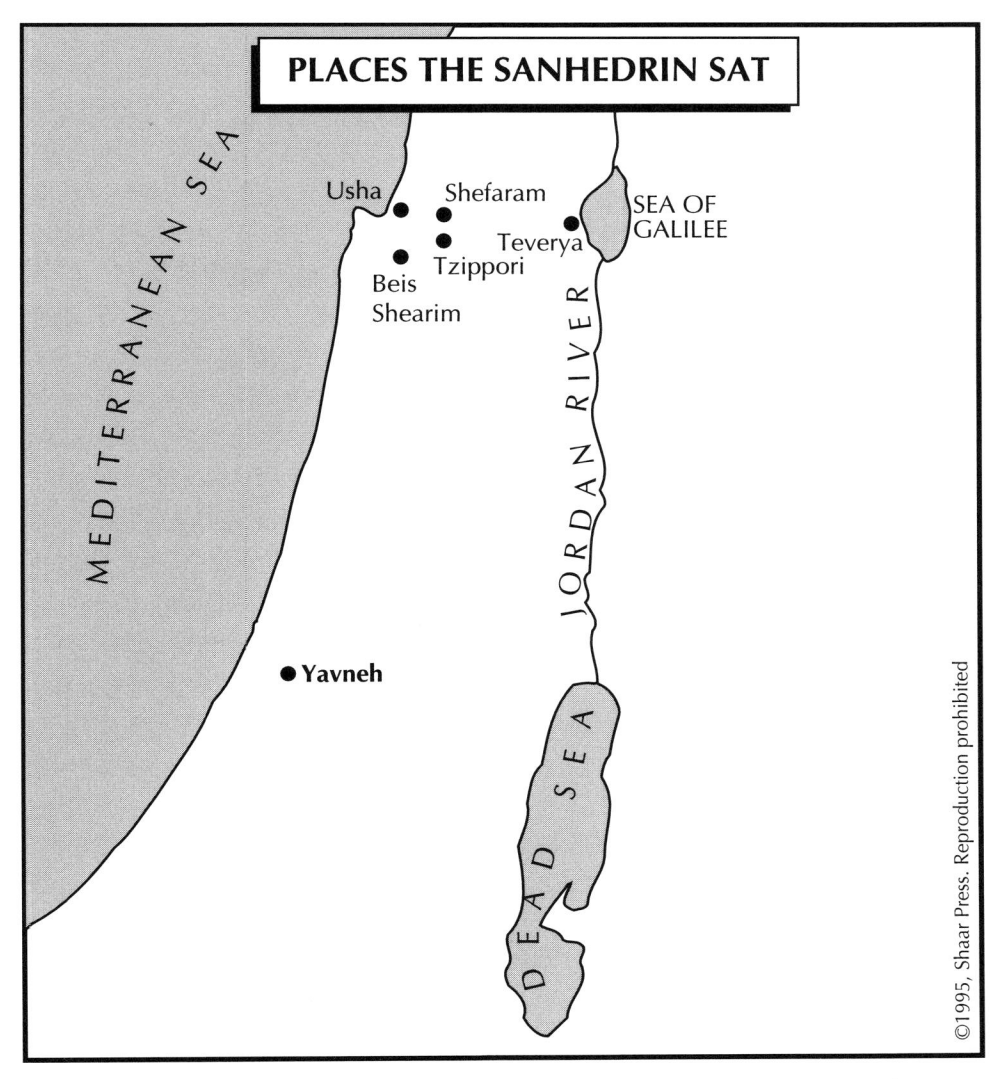

- Usha
- Shefaram
- Teverya
- Tzippori
- Beis Shearim
- Yavneh

MEDITERRANEAN SEA
SEA OF GALILEE
JORDAN RIVER
DEAD SEA

©1995, Shaar Press. Reproduction prohibited

community, with continuing independence of thought and behavior, which, though beaten militarily, was not cowed spiritually or nationally. Thus, the Romans began now to restrict the Jewish institutions at Yavneh in the use of their powers, and the rabbis, cautious as ever not to provoke the wild beast unduly, voluntarily withdrew from Yavneh, meeting there only occasionally and even then surreptitiously. This in turn caused a lack of communication among the scholars and led to their inability to arrive at quick and definite decisions on pressing legal and social matters. This lack of cohesion caused internal strife and deep divisions among the leaders of the Sanhedrin and the people.[26]

---

26. For a fuller exposition of the effect of Roman intimidation on the rabbis of Yavneh and the ensuing split between them, see HaLevy, Volume V (new Volume III), from p. 138 onward.

Disputes among the leaders of Yavneh that would have been reconciled or definitively settled through the concentration of the rabbis in the city were now left to simmer.

The main figures at Yavneh were Rabban Gamliel II, Rabbi Eliezer ben Hyrcanus and Rabbi Yehoshua ben Chananyah. While Rabban Gamliel II served as the *Nasi*, head of the Sanhedrin and titular head of the people, Rabbi Eliezer served as head of the Beis HaVaad, the rabbinic convocation that formulated policy and halachic decisions. Rabbi Eliezer, who was the brother-in-law of Rabban Gamliel, was known as the greatest scholar of the age,[27] and he was a very strong and independent personality.

A Talmud-period oven in Sepphorus

The rule of the majority in halachic disputes, which is implied clearly in the Torah,[28] was zealously upheld by Rabban Gamliel II and the other rabbis of Yavneh. There arose a halachic issue,[29] concerning which Rabbi Eliezer took a very strong stand. The majority of the rabbis opposed his view, even after Rabbi Eliezer invoked supernatural phenomena to support his decision.[30] Rabbi Eliezer, convinced of the correctness of his view, steadfastly refused to accede to the majority opinion. This was an open breach of the long-standing policy of majority rule at Yavneh and was also viewed as a denigration of the authority of the *Nasi*, Rabban Gamliel II. Because of the seriousness of the matter and the fact that the actions of Rabbi Eliezer, the foremost sage of the generation, could not be ignored, the rabbis of Yavneh were forced to proclaim a ban (*cherem*) against Rabbi Eliezer until he retracted. Retract he would not, and he died still under the ban of his colleagues. This matter deeply wounded the prestige of Yavneh and weakened the internal structure of the rabbinic rule of the country.

---

27. Mishnah, *Avos* 2:8.
28. *Shemos* 23:2.
29. The issue concerned an earthenware clay oven and the means of its ritual purification. There have been theories offered that this apparently prosaic matter masked a far more complicated dispute regarding rabbinic approval of an attempt at violent overthrow of Roman rule. See Naftul, *Hatalmud V'Yotzrov*, Volume I, p. 48.
30. See Talmud, *Bava Metzia* 59a-b.

The New Nasi

THE BANNING OF Rabbi Eliezer did not cool the disputes at Yavneh. An even more contentious series of differences arose between Rabban Gamliel II and other rabbis of Yavneh, particularly with Rabbi Yehoshua ben Chananyah. A number of incidents occurred wherein Rabban Gamliel II publicly revoked the decisions of Rabbi Yehoshua ben Chananyah and acted very decisively against him in a personal vein.[31]

The sages were faced with a serious dilemma. They knew that Rabban Gamliel was selfless and that he imposed his authority only to preserve the status of the Sanhedrin and to prevent halachic anarchy in the wake of the destruction of the Temple. His colleagues understood his motivation but felt that they had to defend the honor of Rabbi Yehoshua. The rabbis of Yavneh rallied around Rabbi Yehoshua and voted to depose Rabban Gamliel II as *Nasi*. This occurred approximately eighteen months after the banning of Rabbi Eliezer. Not wishing to make the rift completely irreconcilable, the rabbis refused to install Rabbi Yehoshua in Rabban Gamliel II's stead, but rather chose Rabbi Elazar ben Azaryah as *Nasi*. Despite his youth,[32] Rabbi Elazar performed well in a difficult role. Both he and eventually Rabban Gamliel II himself would emerge as the saving heroes of this sad drama.

The day of the dramatic removal of Rabban Gamliel II as *Nasi* has remained embedded in Jewish thought and writings as "that day" (*bo bayom*). On "that day" a basic change in the makeup of the yeshivah at Yavneh occurred. The rigorous entrance requirements established by Rabban Gamliel II[33] for admittance to the yeshivah were relaxed, and on "that day" many desks and benches, and hence students, were added in the study hall. Also on "that day," because of the presence of so many of the wise men of Torah together at one place and time, halachic decisions were clearly taken, half-forgotten precedents were remembered and clarified, and a cogent record of

---

31. See Talmud, *Rosh HaShanah* 25a; *Bchoros* 36a; *Brachos* 27b.
32. See Talmud, *Brachos* 27b. The tradition of Israel is that Rabbi Elazar ben Azaryah was under twenty-five years old when appointed *Nasi*.
33. See Talmud, *Brachos* 28a.

Ruins at Tzippori

the proceedings was prepared and perpetuated.[34] It is interesting and uplifting to note that both Rabban Gamliel II and Rabbi Yehoshua, in their devotion to the preservation of Torah and the Jewish people no matter what the personal cost, participated in all of the sessions of "that day" without rancor or dissension! Rabban Gamliel II, in an inspiring display of humility and devotion to a higher cause, attended the study hall and sat with his colleagues as if he had never been Rabbi Elazar ben Azaryah's superior. They, on the other hand, joined in the discussion with undiminished respect for the man who had once been their superior and was now their peer.

Changes in Yavneh

THE DISPUTES INVOLVING Rabbi Eliezer, Rabbi Yehoshua and Rabban Gamliel II weakened the strength of the spiritual center at Yavneh. Even though Rabban Gamliel II was later (approximately in the year 85) reconciled with the other rabbis at Yavneh, and even reinstated as *Nasi* (albeit on a somewhat more limited basis than before),[35] much of the lustre of

---

34. The volume of Mishnah known as *Edyos* (*Testimonies*) is primarily a record of the halachic deliberations of "that day."

35. Rabban Gamliel II shared power with his successor Rabbi Elazar ben Azaryah. Rabban Gamliel II led the institutions and delivered the lectures at Yavneh for three weeks (Sabbaths) of the month, with Rabbi Elazar ben Azaryah doing so for the fourth week (Sabbath) of the month. See Talmud, *Brachos* 28a.

Mikveh at Tzippori

office was now lacking. Many of the sages, chief among them Rabbi Yehoshua, again left Yavneh for other cities in the Land of Israel where new centers of learning and leadership were now rising. A new generation of scholars, led by Rabbi Akiva, Rabbi Tarfon, Rabbi Yosi HaGalili, Rabbi Yishmael, Rabbi Yochanan ben Beroka, and Rabbi Elazar ben Chisma, emerged and took leading roles in the administration of Jewish life. The changing of the guard within Yavneh also rekindled Roman suspicions regarding the role of Yavneh.

The Romans were not pleased to see a new, younger and apparently more militant Jewish leadership arise in Yavneh. The year 86 saw clashes between Roman soldiers and Jewish groups in Judah, and the Romans now openly brought pressure on the yeshivah and Sanhedrin at Yavneh to disband. The ferocious Domitian still reigned as emperor and he was an open and avowed enemy of the Jews and especially of Yavneh and what it represented. Thus, Rabban Gamliel II and the rabbis left Yavneh and reestablished the Sanhedrin in the Galilean town of Usha, where it remained for ten years (86-96). However, it appears to have been convened there only on a sporadic and infrequent basis because of the constant threats of the Romans. Rabban Gamliel II was himself targeted by the Romans for execution, as was anyone else who claimed descent from Hillel and the House of David.[36] As such, he lived the remainder of his life in constant movement and long periods of hiding. The Talmud mentions his presence in Tiberias, and it is logical to assume that he spent most of his time

---

36. See HaLevy, old Volume 5 (new Volume 3), p. 35; Naftul, Volume 1, p.71, both quoting Eusebius' History of the Early Church, Chapter III, section 20.

there rather than in Usha.[37] The situation in the Land of Israel was very tense as Domitian proposed and then enforced a special punitive tax on the Jews there. Everyone felt that a storm cloud was about to burst over the Jewish people and their homeland.

Nerva

TO THE RELIEF OF MOST EVERYONE Domitian was assassinated in the year 96. He was succeeded by a much gentler and tolerant man, Nerva. Nerva combined in himself the best potential qualities of Rome — organization, moderation, tolerance and farsighted patience, and in the two years of his reign the situation of the Jews in the Land of Israel improved dramatically.

Nerva repealed the enforcement of Domitian's draconian tax on the Jews and relaxed almost all of the past century's decrees against them.[38] He also removed conversion to Judaism from the Roman list of crimes. He disbanded much of the apparatus of secret police and informers (always part of the baggage of insecure, megalomaniac dictators) and brought a serenity to Roman-Jewish relations.

---

37. See Talmud, *Shabbos* 115a; *Eruvin* 101b; *Tosefta, Trumos,* Chapter 2, section 13.

38. Nerva was so proud of his fair behavior towards the Jews that the royal coin minted during his reign had his picture on one side and the legend, "The Disgrace of the Jewish Tax Removed," on the other side.

11
The Rise of Christianity

THE FIRST CENTURY of the Common Era saw the rise of a new religion, Christianity, that would eventually dominate Western civilization and spread throughout the world. It is beyond the purview of this book to give a detailed history of Christianity and its development or to analyze its dogmas and theological beliefs. Other Jewish history books even ignore the rise of Christianity,[1] and the only references that are made to Christianity are in conjunction with the bloody history of the Church in its later relationship with Jews and Judaism. I am convinced that some knowledge regarding the beginnings of Christianity is essential in order to have a grasp of Jewish life as it was in the centuries after the destruction of the Temple, the period of the Mishnah and the Talmud. In fact, it is most difficult to deal with the realities of our present world, two millennia after the beginnings of Christianity, without recourse to the facts and ideas of that far-distant era of the first centuries of the Common Era.

Roots of the Religion

IN THE CENTURY OF the destruction of the Temple there were Jews who advanced a new messianic message. It was based upon the teachings of a Jew, Yeshu (Jesus in Greek) of Nazareth, who was executed by the Romans for preaching sedition, some time before the destruction of the

---

1. The Talmud itself practically ignores Christianity, devoting very few paragraphs to the beliefs and rise of Christianity. Later in this book, some possible explanations of this policy of the rabbis of the Mishnah and the Talmud will be presented.

Temple.[2] The followers and disciples of this man, all of whom were Jews, were led by James, the brother of Yeshu; Peter (originally Simon), a fisherman of Galilee; and Paul (originally Saul) of Tarsus.

James and Peter saw themselves as full-fledged Jews, bound by the laws and traditions of the Torah and Israel. To their Judaism they added a belief in Yeshu as being the Messiah, as someone already resurrected from the dead, and they eventually expanded his role into a being who possessed a special and actual kinship, so to speak, with God. They also adopted many of the extreme views and ascetic customs of the Essenes, with immersion in water (baptism) as a symbol of purity and faith becoming a requirement.

As is true of most of the beliefs and rituals of early Christianity, this symbol of entrance into the faith was borrowed from Jewish law and custom regarding the acceptance of converts. However, as again was true regarding almost all Christian rituals borrowed from Judaism, the emphasis and perspective on this water-immersion ceremony was somewhat distorted and eventually completely de-Judaized. But Peter and James nevertheless saw Christianity as Judaism and not as a new religion. They were not interested in pagan converts to Christianity if those converts did not agree to follow the "Law of Moses" and abide by the commandments of the Torah. Circumcision, dietary laws, strict Sabbath observance on Saturday, loyalty to the Land of Israel, all

---

2. The actual time of Yeshu's life is unclear. There is an opinion in the Talmud that he was a contemporary of Rabbi Yehoshua ben Perachyah, which would place him in c. 165 B.C.E. — in other words, more than a century earlier than popularly assumed! This opinion was restated by Rabbi Moshe ben Nachman (Ramban) during his debate with the Church leaders of Barcelona, Spain, in 1267. However, most scholars, both Jewish and non-Jewish, do posit Yeshu's execution in c. 35 C.E., and that is the opinion that I follow in this book. There exists also a school of scholars who question whether a historical person such as Yeshu ever existed.

Much ink has been spilled by scholars and historians over the centuries concerning the role of the Jewish police or criminal courts in the execution of Yeshu, and much Jewish blood has been spilled over the same centuries because of the calumny that the Jews are "Christ-killers." The Sanhedrin had stopped judging capital cases in about 30 C.E., several years before his execution, so that even if Jews had been involved, they would have acted as tools of the Romans rather than as "Jewish" authorities. The life and death of Yeshu are so surrounded by historical fog that no clear picture can emerge of his activities and the circumstances of his death. The Gospels (the first four books of the New Testament, which set forth the basic tenets of Christianity and are interspersed with anecdotes about the life of Yeshu) themselves are contradictory in their stories of Yeshu, and therefore the alleged events are the stuff of unverifiable legend.

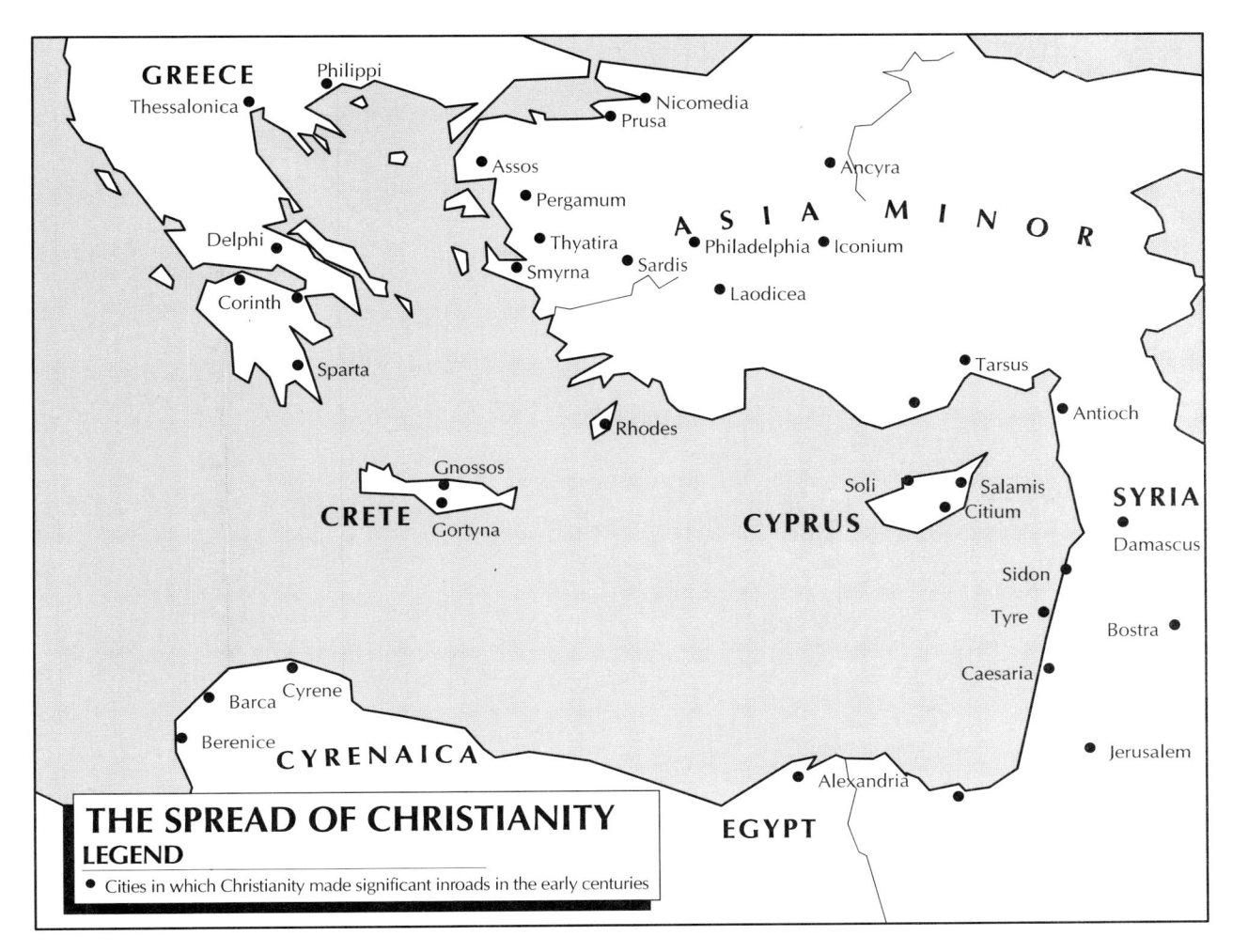

THE SPREAD OF CHRISTIANITY
LEGEND
• Cities in which Christianity made significant inroads in the early centuries

were part of their Christianity. If this view of Christianity had become dominant, Christianity in all likelihood would soon have disappeared, not being very attractive to most Jews who were loyal to Judaism or to most pagans who abhorred any Jewish ways and had no special regard for the "Law of Moses."

Paul

PAUL WAS OF A MUCH DIFFERENT mind and of much sterner stuff than Peter and James. Perhaps because of his background as a student of the rabbis and the Pharisees, Paul realized early on that the Jews would not accept Christianity, no matter what "miracles" or messianic proofs were presented. He was aware of their intense loyalty to the Torah and its precepts, among them the rejection of the deification of any man. Judaism taught that God was God and man was man, and the two were not to be confused with one another. Paul saw more clearly than Peter and James that the future spread of Christianity would lie in its ability to appeal to the pagan Roman world, and it was to converting the members of that world that he set his prodigious energies and tenacity. Paul himself clearly stated his mission: "The Gospel to the uncircumcised (pagans) was entrusted to me, even as the Gospel to the circumcised (Jews) was to Peter."[3]

Paul was especially encouraged to take his message to the non-Jewish world by the fact that the early successes of the Christians in winning over their fellow Jews soon petered out as the Christians met stronger and stronger opposition to their doctrines and methods from the rabbis and the masses. Thus, Christianity was forced to look for converts outside of the Jewish people. In order to be successful in winning the non-Jewish world to their faith, the Christians had to transform themselves effectively to appear as non-Jews in the eyes of the pagan society. In this they were aided by the Jews, who openly rejected them and attempted to separate all Christians from their midst,[4] and by the new doctrines and redefinition of Christianity postulated by Paul.

A Series of Paradoxes

PAUL ADVOCATED a radical break with the forms of traditional Judaism. He thought of himself as an expert in Jewish law[5] and was a convert to Christianity by means of visions and miracles. He claimed that originally, as a

---

3. *Galatians*, Chapter 2, verse 7.
4. The nineteenth blessing of the Amidah prayer was instituted by the rabbis of Yavneh, under the leadership of Rabban Gamliel II in c. 85. The blessing known as *Birchas HaMinim* (the blessing recited to oppose the influence of the *minim,* the early Jewish Christians) was composed by Shmuel HaKattan and immediately became part of the daily Jewish prayer service. It included a strong denunciation of the tactics and behavior of the early Christians (see Talmud, *Brachos* 28b.) Anyone refusing to recite this blessing publicly was suspected of being a Christian (*min*) and thereafter excluded from the Jewish community. Thus, by the end of the first century of Christianity, its hopes for winning over the Jewish people to its banner were dashed. For a beautifully poetic assessment of the life and accomplishments of Shmuel HaKattan, see *Be'er HaTalmud* by Eliezer Shteinman, Masada Publishing, Tel Aviv, 1967, Volume I, pp. 264-8.
5. *Galatians*, Chapter 1, verses 13-14.

Jew, he had been zealous in persecuting the early Jewish Christians. Now, however, as a new convert he displayed a truly zealous tendency towards excess that sometimes marks those who have only recently and suddenly discovered the "truth."

He now denigrated everything Jewish, ridiculed the Torah and its commandments and proclaimed that Christianity was for the pagan and the uncircumcised since the Jews rejected it. He stated that none of the rituals of Judaism — circumcision, Sabbath observance, dietary laws, etc. — had any further validity and that even the Jews should "forsake Moses...[and] not circumcise their children, neither to follow their [Jewish] customs."[6] He proclaimed that the essence of the revelation of God to Israel on Sinai had been fulfilled by the coming of Christianity and that Judaism should therefore voluntarily abdicate its historic role and godly mission in civilization in favor of Christianity. No longer was the form — the Torah, the laws and commandments, the ritual taught at Sinai — important or even valid, but rather the spirit, the ideals, the belief in the Christian God alone would be sufficient for salvation.

But however much Paul ranted against Judaism and the Jews, he could not escape the reality that much basic Christian doctrine was based upon Jewish beliefs, traditions and teachings. The ideas of love, compassion, kindness to the stranger and the lowly, immortality of the soul, the resurrection of the dead, faith in one, single, exclusive Creator, self-discipline in sexual and physical matters, reverence for life and holiness of human purpose, all were Jewish ideas, and it was these tenets that formed the core of early Christian belief. But the additional layers of Christian thought became a minefield of contradictions and paradoxes that Christianity itself could not reconcile.

Throughout the two millennia of its existence, Christianity has waged war upon itself, basically because it never clearly defined itself to the satisfaction of all its would-be adherents. The concepts of the two natures of Yeshu (physical and godly), the dogmas of the Trinity (three separate parts making up one indivisible Divine Being), the virgin birth of Yeshu and the role of his

---

6. *Acts*, Chapter 21, verses 20-1. However, this may be a claim about Paul himself, not necessarily what he taught. Many interpreters claim (in the light of *Corinthians*) that Paul advocated continued observance of the Torah for Jews and abrogation of the law for non-Jews.

mother, Mary,[7] and the theory of Original Sin, the incorporation of much pagan ritual and symbolism in Christianity, the role of purgatory and Hell, the death of the Messiah (if not of one piece of God, so to speak) all are vexing problems in Christian thought and history. By the second century of Christianity numerous disputes and struggles were underway regarding all of these issues.

In Christianity, what was correct dogma and what was heretical thought was often decided by the sword and not by debate and reasoned belief. The Jews rejected the ideas of Christianity, deeming them to be blasphemous both to God and to man. The Jewish opposition to Christian beliefs was loud and public. This vociferous rejection of Christianity by the very people of Yeshu and his disciples left in Christianity a very deep-rooted infection that festered in hatred throughout the Christian world and periodically erupted in murderous persecution of the Jews. The Christians hated the Jews not so much for their alleged participation in the death of Yeshu in c. 35, but rather because the Jews persisted in denying his validity and that of his religion for millennia after his death.

Too Much the Same

IN THE WORDS OF A SECULAR historian, "The Jews could not concede the divinity of [Yeshu] as a God-made-man without repudiating the central tenet of their belief. The Christians could not concede that [Yeshu] was anything less than God without repudiating the essence and purpose of their movement. If [Yeshu] was not God, Christianity was nothing. If [Yeshu] was God, then Judaism was false. There could be absolutely no compromise on this point. Each faith was thus a threat to the

---

7. The concept of the virgin birth is mentioned in only one of the four Gospels, that of *Luke*. Luke was a Greek, unlike the authors of the other three Gospels, who were all Jewish. The idea that great people were somehow born of a virgin had wide credence in the Greek and Roman world, long before the advent of Christianity. The adoration of Mary as the mother of Yeshu also fits the pattern of thought prevalent in the Greco-Roman world and earlier pagan times that lionized and even deified mothers of great men. To the Jews, the idea of a virgin birth was untenable, and when associated with supposed deity, it became anathema. The belief in the special role of Mary, and concomitantly in the concept of the virgin birth of Yeshu, became main theological points of contention within Christianity itself during the Reformation and thereafter.

other."[8] But Christianity borrowed very heavily from Judaism. It took as its own the Bible, already translated into Greek, and this "old testament" became the foundation rock of the new faith. It incorporated into its way of life the idea of a Sabbath day, though eventually moving it to Sunday from the traditional Saturday Sabbath of Israel. Included in Christianity were other trappings taken from Judaism, such as "...feast-days, incense and burning lamps, psalms, hymns and choral music, vestments and prayers, priests and martyrs, the reading of the sacred books and the institution of the synagogue (transformed into the church)."[9] Rabbinic and scholarly authority was now transferred to bishops and popes. It is clear that it was this very strong nature of sameness and familiarity shared by Judaism and Christianity that helped fuel the bitter enmity that Christians displayed toward Jews throughout history. Foolish humanity hates those who are a little different from themselves with a far greater passion than they hate those who are vastly different from themselves.

A Widening Gap

BY THE YEAR 50 C.E. Paul had established himself as the chief spokesman of Christianity, at least as far as the pagan world was concerned. He now took a minor, deviant Jewish sect and transformed it into a world religion. Paul traveled throughout the Mediterranean world, organizing new Christian cells and strengthening the existing ones. Paul was persecuted for his missionary activities. He claims to have been scourged by Roman authorities, beaten with rods by the orders of judges in Greek cities and flogged with thirty-nine blows by angered Jewish congregations. His life was constantly in danger but he persevered, and eventually his brand of Christianity, tailored for appeal to the pagan world, began to take root throughout the Roman world, even in the seat of power, Rome itself.

Paul never married, had no family and was solely committed to his goal of propagandizing for his new-found faith. Because he never married, he brought into Christianity a heavy emphasis regarding sins

---
8. *A History of the Jews* by Paul Johnson, Harper & Row, 1987, p. 145.
9. Ibid.

of the flesh and the desirability of a celibate way of life. Over the centuries this idea of celibacy, at least for the clergy of Christianity, took hold. Much of the angst of the modern world over sexual matters can be traced to this distorted view of human sexuality as projected by Christianity during its early, formative years. Thus, Paul's personal problems and prejudices somehow became the burden of all later Christian society as well.

Paul's hatred of the Jews also stemmed from his personality and experiences. The rejection of Christianity by the Jews engendered in him a vitriolic reaction. Paul downplayed Yeshu's Jewishness and made him the "servant of man" and no longer the "servant of Israel." He pandered to the anti-Jewish prejudices of the Greco-Roman world, insisting that Jews were no longer the people of God and raising the gentiles to a far higher plane of civilization and humanity than the Jews. Paul was executed in Rome in c. 64 C.E. after the great fire had destroyed Nero's city. By that time he no longer saw himself as a Jew but rather as a convert to a new universal religion which he himself had substantially fashioned. "From the end of Paul's lifetime onward Jews and Christians lived in two separate worlds, there being between them no relation except that of kinsmen who have grown apart; hence animosity and conflict between them increased."[10]

One Good Word

THE MOST EXPLICIT ASSESSMENT of Judaism's view of any positive aspect of Christianity was stated by Rabbi Moshe ben Maimon in the final section of his monumental code of Jewish law, *Mishneh Torah*. Looking back over the then-twelve centuries of Christian society, Rabbi Moshe ben Maimon stated that Christianity's main contribution to civilization was that it introduced and popularized the concept of the Messiah, and the subsequent utopian messianic era, in a pagan world originally far from such thoughts and hopes. Jewry felt that on the whole Christianity had strayed too far in adapting itself to the pagan world it conquered, but it certainly was an improvement over paganism.

---

10. *From Yeshu to Paul* by Joseph Klausner, Beacon Press, 1961, p. 599.

12
Bar Kochba

NERVA BECAME EMPEROR in early September of 96, but he was old and sick, and so a leading rabbinic delegation immediately set sail from Judah to Rome in that very same month, spending the holiday of Succos on board ship.[1]

The visit of this second rabbinic delegation[2] to Rome was much more successful than that of the previous delegation, achieving a lowering of the rate of the special "Jew tax" which was still in force. Indeed, Nerva relaxed almost all of the decrees made in the past century against the Jews. Even more importantly, the appearance of the great rabbis of Israel at the Roman court made a great impression upon the higher echelons of Roman society. A trend towards converting to Judaism had developed amongst aristocratic Romans in the first century of the Common Era and was reflected even in the royal families of Rome.[3] With the appearance in Rome of the impressive rabbinic leadership of the Jews, this trend gained momentum. Titus and Domitian had executed those who converted. Nerva tolerated and privately respected them.

So the Jews rejoiced in imperial Rome's new attitude towards them, and the Sanhedrin took the opportunity provided by Nerva's reign to return to Yavneh from Usha. Alas, after only two years of rule, Nerva died and was replaced by Trajan.

The reign of Trajan would be marked by another great and unsuccessful Jewish war against Rome. It would also mark the beginning

---

1. Talmud, *Succah* 23a and 41b.
2. The members of this delegation to Rome were Rabban Gamliel of Yavneh, Rabbi Yehoshua, Rabbi Elazar ben Azaryah and Rabbi Akiva.
3. The great Onkelos, the translator of the Bible into Aramaic, was a close relative of Titus and became the prototype of the "righteous convert" of the time. See Talmud, *Gittin* 56b, and *Avodah Zarah* 11a.

Trajan

of the millennia-long struggle of the Jewish people and Judaism against Christianity, a religion which sprang from Jews and Judaism but rapidly became a non-Jewish faith, both in terms of constituency and beliefs. The situations and circumstances which allowed Yavneh to be the haven of Israel after the destruction of the Temple and Jerusalem were now changing. Jewish survival in the Land of Israel was again in the balance as the second century of the Common Era began.

Although Trajan, a fellow Senator, had been adopted as a son by Domitian,[4] he was cut from a much different and inferior cloth. Nerva was a man of peace, and Trajan, a soldier from earliest youth, was violent and reveled in war. Therefore, the move back to Yavneh was to be of short duration. Trajan had no tolerance for the independent ways and attitudes of the Jews of Judah. He resented the Jews' declaration of superiority in matters of religion and social morals, and he opposed the continued proselytization of pagan Rome by Jews[5] as well as Christians.

When Trajan embarked upon a war of conquest against the Parthians, he felt that Judah — which, in spite of Roman conquest, still felt itself somehow equal to Rome — would undoubtedly undermine the necessary rear-echelon logistical structure for such a campaign. Instead of compromising with Jewish interests and winning the Jews as an ally against Parthia, he determined to crush any independent form of Jewish life in Judah once and for all. He began by removing Agrippa II,[6] the great-grandson of Herod and Miriam, from the rule of the Galilee, and placed that province under the direct rule of Rome. Even though Agrippa II and his sister, Bernice, were

---

4. It was common for Roman emperors to attempt to choose their successors to the throne by means of officially "adopting" that person as a son. Sometimes, as in the case of Trajan and later Hadrian, the "adoption" took place even at the deathbed of the old emperor.

5. Even though active proselytization on behalf of Judaism was contrary to rabbinic law and tradition, it seems that there were many Jews who were willing to teach and popularize Judaism amongst the Roman aristocracy of the time. The Talmud itself, in discussing Hillel and Shammai, indicates that there were variant philosophies extant among the rabbis themselves in their approach to potential converts to Judaism.

6. There is an historical theory that this deposition of Agrippa II may have taken place earlier, in 95, under the reign of Domitian. However, most Jewish historians attribute Agrippa's demotion to Trajan.

hardly considered Jewish rulers in the eyes of the rabbis, as far as Rome was concerned they were viewed as Jewish nobility and hence distrusted by Trajan.[7]

Yavneh Disbanded

IT WAS AT THIS TIME, c. 100 C.E., that Trajan also ended the autonomous government of the Nabateans in the southern Negev desert and brought its territory under direct Roman rule as part of the province of Arabia. By the year 103 there were no autonomous territories in the area of the Land of Israel.

Trajan now turned his attention directly against the Jewish leadership of Judah and particularly persecuted Rabban Gamliel II of Yavneh and his family. Trajan was provoked at the restoration, apparently without his express imperial permission, of the central yeshivah and Sanhedrin in Yavneh, after its earlier exile to Usha in the Galilee. He looked suspiciously at the growing power of the rabbis and was particularly disturbed by their tenacious opposition to all forms of Roman culture and life-style. Therefore, by the beginning of the year 105, the rabbis once again were forced to disband the center at Yavneh, and they attempted to return to Usha. The trek would be a long one, and more than a decade would pass before Usha again became the center of Jewish life in the Land of Israel.

Rabban Gamliel II, under particular pressure, escaped to Lod (Lydda), where Rabbi Tarfon had his yeshivah and rabbinic court. There in Lod, a group of five rabbis[8]

Above: Trajan's Column
Below: Detail of Trajan's Column

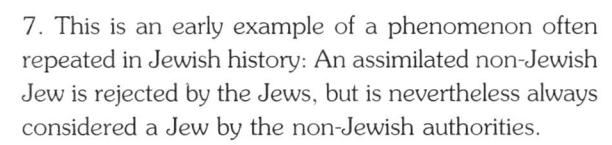

---

7. This is an early example of a phenomenon often repeated in Jewish history: An assimilated non-Jewish Jew is rejected by the Jews, but is nevertheless always considered a Jew by the non-Jewish authorities.

8. The five scholars who comprised this group were Rabban Gamliel II, Rabbi Tarfon, Rabbi Akiva, Rabbi Yehoshua and Rabbi Elazar ben Azaryah. It is interesting to note that Rabbi Eliezer, still under rabbinic ban, also resided in Lod at this time. See Talmud, *Sanhedrin* 32b. Also see Talmud, *Bava Metzia* 59b, and *Moed Katan* 27a, regarding the sudden death of Rabban Gamliel II.

formed what could be termed an executive committee to wield supreme rabbinic authority until the restoration of the entire Sanhedrin at Usha. However, with the sudden and unexpected death of Rabban Gamliel II later that year,[9] the center at Lod was weakened. Rabban Gamliel II was succeeded by his colleague, Rabbi Elazar ben Azaryah, as head of the yeshivah and Sanhedrin. Rabban Gamliel II's own son, Shimon, was in hiding from the Roman police, and thus could not then be considered a candidate to succeed his father. The rabbis also felt that having a *Nasi* who was not descended from the House of David and hence not "royal" — Rabbi Elazar ben Azaryah — could somehow soften the Roman persecution of the rabbis. This hope would prove futile.

Trajan's Arch

Lod

RABBI ELAZAR BEN AZARYAH attempted to expand and strengthen the influence of the center at Lod. He enlarged the executive committee to include thirty-two scholars,[10] and he planned to make Lod the focal point and rallying place for the Jews of Judah. Trajan thought otherwise, and after a few years of increasing Roman pressure, Rabbi Elazar ben Azaryah left Lod and took up residence in Tzippori (Sepphoris) in the Galilee. There he established a clandestine yeshivah and gathered a new generation of scholars to study under him, away from the malevolent and watchful eye of Rome.[11] His great colleagues, Rabbi Tarfon

---

9. Scholars are in conflict regarding the date of death of Rabban Gamliel II. The estimates range from 105 to 117. The earlier date seems more probable.
10. See *Tosefta, Mikvaos,* at the conclusion of Chapter 8.
11. See *Tosefta, Kelim, Bava Basra,* Chapter 2, section 2.

and Rabbi Akiva, remained in Lod and there operated a yeshivah in hiding in the attic of Beis Nitzah.[12] A spirit of gloom hung over Judah, and the rabbis braced themselves for the coming life-and-death struggle with Rome. Trajan would soon strike major blows in his attempt to end Jewish spiritual independence throughout the Roman Empire, just as Titus' blows had earlier ended Judah's national independence.

Roman Fury Unleashed

THE WAR AGAINST THE JEWS would be conducted by Trajan on three fronts — Mesopotamia, Israel and Egypt/Cyrenaica (Cyrene). In 114 Trajan led the Roman legions against the Parthian Empire, which embraced the land mass of present-day Iran, Afghanistan, Pakistan, Turkish Armenia and parts of Iraq/Babylonia.

By the year 115 the Romans had conquered most of this vast area, and Trajan was ready to declare victory and return to his Roman palace. But the Parthians stubbornly refused to accept Roman victory and rule, and in 116 a serious renewal of the war began. This time the Roman forces, their supply lines seriously overextended and their soldiers exhausted by two years of war in a most inhospitable society and climate, were badly mauled by the Parthian troops. The Romans began a long, slow and bloody withdrawal back into Asia Minor. They were constantly harassed by the local populace, most of whom sided with the Parthians. This was especially true of the Jews of Babylonia, who openly fought against Roman rule.

Trajan, enraged by having his victory evaporate, turned his wrath against the Jews living in present-day southern Turkey, northern Iraq and Syria. He appointed one of his most ruthless legion commanders, Lucius Quietus, to suppress this Jewish uprising against Rome. Trajan's instructions were to destroy the Jewish population of Asia Minor, and Lucius Quietus set himself to the carnage with a gleeful vengeance. Entire Jewish populations of major cities were put to death,[13] with the leaders of those communities horribly tortured to death. After completing his work in Mesopotamia, Lucius Quietus

---

12. See Talmud, *Sanhedrin* 74a, and *Kiddushin* 40b.
13. The Jewish populations of Edessa, Netzivin (Nisbis) and Antioch bore the brunt of Lucius Quietus' evil fury.

JEWISH UPRISINGS AGAINST ROME 66-135 C.E.

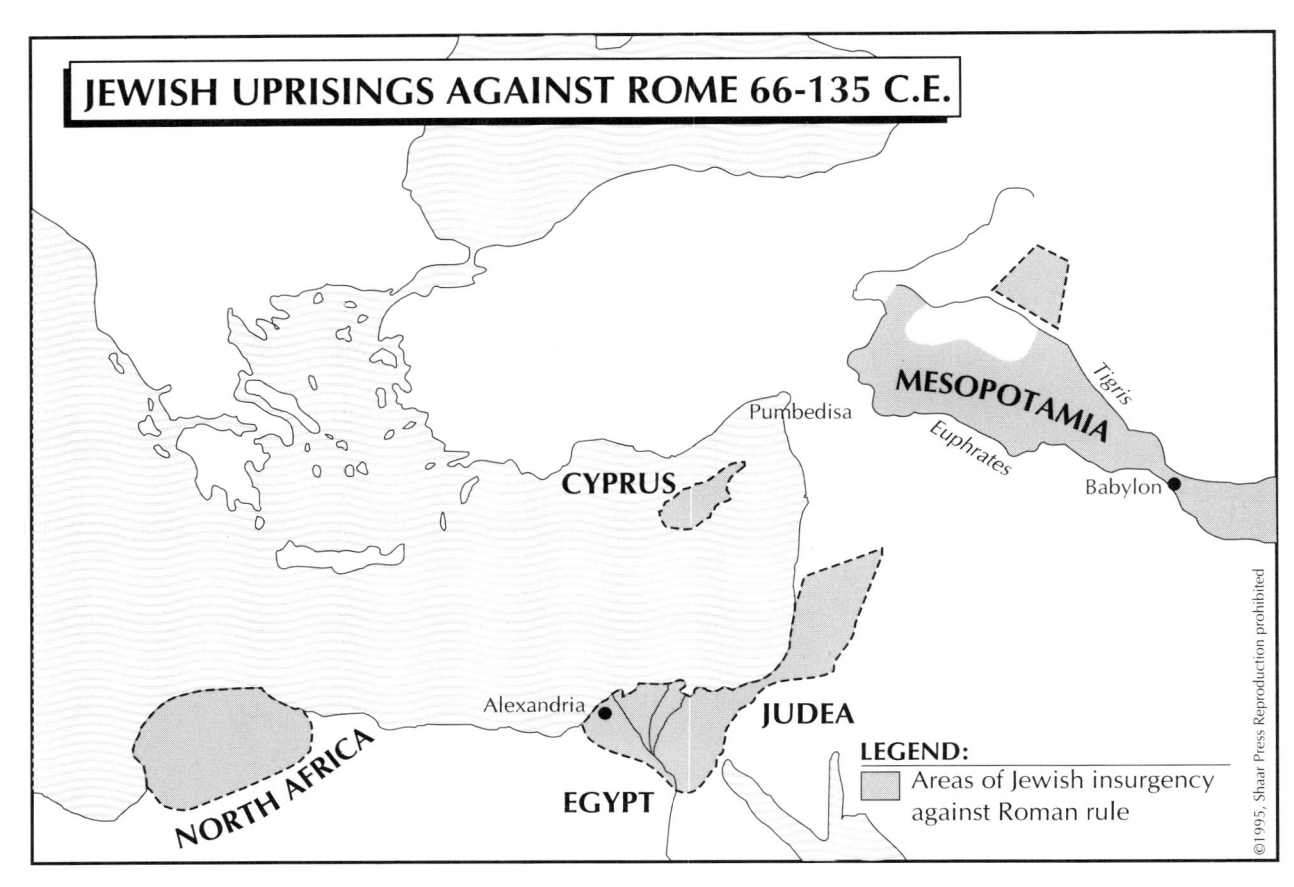

was appointed governor of Judah, where he would continue his persecution of the Jews.

The Jews Revolt

QUIETUS QUICKLY BROUGHT terror and death to the Jews of Judah. He executed many Jewish leaders and destroyed the rabbinic center at Lod.[14] Rabbi Akiva and Rabbi Tarfon fled and went into hiding, their students scattering over the Land of Israel to escape persecution. The Roman fury against the Jews reached the large and influential Jewish communities of Egypt and Cyrenaica (in Libya). The Jews there had earlier taken up arms to defend themselves against the growing violence of their Hellenist neighbors. The roots of Greek/Hellenist anti-Semitism in Alexandria and Egypt were old and deep, dating back to the times of the Ptolemys. The year 115 saw violent Greek attacks

---
14. See Talmud, *Taanis* 18b.

against Jewish communities throughout Egypt and Cyrenaica, which were answered with equally violent attacks by the Jews against the resident Hellenist population. The armed might of the Jewish communities prevailed, and there were thousands of casualties in the struggle.

The Romans, upon learning of the Jewish successes at arms, soon sent special contingents of troops to Egypt and Cyrenaica to quell the uprisings and unrest. These Roman troops were especially brutal in their treatment of the Jews. The Jewish communities in Cyrenaica were totally destroyed, and in fact the entire area was left a wasteland.

By the year 117, the great Jewish community of Alexandria was seriously diminished in numbers, wealth and influence due to this Roman onslaught. After a rebellion against Rome by the Jews of Cyprus in 116, the Jewish presence on that island was also completely eliminated.[15] The conflagration which engulfed the Jewish communities of the nearby Diaspora almost destroyed all Jewish strength and influence in the Roman Empire.

Hadrian

WHEN THE MOTIVATIONS for the Jewish revolts throughout the Roman Empire during the reign of Trajan are assessed, there are two factors that appear dominant. The first is the bitter and long-smoldering Jewish hatred of Rome itself and all the evil it represented. The rabbis called Rome "the evil kingdom," and they meant it. Almost everything that Roman culture found beautiful and desirable, the Jews found disgusting and repulsive. When coupled with the natural feelings of vengeance against Rome for destroying their national entity and holy Temple, this Jewish antipathy towards Rome easily exploded into violent rebellion.

Secondly, the time was one of great messianic expectations. As pointed out in the previous chapter, messianic fervor was the norm throughout the Jewish world of Rome. The Jews somehow felt that the messianic redemption was now at hand and that the fall of Rome was imminent. As such, a sense of impatience with the status quo

---

15. An echo of this slaughter is found in Talmud Yerushalmi, *Succah,* Chapter 5, section 1.

pervaded the Jewish world. The improbable — the defeat of mighty Rome by small Israel — seemed somehow likely, for these were undoubtedly extraordinary times. These underlying causes, which shaped Jewish behavior in the Diaspora during the century following the sacking of Jerusalem, were present in Judah as well and would soon find violent expression there in the great war of Bar Kochba against Rome.

Trajan became ill in 117 and, in order to regain his health, left the army he had led against the Parthians in an attempt to return to Rome. However, death overtook him in the city of Selenius, on the Mediterranean coast of present-day Turkey. His main general and nephew as well as newly adopted son,[16] Hadrian, still stationed with the army facing the Parthians, was chosen emperor by those troops, and his accession to the imperial throne of Rome was then confirmed by the Roman Senate in August 117.

The Jews were hopeful that this change in Rome's leadership would augur well for them. The initial indications from Hadrian were heartening, for he withdrew the Roman legions from the Parthian front, which ended the Roman persecutions of the Jews of Mesopotamia and removed any further threat to the autonomy of the large and flourishing Jewish community of Babylonia. Hadrian arrested and executed the brutal and hated Lucius Quietus and thereby relaxed the heavy hand of Roman domination over Jewish life throughout Israel. The Jews felt that Hadrian would be a just and tolerant ruler, more in the mold of Nerva than in the likeness of his predecessor, Trajan. Some of this Jewish optimism was fueled by the fact that Rabbi Yehoshua, one of the leading members of the rabbinic leadership of Judah, knew Hadrian and had a cordial relationship with him.[17] And Hadrian was now about to make a gesture towards the Jews which would send their hopes soaring and reinvigorate their spiritual and political life.

In about the year 122, Hadrian published the "Balfour Declaration" of his day. He announced his decision to allow the Jews to rebuild the Holy Temple and also to repair the destruction of Jerusalem and its walls.[18]

---

16. See note 4 above.
17. See Talmud, *Chagigah* 5b and *Shabbos* 119a.
18. See *Midrash, Bereishis Rabbah,* Chapter 64, section 8.

Jewish excitement reached a fever pitch. Monies were collected throughout the Jewish world to help finance this dramatic project. Jews began to return to Israel from everywhere in the Roman Empire, and there was a great surge of Jewish pride and enthusiasm generally. Jews felt that this coming Temple would be in line with that of Ezra, also built by the permission of a foreign occupying power of the Land of Israel, and would, by Ezra's precedent, therefore fulfill all necessary ritual and legal requirements of the Torah. Jews were most forward in pointing out to their Christian rivals that the rebuilt Temple would of necessity negate basic Christian beliefs in the rejection of Jewry by God.

Apparently, the reaction to Hadrian's declaration was so great, from Jew and non-Jew alike, that Hadrian began to have second thoughts regarding the matter. He now realized that what he thought to be a clever and inexpensive maneuver on the part of Rome to win Jewish loyalty, the Jews considered to be a practical grant of independence and self-rule, both physically and spiritually. Hadrian's doubts were reinforced by the lobbying efforts of the non-Jewish populations in Israel, particularly of the Samaritans and Christians, who vehemently opposed the Jewish rebuilding of the Temple and the city walls of Jerusalem. Hadrian, embarrassed to openly revoke his own imperial decree, therefore added such cumbersome conditions to his offer to the Jews as to prevent the decree from ever coming to fulfillment.[19] Thus, the great hopes for the future that the Jews invested in Hadrian began to evaporate.

The Sanhedrin Reconvenes

AS A RESULT OF THE OPTIMISM engendered amongst the Jews at the beginning of Hadrian's reign, the rabbis and the Sanhedrin had come forth from their scattered hiding places and reconstituted the central body of rabbinic authority once more at Usha, in the Galilee. (Apparently the rabbis were still fearful of returning to their original base at Yavneh and preferred the lower-profile location of Usha.) In about 122 the Sanhedrin was reconvened at Usha.

---

19. Ibid.

Many of the old lions who had guided the Jewish people during the dark times after the destruction of the Temple were no longer alive. Rabban Gamliel II, Rabbi Eliezer, Rabbi Yehoshua, Rabbi Elazar ben Azaryah, Rabbi Tarfon, all were not present at Usha. Rabbi Shimon ben Gamliel II, the son of Rabban Gamliel II, did not dare assume a leading role in the Usha center due to the continuing objection of Rome to allowing a Davidic descendant to lead the Jews. Thus, the mantle of authority fell upon the aged[20] but responsible shoulders of Rabbi Akiva.

Rabbi Akiva revitalized the yeshivah and Sanhedrin at Usha, and together with his colleague Rabbi Yishmael and their disciples, such as Rabbis Chanina ben Tradyon, Elazar ben Parta, Yosi HaGalili, Yehudah ben Illai'i, Meir, Yochanan ben Nuri, Yesheivov HaSofer, Shimon ben Azai, Shimon ben Zoma and Shimon ben Yochai, led a revival of study and Jewish spirit throughout the Land of Israel. Rabbi Akiva was the main personality of the time, beloved and respected by all Israel, his advice and opinions reckoned with by the Roman rulers, and he therefore wielded great personal power and influence in the Jewish world. It was during these early years of this reconvening of the center at Usha, when relative calm yet pervaded the Land of Israel, that the rabbis promulgated a series of social compacts which came to be known as "*takanos (ordinances of)* Usha." But as already seen above, Hadrian's volatility in his attitude towards the Jews hung as a foreboding cloud over all of the deliberations at Usha.

A Third Rebellion

IN THIS SECTION two great Jewish rebellions against Rome have been described. One was during the time of Vespasian and Titus, which resulted in the destruction of the Temple and Jersualem. The other occurred during the reign of Trajan, which caused the deaths of hundreds of thousands of Jews throughout the Roman Empire, particularly in Asia Minor, Egypt and Cyprus. But now a third rebellion of the Jews against Rome would erupt during the reign of Hadrian. It would be far more bloody and perhaps even more consequential for the Jews

---

20. Jewish tradition tells us that Rabbi Akiva was more than hundred years old when he was martyred in c. 135.

than its two predecessors. This rebellion would be the last attempt by Jews to restore a Jewish national entity through force of arms for the next eighteen hundred years, and its failure would force Israel to accept the inevitability of a long, painful and continuing state of exile.

Both the actual causal incident and the date of the beginning of this third great Jewish war against Rome are unclear. Conventional historical wisdom places the onus of sparking the rebellion on Hadrian's decision to construct a new Roman city, Aelia Capitolina, on the site of Jerusalem, while concurrently building a temple to Jupiter on the spot of the Holy Temple on Mount Moriah.

When that decision was actually publicized is a matter of conjecture. Most scholars say the rebellion began in 126 and was over by 135. There are others who date the beginning of the rebellion in 128, and still others date it as late as 130. The end of the rebellion, marked by the destruction of the last Jewish fortress of Beitar, is said by some scholars to have occurred in 133 and not 135, while still others date the end of the war as late as 136-137.[21]

Hadrian himself spent two years[22] in the Land of Israel surveying the situation of the Romans in Asia Minor and the Middle East. Apparently, while in Judah itself, his attitude towards the Jews and Judaism became extremely inimical. He now promulgated laws against circumcision,[23] the observance of the Sabbath and family purity and public prayer. The Jews saw themselves to be in the same circumstances as those that had provoked the Hasmonean rebellion against the Syrian Greeks almost three centuries earlier. And they responded in the same fashion — by war and revolt.

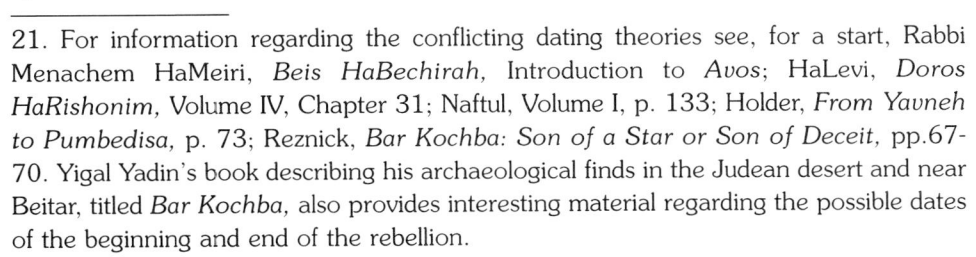

Coin minted by Hadrian

---

21. For information regarding the conflicting dating theories see, for a start, Rabbi Menachem HaMeiri, *Beis HaBechirah,* Introduction to *Avos*; HaLevi, *Doros HaRishonim,* Volume IV, Chapter 31; Naftul, Volume I, p. 133; Holder, *From Yavneh to Pumbedisa,* p. 73; Reznick, *Bar Kochba: Son of a Star or Son of Deceit,* pp.67-70. Yigal Yadin's book describing his archaeological finds in the Judean desert and near Beitar, titled *Bar Kochba,* also provides interesting material regarding the possible dates of the beginning and end of the rebellion.

22. Which two years? The four main theories are 124-126; 126-128; 128-130; and 130-132. This problem is naturally part of the discussion regarding the dates of the rebellion itself, as outlined above.

23. The Romans, like the Greeks before them, believed circumcision to be a primitive, uncivilized act of self-mutilation. The abolition of this covenant of Abraham was seen by the Romans as a necessary first step in their attempt to "civilize" the Jews. While slavery, conquest, debauchery, gladiator sports and public torture of human beings were acceptable in the elite, cultured civilization of Rome, only circumcision was not.

High Hopes

EVERY REVOLUTION HAS A spontaneous aspect to it. But in order for it to have a chance at success, the revolution requires determined, even harsh, leadership. The hateful decrees of Hadrian and the draconian methods by which he enforced them guaranteed popular, spontaneous support for a war against Rome. The determined leadership came from a now-legendary but then still obscure Jew named Shimon ben Kosiba, who was renamed *Bar Kochba* — "Son of the Star."[24] Rabbi Akiva was a staunch backer of his, proclaiming him to be worthy of being the Messiah of Israel and rallying the people to his banner. Shimon was a person of immense physical strength and spiritual influence.

He gathered about him an army of power and numbers, and the Jewish people, believing in the God of their fathers and the messianic qualities of their leader, were confident of success, even against the mighty Roman Empire. Indeed, Bar Kochba did meet with great initial success. The Roman legions retreated in front of his attacks, and much of Judah (though not the Galilee) was freed of Roman control. The Roman commander in Judah, Tinneius Rufus, seeing that Bar Kochba and his forces had outflanked the Roman defenders of Jerusalem, ordered the Roman forces defending that city back to Caesarea, there to replenish their forces and to plan the counterattack against Bar Kochba.

Jerusalem was now undefended, and with great joy and thanksgiving, Bar Kochba and his men entered the Holy City. There they proclaimed the establishment of the new commonwealth of Judah, with Jerusalem as its capital. The commonwealth would survive only

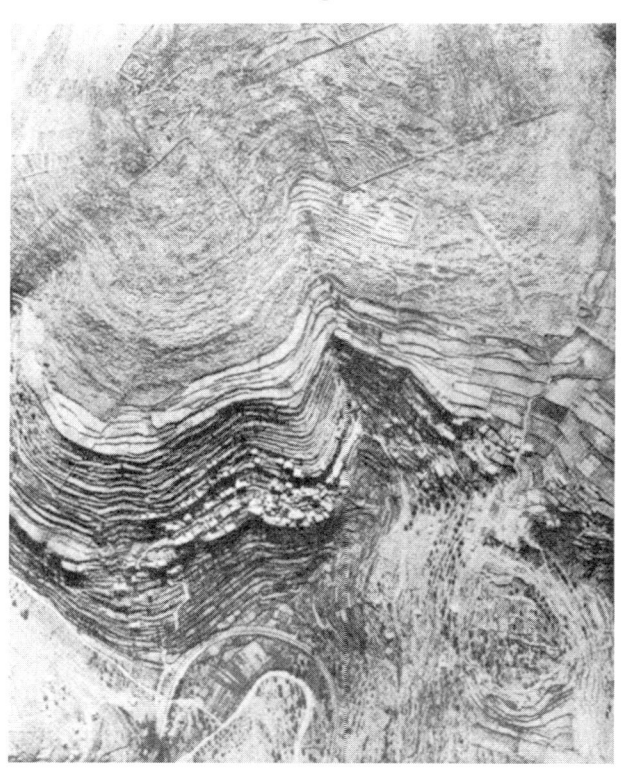

Aerial view of ruins at Beitar, with the area of the two Roman camps still visible

---

24. The "star" referred to is based on the phrase from the Bible (*Bamidbar* 24:17), "A star shall step forth from Jacob," which Jewish tradition has always understood to be a prophetic reference to the Messiah.

210 ☐ ECHOES OF GLORY

thirty months. But during that time Bar Kochba minted coins, established the trappings of government and began to clear the ruins of the Temple in preparation for the construction of the Third Temple. Jewish hopes for complete triumph ran high, but it was not to be.

The Fall of Beitar

BAR KOCHBA'S KINGDOM was barely established when Hadrian immediately sent large Roman reinforcements to Judah to snuff out the independent Jewish state. The Roman legions, advancing cautiously from Caesarea towards Jerusalem, sustained some major defeats despite their tactics and numbers. Bar Kochba's forces took a heavy toll upon Hadrian's army.[25] But the Romans were too powerful and numerous for the Jews, and the hoped-for miraculous messianic deliverance never occurred. After a year's siege, Jerusalem once again was under Roman rule.

Bar Kochba, now dispirited and paranoid, retreated to the great fortress city of Beitar, planning to fight to the death. His behavior became more and more despotic and erratic, and Rabbi Akiva, his main patron and supporter, was forced to admit publicly that Shimon ben Kosiba was no longer worthy to be a candidate for messianic recognition. In Beitar, Bar Kochba quarreled bitterly with the rabbis, whom he suspected of disloyalty to him, and he even had his own uncle, the famous scholar Rabbi Elazar HaModa'i, executed on false charges of treason. This brutal and immoral act lost for Bar Kochba any remaining rabbinic support. Treason did abound in Beitar, but it was another Jew not associated with the rabbis who betrayed the defenses to the Roman legions. Beitar fell on the ninth day of Av, that infamously sad day on the Jewish historical calendar, and Bar Kochba and all the inhabitants of Beitar were put to the sword. Both Jewish and Roman sources place the number of Jewish dead resulting from the sack of Beitar and its aftermath in the hundreds of thousands.[26] Thus did this final Jewish bid for national independence from Rome end in a sea of blood and tears.

Coins of Bar Kochba

---

25. In fact, the famous XXII Legion of Rome was completely annihilated by Bar Kochba, and its standard was never again raised within the armed forces of Rome.
26. See Talmud, *Gittin* 57a, and Talmud Yerushalmi, *Taanis* Chapter 4, section 5.

Artifacts from the Bar Kochba era

A letter from Bar Kochba

A Failed Promise

THE BAR KOCHBA EXPERIENCE would be the first of many unrealized opportunities in Jewish post-Second Temple history. Due to his acts of bravery on behalf of the Jewish people and his initial successes, he would fare better in Jewish memory than later false messiahs, but Bar Kochba was nevertheless a bitter disappointment of major proportions to the Jewish people. It would not be he, the warrior and failed messiah, who would become the legendary hero of his people. Rather, it would be his original aged supporter, the great sage of Israel, Rabbi Akiva, who would emerge as the dominant heroic Jewish figure of that terrible time. Bar Kochba was unable to defeat Rome. Rabbi Akiva was able to do so.

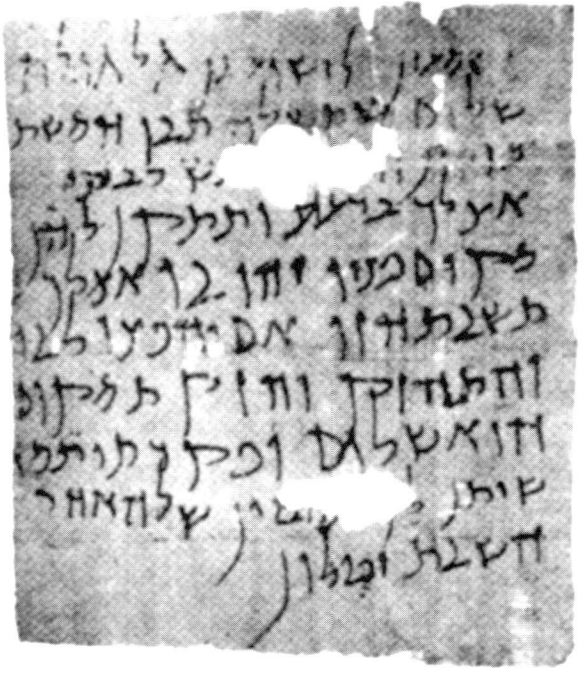

212 ☐ ECHOES OF GLORY

13

Rabbi Akiva and the Aftermath of Bar Kochba's Defeat

IN EVERY GENERATION there are people of influence and power who dominate the story of that time. However, there are also people of such influence and social power that they remain dominant figures in civilization for all later times as well. Rabbi Akiva ben Yosef, the great sage and leader of Israel, is such a person.

The bond of love forged between Rabbi Akiva and the Jewish people remains as strong and lasting today as it was when it was first created almost nineteen centuries ago, for Rabbi Akiva represented in his personality all the life values and character strengths that Torah imparts to humans. Rabbi Akiva was so much the epitome of Torah that the Talmud has Moses stating to God, upon peering far into the prophetic future and seeing the personal greatness of Rabbi Akiva, "Lord of the universe, You have such a person as Rabbi Akiva through whom You could grant the Torah to Israel, and You have instead chosen to do so through me?!"[1]

Unschooled and ignorant of Torah knowledge until after his marriage, the moment he began to study Torah at the yeshivah of Rabbi Eliezer, he pursued it with unwavering fervor. Rabbi Akiva rose by dint of his personal commitment and intellectual brilliance to represent Torah scholarship unparalleled, so much so that his older colleague and frequent disputant, Rabbi Tarfon, upon being convinced of the correctness of one of Rabbi Akiva's halachic opinions, retracted his own ruling in the matter and stated, "Akiva, leaving you [and your Torah decisions] is as [serious as] leaving life

---

1. *Menachos* 29b.

itself!"[2] The rabbis of the Talmud established the halachic rule that the law of Israel would always conform with Rabbi Akiva's opinion unless many of his colleagues openly disagreed with him.[3] There were many others, in his time and after, who were great and famous Torah scholars, but Rabbi Akiva did not simply study Torah, teach Torah and organize the laws and traditions of Torah — Rabbi Akiva *was* Torah, to such a unique degree that it was he who became enshrined in the hearts of the Jews ever after.

Rabbi Akiva was gentleness and compassion incarnate. His devotion to and appreciation of his beloved wife, Rachel, is encapsulated in the phrase that he shared with his students: "All that is mine [in Torah greatness] and all that is yours [in what you have learned from me] is truly hers."[4]

Originally of poor and humble circumstances, and a descendant of converts, he became a very wealthy man later in life. He also represented the Jews and the Torah to the Roman aristocracy, upholding in debate and action the truth and nobility of his faith and his people. Yet in spite of his changed and improved circumstances, he always remained the representative of the poor and the lowly,[5] their champion and benefactor. To him the commandment "Love your fellow as yourself"[6] was the great general rule of the Torah and its standard for Jewish behavior.[7] Yet Rabbi Akiva was the man of steel when necessary, unbending in devotion to the Torah and people of Israel.

It was he who rallied the Jews to the cause of Bar Kochba and Jewish independence. His tenacity and inner strength was unbounded. The defeat of Bar Kochba, the disappointment of the failed potential messiah, the awful slaughter that marked the fall of Beitar, the death of 24,000 of his own students in little more than a month's time,[8] the internal quarrels and disputes that then threatened to erode the strength of the remnant of Jewry, the cruelty of Rome and its

---

2. Talmud, *Kiddushin* 66b.

3. Talmud, *Eruvin* 46b.

4. Talmud, *Kesubos* 63a.

5. Talmud, *Kiddushin* 27a.

6. *Vayikra* 19:18.

7. Jerusalem Talmud, *Nedarim,* Chapter 9, section 4.

8. This is the basis for the period of semi-mourning that Jews observe between the holidays of *Pesach* and *Shavuos.*

seemingly never-ending domination over Israel, all did not dim his spirit, weaken his faith, or impeach his love for the God, people and Land of Israel.

Rabbi Akiva was always optimistic and accepting. His great teacher, Nachum Ish Gamzu, had taught him that "everything that God does is for the best,"[9] and Rabbi Akiva never wavered from that faith. "The world is always judged kindly"[10] was his motto. Others might weep and despair when viewing the ruins of Jerusalem and the Temple, but Rabbi Akiva, seeing beyond today's ruins into the time of tomorrow's rebuilding, smiled in contemplation of the future.[11] In all later generations, Jews in terribly difficult times of seeming despair would look back to Rabbi Akiva for inspiration and succor.

A True Martyr

RABBI AKIVA ALSO SERVES as the prime example of martyrdom in Jewish life. There were many Jews who died for their faith long before Rabbi Akiva's arrival on the scene. As noted earlier, the era of the Hellenists and the Hasmoneans was replete with stories of excruciating martyrdom suffered by Jews in observance and defense of their faith — but Rabbi Akiva's execution on Yom Kippur[12] (c. 136) in the hippodrome of Caesarea marked a definitive moment of Jewish martyrdom. The old man, his skin flayed by iron combs, his people hounded and persecuted by mighty Rome, views himself and his career not as defeated but as triumphant. His last words — "Hear O Israel, the Lord our God, the Lord is One" — are not uttered in the agony of loss or the despair of abandonment, but in the serenity of faith and soul.

All of his years as a student and teacher of Torah, the Angel of Death had been his constant companion, and Rabbi Akiva fully un-

---

9. Talmud, *Berachos* 60b.
10. Mishnah, *Avos,* Chapter 3, section 17.
11. Talmud, *Makkos* 24a-b.
12. There is another tradition amongst Jews that Rabbi Akiva was executed on 5 Tishrei, five days before Yom Kippur. There is a third tradition that he was executed on 9 Tishrei, the day preceeding Yom Kippur. See A. Stern, *Malitzei Esh* (Jerusalem, 1975).

Tomb of Rabbi Akiva

derstood that his path of teaching Torah and supporting Jewish independence against Roman tyranny could eventually lead to his agonizing martyrdom.[13] But he never wavered or flinched. Tradition has his holy body whisked away from Caesarea to Tiberias by angels, there to be buried in the cemetery-mountain near the graves of his beloved students. The folk appreciation, "Fortunate are you, Rabbi Akiva, that you are martyred for the sake of Torah,"[14] placed a different meaning on such martyrdom for all later generations of Jews. To be Rabbi Akiva's partner, to emulate his greatness, to share his optimism and hope, to be nurtured from the wellsprings of his devotion to God and Israel, all of this made martyrdom acceptable to Jews throughout the ages. Only the willingness and ability of Jews — great and simple, scholarly and untutored, those physically strong and those broken of body — to die for Judaism made it possible for Jewish life to survive and prosper throughout the long night of exile. And it was this ability and strength of character that Rabbi Akiva left as his final gift to his beloved people.

Rabbi Akiva's martyrdom was part of the unrelenting persecution of Jews and Judaism that became Roman policy in conquered Judah after Bar Kochba's defeat and the destruction of Beitar.

The Romans had decided to rid themselves of their Jewish prob-

---

13. Talmud, *Berachos* 61b.
14. Ibid.

lem, primarily in Judah, once and for all. They therefore, really for the first time, concentrated not so much on the Jews as a people but on Judaism and its Torah. Their plan was to eliminate the scholars and sages of Israel, who were, after all, the true leaders of the Jews, and to forbid the practice of Judaism, the lifeblood of Israel, thus guaranteeing the Jews' demise as a counterforce to Roman culture and hegemony. The Sabbath, circumcision, public study and teaching of Torah, as well as observances of all Jewish ritual and customs, were forbidden. Thousands of Jews were executed during this time of terror, the rabbis and their yeshivas were decimated and dispersed, and the survivors were driven underground. The rabbis felt their world "desolate,"[15] but in the face of this implacable enemy they nevertheless did not collapse in their faith and tenacity of spirit. Indeed, many great men, in addition to Rabbi Akiva, were martyred for the sake of Judaism,[16] but even these tragedies did not fatally discourage the people. Somehow the determination of the Jews to survive as Jews did not falter.

New leaders and scholars would arise, many of them disciples of Rabbi Akiva, who would take upon themselves the arduous task of rebuilding the Jewish people, spiritually and physically. Rabbi Meir, Rabbi Yehudah ben Il'ai, Rabbi Nassan HaBavli, Rabbi Reuven ben Itztrobuli, Rabbi Shimon bar Yochai and Rabbi Yossi are some of the new leaders who would come to the fore to save Israel in this desperate hour. With the spirit and example of Rabbi Akiva as their inspiration and in spite of great personal risk, these men would fight the Romans and their decrees, first in a clandestine fashion, but later openly and boldly. And eventually they would prevail in the struggle.

Rabbi Akiva's Disciples

THIS LASTING LEGACY of Rabbi Akiva to Israel, tenacity in the face of anything, is also represented in the words of his student, Rabbi Yehudah: "The world was desolate until Rabbi Akiva came to our rabbis in the south [of

---

15. Talmud, *Yevamos* 62a.
16. The legendary tale of the *"Ten Martyrs of Israel"* mentioned in the Midrash and in the Ashkenazic prayer liturgy of *Yom Kippur* and *Tisha B'Av* is a reference to the scholarly victims of Hadrian's draconian persecutions after the fall of Beitar, even though not all of the ten martyrs described therein are actually of that time period.

Tomb of Rabbi Meir in Tiberias

Israel] and there taught Torah to Rabbi Meir, Rabbi Yehudah, Rabbi Yossi, Rabbi Shimon bar Yochai and Rabbi Elazar ben Shamua. He said to them, 'My first group of disciples [the 24,000 who died as described above] died because they were narrow-visioned and unaccommodating one to another. Be careful not to follow their example. Instead, rise [jointly] and fill the entire Land of Israel with Torah.' "[17]

And rise they did. Rabbi Meir, the greatest and yet most enigmatic of Rabbi Akiva's disciples,[18] created the body of halachic opinion that was a main repository of the Oral Law and upon which Rabbi Yehudah HaNasi, in a following generation, would base much of his monumental work, the *Mishnah*. The rabbis stated that any Mishnah that Rabbi Yehudah HaNasi quoted anonymously was from the school of Rabbi Meir.[19]

Rabbi Meir, descended from converts to Judaism, was married to one of the legendary women in Jewish history, Beruriah, the daughter of the martyred saint and scholar Rabbi Chanina ben Tradyon. Dogged by personal tragedies and almost unbelievable family reverses, he was nevertheless Meir — *the light* of Israel — to his people. He is also the miracle worker of Jewish tradition, Rabbi Meir *Baal HaNess* ("*Controller of Miracles*"), and his maxim "God of Meir, an-

---

17. Talmud, *Yevamos* 62a.
18. Talmud, *Eruvin* 13b.
19. Talmud, *Sanhedrin* 86a.

swer me" remains the hope of Jews in distress until today. His love for Jews and the Land of Israel was boundless, and when he died in Asia Minor, forced to flee there by personal troubles, internecine conflict and Roman persecution, he ordered his body to be buried at the Mediterranean seashore so that, through the medium of the connecting waters, he would be reunited with his beloved Land of Israel.[20]

Acher

AS COULD BE EXPECTED after such a monumental historical disaster as the destruction of Beitar and the attendant brutal persecution of Jews and Judaism by the Romans, there were Jews who lost hope and faith. Just as in modern Jewish history, when the Holocaust engendered searing questions of faith throughout the Jewish world, so too in the generation of Beitar did the oppression of Rome cause many Jews to question the Divine Will and plan.

Foremost amongst those whose faith was shaken by the Roman persecution of the rabbis of Israel was the great scholar and one of the teachers of Rabbi Meir, Elisha ben Avuyah. In despair and doubt, Elisha abandoned the practice of Judaism and came to be called by the rabbis *Acher ("the Other/Different/ Changed One")*. His example was a dangerous one, especially in such volatile and difficult times, and the rabbis made an example of his apostasy and shunned him in order to prevent his behavior from further eroding the faith of Israel amongst less scholarly Jews. However, Rabbi Meir did not abandon his isolated and now embittered friend and mentor. He continued to maintain contact with him, even discussing complicated matters of halachic decision with him. Rabbi Meir attempted always to win Elisha back and even after Elisha's death interceded with heaven on his behalf. But Elisha, like many other tragic apostates in Jewish history, had by then completely given up on himself, and Rabbi Meir's efforts were therefore not as successful as he had hoped.

---

20. Jewish tradition also has his body later being reinterred in the Land of Israel, on a hill near Tiberias facing the presumed cave of burial of his great mentor, Rabbi Akiva.

Ambivalence Towards Rome

IN THIS CLIMATE OF DEFEAT, doubt and despair, the rabbis themselves were of different minds as to what policy ought to be pursued with Rome. After the period of total fury against the Jews that followed Beitar, the Roman oppression began to slacken. Hadrian himself died in 139 and was succeeded by the more moderate and cautious Antoninus Pius.

The Roman administration that persecuted the Jews in the Land of Israel was still in place, but it also began to relax its strong hand while awaiting new direction from Rome. By 142, Tinneius Rufus, the cruel procurator of Judah,[21] was removed from office. Antoninus Pius rethought the hateful policies of his predecessor and, though the anti-Jewish laws were not yet officially revoked, the Jews of Judah became more hopeful. But times were still treacherous.

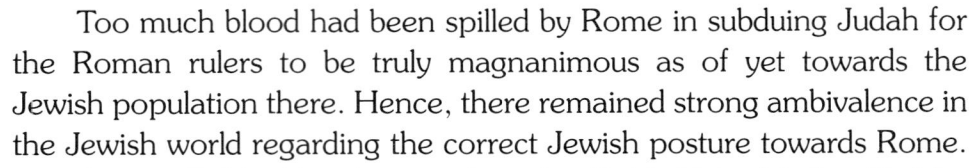

Too much blood had been spilled by Rome in subduing Judah for the Roman rulers to be truly magnanimous as of yet towards the Jewish population there. Hence, there remained strong ambivalence in the Jewish world regarding the correct Jewish posture towards Rome.

Among Rabbi Akiva's great disciples, Rabbi Yehudah (bar Il'ai) favored a more conciliatory, cooperative and complimentary attitude towards Rome, its government and achievements. Because of this, Rome now saw him as the leading spokesman for Jewish interests in Judah and granted him official status.[22] Rabbi Yossi (ben Chalafta) was of a much less positive frame of mind regarding Rome, essentially advocating a position of non-cooperative passivity towards Roman interests and policies.[23] Rabbi Shimon bar Yochai was vehement in his opposition to Rome, refusing any accommodation to it.[24] The Romans, always sensitive to criticism and possible subversion, exiled Rabbi Yossi to Sepphoris in the Galilee and condemned Rabbi Shimon to death. Rabbi Shimon fled and was forced into hiding, but was miraculously sustained in his lonely desert cave by water and fruit. There, in isolated seclusion, he developed into the legendary holy

Antoninus Pius

---

21. In contemporary terms, we could say that Tinneius Rufus was Hadrian's Himmler.
22. Talmud, *Shabbos* 33b.
23. Ibid.
24. Ibid.

man of Israel, to whom tradition ascribes the great work of mystic *Kabbala,* the *Zohar.*[25] But it would be years before he could safely leave his hiding place and resume his leadership role amongst the rabbis of Judah.

Hope for Peace

AS LONG AS THE HATEFUL DECREES of Hadrian remained in effect, the rabbis cautiously searched for an opening that would allow them to entreat Rome for the final repeal. Rabbi Reuven ben Itztrobuli headed a distinguished delegation of rabbis,[26] about 148, in an initial, exploratory attempt to petition Rome. Unfortunately, this attempt was met with failure. Seven years later, another delegation of great rabbis from Judah journeyed to Rome. This one was headed by a most unlikely leader, Rabbi Shimon bar Yochai, only recently returned to public life after his years of hiding and solitude. Remarkably, this rabbinic delegation was blessed with success. The Roman paranoia regarding the Jews had subsided, and the cold rationality of having Judah as a peaceful province rather than maintaining it as a hotbed of violence took hold of the Roman deliberations. And most importantly, Antoninus Pius was not Hadrian. Time and circumstances had also moderated Rabbi Shimon's view of Rome and his opinion about how the Jewish community should react towards the conqueror.[27] An era of good feelings between Rome and Jerusalem seemed possible now.

The cave of R' Shimon bar Yochai

Hadrian

---

25. See this author's *Herald of Destiny* (*Shaar Press,* Brooklyn, 1993), p. 230, ff., regarding the issue of authorship and publication of the *Zohar.*

26. Missing from any public role during the early years of Antoninus Pius' reign was Rabban Shimon ben Gamliel II. Hunted by the Romans during the last years of Hadrian, Rabban Shimon ben Gamliel II, as his father before him, was prevented for much of his life from asserting publicly his hereditary role of authority as the *Nasi* — the head of the Sanhedrin and the princely leader of Israel. Therefore, the leadership of Israel was perforce asserted by others.

27. Rabbi Shimon bar Yochai's own son, the famed Rabbi Elazar ben Shimon, would within a few years already find employment in the service of the Roman administration in Judah! See Talmud, *Bava Metzia* 83b.

The Power of the *Nasi*

IN ABOUT 158 THE RABBIS attempted to return the Sanhedrin and main yeshivah in Judah to Yavneh, its traditional home. The Yavneh group was headed by Rabbi Yehudah, Rabbi Yossi, Rabbi Shimon bar Yochai, Rabbi Elazar ben Yossi and Rabbi Yehoshua ben Korcha.[28] Rabban Shimon ben Gamliel II still remained in his secluded Galilean home, not daring an open return to Yavneh. However, his young son Yehudah, who would later become the leader and teacher of all Israel as Rabbi Yehudah HaNasi (Rebbi) did come to Yavneh to study.[29]

The experiment of reestablishing Yavneh's primacy proved politically premature, and the center of the Sanhedrin was forced to continue to remain in Usha in the Galilee. But the rabbis now felt that the failure of Yavneh could endanger Usha as well. They therefore transferred the seat of the Sanhedrin to Shefar'am, a smaller village also in the Galilee, a locale less likely to be seen as a provocation by the Roman authorities.

Even there, close to his own home, Rabban Shimon ben Gamliel II did not take control of the Sanhedrin. Though he remained the *Nasi*, he was unable to exercise any of the powers of that office effectively. This anomaly would lead to a serious dispute among the rabbis, similar in scope, if not in intensity, to the one that had wracked the reign of Rabban Gamliel II of Yavneh fifty years earlier.

During the years of Hadrian's persecution of the rabbis, many of the scholars left the Land of Israel to find refuge in the Diaspora, especially in Babylonia. The scattering of the scholars served further to diminish the base of authority of the *Nasi* in Judah, since in a practical sense these great men were no longer under his personal, local jurisdiction.

When the persecutions diminished under the reign of Antoninus Pius, many of the Babylonian scholars came west to the Land of Israel again. However, their years in Babylonia and other Jewish communi-

---

28. He was the son of Rabbi Akiva, but was always euphemistically referred to as the son of *Korcha* ("the Bald One," i.e., Akiva) to avoid name recognition by Rome and its possible revenge against the family of Rabbi Akiva.

29. *Midrash Rabbah, Bereishis,* Chapter 76, section 7. Also see Naftul, Volume I, p. 161.

ties had given them a new spirit of independence vis-a-vis the authority of the *Nasi* in Judah. When Rabban Shimon ben Gamliel II attempted to bolster the authority and prestige of his office as the Sanhedrin was being reconstituted at Shefar'am, he met with determined opposition. His two main antagonists were Rabbi Nassan ("the Babylonian") and Rabbi Meir.[30] The dispute over the powers of the *Nasi* eventually caused Rabbi Meir to retire from public life and, when personal tragedy occurred in his domestic life, even to leave the Land of Israel. The Roman authorities exploited the rift in the Sanhedrin by their own new decrees and diminished the powers and the role of the *Nasi* as the temporal leader of Israel. Thus, Rabban Shimon ben Gamliel II's attempt to strengthen the position of *Nasi* led to a setback. It would not be until decades later that Rabban Shimon ben Gamliel II's son, Rabbi Yehudah (Rabbi), would be successful in restoring the full traditional powers of the *Nasi* to the office.

Antoninus and Rabbi

ANTONINUS PIUS DIED in 161 and was succeeded by his son-in-law, the gifted philosopher-emperor, Marcus Aurelius Antoninus. Marcus Aurelius was a man of many talents and superior intellect. He was a firm ruler, a warrior when necessary, and an able and efficient administrator. His abilities were immediately tested in 162 when the Parthians again made war against Rome on the eastern borders of the empire. Aurelius dispatched the famed Roman general Lucius Verus to conduct the campaign. Astutely enough, Marcus Aurelius realized that Judah was a necessary base for the pursuit of the war against the Parthians. He therefore moved to mollify the Jews of Judah in order to secure their allegiance to the Roman war effort. That war, which was not successfully completed until 166, allowed Marcus Aurelius to come into contact with the Jewish leaders of Judah.

Marcus Aurelius

Meanwhile, after the death of Rabban Shimon ben Gamliel II in

---

30. See Talmud, *Horios* 13b.

about 163, his son Rabbi Yehudah (Rabbi) became *Nasi*. This remarkable person overshadowed all of his compatriots, so that within a short period of time he was recognized as the temporal and spiritual leader of Judah. All matters of public policy were left to his review and decision. Providentially, in the course of the Parthian war, Marcus Aurelius met Rabbi, and they became friends and eventually confidants. Jewish tradition viewed this friendship between the philosopher-emperor of Rome and the holy teacher of Israel as the symbolic reunification of Esau and Jacob, the sons of Isaac and Rebecca of long ago. Their individual intellects, wealth and talents complemented each other to such a degree that "Antoninus (the name that Marcus Aurelius is known by in Jewish tradition)[31] and Rabbi" became an inseparable pair in Jewish lore.

The friendship of the Roman emperor with the *Nasi* of Israel naturally brought about a period of tranquility and harmony in Roman-Jewish relations. All of the decrees of Hadrian were now completely removed from the Roman law books, and Rome ruled Judah with a soft hand and a cooperative spirit.

The land itself experienced a physical, economic and spiritual rebirth. The Babylonian and other Diaspora scholars flocked to Rabbi's yeshivah at Beis She'arim in the Galilee, and he and his court became the acknowledged center of world Jewish life. Marcus Aurelius consulted with his friend in Judah on matters of state policy as well as on personal questions.[32] His philosophic bent and inquiring mind demanded that he take advantage of a resource such as that which Rabbi represented. The years of Marcus Aurelius' reign, ending in his death in 180, was the high-water mark in the intercourse between Rome and the Jews. The Jews, under the leadership of Rabbi, would use this period of blissful respite to prepare themselves for the struggle of darker days surely lurking around the corner.

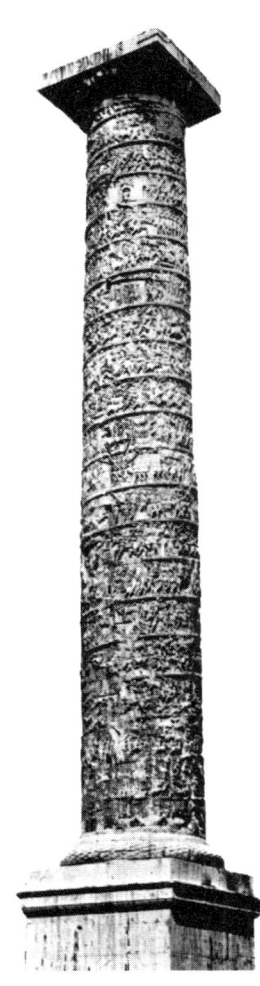

Marcus Aurelius' column in Rome

---

31. Most Jewish historians have identified the "Antoninus" of the Talmud, who was the friend of Rabbi, with Marcus Aurelius. However, there are those who prefer to believe that the Talmud's "Antoninus" was in fact Antoninus Pius, the emperor who preceded Marcus Aurelius on the Roman throne. This latter position is difficult to maintain because of the chronology of Rabbi and the less-than-sanguine character of Antoninus Pius as compared with that of Marcus Aurelius. There is also an opinion that "Antoninus" is the son of Marcus Aurelius, Commodus.

32. There is a tradition amongst Jews that Marcus Aurelius even considered conversion to Judaism for himself and the royal family, but was dissuaded by Rabbi.

In 165 an epidemic of the plague swept the Roman world. It would not abate until it ran its natural course in 167. Tens of thousands died, and no one knew why. It was only because of the wisdom and rationality of Marcus Aurelius, who allowed no scapegoating for this natural disaster to occur, that Jews and other minorities were spared persecution over this outbreak of disease. The father of modern medicine, Galen,[33] flourished during this time, and the first hesitant steps towards knowing and understanding human physiology began with him, under the encouragement of Marcus Aurelius.

Even during the reign of Marcus Aurelius, however, the Roman authorities continued their ruthless attempt to suppress Christianity, which had made significant inroads amongst Roman society, including people of both high and low class. Rome actually felt itself more threatened by the spread of the new religion in the empire than by the armed forces of its enemies constantly probing its outermost borders. The fact that the Jews enjoyed the benign favor of the emperor at the very same time that Christians were being martyred[34] for their faith by Rome only served to exacerbate the poor relations between the early Church fathers and the Jews. Eventually, dire consequences resulted from this.

Marcus Aurelius' reign was also marked by an ongoing major war with the Germanic tribes of central Europe. From 168 till 175 the bitter struggle raged, with Rome finally subduing its barbarian enemies. Marcus Aurelius sensed that Christianity from within and the unrelenting pressure of the barbarian tribes from without would eventually defeat Rome. But he was determined that it would not happen on his watch.

In his famous philosophic work,[35] Marcus Aurelius already envisioned a world without empires. He sought to build a strong inner person who would be able to weather all external storms and, based on rationality and inner morality, produce a better world. But alas, the forces of history that succeeded him would not yet allow for such a sanguine future. Nevertheless, his association with Rabbi Yehudah HaNasi contributed to a major accomplishment, the composing of the *Mishnah*. In the following chapter, I will discuss that work and further expound upon the life of Rabbi Yehudah HaNasi, the leading person behind it.

---

33. Probably a Hellenistic Egyptian.
34. In 165, the famous Christian leader of the early Church, Justin Martyr, was executed in heinous fashion by the Roman authorities.
35. *Meditations,* composed in six years of intensive effort, from 174 to 180.

Section IV

Torah Remains Eternal

14
Mishnah

RABBI YEHUDAH HANASI (*The Prince*), whom we mentioned in the previous chapter, is one of those historic personages whose influence and accomplishments remain important even in much later times. In this respect he is the disciple and image of Rabbi Akiva even though he never met that great sage of Israel.

Rabbi Yehudah HaNasi was the son of Rabbi Shimon ben Gamliel II. He incorporated within himself intellect, leadership qualities, personal charisma, holy behavior[1] and an overriding sense of responsibility for the destiny of the Jewish people. Because of this unique combination of outstanding personal characteristics, he became known throughout the Jewish world and centuries as *Rabbi*, our teacher, mentor and guide. However, it was Rabbi's friendship with Marcus Aurelius and with his son and successor, Commodus,[2] that allowed Rabbi to take the necessary steps to guarantee Jewish survival. The window of tranquility in Judah, which lasted only decades (170-200), nevertheless afforded Rabbi and his colleagues the opportunity to solidify the position of the scholars and yeshivos, free from Roman interference and persecution. Rabbi would make good use of the respite afforded the Jews in Judah.

Commodus

---

1. Rabbi Yehudah HaNasi was also known as *Rabbeinu HaKadosh* (*Our Holy Teacher*). His reputation for sanctity was exemplary even in a time when there were many outstanding holy scholars among the Jewish people.
2. Commodus succeeded to the throne of Rome after the death of Marcus Aurelius in 180. He ruled until his assassination in 192. Neither in intellect nor in disposition was he his father's son. Nevertheless, though he was considered a cruel and intolerant emperor by most, he remained friendly and well disposed towards Rabbi and the Jewish people.

Rabbi's Project

RABBI YEHUDAH HANASI'S main base was in Beis She'arim, a village in the Galilee.[3] He gathered around him in Galilee the scholars of Israel and reestablished a main yeshivah, a new Yavneh. This great accomplishment of unifying the previously scattered schools of the major teachers of Israel and thereby giving central authority to the reconstituted Galilean Sanhedrin allowed Rabbi to pursue an even more ambitious and far-reaching project — that of codifying and committing to writing the great number of disparate rules, interpretations and practical definitions of the Torah which were encompassed under the Oral Law.

As explained earlier, the Oral Law, transmitted from Moses through the generations of Jewish life, was never edited and placed in a book form for mass public use. The Oral Law itself contained a biblical stricture which apparently prevented the written Torah from being transmitted orally and the

---

3. There are well-preserved ruins of a synagogue, homes, and burial caves that may be seen at Beis She'arim today.

Tombstone in Beis She'arim marks the grave of two girls, a daughter of Rabbi Shimon ben Gamliel and a daughter of Rabbi Yehudah HaNasi

Entrance to the burial niches at Beis She'arim

230 ☐ ECHOES OF GLORY

Synagogue at Beis She'arim — arch at entrance

Oral Law from being transmitted in a public, written, book form.[4] However, Rabbi, with the concurrence of his rabbinic colleagues, took the bold step of permitting the Oral Law to be codified and published in the form of a book to be used for public reference and study.[5] This book came to be known as *Mishnah*.

Notebooks of the Scholars

RABBI'S MISHNAH WAS NOT born fully formed by his efforts alone. From the time of Ezra and the Men of the Great Assembly onward, individual scholars had composed notebooks that formed the basis of their lectures and studies.[6] Over time, these notebooks became generally available

---

4. See Talmud, *Gittin* 60.

5. The legal justification for allowing the Oral Law to be recorded in writing as a book was based upon the verse in Psalms (119:126), "It is a time to perform for God; they have nullified Your Torah." The Rabbis interpreted this to mean that in extreme emergency situations the rabbinic leaders of Israel may, so to speak, "nullify Your Torah in order to perform for God." See Talmud, *Gittin* 60a, *Berachos* 54a, and *Yoma* 69a for examples of this rabbinic right put into action. Needless to say, the attempted use of this prerogative by the rabbis of any age would be subject to careful debate, scrutiny and even controversy. Only the leadership of such an exceptional person as Rabbi Yehudah HaNasi enabled such a major departure from previous tradition as the publication of the Oral Law in book form — Mishnah — to become accepted as legitimate and recognized by all of the rabbis of Israel.

6. The two great works regarding the formation of the Mishnah and its evolution are, in my opinion, *Doros HaRishonim* by Rabbi Yitzchak Isaac HaLevi and *Yesod HaMishnah V'Arichasa* by Rabbi Reuven Margolis. Both works have been reprinted numerous times by Israeli publishing houses and are widely available.

ORDERS AND TRACTATES

	TRACTATE	TOPIC
SEDER ZERAIM	BERACHOS	Blessings and prayers
	PEAH	The "corner of the field" left for the poor to harvest
	DEMAI	The laws of produce, about which there is doubt whether tithes were taken
	KILAYIM	Forbidden mixtures of seeds, animals, and cloth
	SHEVIIS	The Sabbatical year, when the land is given a rest from agricultural work
	TERUMOS	Produce set aside for the *Kohanim*
	MAASEROS	The tithe set aside for the Levites
	MAASER SHENI	The tithe set aside to be eaten in Jerusalem
	CHALLAH	The portion of dough set aside for the *Kohanim*
	ORLAH	Laws of fruit produced by a tree during its first four years
	BIKKURIM	First-fruits, brought to the Temple for a special ceremony
SEDER MOED	SHABBOS	Laws of the weekly Day of Rest
	ERUVIN	Laws concerning the *techum Shabbos* and carrying within enclosed areas
	PESACHIM	Laws of the Pesach festival and its offerings
	SHEKALIM	The donation required of every Jew for the upkeep of the Temple and purchase of communal offerings
	YOMA	Laws of Yom Kippur
	SUCCAH	Laws of the Succos festival
	BEITZAH	Laws of *Yom Tov*
	ROSH HASHANAH	Determination of the calendar; laws of the *shofar* and the prayers for Rosh HaShanah
	TAANIS	Laws of the public fasts
	MEGILLAH	Reading the Torah and the Scroll of Esther in the synagogue; the Purim festival
	MOED KATAN	The Intermediate Days of the festivals; laws of mourning
	CHAGIGAH	Laws of the festival sacrifices
SEDER NASHIM	YEVAMOS	Levirate marriage
	KESUBOS	Marriage obligations and the marriage contract
	NEDARIM	Vows
	NAZIR	Laws of the nazirite
	SOTAH	Concerning the Temple ceremony to test a woman suspected of adultery
	GITTIN	Laws of divorce
	KIDDUSHIN	Laws of marriage

232 ☐ ECHOES OF GLORY

OF THE MISHNAH

	TRACTATE	TOPIC
SEDER NEZIKIN	BAVA KAMMA	Civil damages
	BAVA METZIA	Responsibility in regard to found, borrowed, or rented property; loans, employees, rentals
	BAVA BASRA	Rights and responsibilities of neighbors; other civil cases; inheritance
	SANHEDRIN	The court system; the various capital punishments
	MAKKOS	Offenses punishable by lashing
	SHEVUOS	Oaths
	EDUYOS	Various testimonies given by *Tannaim*
	AVODAH ZARAH	Idolatry; laws concerning gentiles
	AVOS	Basic moral and ethical principles
	HORAYOS	Offerings in cases of erroneous rulings
SEDER KODASHIM	ZEVACHIM	Animal sacrifices
	MENACHOS	Sacrifices of flour and other produce
	CHULLIN	Kosher slaughter and other dietary laws
	BECHOROS	Laws of firstborn animals and of the firstborn son
	ARACHIN	Pledges of Temple donations based on the value assigned to persons
	TEMURAH	Laws regarding substitution of one sacrificial animal for another
	KEREISOS	Transgressions punishable by *kares* (Divine extirpation)
	MEILAH	Prohibition against personal use of Temple property
	TAMID	Description of the daily routine in the Temple
	MIDDOS	The dimensions of the Temple and its furnishings
	KINNIM	Bird sacrifices
SEDER TAHAROS	KEILIM	Ritual purity of vessels
	OHALOS	The *tumah* (ritual impurity) of corpses
	NEGAIM	The *tumah* of the skin conditions known as *tzara'as*
	PARAH	Laws of the Red Cow; mixture of its ashes with well water
	TAHAROS	Various rules regarding the *tumah* of foods and liquids
	MIKVAOS	Regarding *mikveh* and immersion in it
	NIDDAH	The *tumah* of menstruation
	MACHSHIRIN	How foods and liquids become *tamei* (ritually impure)
	ZAVIM	Bodily emissions that cause *tumah*
	TEVUL YOM	The status of *tumah* from immersion until sunset
	YADAYIM	Ritual washing of hands
	UKTZIN	Which parts of plants can become *tamei*

TORAH REMAINS ETERNAL

amongst the scholars and students of the yeshivos. These written notes were used as student reference texts and memory aids, while the main study of the contents of the Oral Law remained, as before, transmitted personally from one generation to the next by oral study and debate.

These earlier notebooks were identified with certain periods of time and specific scholars. Thus, the notes of the *Zugos* were known under the general heading of *Mishnah Rishonah* (*the First Mishnah*), while other, later notebooks were known as the *Mishnah of Rabbi Akiva,* or in a still later generation as the *Mishnah of Rabbi Meir.* All of this earlier scholarship and work formed the base upon which Rabbi Yehudah HaNasi built and edited the Mishnah in its final form. But even though the Mishnah contained the work of previous generations, the spirit and unity of the book, its classic, concise style and soaring Hebrew language, its nuances and choices of opinions, all were the reflections of the intellect, holiness and authority of Rabbi.

Sections of the Mishnah

THE BASIC STRUCTURE of the Mishnah, which became the skeletal form of the Talmud, consists of six main sections (*shisha sedarim* in Hebrew, or in its abbreviated form, *shas*).[7] These sections are 1) *Zeraim* (containing the laws of blessings and prayer as well as the Torah's rules of agriculture which apply primarily in the Land of Israel), 2) *Moed* (including the laws of the Sabbath and holy days of the year), 3) *Nashim* (dealing with the laws of domestic relations, vows and the *nazir*), 4) *Nezikim* (treating the laws of torts, criminal law, commercial transactions, partnerships and inheritance), 5) *Kodashim* (involving the laws of the Temple and its services and sacrifices, as well as the rules of kosher food) and 6) *Taharos* (describing the laws of family, Temple and priestly purity and defilement, and of the methods allowing for purification from such defilement).

---

7. The word *Shas* has become synonymous with Talmud even though its strict origins refer to Mishnah and not necessarily Talmud. Nevertheless, since the Talmud adopted the order and structure of the Mishnah, and the Talmud eventually dwarfed the Mishnah in size and scope, *shas* soon came to refer to the Talmud. Thus, a Talmudic scholar was known in Yiddish as a "*Shas Yid.*"

Each of these six main sections was further subdivided into individual volumes (*mesechtos*), each dealing with detailed subject matter categorized for easy associative memory and halachic determination. It is commonly accepted that there are sixty-three separate tractates to the Mishnah (and consequently to the Talmud as well).[8] Thus was the entire Oral Law formally codified, organized and presented in public book form[9] for the first time in Jewish history, under the direction, and bearing the personal imprint, of Rabbi Yehudah HaNasi.

Migration from the Homeland

IT IS IRONIC THAT DURING THIS TIME of Rabbi, the great Nasi and leader of the Jewish community in the Holy Land, the beginning of the millennia-long decline of Jewish settlement in the homeland began. Nevertheless, even though Marcus Aurelius and Commodus relaxed the Roman hand of oppression over Judah, the Jews instinctively realized that there was no longer any real opportunity for autonomous Jewish national life in Judah. The Roman population and influence were so dominant as to thwart any Jewish assertion of self-government.

At the beginning of the third century of the Common Era, the Jews enjoyed greater political, social and economic benefits in Babylonia than they did in their homeland. Thus, even during the life of Rabbi, many

Mishnah with Rambam's commentary, written in Hebrew transliteration of Arabic, in Rambam's own handwriting

---

8. There are opinions that there are actually only sixty or sixty-one tractates, depending on whether *Bava Kamma*, *Bava Metzia* and *Bava Basra* are to be counted as three volumes or as one, and whether *Sanhedrin* and *Makkos* are to be counted separately or as one volume.

9. There are doubts as to whether, even in the lifetime of Rabbi, the Mishnah was committed to book form in writing or only formulated as an oral document. See Rashi's commentary to Talmud, *Eruvin* 62a and *Kiddushin* 13a, from which one may deduce that the Mishnah was only organized in the time of Rabbi but not actually written in book form as of yet. However, see Rashi again in Talmud, *Kiddushin* 51b, where he clearly implies that there was a written text of Mishnah in the generation immediately after Rabbi.

great scholars migrated from Judah to the Jewish communities of the Diaspora, mainly to Babylonia and secondarily to Syria and Asia Minor.

One of the motivating causes of Rabbi's action in publicizing the Mishnah was his own awareness that the center of Jewish life was moving away from Judah and that the authority of the *Nasi* and the rabbis of the Holy Land in later generations would be far less than what he was able to command in his lifetime. The Mishnah was to be the last great, universally studied contribution of the Jews in the Land of Israel to the development of Torah scholarship for millennia.[10] As such, it had the bittersweet distinction of marking the end of the era of the Second Commonwealth in Jewish history.

Roman water tunnel in Tzippori

Rabbi Chiya

THE LAST SEVENTEEN YEARS of his life Rabbi spent in Tzippori (Sepphoris), away from his original home and center at Beis She'arim. Though no particular reason for this move is clearly mentioned in historical sources, it seems that Rabbi's deteriorating health and the growing uncertainty regarding ultimate Roman intentions towards the Sanhedrin contributed to this change of venue.

Rabbi's student-colleague and friend, the great Rabbi Chiya, was the emissary of Rabbi to the next generation of scholars, as well as to the masses of Israel. Rabbi Chiya foresaw the occurrence of times in which it would be necessary to rebuild Torah from scratch. Undaunted,

---

10. *Talmud Yerushalmi,* the "Jerusalem Talmud," was completed and edited in the fourth century of the Common Era, almost two centuries after the Mishnah. However, it was soon dwarfed both in size and prominence by the *Talmud Bavli,* the "Babylonian Talmud," and for long centuries it was studied by only a chosen few scholars. See below, the chapter "Talmud," for a more detailed discussion of these two works and their relative influence vis-á-vis one another.

he prepared a program for so doing, concerning which Rabbi exclaimed, "How great are the works of Chiya!"[11] Rabbi Chiya was the main catalyst in the creation of the *baraisos*[12] and in the establishment of the great yeshivos in Babylonia and in Israel[13] after the death of Rabbi.

Rabbi's Legacy

JUST BEFORE HIS DEATH, Rabbi separated the positions of official authority that had been combined within his one person and distributed them to two of his sons and one of his disciples. The position of *Nasi* was granted to his son Gamliel (III), while the title of *chacham* (wise man/adjudicator of laws) was given to his other son, Shimon. Rabbi's disciple, Rabbi Chanina bar Chama, was appointed as Rosh Yeshivah at Rabbi's yeshivah.

The Talmud tells us that at his death, Rabbi, the aristocrat who possessed high position, great power and untold wealth, was able to raise his ten fingers skyward and proclaim, "Lord of the universe, You are well aware that I have struggled through the use of these, my ten fingers, to advance the cause of Torah, and that I have not attempted to benefit from this world whatsoever, even to the extent of my smallest finger!"[14] Rabbi combined within himself all spiritual and human greatness and wealth.[15] Yet when he died, the rabbis said that after Rabbi was gone, all models of true humility, holiness, and fear of sin disappeared forever.[16] All later Jewish survival was a product of Rabbi's ten fingers — of his Mishnah.

---

11. Talmud, *Bava Metzia* 85a.

12. A compilation of laws and cases of the Oral Law that explain, complement and/or complete statements and decisions of the Mishnah. The *baraisos* form the basis for all Talmudic discussion of halachic issues. See Talmud, *Chullin* 141a, for Rabbi Chiya's role in the formulation of the *baraisos*.

13. Rabbi Chiya was born and bred in Babylonia. He immigrated to the Land of Israel, together with his sons, to study Torah with Rabbi. In fact, Rabbi sustained Rabbi Chiya, who had no other financial basis in the Land of Israel. He traveled often between the centers of Jewish life in Babylonia and the Galilee, and was thus an accepted representative of both traditions of Torah study and methodology. He settled in Tiberias, and he and his two sons, Yehudah and Chizkiah, are buried there in the ancient Jewish cemetery.

14. Talmud, *Kesubos* 104a.

15. Talmud, *Gittin* 59a.

16. Talmud, *Sotah* 49a. There are alternate texts suggesting that since the statement appears in the Mishnah itself, perhaps Rabbi is not the subject of that epitaph.

15
The Valley of Babylonia

EVEN AFTER THE DEATH of Rabbi Yehudah HaNasi, the Jewish community in Israel would continue to exist in force for another three centuries; however, at that *Nasi's* death (at the beginning of the third century), the role of central leadership in Jewish life passed from Israel to Babylonia.

Babylonia was already an ancient Jewish community, more than seven hundred years old, when the Mishnah was completed and published. It was well established, its leaders always having been direct descendants of the royal house of David, and the community long having possessed a proud heritage of intense Jewish life. At the same time, as long as the Temple stood in Jerusalem, Babylonian Jewry had been happy with and reconciled to the dominating role in the Jewish world played by Judah. Nevertheless, near the beginning of the second century, with the Temple in ruins and the hand of the Roman oppressor heavy upon the Jewish community in the Land of Israel, the Jewish community of Babylonia, of necessity, had begun to envision itself as becoming the premier player in Jewish life. And thus it was that indeed, in the early part of the third century, it started to assume this role, the development of which we shall now trace.

Conditions in Babylonia

THE JEWISH COMMUNITY in Babylonia was both uniquely suited — and unsuited — for this new position. Usually, the prospect of beginning life anew in a foreign country presents difficulties in terms of unfamiliar language and surroundings. However, among the assets of Babylonia were the similarity of its language, Aramaic, to Hebrew,[1] and the psycholog-

---
1. See Talmud, *Pesachim* 87b.

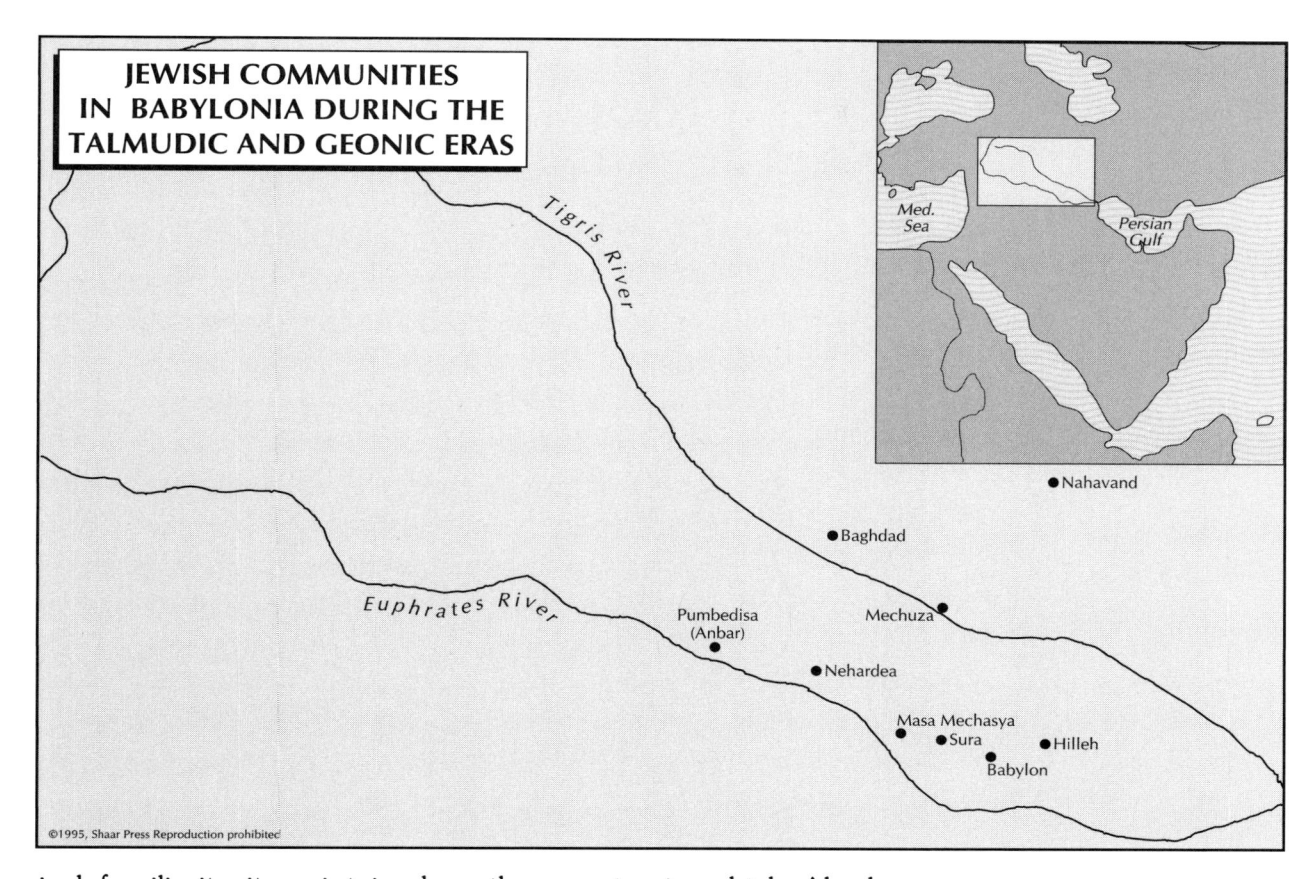

JEWISH COMMUNITIES IN BABYLONIA DURING THE TALMUDIC AND GEONIC ERAS

ical familiarity it maintained as the country in which Abraham was born.[2] Moreover, since the Jews of Babylonia were of more modest financial means, demands and life-style, life there was more conducive to strengthening and maintaining Torah values.[3] Most importantly, the government of Babylonia, though titularly subservient to Rome, never really enforced any harsh decrees against the Jews, and in fact allowed the Jewish Babylonian community full autonomy in many areas of religious, social and even economic life. Also important is the fact that Christianity, which by the third century had already undertaken a very anti-Jewish tinge, for some reason did not flourish in Babylonia.

On the other hand, Babylonia's material poverty[4] was also a disadvantage in that it limited the establishment of yeshivos.[5]

---

2. Ibid.

3. See Talmud, *Chagigah* 9b.

4. See Talmud, *Kiddushin* 49b.

5. There are numerous instances in Jewish history when a certain factor in society would simultaneously be a boon and a detriment to Jewish life. Jews rising to high public office in non-Jewish governments, the ongoing ability to corrupt non-Jewish public officials with bribes to subvert enforcement of onerous anti-Jewish laws, and the geographic

Another disadvantage of Babylonia was its unhealthy climate, damp and hot.[6] In addition, the lack of general culture in Babylonia, in contradistinction to the avant-garde continuing cultural ferment that existed in Egypt, Judah and other Greco-Roman centers in the Jewish Diaspora, created a less stimulating intellectual climate for the Jewish population. This reflected itself even in Torah studies.

For hundreds of years, until the arrival of Rabbi Yehudah HaNasi's disciples in the third century of the Common Era, Babylonian Jewry first tolerated and later accepted a relatively low level of Torah scholarship, and sometimes even illiteracy, among much of its population.[7] However, there was a very sizable reservoir of distinguished Torah scholars throughout the period of the Second Temple and beyond. Places like Nehardea and Ginzik were scholarly in R' Akiva's time, and the *Tanna* R' Yehudah ben Beseira lived in the Babylonian city of Netzivin. Be that as it may, the general level of Torah scholarship there would now change drastically for the better with the appearance on the scene of one of the great heroes of the Talmud — Abba the son of Aibo, (because of his height he was commonly called *Abba Aricha*, "Long Abba"), known forever by his descriptive and honorary title — Rav.[8]

Rav

RAV FOUND MUCH OF Babylonia to be a Torah wasteland, "a valley untended."[9] He is the one who tended that valley, built protective fences to safeguard its Torah crops and turned Babylonia into the central community of the

---

concentration of numerous Jews in one given area, lending cohesion and vulnerability at one time, are but some examples of this paradox of our experience.

6. See Talmud, *Shabbos* 105b.

7. On the other hand (in another example of the paradox of history mentioned in note 5 above), in Babylonia the lack of an intellectual climate competing with Torah studies allowed its Jews to devote their study efforts exclusively to Torah, once Rav established the necessary educational infrastructure. Lack of a competing intellectual system again occurred in Jewish life in Ashkenazic France and Germany from the eleventh through the fourteenth centuries, and in Eastern Europe from the fourteenth through the eighteenth centuries. In those times, too, the situation eventually cut both ways.

8. Just as Rabbi Yehudah HaNasi was known universally in the Jewish world as Rabbi, so too was his disciple, Abba Aricha, known in a later generation simply as Rav (the Rabbi/Teacher/Master.)

9. See Talmud, *Eruvin* 6a.

Jewish world for the next eight centuries. Rav himself was Babylonian by birth. However, he spent much of his life in the Land of Israel, studying there under the tutelage of his distinguished and beloved uncle, Rabbi Chiya,[10] and even more importantly in the yeshivah of Rabbi.

Rav eventually became one of Rabbi's foremost disciples, and his prowess in Torah scholarship was of such magnitude that he was deemed to be a *Tanna,* a colleague of the rabbis of the Mishnah,[11] even though his generation was counted as being one of *amoraim,* men of the Talmud no longer maintaining the stature of *tannaim,* the men of the Mishnah.

Rav had returned to Babylonia about 190, during the lifetime of Rabbi, hoping to establish a major yeshivah there and improve the spiritual situation. However, for reasons unknown to us, Rav's original attempts to reestablish himself in Babylonia were unsuccessful. Only after the death of Rabbi Yehudah HaNasi, when Rav himself was already past sixty years of age, did his renewed attempt to create a strong center of Torah leadership prove successful. This was about 220, when Rav left the yeshivah of Rabbi, whose son, Rabban Gamliel III,[12] now directed it.

When Rav arrived to settle permanently in Babylonia, two great scholars were the leaders of the Jewish community there, which was centered in Nehardea. One was Karna. The other was Mar Shmuel, who was much younger than Rav, headed a yeshivah, and was also a noted astronomer and doctor. Eventually he and Rav would combine to create the major Torah institutions in Babylonia.[13] Rav felt uncomfortable in Nehardea. The leadership of the community accorded him great respect because of his reputation as an outstanding Torah scholar. The temporal leader of Babylonian Jewry, the Reish Galusa (the

---

10. Rav always referred to his uncle, Rabbi Chiya, as *chavivi,* "my beloved." See Talmud, *Bava Metzia* 76b.

11. See Talmud, *Eruvin* 50b.

12. Rav never received the *semichah* (ordination) which would have qualified him to become a member of the Sanhedrin, in spite of his greatness in Torah scholarship. See Talmud, *Sanhedrin* 5a, regarding Rabbi's refusal to grant such ordination to Rav. After Rabbi's death, Rav petitioned Rabban Gamliel III (Rabbi's son and successor as *Nasi* in Judah), to grant him the coveted *semichah.* Rabban Gamliel III also refused, stating, "I cannot grant you more than my father did." See Talmud Yerushalmi, *Chagigah,* Chapter 1, section 8. After Rabban Gamliel's refusal to grant him *semichah,* Rav left Israel and settled in Babylonia permanently.

13. Their personal relationship began on a rocky note, but later they became fast friends and honored compatriots. See Talmud, *Shabbos* 108a, and *Bava Kamma* 80b.

Exilarch),[14] appointed him to the symbolically important position of *agronomos,* the local supervisor of weights and measures, in order to provide him with a livelihood and an opportunity to integrate himself into the Nehardea community. However, Rav refused the Exilarch's demand that he undertake, as *agronomos,* other supervisory tasks. This was despite Karna's entreaties to obey the Exilarch. The Exilarch, enraged by the affront to his dignity, arrested Rav and imprisoned him for a short time.[15] After this, Rav no longer served in a governmental position.

The Sidra

IN NEHARDEA, aside from the yeshivah of Mar Shmuel, there existed an ancient school of Torah scholarship called the *Sidra.* At the *Sidra,* the Torah portion of the week was explained, debated and expanded upon by the Torah scholars of the community, all in the light of the Oral Law. It was not a school for young scholars, but a center for exposition of the Oral Law amongst proven scholars.

The *Sidra* was a uniquely Babylonian institution, and the head of the *Sidra* was always a man of power and note. When the head of the *Sidra* taught or lectured, he had a *meturgaman* (literally, *expounder,* though the word has a much broader meaning in its actual Talmudic usage) who would transmit his thoughts and message to the listeners. As a rule, the head of the *Sidra* tolerated very little originality or creativity on the part of the *meturgaman* fulfilling his role as translator. The head of the *Sidra* in Nehardea at that time was Rabbi Shila, and he engaged Rav to serve as the *meturgaman* at the *Sidra.* However, Rav proved too original and creative in this task and could not restrict himself to dry translation. Thus he was forced to resign the post.[16] Rav, disappointed by his experiences in Nehardea, now looked to other cities in Babylonia for his future. This was only an apparent setback. Actually, a great general benefit would now accrue to Jewry, since Rav would go on to create, in the town of Sura, what would become world Jewry's main Torah center for centuries.

---

14. The creation of the office of Reish Galusa, or Exilarch, will be explained later in this chapter.
15. See Talmud Yerushalmi, *Bava Basra,* Chapter 5, section 5.
16. See Talmud, *Yoma* 20b.

Hutzal

FROM NEHARDEA RAV TRAVELED to Hutzal, one of the famous ancient Jewish cities in Babylonia.[17] There in Hutzal Rav found a warm welcome and an appreciation of his talents and greatness. A yeshivah had been founded there almost a century earlier by Rabbi Achai, and after his death[18] it was still called by his name. The students of the yeshivah, upon hearing of Rav's arrival, petitioned that he become the head teacher. Rav agreed and spent some time in this leading role,[19] where he attracted a wide student following.

His strong personality, his care for the students, his intellectual brilliance and outstanding erudition, the research and preparation that his lectures reflected and his phenomenal ability to inspire the next generation to attempt to emulate him all brought him fame and more students. Rabbi Asi, who also headed a yeshivah in Hutzal, was then already aged,[20] and he encouraged many of his best younger students to study with Rav at Rabbi Achai's yeshivah. Rav saw his future at Hutzal. However, this was not to be.

Nehardea

IN ABOUT 228, RABBI SHILA, the head of the *Sidra* in Nehardea, died. The question naturally arose as to who would succeed him in what was potentially the most influential Torah position in Babylonia. Rav and Mar

---

17. In Hutzal there was a synagogue whose foundation was laid by the prophet Yechezkel at the destruction of the First Temple. In Nehardea there was a synagogue whose foundation, laid even prior to the destruction of the First Temple, contained stones and earth from Jerusalem. The Talmud, *Megillah* 29a, states that God's spirit, so to speak, was found in Babylonia in those two synagogues. The custom of using a Jerusalem-stone cornerstone for Jewish buildings in the Diaspora has been renewed in the latter half of the twentieth century.

18. Rabbi Achai died shortly after Rabbi Yehudah HaNasi. See Talmud, *Kiddushin* 72a. Rabbi Achai was a son of Rabbi Yoshiyah.

19. See Talmud Yerushalmi, *Succah,* Chapter 4, section 2.

20. Rav Asi, too, was a member of the transitional generation after Rabbi that transferred Torah between Babylonia and Judah. He is buried in the ancient Jewish cemetery near Tiberias.

Shmuel were both candidates for the position. For many reasons, the position was offered first to Rav. Rav, however, deferred in favor of Mar Shmuel, pointing out that Mar Shmuel was a native of Nehardea and had already headed religious and educational institutions in the city. Mar Shmuel became the leader of Jewish education in Nehardea and, in a greater sense, the partner of Rav in creating Babylonia as the center of Torah for generations to come.

Mar Shmuel created a great yeshivah in Nehardea and, until his death in 254, was a strong force in the Jewish renaissance in Babylonia in the third and fourth centuries of the Common Era. His grandchildren were great scholars and well-known Talmudic teachers, and his daughters also became famous in Talmudic literature.[21] Rav's refusal to accept the post of head of the *Sidra* in Nehardea also made it impossible for him to remain in the nearby town of Hutzal, since technically Hutzal was under the jurisdiction of Nehardea. Rav therefore moved to his final destination in Babylonia, the city of Sura.

Sura

SURA WAS A CITY in southern Babylonia, in an agricultural area not far from Rav's own birthplace. It was also near another town that would become famous in Jewish Babylonia, Masa Mechasya.[22]

The climate of Sura was semi-tropical, with areas of swamps surrounding the city. The spiritual climate was also murky, with the Jewish population on the whole unlearned in Torah and ignorant of Jewish practice. Rav, however, created a new atmosphere in Sura. He established a great *Sidra* which soon grew into the largest yeshivah in Babylonia, attracting thousands of students. Many of them stayed only temporarily, but it appears that the yeshivah always had

---

21. Shmuel's two daughters were kidnapped and forcibly married to two non-Jews, who later converted to Judaism. They became well known for their piety and loyalty to the Jews, and their sons became great Torah scholars under the direction of their grandfather, Mar Shmuel. Interestingly enough, the Talmud almost always refers to the grandsons as "the children of Mar Shmuel's daughters," not mentioning their fathers' names.

22. There are those who believe that Sura and Masa Mechasya are one and the same town. However, see Talmud, *Beitzah* 29a, where it appears that they were separate communities. Naftul (Vol. II, p.115) theorizes that they were twin cities, or that Masa Mechasya was a suburb of Sura.

1,200 permanent students[23] and that their caliber was extremely high.[24]

Sura and Masa Mechasya became famous for Torah, not only in Babylonia but throughout the Jewish world. The Jewish people coined a phrase to illustrate their love of Rav, Sura/Masa Mechasya, and the study of Torah: "Better to sit on the garbage landfill of Masa Mechasya than in the great palaces of Pumbedisa (a wealthy city of Jews that at that time had no major yeshivos as yet)."[25]

It was during Rav's tenure in Sura that the institution of *Yarchei Kallah* became established and popular. The *Yarchei Kallah* was an activity in which tens of thousands of alumni traveled to Sura and Nehardea to study Torah during the spring and autumn months of Adar and Elul every year.

The yeshivah building in Sura was large and majestic, with gardens which provided food and added beauty surrounding it.[26] Rav made Torah study a universal project for Jews of all ages and stages of life and station. The yeshivah that he founded in Sura/Masa Mechasya survived for almost a millennia and was the center of Jewish learning, life and law for much of that time. No comparable institution in Jewish history enjoyed such a long existence and continuing influence. Rav and Sura became inseparable in the story of Torah and Israel, and his tall shadow stretches over us even today.

The Mantle Passes to Babylonia

RAV DIED IN HIS EIGHTY-FIFTH YEAR, in the year 247 of the Common Era. It was mainly by dint of his personality and Torah greatness that by that time the center of Jewish life and leadership had shifted from the Land of Israel to Babylonia. Rav's cousins, Rabbah bar Bar Chana in Babylonia, and Chizkiyah the son of Rabbi Chiya and his brother Yehudah in the Land of Israel, also raised the banner of Torah after the death of Rabbi. But

---

23. See Talmud, *Kesubos,* 106a.
24. Eliezer Shteinman, in his work, *Be'er HaTalmud* (Tel Aviv, 1965, Volume 3, p. 236) lists thirty-four disciples of Rav who became leaders of the Babylonian Jewish community in the following generation. All of them were participants in the organization and editing of the Babylonian Talmud.
25. See Talmud, *Kerisos* 6a.
26. See Talmud, *Kiddushin* 39a.

it was Rav who guaranteed the continuity and expansion of the Mishnah through contributing to the developing Talmud of his time, and whose yeshivah became the lighthouse for the Jewish exile.

In the Land of Israel, meanwhile, the embers of the great fire of Torah lit there by Ezra and nurtured and preserved until the time of Rabbi were now dying out. Great men such as Rabbi Yochanan[27] and his brother-in-law Rabbi Shimon ben Lakish, Rabbi Chanina bar Chama, Rabbi Yanai,[28] Rabbi Levi ben Sisas[29] and Rabbi Yoshiah remained in the Galilee, particularly in Tiberias and its environs, and helped Rabban Gamliel III, the son of Rabbi, in his task of providing leadership for the Jewish world. Rabban Gamliel III died soon after taking office, and he was in turn succeeded by his son Yehudah.[30]

This Rabbi Yehudah Nesiah I was the last of the heads of the great Beis Din in the Land of Israel, and it was after his death in about 228 that the Babylonian yeshivos and Jewish communities felt themselves independent in all matters of the rule of the *Nasi* in the Land of Israel. Rabbi Yehudah Nesiah I was in turn succeeded by his son, Rabban Gamliel IV. Rabban Gamliel IV was also succeeded by his son, Rabbi Yehudah Nesiah II. Neither Rabban Gamliel IV nor Rabbi Yehudah Nesiah II were of the stature of Rav, Mar Shmuel, and their disciples in Babylonia, and thus, almost by default, the great house of Hillel that had served as the spiritual rulers of Israel for over 260 years now relinquished its role to the scholars of Babylonia.

Part of the blame for the decline of the Jewish community of the Land of Israel in the third century is directly traceable to the political instability and wave of assassinations that wracked the Roman government. The emperor Caracalla was murdered in the year 217. His murderer, Macrinus, succeeded to the throne but was in turn assassinated one year later. Heliogabulus now became emperor, but he too was murdered in 222. Alexander Severus then became emperor, and he was able to stabilize the Roman government under his thirteen-year rule, until 235.

From 235 till 284 complete anarchy again reigned, with nine-

---

27. The founder and main organizer of Talmud Yerushalmi.
28. The father-in-law of Rav's cousin and Rabbi Chiya's son, Yehudah.
29. Known more simply in the Babylonian Talmud as Levi. He, too, eventually left the Land of Israel and settled in Babylonia.
30. He was called Rabbi Yehudah Nesiah to differentiate him from his peerless grandfather, Rabbi Yehudah HaNasi.

Severus at the Senate

teen different men occupying the emperor's throne. Judah, under direct Roman rule, was despoiled by the constant turmoil of the Roman rulers. The community was practically taxed out of existence, and the Romans continued to use it as a staging area for their never-ending war with the Parthians. In such a situation it is no wonder that the influence, power and prestige of the Jewish community of the Land of Israel declined so precipitously. Babylonia, on the other hand, which was not really under direct Roman rule, was placed out of harm's way. Its rulers and governing bodies were on the whole autonomous, tolerant and self-sufficient, and as such, the Jews of Babylonia lived in a shielded and protected environment.[31] This greatly facilitated Rav and Mar Shmuel and their disciples in strengthening the Jewish community of Babylonia, both physically and spiritually.

Rav's Work

RAV CONTINUED THE WORK of his mentor, Rabbi, in organizing and formulating the language of the Oral Law. Aside from his foundation work on what would emerge centuries later as the Talmud, Rav also edited a number

---

31. There were, however, some outbreaks of persecution, especially by the invading Zoroastrian believers who periodically terrorized the Babylonian population, both Jewish and non-Jewish.

of other major works. These include: 1) *Sifra d'Bei Rav*,[32] an halachic commentary to *Leviticus,* a companion work to the Mishnah in understanding the ritual laws of purity and Temple service; 2) *Sifrei d'Bei Rav,* the same type of commentary as Rav's *Sifra,* but covering *Numbers* and *Deuteronomy;* 3) *Mechilta,*[33] again the same type of commentary, but covering *Exodus;* 4) *Aggadata d'Bei Rav*, a collection of *aggadic* interpretations, parables and moral lessons based on the Bible; and 5) *Tosefta*[34] a commentary on certain tractates of the *Mishnah,* adding to the previous *Tosefta* of Rabbi Oshiya, which in itself was an addition to the Mishnah of Rabbi Yehudah HaNasi.

These important works of scholarship remain vital to students of Torah today and have been reprinted many times over the centuries.

Tekiasa D'Bei Rav from a 14th-century Viennese machzor

They also serve as the basis for hundreds of other books explaining and commenting on the Oral Law themselves and are the subject of dozens of super-commentaries. One may say that the books produced from the "School of Rav" set the pattern for all later works expounding the Oral Law, and indeed, they form the skeleton of the great structure of the Talmud.

Rav's Prayers

BUT RAV, AS THE TORAH itself, was more than intellect, scholarship and academic discipline. Rav was also heart, emotion, compassion, poetry, beauty, sensitivity and spirituality. Rav was the major contributor to the *Siddur/Machzor* prayerbook of Israel, after the creation of this prayerbook by the Men of the Great Assembly six centuries earlier.

---

32. The work is also known as *Toras Kohanim, The Laws Regarding the Priests (and the Temple).*
33. See the commentary of Rashbam, Rabbi Shmuel ben Meir, to Talmud, *Bava Basra* 124b, where he credits Rav with the authorship of the *Mechilta.*
34. Also called *K'savos d'Bei Rav (The Writings of the School of Rav).*

His *Tekiasa d'Bei Rav,* the prayers that accompany the sounding of the shofar during the *Mussaf* service on *Rosh HaShanah,* is Jewish history's finest example of holy Hebrew poetry.

> *You alone remember the forming of the universe*
> > *and account for all the creatures of yore.*
>
> *Before You are revealed all secrets*
> > *and the vast mysteries from the beginning of time.*
>
> *There is no forgetting by Your Heavenly Throne,*
> > *nor is anything hidden from You.*
>
> *You recall everything that has occurred,*
> > *and nothing created is concealed from You...*
>
> *This day is the beginning of Your works,*
> > *a reminder of that first day of creation.*
>
> *For it is a statute unto Israel,*
> > *a day of judgment by the God of Jacob.*
>
> *And regarding the nations shall it be said today:*
> > *Which shall be to the sword and which to peace?*
> > *Which to hunger and which to plenty?*
>
> *And Your creatures are remembered by You today*
> > *for life or for death.*
>
> *Who is not remembered and judged before you today?*
> *...Fortunate is the man who does not forget you,*
> > *and the son of man who strengthens himself*
> > *through belief in You.*
>
> *For those who seek You will never falter,*
> > *And those who trust in You will never need be shamed.*[35]

Rav also revived one of the basic prayers of the *Siddur, Aleinu.*[36] This prayer is recited three times daily in the prayer services of the Jews and also appears in the *Mussaf* services of *Rosh HaShanah* and *Yom Kippur.* It affirms the uniqueness of the Jewish people and its appreciation of God's special providence over Israel. It also affirms the pure monotheism of Judaism and the hope for the eventual brotherhood of man in the service of God. The *Todiaynu* prayer (recited at the end

---

35. I am embarrassed beyond words about how much is lost in translation. Nevertheless, I believe that a flavor of Rav's profound poetry still shines through.

36. Jewish tradition also ascribes authorship of this prayer to Yehoshua bin Nun at the conquest of Jericho. It apparently was forgotten by the masses over the centuries and was reintroduced and popularized by Rav.

Aleinu from a 15th-century Italian siddur

of a Shabbos followed by a *Yom Tov*) is also of Rav's composition, and is referred to in the Talmud[37] as a "precious gem." Additionally, the famous private *Prayer of Rav* for life, health, wealth, happiness, spiritual growth and material goodness was adopted by the Jewish people as the most fitting prayer to accompany the announcement of the new moon on the Shabbos before every *Rosh Chodesh*.[38]

In every area and facet of Jewish life throughout Israel's long history, Rav's words, spirit, advice and presence have accompanied the Jewish people. Rav is the fitting heir to the mantle of greatness and unending inspiration of Ezra, Hillel, Rabban Yochanan ben Zakkai, Rabbi Akiva and Rabbi Yehudah HaNasi. Without Rav, one cannot imagine Jewish existence and survival.

Rav's Disciples

RAV HAD THREE SONS and three daughters. His oldest son, Chiya, is mentioned in the Talmud often as a scholar of note. His second son, Aibo, is mentioned as a man of commerce.[39] His sons-in-law were all scholars and are mentioned in the Talmud, as well as a number of his grandchildren.[40] But Rav's legacy was transmitted mainly through his disciples, namely Rav Huna, Rav Kahana, Rav Chisda, Rav Yirmiyah, Rav Hamnunah, and Rav Chama bar Guria. They strengthened the great yeshivah at Sura, established other yeshivos in Babylonia and trained thousands of others as students of the Oral Law, all of whom, whether well-known or anonymous, participated in the creation of the Talmud and helped shape it into its final form.

---

37. See Talmud, *Berachos* 33b.
38. See Talmud, *Berachos* 16b. The only month before which this prayer is omitted is Tishrei, whose *Rosh Chodesh* is *Rosh HaShanah*.
39. See Talmud, *Pesachim* 113a.
40. See Talmud, *Chullin* 92a.

King Shapur triumphs over Valerian and the Romans

The Sassanian King

DURING THE LATTER DAYS of Rav, Babylonia was conquered for a short while by the Parthians, who went on to defeat the Romans and establish the Sassanian dynasty. The Sassanians were fanatical Zoroastrians and initially persecuted the Jews of Babylonia, but this lasted only a few years.

In 241, King Shapur I[41] ascended the Sassanian throne and proved to be a person of tolerance and wisdom. He became friends with Mar Shmuel and used many Jews as counselors and advisers. The king knew much about Jewish law, custom and ritual, and is mentioned respectfully in the Talmud.[42] Under his reign, the pattern of friendly rule over the Jews in Babylonia was reestablished, a pattern that survived for centuries after the demise of the Sassanian dynasty.

Sura and Pumbedisa

UPON RAV'S DEATH, Mar Shmuel became the leader of the Babylonian Jewish community. His yeshivah at Nehardea had also grown very large. In fact, after Rav's death, many of the Sura students left to study with Mar Shmuel in Nehardea. The system of two large and competing yeshivos in Babylonia would continue for over eight centuries.

---

41. In the Talmud he is called *Shvor Malka*.
42. See Talmud, *Avodah Zarah* 76b and *Bava Basra* 115b.

The yeshiva in Nehardea would decline after the death of Mar Shmuel in 254, eventually to be supplanted as the second yeshivah in Babylonia by a school founded by Rav Yehudah ben Yechezkel (a student of Rav's) in the city of Pumbedisa. From 350 to the end of the great Babylonian Torah center in 1050, Sura and Pumbedisa would remain the two main schools of Torah in Babylonia. The competition between the two guaranteed scholarship and intellectual ferment. It would at times also cause bitter dispute and disunity in Babylonian Jewry.

The Exilarch

THE HEADS OF THE yeshivos of Babylonia, although recognized by the people as the spiritual leaders of the community, did not form the temporal authority of the Jewish communities. That power lay with the ancient institution of the *Reish Galusa,* the Head of the Exile. The men who served in this office were direct descendants of the Davidian dynasty of the Kingdom of Judah of First Temple times. They saw themselves as the rightful heirs to the throne of David and Solomon, and they conducted regal courts and lived in luxurious palaces while awaiting the redemption of the Jews from exile.

The institution of *Reish Galusa,* or Exilarch, began when Ezra, Nechemiah, Zerubavel and the Men of the Great Assembly reestablished the Jewish state in the Holy Land. The Head of the Exile, who remained in Babylonia, established a parallel Jewish "state" in Babylonia. The Babylonian authorities actually allowed an autonomous Jewish power, with all the trappings of government and royalty, to govern the country's large Jewish population. Apparently, the Babylonian government preferred that situation to the prospect of having to govern that often cantankerous minority itself. Thus, the *Reish Galusa* maintained legal power, a police force under his own jurisdiction, powers of taxation and the influence and strength that the ability to hire and fire always brings. For almost eight hundred years, the *Reish Galusa* and the heads of the yeshivos (who from the sixth century onwards bore the title *Geonim*) coexisted while naturally competing for power and influence over the Babylonian Jewish community. As can be imagined, this made for some interesting moments in the story of Babylonian Jewry.

Little is known about most of the men who served in the position of *Reish Galusa* over this long span of time. What is known is that they were not all of equal quality. Some were scholars, while others were boors. Some were modest and unassuming, respectful of the Torah scholars of their time and cooperative with the heads of the yeshivos. Others were haughty and arrogant, paranoid over imagined and perhaps real slights, and prone to engage in constant battle with the yeshivah heads. As is always the case in life, it was not the institution that determined the social climate of the times, but the temperament of the one who occupied the post. That factor is what set the tone of debate and congeniality in public communal matters in Babylonia.

Rav Huna and Mar Ukva

IN THE GENERATION OF RABBI, Babylonia's *Reish Galusa* was the great scholar Rav Huna.[43] Rabbi respected him highly and even said that were Rav Huna to emigrate to the Land of Israel, he would defer to him his position in the Yeshivah.[44] Upon the death of Rav Huna, Mar Ukva became the *Reish Galusa*. A distinguished Torah scholar, he cooperated with Rav and Mar Shmuel in achieving the revitalization of Babylonian Jewry in the third century. He is celebrated in the Talmud for his acts of charity,[45] his modesty and deference to the heads of the yeshivos of his time, especially Mar Shmuel,[46] and his authority in halachic matters.[47]

The history of Israel, especially that of the turbulent early centuries of the Common Era, testifies to God's providence in supplying the Jewish people with the right man at the right time and place in order to insure Jewish survival. Mar Ukva is an example of this. For without Mar Ukva's aid and support, Rav and Mar Shmuel would have found the creation and expansion of their yeshivos a much more overwhelming task than it was. It is no wonder, therefore, that Mar Ukva is remembered so fondly in the Talmud and in the writings of the later *Geonim*.

---

43. Not to be confused with the more famous Rav Huna, quoted innumerable times in the Talmud, who was a disciple and student of both Rav and Mar Shmuel. See Naftul, Vol. I, p. 206.
44. Talmud Yerushalmi, *Kilayim,* Chapter 9, section 3.
45. See Talmud, *Kesubos* 67b.
46. See Talmud, *Mo'ed Katan* 16b.
47. See Talmud, *Kiddushin* 44b.

Mar Ukva was blessed with long life, surviving both Rav and Mar Shmuel. He remained the *Reish Galusa* during the time of their successors, Rav Huna, Rav Yehudah and Rav Chisda. His presence and influence undoubtedly contributed to the smooth transition from the first generation of Babylonian *Amoraim* — that of Rav and Mar Shmuel — to the second. This set a precedent of actual seamlessness of succession among the generations of the *Amoraim,* reflected in the style of the Talmud itself, wherein the staged Torah discussions among different generations of scholars take place on the Talmudic page with no awkwardness or difficulty. Personages such as Mar Ukva bridged the generations, uniting them and allowing the yeshivos to grow and prosper, all through the benevolence of the temporal authority of the Babylonian Jewish community.

Rabbi Yochanan

OVERLAPPING THE PERIOD of Rav and Mar Shmuel in Babylonia was the period which Rabbi Yochanan dominated as leader in the Land of Israel. One of the major scholars of the period, Rabbi Yochanan was a student of Rabbi, Rabbi Yehoshua ben Levi, Rabbi Yanai and others. Rabbi Yochanan was the driving force in the development of the *Talmud Yerushalmi* (Jerusalem Talmud), which would be completed and edited by his students' students two generations later. Rabbi Yochanan, together with most of the remaining scholars of the Land of Israel, found his home and learning center in the environs of Tiberias. Tiberias was the final venue of the Sanhedrin in the Land of Israel, where it continued to function until its demise in the fourth century.

Rabbi Yochanan, his brother-in-law Rabbi Shimon ben Lakish[48] and Rabbi Elazar ben P'das were the leading Torah teachers in the Land of Israel during the first half of the third century. But as great as the men of Tiberias were in Torah knowledge, the center of Torah scholarship was now firmly in place in Babylonia. Thus, the Torah joined the Jewish people in its exile from the Holy Land.

---

48. See Talmud, *Bava Metzia* 84a, for the wondrous story of how Rabbi Yochanan took Reish Lakish, a highwayman and gladiator, and remade him into Rabbi Shimon ben Lakish, the great scholar of Israel.

16
Rome Declines and Dies

THE IMMUTABLE RULE regarding civilizations and empires is that they inevitably decline and end. The Roman Empire, which ruled most of the known world of its day for over half a millennium, began its irreversible slide into the ash heap of history in the middle of the third century. By the early part of the fifth century the city of Rome would be sacked, and the western part of the Roman Empire would be no more. The eastern part of the former empire, centered on Byzantium / Constantinople, would continue to survive many centuries longer, but only as an empty shell of its former self.

The turmoil engendered by such a great upheaval would touch the Jews living in the domains of the empire as well. But in their relatively safe haven of Babylonia, most of world Jewry rode out the storm safely. The development of the Talmud continued unabated and relatively unaffected. The irony of Rabbi Akiva outliving his Roman tormentors, in an historic sense, was not lost on the scholars and masses of Israel. There would be precious few tears shed by Jews over the fall of Rome and its empire. The Jews saw this cataclysmic event as part of God's continuing rule over man. It demonstrated a long-suspended verdict finally meted out on behalf of victims who suffered through centuries of Roman aggression and dominion. The Jews sensed that their Talmud would prove more vital than the spears and standards of the Roman legions.

The increasing toll of the border wars Rome was forced to fight sapped much of the will and energy of its army and populace. As in all mature civilizations, a population raised for long generations on the expectation of bread and circuses eventually loses direction, identity, patriotism and a clear vision of its purposes and goals. In addition, the penetration of Christianity throughout the Roman Empire took on epidemic proportions.

The other-worldliness and denial of self that characterized early Christianity made the maintenance of empire and power meaningless and irrelevant to millions of Roman citizens, freedmen and slaves. The idols of paganism, long known to be worthless already in the classical world, finally crumbled before the spirituality and universalistic monotheism (albeit flawed and imperfect) of Christianity.

In modern times, many avowed and ideological anti-Semites also would eventually become anti-Christians, because they would see the viable forces of Christianity as the product and result of the ideas and influences on civilization stemming from Judaism, which they so despised.[1] Indeed, it is through Christianity that Jewish ideas did eventually penetrate and come to dominate Roman society, and to cause indirectly the changes in that society's attitudes which inexorably led to its own demise. But Rome's death would be a long and slow one.

The Yeshivos in Tiberias and Caesarea

AFTER ALMOST 50 YEARS of anarchy, Diocletian was able to restore central authority to the Roman government. He ruled as emperor from 284 till 306. Diocletian spent time in the Land of Israel, residing near Tiberias, and even met with Rabbi Yehudah Nesiah II.[2] Although Diocletian's relationships with the Jews were cool, he did not especially discriminate against or persecute them. Nonetheless, during his reign the Jewish community in the Land of Israel continued its slow decline.

Both Rabbi Yochanan and Rabbi Elazar ben P'das died about 288, and Rabbi Ami and Rabbi Asi, members of distinguished priestly families, now jointly headed the yeshivah in Tiberias. A second yeshivah existed in Caesarea, a city which was the center of Roman administration but was heavily infiltrated by Christians who openly proselytized the

---

1. Hitler and his henchmen, as well as many of the anti-Jewish radicals in the French and the Russian revolutions, are examples of this type of thinking. Christianity has always had a difficult time coming to grips with its Jewish origins on one hand and its pagan Roman trappings on the other. The continued survival of Judaism in an overwhelmingly Christian society also contributed to the continuing Christian dilemma regarding the Jewish "problem."

2. See Talmud Yerushalmi, *Terumos*, Chapter 8, section 4.

Tombs of R' Ami and R' Asi

Roman aristocracy living there. It was therefore a most unlikely home for a yeshivah. But in c. 290, Rabbi Abbahu, one of the disciples of Rabbi Yochanan, was able to establish such an institute of learning there.

Rabbi Abbahu maintained good relations with the Roman authorities, and his yeshivah would prove successful. In fact, it became one of the last main houses of Jewish learning in the Land of Israel for the coming centuries. It survived the pogrom that destroyed the Jewish center in Tiberias in 305; it outlived Rabbi Yehudah Nesiah II, who died the same year. Rabbi Abbahu himself died in about 310. The yeshivah in Caesarea then closed, and there was an attempt, led by Rabbi Yirmiyahu, Rabbi Yonah and Rabbi Yossi, to reestablish that yeshivah center at Tiberias. This effort met with mixed results, and the Tiberias yeshivah was again destroyed by the Romans in 323, when persecution of the Jews began in earnest under the new emperor, Constantine.

Decline of the Samaritans

IT WAS DURING THE REIGN of Diocletian that the Samaritans were finally expelled from the ranks of the Jewish people. They had surreptitiously readopted forms of paganism and had become allies of the Romans and the Christians in opposing Judaism. They became open and uncompromising enemies of the Jewish community in the Land of Israel. Thus ended a six-century struggle by the Jewish sages to define the status of the Samaritans vis-á-vis Judaism. The Samaritans now left Judaism and shrank into a minute sect with no further major

A Samaritan encampment on Mount Gerizim

influence on either Judaism or Christianity. Today, their temple on Mount Gerizim, outside Shechem (Nablus) in the Land of Israel is the only remnant of their former power and position in that country.

Destruction of Nehardea

MEANWHILE, IN CONTRAST to the declining Jewish community in Israel, the Babylonian Jewish community continued to grow and intensify. Rav's disciples expanded his yeshivah at Sura, and it became Babylonia's center of Jewish scholarship. Many scholars from the Land of Israel as well, fleeing the difficult circumstances there and wishing for a more tranquil atmosphere in which to study Torah, came to Sura.

Rav's disciple, Rav Huna,[3] became the head of the yeshivah in Sura in about 250 and served in that post forty years. Under his leadership, Sura attracted thousands of students, with many hundreds studying there at any given time on a full-time, intensive and permanent basis.[4]

Contributing to the growth and greatness of Sura was the unfortunate destruction of Nehardea's Jewish community and of Mar Shmuel's yeshivah there. This happened in 259, five years after the death of Mar

---

3. Not the Rabbi Huna who was the *Reish Galusa* during the time of Rav and Mar Shmuel, though apparently he was a member of that *Reish Galusa's* family.
4. See Talmud, *Kesubos* 106a.

Shmuel. The king of Palmyra,[5] Septimus Odenathus,[6] took advantage of the continuing turmoil in Rome and conquered, along with large parts of Syria and Babylonia, the northern part of the Land of Israel, whereupon he proceeded to sack Nehardea, and with it its great yeshivah. Although the rule of Palmyra was only brief, if bloody, and the situation in Babylonia soon returned to its accustomed tranquility, the Jewish community of Nehardea and its great yeshivah never recovered. The greatness of Nehardea as the "second" center of learning would now be transferred to another city in Babylonia, Pumbedisa.

Growth of Pumbedisa

IN ABOUT 257, AFTER THE DEATH OF Mar Shmuel but before the destruction of Nehardea, a disciple of Rav's, Rabbi Yehudah bar Yechezkel,[7] had opened a small yeshivah in Pumbedisa. Rabbi Yehuda was one of the outstanding Torah scholars in Babylonia and soon attracted a large following of students to his yeshivah. After the closing of the yeshivah in Nehardea, Rabbi Yehuda's yeshivah in Pumbedisa became ever more popular, and it eventually became a major Torah center in Babylonia, second only to Sura in fame and numbers.

For the next eight centuries Sura and Pumbedisa would be the two main Torah centers of Babylonia, competing with each other, sometimes bitterly, but usually in a more friendly fashion. There would be times during the period of the *Geonim*,[8] and even earlier, that Pumbedisa would overshadow Sura in influence and power. But overall, in the long history of Babylonian Jewry, Sura has the primary place of honor.

When Rav Huna died in about 298, Rabbi Yehudah became the leader of the Torah scholars in Babylonia. However, Rabbi Yehudah himself died just one year later, so that the remaining leaders of Babylonian Jewry could no longer communicate with disciples of Rav and Mar Shmuel, but only with their disciples' disciples.

---

5. A city-state located in what is today eastern Syria, built upon a lush oasis.
6. The Talmud, *Kesubos* 51b, refers to him as King Netzar.
7. He also studied under Mar Shmuel in Nehardea after Rav's death.
8. See the later chapter in this book on the beginnings of the period of the *Geonim*. The *Geonim* were the heads of the Babylonian yeshivos from the seventh till the eleventh centuries and also claimed temporal powers.

Constantine

WHEN DIOCLETIAN RETIRED from the throne of Rome in 306, he was convinced that he had finally brought permanent stability to the empire. However, his hopes were rudely dashed, for within a few months of his retirement civil war again engulfed the Roman world.

From 306 till 324, no less than six Roman generals proclaimed themselves emperor and warred for power. The eventual victor and emperor was Constantine the Great.[9]

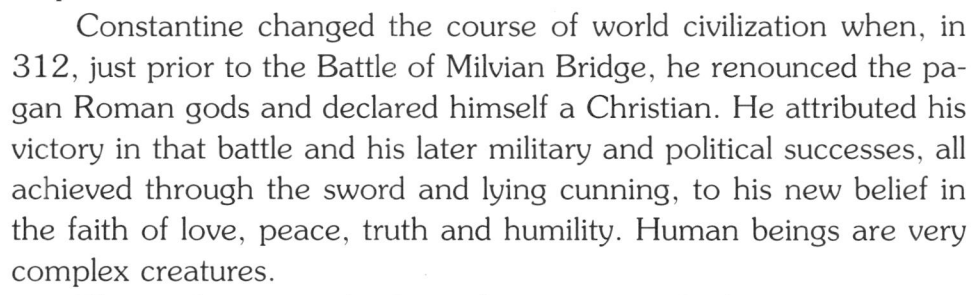

Constantine changed the course of world civilization when, in 312, just prior to the Battle of Milvian Bridge, he renounced the pagan Roman gods and declared himself a Christian. He attributed his victory in that battle and his later military and political successes, all achieved through the sword and lying cunning, to his new belief in the faith of love, peace, truth and humility. Human beings are very complex creatures.

The ending period of Diocletian's reign had witnessed great Roman persecution of the Christians, with a reign of terror against Christians and Christianity spreading throughout the Roman world from 303 until 305. But the Christians proved steadfast in their faith, and in spite of the martyrdom of tens of thousands, their new religion continued to grow and gain new adherents. However, as is natural in all such affairs, the Christians harbored a great deal of ill will toward those who persecuted them.[10]

Constantine's conversion brought about the institution of Christianity as the official religion of Rome. The pagan temples were converted to churches, Christian basilicas were built in Rome[11] and the methods of persecution used by Roman authority against Christians only a few short years before were now used by that same authority to persecute non-Christians.

Constantine

---

9. Always beware of "the Greats."
10. The Christians would not forget their experiences when they came to power. Much of the venom spewed forth by Justin Martyr and other early Church fathers can be traced to the "great persecution" of those years. Indeed, throughout the centuries Christians have often justified their own persecution of others by claiming, truthfully or otherwise, that their victims' ancestors had persecuted Christians.
11. A massive basilica in Rome, built before Constantine, was nine years in the making, from 313 till 322.

THE DIVISION OF THE ROMAN EMPIRE

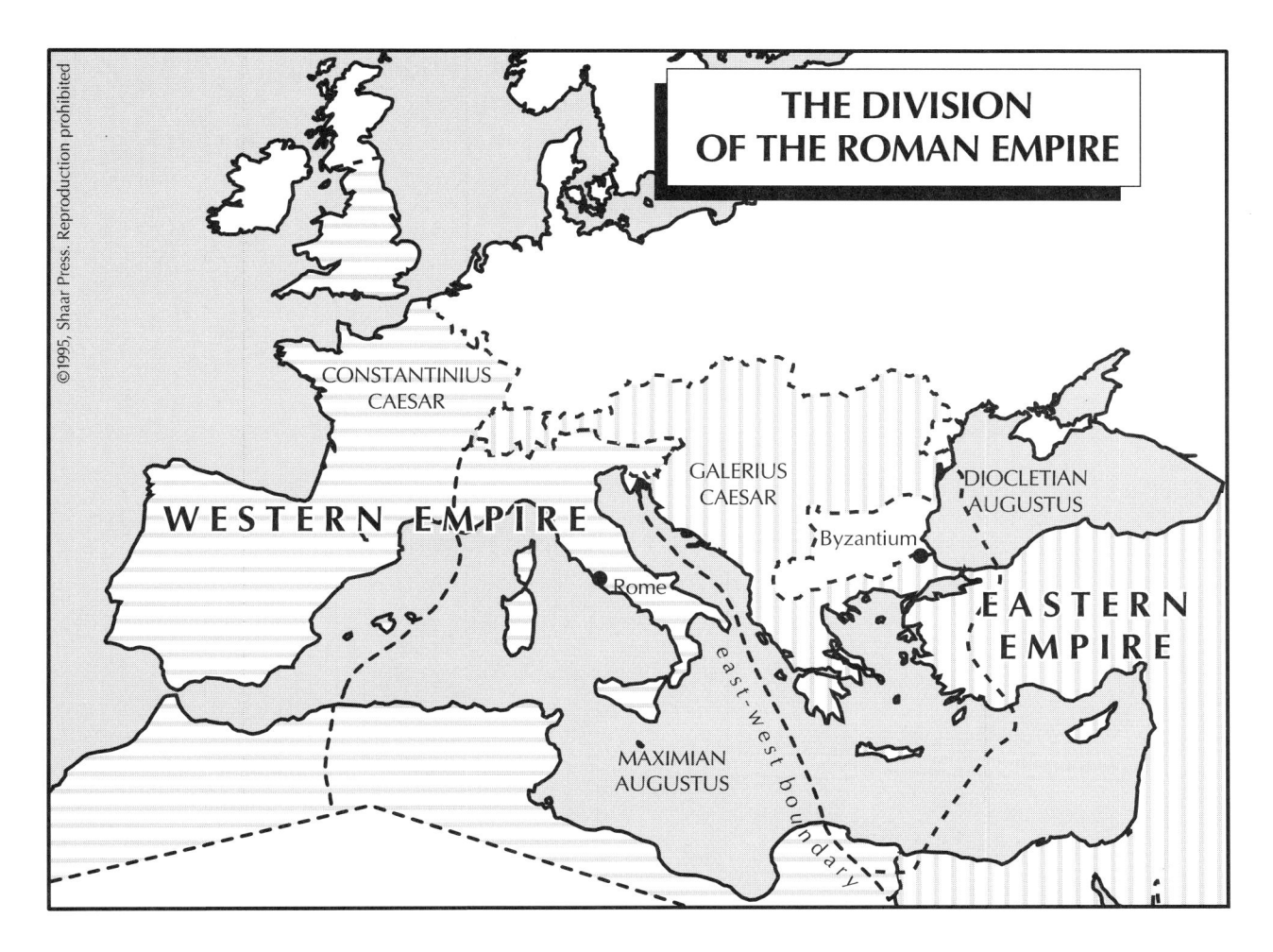

(Map showing the division of the Roman Empire, with labels: CONSTANTINIUS CAESAR, WESTERN EMPIRE, GALERIUS CAESAR, DIOCLETIAN AUGUSTUS, Byzantium, Rome, EASTERN EMPIRE, MAXIMIAN AUGUSTUS, east-west boundary)

By the year 324, Constantine had consolidated his power. He now began the building of his great new city, which he envisioned as becoming the new capital of the Roman Empire. He "modestly" named it Constantinople, and it arose and enveloped the ancient city of Byzantium on the Straits of the Bosporus.[12] In 330, Constantine shifted the seat of Roman government to Constantinople and took up physical residence there.

The Roman Empire now became two. The Western Empire, headquartered and centered in Rome, controlled Italy, most of Europe and North Africa. The Eastern Empire, with its capital in Constantinople, governed Asia Minor, Greece, Syria and the Land of Israel. Constantine was emperor over both pieces of Rome, but his successors would be unable to maintain this hegemony.

Not only did Rome split into two, but so did the Christian faith.

---
12. Byzantium is the modern-day city of Istanbul, Turkey.

The Western Church, the heir to the Western Roman Empire, adopted Rome as its "Eternal City" and eventually called itself the Roman Catholic Church. It also adopted the language of its Roman oppressor, making Latin its "holy tongue." The Eastern Church, itself riven by schisms and sectarianism, became the Christian Orthodox Church.[13] The two empires would soon war with each other, and so would the two churches.

Decline of the Jews in Israel

CONSTANTINE WAS VERY ANTI-JEWISH. His original pagan bigotry against Jews was more than reinforced after his conversion to Christianity. He ruthlessly persecuted the Jews living in the Land of Israel. It was under his reign that all the yeshivos and centers of Jewish life in the Land of Israel were destroyed. By 324, Jewish life in the Holy Land was a wasteland. Rabban Gamliel V, the son of Rabbi Yehudah Nesiah II, died in 308, and was succeeded by his son, Rabbi Yehudah Nesiah III.

During the persecutions, Rabbi Yehudah Nesiah III escaped Tiberias and settled in Caesarea together with a small number of scholars and other Jewish families. Even these few remnants of the great Jewish community of the Second Commonwealth were hounded and persecuted by Constantine's decrees.

Rabbi Yehudah Nesiah III conducted the yeshivah in Caesarea together with Rav Mani. But Rav Mani soon returned to Tiberias to reopen the yeshivah there. In about 325 he was forced to close the Tiberias yeshivah and join the smaller yeshivah of Tzippori (Sepphoris, in the Galilee), where, because of his stature and age, he became the head of the school, with Rabbi Chanina, the previous head of the yeshivah, magnanimously deferring to him. But these events were all only the death throes of the Jewish community in the Land of Israel.

The rabbis of the fourth century, far-seeing and not despairing in spite of the bitterness of their time, completed two great projects before the community of the Land of Israel disappeared from Jewish history for many hundreds of years. The first project was the completion of Talmud Yerushalmi, edited in its final, present-day

---

13. Its main divisions are Greek, Serbian, Armenian and Russian Orthodox.

form[14] in about 350. Rav Mani died at that time, and with his death the yeshivah at Tzippori closed. Thus, a book — the Talmud Yerushalmi — remains as the final memorial of the yeshivos of the Land of Israel of that era.

The Jewish Calendar

THE SECOND GREAT CONTRIBUTION by this last generation of scholars of the Land of Israel — and especially of Rabbi Yehudah Nesiah III[15] and his son and successor, Hillel II — was the establishment of the system for all future calculating of the Jewish calendar. All of civilization moves upon the basis of the measurement of time. Therefore, without an efficient and correct method of measuring that time — a calendar — man's attempt at progress is perforce thwarted. If this is true in general society, it is doubly true in Jewish society, where the divine rituals, the holy days and the entire pattern of religious daily life necessitate a precise calendar.

The calendar system of the Jewish year is basically lunar, the months being approximately 29½ days long, so that for practical purposes they must alternate as twenty-nine and thirty-day months. However, the matter is complicated by the need to reconcile the lunar calendar to the solar calendar, because of the necessity of having the holiday of Pesach always fall in the early spring. The mechanism of adding a thirteenth month, a leap month, to the calendar at regular intervals was used to solve this problem. In addition, the "birth" of the new moon every month, which would naturally govern the day of the week on which the first day of the month would fall, had to be proclaimed regularly.

The system used from the time of Moses until the fifth century of the Common Era involved the Sanhedrin hearing testimony from witnesses[16] as to the time of the "birth" of the new moon and then

---

14. Parts of the work have been lost to us over the centuries of exile. Rabbi Moshe ben Maimon mentions in his introduction to his *Commentary on the Mishnah* that five of the six sections of Mishnah are covered in Talmud Yerushalmi. However, in our time, the discussions contained in Talmud Yerushalmi are restricted to only four sections.
15. Died c. 351
16. See Talmud, *Rosh HaShanah* 18a - 26b, for a discussion of the procedure used by the Sanhedrin to proclaim the "new moon."

notifying Jewry in the Land of Israel, Babylonia, and the entire Diaspora of its decision. The Sanhedrin also determined which years would be leap years and had the responsibility for all calendar adjustments. Much rabbinic authority maintains that the Sanhedrin also had always taken into account the present-day formula based upon the mathematical and astronomical calculations.[17] As such, the Sanhedrin would never accept testimony seriously conflicting with the mathematical calculations and formulae upon which we solely base the Jewish calendar today.

Signaling the new moon before the establishment of the permanent calendar

Be that as it may, the great Mar Shmuel in the third century already publicly published many of the traditional, necessary calculations and also devised formulae for the implementation of a permanent, eternal calendar for the calculation of years and months in Jewish life.

Mar Shmuel, aside from being the great Torah scholar and head of the yeshivah of Nehardea, was also a doctor, an astronomer of note and an accomplished mathematician. However, as long as the Jewish community in the Land of Israel continued to function and the *Nasi* was able to convoke a Sanhedrin, the ancient method of deciding calendar matters through witnesses on a month-to-month basis continued. By the year 359, however, the system could no longer work, due to the weakening of the Jewish community in the Land of Israel. In that year the *Nasi*, Hillel II, formulated and published the permanent Jewish calendar, and thereby ended the millennia-old method of declaring the "new moon" on the basis of witnesses and Sanhedrin. This formula has proven to be essentially accurate and has not required any major adjustment over the nearly sixteen centuries of its usage, unlike the general Western solar-based calendar, which required extensive revision a number of centuries ago.

The Christian Calendar

UNDOUBTEDLY, ANOTHER REASON for the great importance of Hillel's stable, permanent, widely popularized Jewish calendar was the almost simultaneous promulgation of another new calendar adopted by the early

---

17. And that the rudiments of that formula were known to Jewish scholars from the time of Moses and Sinai.

264 ◻ ECHOES OF GLORY

Church fathers as the basic calendar of Christianity.

In 325, under Constantine's sponsorship, the leaders of the Christian Church convened a meeting in Nicaea,[18] there to decide upon certain basic doctrines of Christianity and to establish a general administration for the Church. The proceedings, decisions and records of this Council of Nicaea were very inimical to Jews and Judaism. The Church felt that its future success was dependent upon distancing itself as far as possible from its Jewish origins. Thus, the Council felt impelled to create a new calendar that would significantly differ in nature and calculation from the Jewish calendar. Easter, Pentecost and other Christian holidays would no longer be based solely on the Jewish calendar, as had been the practice in many Christian communities prior to the Council of Nicaea. If Jewry were not to have a set calendar of its own, and instead had to rely on the monthly proclamations of the Sanhedrin and the time-consuming process of horsemen delivering the news, the new Constantine calendar might have acquired dominance over much of Jewry, especially its unlearned segments. This was prevented by Hillel's promulgation of his clear, understandable, consistent and widely known calendar a short time after the Council of Nicaea's decisions.

Babylonian Leadership

MEANWHILE, IN BABYLONIA, after the death of Rav Huna in 298, his colleague Rav Chisda[19] became the head of the Sura yeshivah. Rav Chisda, eighty-two years old upon assuming office, served as Sura's head until his death ten years later in about 308. Rabbi Yehudah, the head of Pumbedisa, passed away in about 300 and was succeeded by Rabbah bar Nachmani, one of the legendary greats of the Talmud. Rabbah's colleague and eventual successor as head of Pumbedisa was Rav Yosef ben Chiya.[20] Under

---

18. A city in Asia Minor, located in present-day Turkey.
19. See Talmud, *Sanhedrin* 17b, where Rav Huna and Rav Chisda are referred to as "the elders of Sura."
20. The Talmud, *Berachos* 64a, describes Rabbah as an "uprooter of mountains" in his logical and analytical skills, while Rav Yosef was called "Sinai" because of his vast and all-encompassing knowledge of the Oral Law. Rav Yosef deferred to Rabbah, and only upon the death of the latter did he assume a leading role in Pumbedisa. Rav Yosef was sightless for many years.

Rabbah and Rav Yosef, Pumbedisa successfully challenged Sura for dominance in the Babylonian Jewish world.

Babylonia was shielded from the upheaval of Constantine's newly Christianized Roman world by the fact that it was under the control of the Sassanian dynasty, whose rulers kept both Rome and the Christians out of their empire. However, the Jews were forced to pay a price for the protection afforded them. The Sassanian kings, like all governments, always overspent their allowances and budgets, and therefore were constantly seeking new and higher forms of taxation to increase their operating revenues. Taxes against the Jews became especially high.

In 319, a complaint was lodged by the government against Rabbah alleging that his yeshivah and study sessions, especially the semi-annual gatherings of thousands to study Torah for a month, kept many Jews from engaging in work and commerce. They were therefore unable to pay their taxes, depriving the government of revenue.[21] Rabbah was forced to flee from Pumbedisa and died soon after, in 320, a fugitive and alone.[22] Rav Yosef succeeded Rabbah as head of Pumbedisa but only served for two and a half years, dying in 323.

Among the other leaders of Babylonian Jewry in the first quarter of the fourth century was Rav Sheshes,[23] a well-known disciple of Rav Huna of Sura. He conducted a small yeshivah in the town of Shalchi and would gain fame in the Talmud for his educational prowess. The great Rav Nachman bar Yaakov was a colleague of his. Rav Nachman headed a yeshivah in Mechoza. However, he is noted in the Talmud mainly for his legal prowess as a judge in civil cases. The Talmud states categorically that "in civil cases the law always follows the opinion of Rav Nachman."[24] His wife, Yilta, was also one of the famous women of the Talmud and a brilliant person in her own right.[25]

Rav Sheshes and Rav Nachman are also important in the story of the development of the Babylonian Jewish community, for due to their efforts many smaller but no less vital schools of Torah study de-

---

21. The ancient, misguided complaint not unknown today — "Of what value are the yeshivah students and the rabbis to society?" The complaint was actually lodged by a self-hating Jew. The echoes of such distorted thinking and behavior still reverberate in the Jewish world today.
22. See Talmud, *Bava Metzia* 86a.
23. Rav Sheshes, like Rav Yosef, was sightless.
24. See Talmud, *Kesubos* 13a.
25. See, for example, Talmud, *Chullin* 109b.

veloped in Babylonia outside of Sura and Pumbedisa. These yeshivos would produce many of the great leaders of Babylonian Jewry over the next two centuries.

Abbaye and Rava

IN 326 ABBAYE BECAME THE HEAD of the yeshivah in Pumbedisa. Orphaned from both of his parents while yet in infancy, Abbaye was raised by his uncle, Rabbah bar Nachmani, and his aunt, whom Abbaye referred to as his mother. Abbaye himself is also known in the Talmud as "Abba" and as "Nachmani." A child prodigy when he first came to the yeshivah, Abbaye was later chosen by his colleagues to become the head of Pumbedisa,[26] a position he held until his death in 339. Abbaye's main compatriots were Rava, Rav Zeira and Rabbah bar Masneh.[27]

However, Abbaye's name is eternally linked with that of Rava. Abbaye and Rava became in Jewish history the symbol of the Talmud. Their stamp of analysis and discussion appears in countless numbers of debates and discussions that form the Talmud. In fact, the surname of the Talmud is "the discussions of Abbaye and Rava."[28]

Every Jewish child beginning the study of Talmud would always first be introduced to the subject by Abbaye and Rava, and they would continue to accompany him in his study of the Talmud all his life. Abbaye and Rava became household names in the Jewish world in all later centuries, and even among those who were unlettered and unskilled in Talmud, everyone knew and loved Abbaye and Rava.

Rava headed a yeshivah in his community of Machoza after the death of Abbaye, and became the titular head of Pumbedisa as well. In reality it seems that the yeshivah of Pumbedisa relocated to Machoza during Rava's reign.[29] Rava was a powerful leader whose personality imprinted itself on his students and on the pages of the Talmud as well.[30]

---

26. See Talmud, *Horayos* 14a.
27. Ibid.
28. Talmud, *Succah* 28a.
29. Naftul, Vol. VII, p. 333.
30. Rava's great penitential prayer was: "Lord, my God, behold! Even before I was created, I was unworthy; and now that I have been created, it is as though I never was created. I am but dust in my life; how much more so in my death. I stand before You as

His death in 352 signalled the end of an era of creativity and vitality. A new era in Babylonian Jewish life would now begin.

A Warring Family

IN 337 THE PARTHIAN KING Shapur II again opened war against the Roman legions stationed at the borders of his empire. Constantine mobilized a large Roman army to defeat the Parthians once and for all.[31] However, on the way to his planned victory, Constantine died of natural causes.

His three sons, Constans, Constantius and Constantine,[32] all contested for the throne. A bitter civil war broke out, and the family members forgot about the Parthians and instead used the Roman army to slaughter each other. After more than a decade of war and carnage, Constantius emerged as the survivor and proclaimed himself emperor in 350. He proceeded to execute all of the remaining members of Constantine's family, with only two nephews of Constantius surviving, Gallus and Julian.

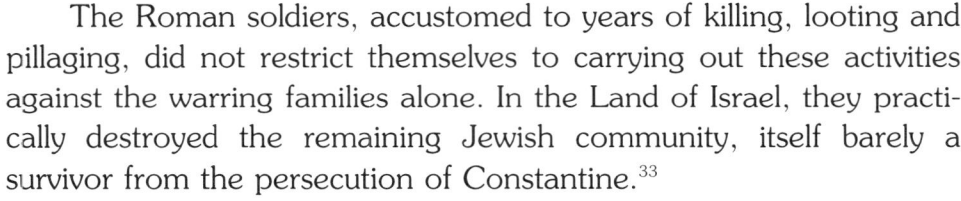

Constantius II, the son of Constantine

The Roman soldiers, accustomed to years of killing, looting and pillaging, did not restrict themselves to carrying out these activities against the warring families alone. In the Land of Israel, they practically destroyed the remaining Jewish community, itself barely a survivor from the persecution of Constantine.[33]

In 351, Constantius appointed his nephew Gallus as the commander of the legions facing the enemy at the Parthian border. A person like Gallus, a dissolute alcoholic, was certainly the wrong choice for such a position. Gallus and his soldiers preferred massacring innocent civilians to fighting the tough Parthian army. The massacres in the Land of Israel were particularly brutal, with individual Jews being hunted down for torture and sport. The Romans justified their behavior by stating that the Jews were engaged in another Bar Kochba-type

---

a vessel overcome with shame and embarrassment." This prayer has been incorporated into the prayer services for *Yom Kippur*.

31. As though there is a "once and for all" in the results of war!

32. The names certainly reflect their father's ego!

33. As mentioned above, 350 is the approximate year of the final editing of Talmud Yerushalmi. The Roman persecution prevented any further work on Talmud Yerushalmi, and only a small yeshivah in Tzippori survived till the fifth century.

revolt.[34] Only in Babylonia, protected behind the Parthian shield of strength and tolerance, were the Jews able to find respite.

"Julian the Apostate"

CONSTANTIUS HIMSELF BECAME frightened by the lawlessness of Gallus' troops in Syria and the Land of Israel. He reasoned, and correctly so, that Gallus and his leading general, Ursicinus, could loose the same band of murderers against him and his house guards. In 354, Constantius recalled Gallus and had him put to death. This left Julian as the only other surviving member of Constantine's family.

Constantius now appointed Julian as the ruler of Gaul and Roman Europe, calling him a Caesar, yet expecting him to be loyal and subservient to him. Gallus had been the wrong man for his task, but Julian was the right man for his. The only problem was that he was *too* right for the job. Constantius, paranoid and haunted by years of the murder of his relatives, became jealous of Julian and now attempted to remove him. But Julian, whose obvious abilities and magnanimous personality gained him wide public and army support, refused to go quietly. He raised an army and marched against his uncle, the emperor. However, before arriving at the gates of Constantinople, he learned that Constantius had died. Thus, Julian's arrival in Constantinople in 360 was not for struggle but for coronation. He now ruled over the entire Roman world.

The Church would brand him "Julian the Apostate," a title that has stuck throughout history. Julian did not believe in Christianity. It is likely that all of the blood shed by Constantine and his sons may have shaken Julian's ability to believe in the redemptive qualities of Christian tenets. In any event, he attempted to reintroduce the old and discredited pantheon of Roman gods as the official religion of the empire.

In his vigorous opposition to Christianity, he set about to dis-

Julian

---

34. There is very scant historical evidence to support this claim. It seems highly unlikely that after the depredations of Constantine and Constantius, the Jewish community, so small and weak in the Land of Israel, would consider the possibility of a revolt against Rome. Also, at this time the calumny that the Jews were guilty of "killing the Son of God" surfaced for the first time as a major complaint. It was used by the Roman Christians to justify their brutally inhumane treatment of the Jews. Tragically, this libelous accusation would have a very long life in the history of Western civilization.

mantle the official Church, which he regarded as subversive to Roman imperial interests. Following the old Middle Eastern adage that "the foe of my enemy is my friend and ally," Julian relaxed many of the discriminatory decrees imposed against the Jews over the preceding forty years. However, since he set out immediately to pursue the war against the Parthians, the Jews were now faced with the dilemma of supporting their Parthian protectors of old or aiding their newly found friend, Julian. The rabbis counseled against open support for Julian and were silent or evasive about his overtures.[35] In 363, Julian died in the campaign against Parthia.[36] The Roman empire was once again plunged into division, war and chaos. The Christians soon regained the upper hand, and the situation of the Jews under Roman domination once again became precarious.

The Empire Weakens

IN 378, THEODOSIUS THE GREAT became emperor of Rome. He ruled until his death in 395 and was the last Roman leader to assert his rule over the entire Western and Eastern Roman Empire. At his death, the empire was officially divided between his two sons, with Theodosius II eventually becoming emperor of the Eastern Roman Empire,[37] naming Constantinople as his capital. The Eastern Empire would last far longer than its sister in the West.

The barbarian tribes of Europe were pressing ever forward, and

Theodosius

---

35. All of this was in spite of Julian's promise to restore Jerusalem and even rebuild the Temple after defeating the Parthians! See Ephraim Urbach's *M'Olamam Shel Chachamim* (Jerusalem, 1988), pp. 408-410, for the background and possible reasons for this rabbinic reticence.

36. The circumstances of his death were suspicious, giving rise to the unending historical rumor that he was poisoned by Christian members of his own household staff. No proof has ever been offered, however, to substantiate this claim.

37. It was during Theodosius II's reign that the post of *Nasi* of the Jewish community in the Land of Israel was abolished in 425. After the death of Hillel II in c. 365, his son Rabban Gamliel VI reigned until c. 385. He in turn was succeeded by his son, Rabbi Yehudah Nesiah, who ruled until c. 400. The final *Nasi* was Rabban Gamliel VII, who died in 425. There is no doubt that the Church was greatly instrumental in the refusal of the emperor to appoint another *Nasi*. The Church could ill afford to have a live and functioning "scion of David" as the titular head of the Jewish community when the Church claimed for itself and its savior the exclusive role of Davidic dynasty.

the Roman legions no longer had the heart or the strength to stop them. In 410, Alaric the Visigoth and his warriors sacked the city of Rome. Even though the Romans were able to rally from this devastating event, it was clear that the very existence of the Western Roman Empire was doomed. That empire would not finally and officially collapse and die until 476, but the last century of Rome was already one of defeat, disorder and disheartened spirit.

It was during this time that Christianity was able to strengthen its grip on Rome, and it began to proselytize the barbarian tribes, intent on conquering Rome as well. Christianity adjusted many of its beliefs and incorporated much of the pagan rituals of these tribes into its own practices to make its drive for universal conversion to Christianity more successful. By the time of his death in 430, Augustine, a father of the Church (Saint Augustine was a bishop in Hippo, Africa, in the fifth century), had produced his vision of a sacred city and greatly influenced the direction of the newly emerging world view of Christianity.

The sack of Rome

Other Church fathers wrote and explained Christian doctrines. The Church thus became stronger intellectually as well as physically and numerically. But the Church continued to be riven with conflicting beliefs and doctrines. Gnostic and Arian heresies abounded, and these disputes were usually settled by the sword. But it was Rome's fall that would damage the Church most materially, for the end of Rome would plunge Europe, and the Church with it, into the five-centuries-long "Dark Ages." Yet, while Rome was falling, Jewish Babylonia was continuing to thrive.

Shifting of the Yeshivos

AFTER THE DEATH OF RAVA IN 352, his colleague, the well-known scholar and leader Rav Nachman bar Yitzchak,[38] became the head of the yeshivah of Pumbedisa. As mentioned above, this yeshivah had

---

38. Not to be confused with the great civil court judge of the previous generation, Rav Nachman bar Yaakov. Rav Nachman bar Yaakov, when referred to in the Talmud, is almost always called Rav Nachman, without his father's name being mentioned. Rav Nachman bar Yitzchak, however, is always referred to with his father's name attached.

moved during the lifetime of Rava to Machoza, and now was restored to its original home of Pumbedisa. Rav Nachman himself died in 356 and was succeeded by Rav Chama of Nehardea, who headed Pumbedisa until his death in 377. Yet, during the twenty-five-year period after Rava's death, Sura reasserted its position of predominance in Babylonian Jewish society.

Rav Papa,[39] a disciple of Abbaye, had founded a yeshivah in Naresh, near Sura, in 352, after the death of Rava. This yeshivah soon absorbed into it the yeshivah in Sura and became known itself as the yeshivah of Sura, although it was now located a few miles outside of that city. Rav Papa was assisted by Rav Huna brei d'Rav Yehoshua, another of the true disciples of Abbaye. The yeshivah in Naresh was very successful and became a main center for Torah scholarship in that generation. However, when Rav Papa died in 371, the yeshivah in Naresh did not continue. Instead, the yeshivah of Sura now moved to another suburb of Sura, Masa Mechasya.

Rav Ashi

THE RABBI AND LEADER of Masa Mechasya was Rav Ashi. He was one of the main architects of the structure of the Talmud and served as its first main editor. He was a product of many different yeshivos and a student of many great teachers. It was perhaps this very diversity of instructors and styles of learning that shaped the uniqueness of Rav Ashi and granted him universal authority in Talmudic matters. His main teachers were Ameimar,[40] himself a disciple of Rav Papa, and Rav Kahana.[41] But Rav Ashi also knew and may have studied under Rava, Rav Nachman bar Yitzchak and even Rabbi Chanina of Tzippori. In any event, Rav Ashi headed the yeshivah of Sura, now located in Masa Mechasya, from 371 till 427. Rav Ashi was blessed with great wealth, which certainly made his management of the yeshivah an easier task. He was also blessed with long life, a gift that enabled him to supply leadership stability to the yeshivah of

---

39. A legendary figure in the Talmud. His sons were great scholars in their own right. Rav Papa is quoted more than a thousand times in the Talmud.
40. He headed a yeshivah in Nehardea.
41. His yeshivah was in Pum Nehara, a city at the mouth of the Euphrates.

Sura, and continuity and structure to his editorial work on the Talmud.

Rav Ashi's compatriot in the yeshivah and in the work on the Talmud was Ravina. Together they organized the vast amount of rabbinic discussion of the past two centuries since the publication of Mishnah, arranged those discussions in a clear and logical fashion, and faithfully recorded the opinions and debates of the great scholars and teachers of all the Babylonian yeshivos until their time. They also included in the Talmud a great deal of anecdotal, aggadic, biographical and historical material of the past centuries of Jewish life. It is this latter material that gives the Talmud its particular human, soulful character and differentiates it from the genre of pure law books.

Mishnah manuscript from the famed Parma collection

Rav Ashi was in many ways a throwback to Rabbi Yehudah HaNasi. In his home, as in Rabbi's, there was to be found Torah and temporal greatness combined. Besides being wealthy, as was Rabbi Yehudah HaNasi, he too was the head of a great yeshivah, was on very good terms with the non-Jewish government, and was possessed of colleagues, students and sons who were able to help him in his great work. And as Rabbi Yehudah HaNasi, he was single-mindedly diligent in carrying out what he perceived as his life's mission.

In his yeshivah, then located in Masa Mechasya, Rav Ashi assigned the students two tractates of Mishnah every year for study, analysis, commentary and debate. As a result of this program, the entire basic Talmudic text was edited and prepared under Rav Ashi in about thirty years. The edition of the Talmud edited by Rav Ashi and Ravina would not be the final edited version we have today. The final form of the Talmud would not emerge until the time of Ravina II in c. 500, but the basic work of organization and editorship was completed by Ravina and Rav Ashi in the early part of the fifth century. Ravina, who was older than Rav Ashi, nevertheless took on a subservient role. Rav Acha, the son of Rava, was also a colleague of Ravina's and participated in the editorial work.

Ravina, like Rav Ashi, was a man of wealth and a trustee of charity to the poor. He died in 420 at the age of eighty. By that time the Talmud had already taken on the basic shape, form and content that would characterize it for the remainder of Jewish history.[42]

Reviving the Yarchei Kallah

RAV ASHI REESTABLISHED the famous *yarchei kallah* in Masa Mechasya, a continuation of the Babylonian tradition that had weakened in the past generations. Jews from all over Babylonia and Asia Minor traveled there to spend a month of Torah study and hear the lectures of the great scholars. The crowds were so immense and the honor of Torah so apparent that Rav Ashi wondered why there was no flood of converts to Judaism from the local non-Jewish population.[43]

This event united the Jewish people in Torah, no matter where they came from, how they earned their living, or what their social or intellectual standing was. Jews in all of their countries of dispersion lived a Talmudic way of life. The common bond that bound the Jewish nation together was this familiarity with and love of the Talmud, its way of life and its value system. Jews may have lived in Morocco, Syria, Spain, Provence, the Rhineland, Bohemia, Italy, Poland, Lithuania or Russia, but in their hearts and minds they were citizens of Sura, Pumbedisa, Nehardea and Masa Mechasya.[44]

---

42. Rashi (Rabbi Shlomo Yitzchaki, an eleventh-century scholar of Troyes, France, and the premier teacher and commentator in the Jewish world of the past millennia) explains the work of Rav Ashi and Ravina thus: "They [Rav Ashi and Ravina] were the last of the *Amoraim*. Until their day there was no organized Talmud. Whenever questions were raised in the study hall regarding the interpretation of a Mishnah or a question regarding an actual case decision, be it regarding monetary law or ritual matters, every *Amora* expressed his opinion. Rav Ashi and Ravina collected all the [records of the] discussions and opinions of the *Amoraim* who preceded them and collated them following the order of the tractates [of the Mishnah], each [record of] discussion being placed following the Mishnah it related to. They then posed the necessary questions [to clarify the issues] and gave the proper answers which the *Amoraim* had proposed, and they and their colleagues established all of this in the Talmud" (Rashi's commentary to Talmud, *Bava Metzia* 86a).

43. See Talmud, *Berachos* 17b.

44. The secularization of much of the Jewish people in the past two centuries has tragically erased this bond of Talmudic unity from the memory, psyche and soul of many Jews. Thus, we are witness to the sad phenomenon of Jews living physically in Tel Aviv and "spiritually" in New York or Paris.

Rav Ashi was the father of this monumental memory system and the way of life that it spawned. His creation, the edited and ordered Talmud, was and remains the key to Jewish survival throughout the ages.

Truce with Parthia

THE POLITICAL SITUATION IN BABYLONIA remained favorable for the Jews during the lifetime of Rav Ashi. In 390, the Romans, realizing the futility of their war against the Parthians and also sensing the growing inherent weakness of their once-invulnerable legions, called a truce in their campaign along the borders of the Parthian Empire.

In 399, King Yazdegerd I became emperor of the Parthian Empire. A wise, benevolent and astute ruler, he was to the Jews of Rav Ashi's Babylonia what Marcus Aurelius had been to the Jews of Rabbi's Land of Israel over two centuries earlier. Rav Ashi knew the king and encouraged his friendship towards his Jewish subjects. Yazdegerd ruled until his death in 421. His successor, Bahram V Gor, also treated the Jews with respect and tolerance. However, he foolishly made war against Rome and was beaten to a standstill. In the peace treaty signed after this struggle, the Parthians were forced to allow Christian missionaries within their borders. This would have dire consequences for the Babylonian Jews a generation later.

Leader of Pumbedisa

DURING THE REIGN OF Rav Ashi in Sura/Masa Mechasya, the yeshivah in Pumbedisa continued to function. After the death of Rav Chama of Nehardea in 377, the yeshivah was headed by Rav Zevid. Later, Rav Dimi of Nehardea, Rafram (the son of Rav Papa), Rav Kahana, and Rav Acha the son of Rava also served as heads of Pumbedisa. Rav Geviha of Bei Kasil, the *Rosh Yeshivah* in Pumbedisa, died in 433 and was succeeded by Rafram of Pumbedisa,[45] who died in 443. He was followed

---

45. Not to be confused with the above-mentioned Rafram, the son of Rav Papa, who headed Pumbedisa some decades earlier.

by Rav Rechumei, and then by Rav Sama bar Rava. Rav Sama's death in 476 coincided with the fall of the Western Roman Empire.

Leaders in Sura

WHEN RAV ASHI DIED IN 427, his successor as head of Sura/Masa Mechasya was his trusted colleague and disciple, Mareimar.[46] Under his reign Sura continued its primacy in Babylonian Jewish life. However, he died only five years after Rav Ashi, in 432, and Rav Idi bar Avin succeeded him. Rav Idi headed Sura for twenty years, until 452. His tenure produced years of stability and continued growth.

After Rav Idi, Rav Nachman bar Huna was installed as *Rosh Yeshivah*. He died in 435. Then, some twenty-eight years after his father's death, Mar bar Rav Ashi[47] finally assumed his father's position as head of Sura. He was the great son of a great father.[48] He continued the editing work on the Talmud that his father and Ravina had initiated. But perhaps as importantly, he served as the solid rock of leadership that the Babylonian Jewish community needed when their politically secure world suddenly began to crumble under the changes brought about by the Christian missionaries then penetrating Babylonian society for the first time.

The pagan Parthians were at one and the same time a ripe target for Christianity and a bitter foe of the new faith invading its borders. The opponents of Christianity, the *magi* and their followers, reacted very belligerently to the fanatical Christian missionaries. Armed clashes between the followers of the faiths soon broke out. King Yazdegerd II, who succeeded his father in 438, had begun his reign as a friend of the Jews. However, the Persian priests soon turned their anti-Christian persecution into an anti-Jewish campaign as well, and the king did not stop them.

In 441, Yazdegerd II opened a new war against the Eastern Roman Empire, now beginning to be known as the Byzantine

A magi

---

46. He is referred to in the Talmud sometimes as Rabbi Yeimar.

47. Although always called Mar bar Rav Ashi in the Talmud, his real, given name (which he used when signing legal documents) was Tavyumi (*Bava Basra* 12b).

48. In all later generations the Jewish expression for a scholar was "a Mar bar Rav Ashi."

Empire, and the Christian missionaries remaining in Parthia were either killed or expelled. At the same time, at the instigation of the *magi* priests, Yazdegerd II instituted laws and decrees against the practice of Judaism, as well as terribly discriminatory laws against individual Jews. The sun of Babylonian Jewry suddenly darkened.

Declining Fortunes in Babylonia

MAR BAR RAV ASHI struggled valiantly to strengthen the Jewish community of Babylonia in its hour of despair. He lobbied for the annulment or at least non-enforcement of many of the anti-Jewish decrees. He endeavored to protect Sura at all costs and continued the intensive Torah learning program there, which had always been its hallmark.

The worsening situation in Babylonia came as a shock to the Jewish community, for nothing of this sort had officially been sanctioned in Babylonia for almost a millennium. Jewish confidence was shattered. Mar bar Rav Ashi attempted to pick up the pieces and rebuild the hopes of the Jewish community.

Yazdegerd II died in 457, and in the ensuing power struggle for succession many of his anti-Jewish decrees were annulled or forgotten. When Mar bar Rav Ashi died in 467, the situation had apparently normalized for the Jews of Babylonia. But the new king, Peroz,[49] after a short respite, once again intensified the campaign against the Jews.

In 470, Peroz arrested and executed three great scholars.[50] Their crime was the open advocacy of Torah learning and Jewish practice.

---

49. He was called "The Wicked" by the Jews of his and later generations.
50. They were Ameimar, a disciple of Rav Ashi; Huna, the son of the then-reigning *Reish Galusa;* and Mesharshya.

THE CHAIN OF TRANSMISSION OF THE ORAL LAW

The Leaders of the Generations of the Tannaim and Amoraim*

THE TANNAIM

Generations of the Second Temple
- ☐ Shimon HaTzaddik
- ☐ Antignos
- ☐ Yose ben Yo'ezer and Yose ben Yochanan ⎫
- ☐ Yehoshua ben Perachyah and Nitai HaArbeli ⎬ THE ZUGOS
- ☐ Yehudah ben Tabbai and Shimon ben Shetach ⎪
- ☐ Shemayah and Avtalyon ⎪
- ☐ Shammai and Hillel ⎭
- ☐ R' Shimon I**
- ☐ Rabban Gamliel**

Destruction of the Second Temple
- ☐ Rabban Shimon II**
- ☐ Rabban Gamliel II**
- ☐ R' Shimon III**

Compilation of the Mishnah
- ☐ R' Yehudah HaNasi**

THE AMORAIM
- ☐ R' Yochanan, Rav, and Shmuel
- ☐ R' Huna
- ☐ Rabbah
- ☐ Rava
- ☐ R' Ashi

* Based on Maimonides' Introduction to *Mishneh Torah*
** Son of his predecessor

Mar bar Rav Ashi had been succeeded by Rabbah Tosfaah, a disciple of Ravina I. When he died in 474, his successor was Ravina II. With him came the close of the Talmudic era in Babylonia. He headed Sura for twenty-six years until his death in 500.

Ravina II was the final main redactor of the Talmud. He lived at a time of deteriorating Jewish fortunes in Babylonia. Even after Peroz died in 484, there were no efforts made by the new ruler, Kavadh I, to ameliorate the Jewish situation. Thus, the time of the collapse of the Western Roman Empire witnessed Jewish (as well as civilized) life in Europe at an end, the Jewish community in the Land of Israel practically non-existent, and the great Babylonian center of Judaism threatened as never before. But it also confirmed the completion of the great work of Torah, the Talmud, that would guide the Jewish people through all its troubles in all future generations.

17
The Talmud — The Book of the Jews

THE JEWISH PEOPLE are known as the "People of the Book." In general world opinion, the phrase refers to the Bible and describes it as the text which is most prized and studied by the Jews. While that is essentially true, it is not completely accurate. The text of the book actually emphasized in day-to-day study is the Talmud, it is as much the book of the people (of Israel) as the Jews are the people of that book.

From the Talmud, one can perceive the true "inside story" of the Jewish people, and its love of Torah and its life of destiny. For, as will be explained later, the Talmud has come to be more than a book. It represents a way of life, a description of human society and its vagaries, a conduit for the never-ending conversation between God and man. It is also the ultimate textbook of Jewish study, for on its pages is recorded the whole sweep of biblical history, all of the details and minutiae of the legal and ritual system of Judaism as embodied in the Oral Law, as well as biographies, anecdotes and insights into the lives of the main figures of Israel, manifesting an abiding belief in the Lord's personal attention to individuals and His never-failing, if sometimes apparently long-delayed, exercise of justice, retribution and reward. It also records psychological analyses, medical diagnoses, business and commercial practices and advice, marital counseling, humor and pathos, and an unflinching assessment of God's demands upon Jews and the Jewish people. Several great descriptions of the Talmud are

Talmud editions through the centuries: A 9th-century manuscript of the Talmud from Munich, Germany

available,[1] but despite them all (the foregoing included), only a true student of Talmud can really appreciate the scope and nobility of this creation. Thus, to all others, in spite of all translations, popularizations and Jewish Studies programs, the Talmud, like the God of Israel, remains hidden, private and to a great extent, misunderstood and improperly interpreted.

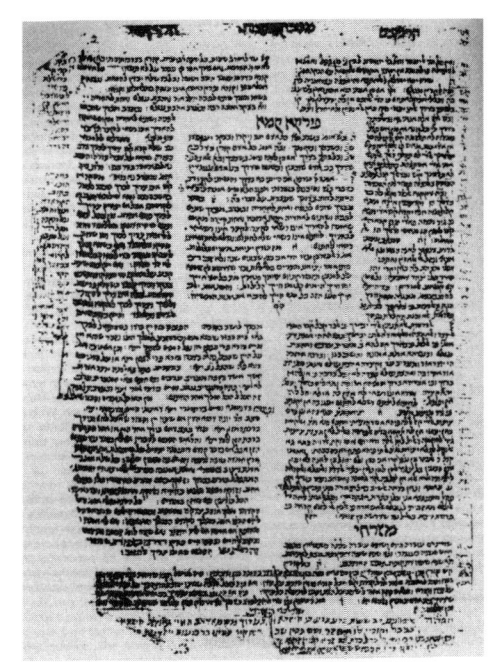

Mishnah manuscript with Ramban's commentary

---

1. The following quote from Harry Austryn Wolfson, in his youth a student at a great European yeshivah and later a leading professor of Jewish and Semitic studies at Harvard University for many decades, is a gem of clarity and emotional tribute to the Talmud and the methodology of its study: "In the Talmudic method of text study, the starting point is the principle that any text that is deemed worthy of serious study must be assumed to have been written with such care and precision that every term, expression, generalization or exception is significant not so much for what it states as for what it implies. The contents of ideas as well as the diction and phraseology in which they are clothed are to enter into the reasoning.

"This method is characteristic of the *Tannaic* interpretation of the Bible from the earliest times; the belief in the divine origin of the Bible was sufficient justification for attaching importance to its external forms of expression. The same method was followed later by the *Amoraim* in their interpretation of the Mishnah and by their successors in the interpretation of the Talmud, and it continued to be applied to the later forms of rabbinic literature. Serious students themselves, accustomed to a rigid form of logical reasoning and to the usage of precise forms of expression, the Talmudic-trained scholars attributed the same quality of precision and exactness to any authoritative work, be it of divine origin or the product of the human mind....[All] phenomena about the text become a matter of investigation. Why does the author use one word rather than another? What need was there for the mentioning of a specific instance as an illustration? Do certain authorities differ or not? If they do, why do they differ? All these are legitimate questions for the Talmudic student of texts. And any attempt to answer these questions calls for ingenuity and skill, the powers of analysis and association, and the ability to set up hypotheses — and all these must be bolstered by a wealth of accurate information and the use of good judgment. No limitation is set upon any subject; problems run into one another; they become intricate and interwoven, one throwing light upon the other. And there is a logic underlying this method of reasoning. It is the very same kind of logic which underlies any sort of scientific research, and by which one is enabled to form hypotheses, to test them and to formulate general laws.

"The Talmudic student approaches the study of texts in the same manner as the scientist approaches the study of nature. Just as the scientist proceeds on the assumption that there is a uniformity and continuity in nature, so the Talmudic student proceeds on the assumption that there is a uniformity and continuity in human reasoning. [The Talmudic method of study] is nothing but the application of the scientific method to the study of texts." (From Wolfson's essay "Cresscas' Critique of Aristotle" [Harvard University Press, Cambridge, Massachusetts, 1929].)

Talmud Yerushalmi

THE TALMUD IS STRUCTURED as a commentary on the Mishnah. There are two versions. The shorter, less studied version is called *Yerushalmi*.[2] It was developed in the third and fourth centuries of the Common Era and, as its name suggests, it was a product of the yeshivos and scholars still remaining in the Land of Israel at that time. It is written in Aramaic, but in the dialect of that language spoken by the Jews of Judah and the Galilee, differing somewhat from the Aramaic dialect spoken by the Jews of Babylonia, which dialect became the basic language of the Talmud Bavli.[3]

The *Yerushalmi*, unlike the *Bavli*, included a discussion of the agricultural laws governing farm life in the Land of Israel. However, it omitted any reference to the sections of Mishnah dealing with the sacrificial Temple services and the attendant laws of ritual purity.[4] For, after the death of Commodus, the son of Marcus Aurelius, the Romans exerted relentless pressure on Jewish life in the Land of Israel, wherein these laws were exclusively relevant.[5] The Yerushalmi suffered from the stifling of its independent expression and the curtailment of its contents by the heavy hand of the Roman occupiers of the country. A detailed discussion of the Temple and its rituals apparently could be seen as subversive by the Roman authorities. The later scholars and commentators on the Talmud and the adjudicators of *halachah* used the *Yerushalmi* as a resource book and a valuable

A manuscript page from Talmud Yerushalmi, Berachos

---

2. Literally, the "Jerusalem Talmud." It is also known as the "Palestinian Talmud."
3. Literally, the "Babylonian Talmud."
4. The order of *Kodashim* and most of the order of *Taharos*.
5. Severus and his descendants ruled the empire from 193 to 235, and they were ill remembered by the Romans and even more so by the Jews of Judah. Dio Cassius, the famous Roman historian and a contemporary of the Severan dynasty, described its rule as follows: "Our history and the affairs of the Romans descend from an age of gold (the times of Marcus Aurelius and Commodus) to one of iron and rust."

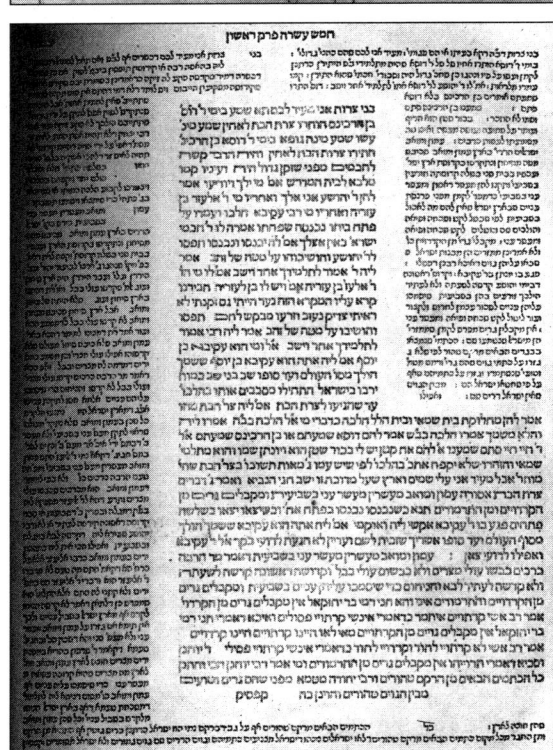

Talmud editions through the centuries: Top L-R: Tractate Avodah Zara, Ubeda, Spain, 1290; The Soncino Edition, Tractate Beitzah, Italy, 1484. Bottom L-R: The Bomberg edition, the first complete edition of the Talmud to be printed, Tractate Yevamos, Venice, c. 1520; The Amsterdam edition, Tractate Bava Kamma, Amsterdam, 1764.

source of tradition regarding the Oral Law; but it was never regarded as ultimately decisive by itself.[6]

Talmud Bavli

THEREFORE, WHEN WE REFER TO the Talmud, the Talmud Bavli is meant. This gigantic piece of scholarship was composed over a time span of 350 years, in the Babylonian yeshivos and Jewish communities. On its pages generations of scholars[7] debate with each other on matters of Jewish law and life. The Talmud knows of no separation of time or place in its discussions and deliberations. The way the text runs, scholars who never saw each other, who lived in different communities and centuries, nevertheless are represented as speaking to, explaining to and debating with one another.

The Babylonian Talmud is unhurried, thorough in its review of any problem, willing to allow matters to remain in doubt if the clear, logical and correct solution is not ultimately present. Above all, it is analytical to the nth degree. Because of this, the Babylonian Talmud can be deceiving to those who approach it with a superficial, even if scholarly based, method of study. For without concentrated effort and rigid methods of traditional analysis and study, the Talmud will not easily give up its secrets. It is finely organized, yet will, at any given moment, apparently stray far away from the original topic under discussion, only to return to it eventually with a fresh approach and a new vision.

True to its Oral Law origins, the Talmud allows associative memory to dictate much of its intricate changes of direction. When quoting the opinion of one of the rabbis on any given subject, it may leave the topic at hand and pursue other opinions of that scholar on completely unrelated topics. The entire gamut of all Torah subjects is up for discussion and reconciliation at any one time, and the student of the Talmud is somehow presumed to be knowledgeable of all the issues

---

6. See the *Book of Halachos* by Rabbi Yitzchak AlFasi, at the conclusion of tractate *Eruvin,* concerning the relative lack of scholarly authority of *Yerushalmi* vis-á-vis *Bavli.*

7. The roughly seven generations of the rabbis of the Talmud (spanning approximately 350 years) are called *Amoraim,* in contradistinction to the rabbis of the Mishnah, who are called *Tannaim.*

of the entire Talmud even before he begins its study! No wonder the rabbis referred to the Talmud as a vast sea in whose waters one must quickly become an excellent swimmer so as not to drown.

Aggadah

AS A SOURCE WORK for all past Jewish history, the Talmud fleshes out for us the lives of the extraordinary people who populate the Bible. It is only the Talmud that allows a truly Jewish glimpse into the human, psychological and political aspects of the events recounted in the Bible.

A noted historian[8] once wrote regarding the art of historical writing, "Everyone is today aware of the fundamental difference between ... those historians who paint portraits ... that are rounded and three-dimensional, so that we believe ... that we are able to tell what it would have been like to have lived in such conditions, and on the other [hand], antiquaries, chroniclers, accumulators of facts or statistics ... theorists who look on the use of imagination as opening the door to the horrors of guesswork, subjectivism, journalism, or worse. This all-important distinction rests on ... the faculty ... called 'fantasia,' without which the past cannot ... be resurrected. ... Without 'fantasia' the past remains dead; to bring it to life we need ... to hear men's voices, to conjecture what may have been their experience, their forms of expression, their values, outlook, aims, ways of living; without this we cannot grasp whence we came, how we come to be as we are now, not merely physically or biologically ... but socially, psychologically, morally; without this there can be no genuine self-understanding." Well, the Talmud is replete with the use of that most-desired "fantasia." It is called *Aggadah,* and it is the backbone of all Jewish moral thought, biblical biography and Jewish history.

The Talmud, with its companion aggadic work, the *Midrash,* is therefore able to bind together the Jewish past, present and future seamlessly and in a fashion unaffected by time and circumstance. It is precisely because of this quality that the Talmud itself has remained and continues to remain the book of the Jews.

---

8. Isaiah Berlin in his essay "Giambattista Vico and Cultural History" in *The Crooked Timber of Humanity: Chapters in the History of Ideas,* Henry Hardy (London and New York, 1990).

The Power of the Talmud

THE JEWS ARE THE PEOPLE of the Book of the Talmud also in the sense that the Talmud has had such an influence over their lives for almost two millenia. For the Talmud taught Jews that no occurrence in life and no person in this world is too petty or unworthy of notice and appreciation. Thus, in the Talmud all lines between the legal codifier, the moral arbiter, the practical counselor and the social critic are blurred to disappearance. What emerges is a worldview steeped in holiness and buttressed by faith and goodness, that allows for a life of serenity and worth even under the worst physical circumstances of poverty and persecution.

The survival of the Jewish people in its long and difficult exile is really the story of the power and influence of the Talmud over Israel. The Jews, in all of their lands of dispersion, from Morocco to India, from South Africa to Finland, attempted to live a Talmudic way of life. The Jews loved the Talmud.[9] The Bible was fire, divine, and after a certain level of understanding, obviously beyond true human appreciation and evaluation. The Talmud, however, was human, understanding, comforting, challenging and personal. It tolerated individual creativity and even peculiarity, encouraged mass participation in its study, provided practical advice and guidance, and demanded an attainable level of truth and morality in life. Jews felt good at the open page of the Talmud. They sensed their eternity and worth and felt a close bond and affinity with the towns and yeshiv-

Talmud editions through the centuries: The Vilna edition of the Talmud, the standard edition used today. Top: Tractate Avodah Zara, 1890 Bottom: A standard Talmud page

---

9. Herman Wouk, in his as-yet unpublished diary, 16 January, 1972, explains that he studies Talmud regularly "because by now the Talmud is in my bones. Its elegant and arcane ethical algebra, its soaked-in quintessential Jewishness, its fun, its difficulty, its accumulative virtue, all balance against the cost in time and the so-called 'remoteness from reality'...Anyway, I love it. That's reason enough. My father once said to me, 'If I had enough breath left in me for only one last word, I'd say to you, 'Study the Talmud.' I'm just beginning to understand him. I would say the same thing to my own sons. Above and beyond all its other intellectual and cultural values, the Talmud is, for people like us, 'identity,' pure and ever-springing."

os and personalities of Jewish Babylonia, since their own towns, yeshivos and leading personalities were not much different, even centuries later and continents apart. To be a Jew was and is to be a Talmudic person.

Toward Deeper Understanding

Talmud editions through the centuries: The Schottenstein Edition; contains the Vilna edition with an annotated interpretive elucidation in English (Brooklyn, NY, begun 1990)

THIS ESSAY ON THE OVERALL VIEW of the Talmud in Jewish life is presented at this juncture as an introduction to the description of the facts and personages that physically brought the Talmud into being. I feel that a history book, especially a Jewish history book, definitely needs "fantasia," which should not be only about facts and dates but about identity and imagination. There has been no major work of letters in world history as imaginative and creative as the Talmud. Not to understand the role of the Talmud — nay, not to have studied Talmud and experienced its grip upon its students — may not prevent one from writing a book on Jewish history; but it will certainly cripple the effort. If this is true for the author of a book on Jewish history, it is, in my opinion, valid for the reader of Jewish history books as well. I am aware that not everyone is or can be a student of the Talmud. As such, I have attempted in this chapter, no matter how inadequately, to communicate to all of the readers of this book a sense of the uniqueness and importance of the Talmud in Jewish life throughout the centuries. By achieving an appreciation of the Talmud and its role in Jewish life, a deeper understanding of Jewish agendas and behavior in history can be gained.

Section V

New Challenges, New Lands

18
The Era of Byzantium

THE FALL OF THE CITY OF ROME and the collapse of the Western Empire naturally transferred all the remaining power and glory that was once Rome to Constantinople and the Eastern Empire. By the sixth century, Christianity had already been the official religion of the Eastern Roman Empire for almost two hundred years. The Church in Constantinople was the Orthodox Church,[1] and it was also known as the Byzantine Church after the original name of Constantinople, Byzantium.

The rise of Byzantium made things very difficult for the Jews who lived under its sway. The Byzantine Church was extremely hostile to the Jews and Judaism. Its attitude was partially fueled by the Jews' own revulsion at the adoption of so many Greek, Roman and pagan customs and values by this supposedly monotheistic religion. The veneration of icons and statues, the representation of human forms in the mosaic floors and wall frescoes of the Byzantine churches and homes,[2] the superstition, mystery and demonology of the Eastern Church, all brought about a Jewish attitude of open scorn and condescension towards the Church. The Church resented this Jewish attitude and took violent steps to repress the Jews.

---
1. Basically, it was what is known today as the Greek Orthodox Church.
2. Jewish homes of the period, especially those of the semi-assimilated upper class, also contained such artwork. Eventually, even synagogues allowed these representations on their floors and walls. One of the halachic justifications for allowing these forms of general Byzantine culture into the synagogue was the fact that they were purely flat and two-dimensional. See Tosafos, *Yoma* 54a-b, as well as the chapter on artwork and the synagogue in *Mechkarim B'Sifrus HaTeshuvos* by Y.Z. Kahana (Mosad Horav Kook, Jerusalem, 1965).

The wall of Constantinople

The New Rashei Galusa

THE JEWS IN BABYLONIA were still out of the Byzantines' reach. But they had a wealth of troubles of their own. Although Parthian persecution of the Jews had not intensified, neither had it relaxed. The position of *Reish Galusa* became open to bidding and corruption.

In 508 Huna bar Kahana succeeded to the position. He exhibited cruelty and incompetency, always a deadly combination of traits. He and his entire family died in about 530, under mysterious and suspicious circumstances.

The new *Reish Galusa*, a man by the name of Pachda, bribed the Parthian court to appoint him to the position even though he was not descended from the family of David. The Parthians later removed Pachda from office and appointed a fifteen-year-old nephew of Huna as *Reish Galusa*. This young man was known as Zutra, and later in life as Mar Zutra,[3] and he proved to be a strong, able and worthy possessor of the office. His reign began in 538, and for thirteen years he

---
3. Not to be confused with Mar Zutra, the *Amora*.

provided stable leadership to the Babylonian Jewish community. However, this period of relative bliss ended when, in 551, he organized an army and waged war against marauding tribesmen who were terrorizing parts of the local Jewish population.

His unapproved wars and domination of certain local provinces caused the Parthian king to view Mar Zutra as a rebel and threat to his hegemony. In 558, the king crushed Mar Zutra's forces and put a temporary end to the position of *Reish Galusa*.[4] The general political situation in Babylonia declined in the sixth century, with wars, civil strife, palace intrigues and local warlords dominating the general scene. The Byzantines made constant encroachments on Babylonia, and as a result of all this chaos, the Jews there suffered physical and economic hardship.

The Savoraim

NEVERTHELESS, THE WORK and devotion of the scholars of Jewish Babylonia continued even in this hostile environment. The sixth century was the time of the Savoraim, the men who explained, and in many cases further edited, the Talmud.[5] The work of the Savoraim was basically a product of Pumbedisa, the remaining great center of learning ever since Peroz's forcible closing of the Sura yeshivah in c. 500.

Rabbi Yosei, a disciple of Ravina, headed Pumbedisa until 514. It was during his tenure that the Talmudic text was finalized in the version that is extant today. When Rabbi Yosei died, Sura reopened, but soon closed once more because of government persecution.[6] In 559, the troubles of the Jews of Babylonia forced the temporary closing of Pumbedisa as well.

---

4. There was no official *Reish Galusa* appointed in Babylonia for the next thirty years, and the office would not regain its luster and power until the Moslem Caliphate controlled Babylonia some eighty years later.

5. From the time of the Savoraim onwards, no further explanations or additions were made to the actual text of the Talmud itself. All later commentaries and opinions regarding the Talmud were written as separate works. However, some of the commentaries, such as that of Rashi and the glosses of Tosafos, eventually found themselves always to be included on the same printed page of the Talmud, though naturally not as part of the Talmudic text itself.

6. It would successfully reopen in 591 and enjoy centuries of continuous operation.

The scholars now moved their center of Torah learning to Peroz-Shavur, a suburb of Nehardea. However, the study of Torah continued to decline precipitously in Babylonia,[7] and only with the coming of the Moslem conquerors and the attendant period of the *Geonim* would Babylonia rebuild itself as the greatest Torah center of its time and the dynamic leader of the Jewish world.

Life Under the Byzantines

THE COMBINATION OF ROMAN POWER and fanatical Christian missionary zeal made the Byzantines a fearsome threat to all their neighbors and especially to Jews. The Byzantine Empire wished to reconquer all of the western territories lost to the barbarian tribes who had sacked Rome a century earlier, while at the same time converting the world to their version of Christianity.

As mentioned earlier, the Christian religion was by now badly divided on fundamental doctrines of faith and practice, and the Eastern Orthodox Church of Byzantine was becoming more and more different and estranged from its western counterpart, the Roman (Catholic) Church. In the eastern, Parthian area of the Byzantine Empire, the heresy of the Manichaean brand of Christianity[8] was eliminated by the sword.

The Byzantines conquered the Land of Israel late in the sixth century. However, in 614 the Parthians, under the leadership of Chosoroes II, in turn occupied the Holy Land. Chosoroes II was a powerful warrior, and his rule stabilized the country. However, when he died in 628, the Parthians fell to warring among themselves and, in 629 the Byzantine emperor Heraclius retook the Holy Land, driving out the Parthians.

Even though Heraclius had made magnanimous promises to the Jews remaining in the Land of Israel, his reign proved to be one of persecution and coercion. He attempted to force the small remaining

---

7. See Maimonides' introduction to his monumental *Mishneh Torah* for a description of this difficult time.

8. This was a faith that combined elements of Zoroastrianism with primitive Christian beliefs. First founded by the Persian Christian sage Manes in the third century, it exerted vast sway over the masses for almost three hundred years. Even Augustine admitted to having been influenced by and almost converted to its doctrines.

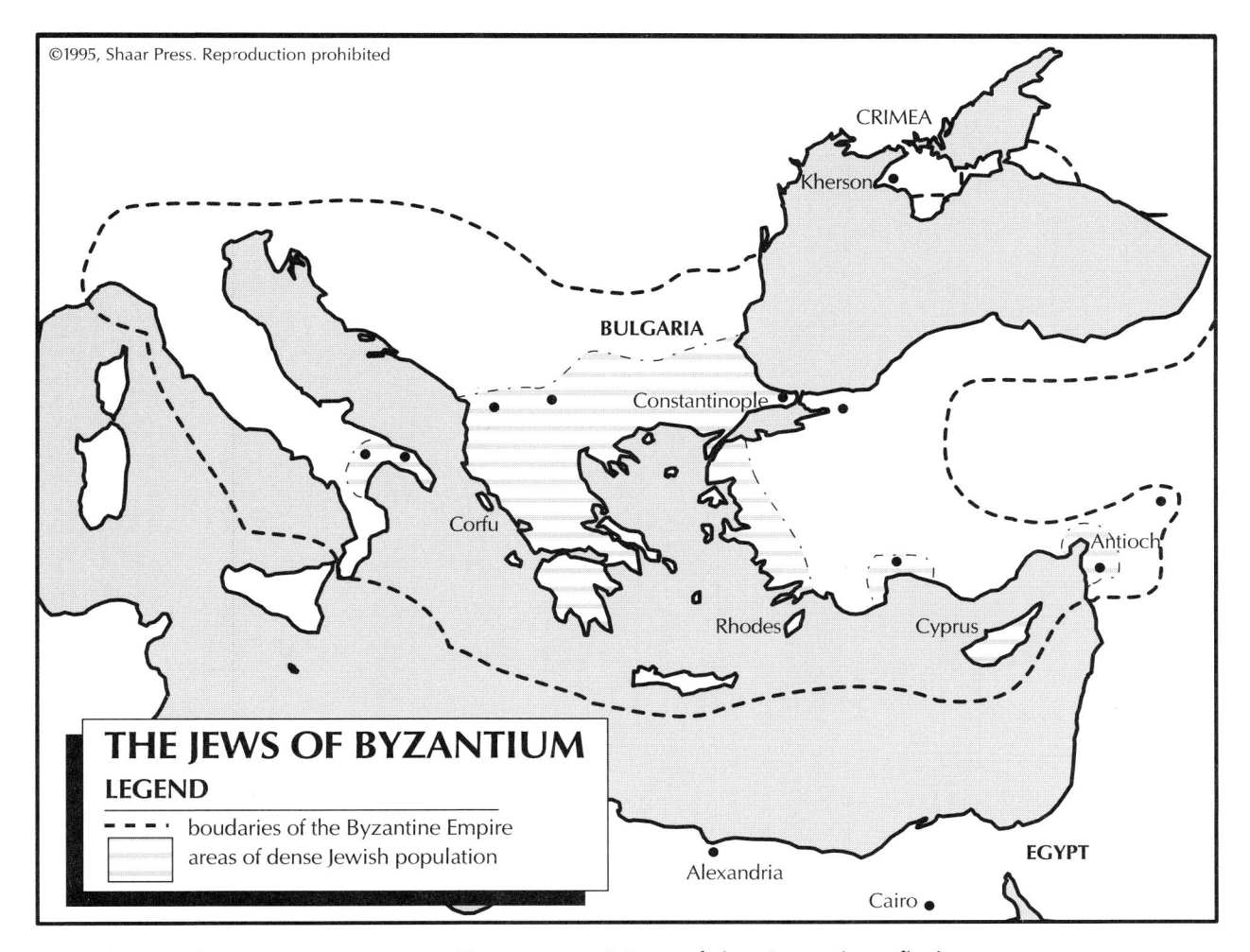

THE JEWS OF BYZANTIUM

LEGEND

- - - - boudaries of the Byzantine Empire
▬▬▬ areas of dense Jewish population

Jewish population to convert to Christianity. Most of the Jews then fled their homeland, while hundreds who remained were martyred because of their refusal to convert. There would be no organized Jewish community in the Land of Israel for almost three hundred years, and there would be no numerically substantial Jewish community in the Land of Israel until the sixteenth century, over eight hundred years later.[9]

The Parthian-Byzantine war, which began in 610 and ended in 629, was in reality the last gasp of these feuding empires as far as the

---

9. However, as will be noted in succeeding chapters, there was always a Jewish presence in the Land of Israel during all of history. During the reign of the Moslems, from the middle of the seventh century onward, individual Jews and their families settled and sometimes even flourished in the country. There were numerous recorded attempts by Jews to live in Jerusalem. These attempts were intermittently successful. In the ninth and tenth centuries, there was an organized, if small, Jewish community in Jerusalem. But only in the sixteenth century was there a rebirth of intensive Jewish life in the Land of Israel, and it was then centered in Safed and Jerusalem.

Middle East was concerned. The Arabs and their sword of Mohammed lay lurking just off stage; naturally, they were noticed by no one. The triumph of the Byzantines in 629 boded evil for the Jews of Babylonia, for now the Eastern Church was determined to settle the Jewish question once and for all.

Great oppressive decrees were promulgated against the observance of Judaism. There was an attempt to apply the onerous decrees of Heraclius, already in force in the Land of Israel, to Babylonian Jewry as well. The recitation of Jewish prayers,[10] the teaching and study of Torah, and the primacy of Hebrew over Greek as the language of the Jews were all threatened. It has been theorized that had the Byzantines conquered and controlled Babylonia for a long period of time, the downfall of the Babylonian Jewish community would have been certain. As it was, the reign of the Byzantines was short-lived, for by 638 they were in full retreat before the Moslem Arabs.

Jews in the Western Empire

THE JEWS WHO LIVED in the Western Roman Empire fell under the domination of the barbarian tribes who destroyed Rome. As these tribes in turn became Christianized, their attitude towards the Jews, which at first had been neutral at worst, turned hostile.[11]

In 589 the Visigoth bishops of Spain were able to have the ruler of that country ban the open practice of Judaism.[12] In 613, the Jews

---

10. The Christians especially objected to the basic Jewish declaration of faith, *Shema Yisrael* (Hear O Israel, the Lord is our God, the Lord is One), on the basis that this statement of God's Oneness was meant to be specifically and purposely anti-Christian. The fact that the prayer antedated Christianity by millennia and is part of the Bible itself (*Deuteronomy* 6:4) meant nothing in a predetermined attitude of hatred and oppression. Byzantine soldiers and police were actually posted at synagogues to prevent the recitation of this and other "hateful" prayers. (Shades of the Communist "progressive world" of the twentieth century!) The Jews and their prayers went underground, and some of the prayers were transferred to different sections of the prayer service where the guards would not expect or notice them. Vestiges of this practice still remain today in the traditional Jewish prayer book.

11. The situation of hate and prejudice was undoubtedly aided by the disappearance of almost all Roman science and culture during this early stage of the "Dark Ages." This is not to say that hatred and persecution of Jews does not occur in societies of culture and science. However, in the "Dark Ages" there was almost no intelligentsia and no one who

were given the choice of conversion to Christianity or expulsion from Spain. Almost all left, in an eerie precursor of the drama of their descendants in the same country 879 years later. (In fact, most of the terribly anti-Jewish laws and decrees of the Visigoth rulers of Spain remained on the books of government throughout the Middle Ages. They were never enforced, but never repealed either. When the Christian Reconquest of Spain drove the Moslems from power in the fourteenth century, the new Christian rulers would then willingly enforce these ancient hatreds.) Jewish communities in Provence, Italy, Sicily and the Balkans were persecuted. Eventually these communities shrank and practically disappeared. They would be rebuilt only many centuries later when the mass westward migration of Jews from Babylonia would take place.

The Roman Catholic Church in the West was as fully oppressive towards the Jews living under its domain as was the Byzantine Church in the East. With the defeat of the Parthians by the Byzantines, the Christian dream of universal hegemony over civilization, albeit tempered by Christianity's own bitter divisions, seemed within reach. But life and history are never predictable, and the rise of Islam would thwart Christianity's reach for world domination.

Jewish Life Under Christianity

THE BYZANTINES LEFT THEIR MARK on Jewish society and the Land of Israel. Their architecture, design, mosaics and fashions are still to be found in the archaeology of the Holy Land. However, their unrelenting intolerance and persecution of Judaism and the Jews produced among Jews a deep and abiding distrust of the Christian world.

Whereas many Jews, even observant and pious ones, adjusted to

---

would at least speak out against the terrible attitude of the Church towards the Jews and towards knowledge generally. As Daniel J. Boorstin puts it in his monumental book *The Discoverers* (New York, 1983, p. 100), "Christianity conquered the Roman Empire and most of Europe. Then we observe a Europe-wide phenomenon of scholarly amnesia, which afflicted the continent from 300 to 1300. During these centuries Christian faith and dogma suppressed the useful image of the world that had been so slowly, so painfully, and so scrupulously drawn . . ."

12. This in a country where Jewish settlement had been recognized and protected for almost five centuries!

A Byzantine-era mosaic on the floor of the Beis Alfa synagogue

living in a Greek or Roman world and playing a role in it,[13] the Jews never adjusted to living in a society dominated by either the Eastern or Western Church. Instead the Jews built their own society, completely isolated, as if hidden in a cocoon, in the midst of Christian society. Until the eighteenth century, Jews and Jewish society were in the Christian world, but never a part of that world.

The memory of Byzantine Christianity remained with the Jews of Babylonia and their descendants even when they had long left the East and moved to North Africa, Spain, Provence, France and Germany. Since they found the Western Church no more hospitable than the Byzantine Church, the Jews rarely differentiated between the two. Thus, even more than the Church rejected the Jews, the Jews rejected the Church and all it stood for. The Jewish attitude towards Christianity in the Middle Ages and later cannot be fully understood without taking the Jewish-Christian experience, both east and west, into account.

The Synagogue

THE CHURCH, BOTH IN ITS BYZANTINE and Roman branches, was especially inimical to the institution of the synagogue. In 397, a law prevented accused people from seeking asylum in a synagogue. In 415, the building of new synagogues in the Roman Empire was expressly banned. In 423, another law stated that if Christians desecrated a synagogue, the Jews would have to vacate it, leaving the Christians to consecrate it as a church!

Justinian, the emperor from 527 to 565, plundered and despoiled synagogues and converted them into churches.[14] Synagogues

---

13. As an example, the city of Tzippori (Sepphoris) existed as a mixed Roman and Jewish city for centuries, with a great deal of interplay within the communities. Nevertheless, it was in Tzippori that Rabbi and his yeshivah did most of the work on the Mishnah, and the city was the seat of the Sanhedrin itself for a period of time.

14. See *Synagogues of Europe*, edited by Carol Herselle Krinsky (New York, 1985), p. 39.

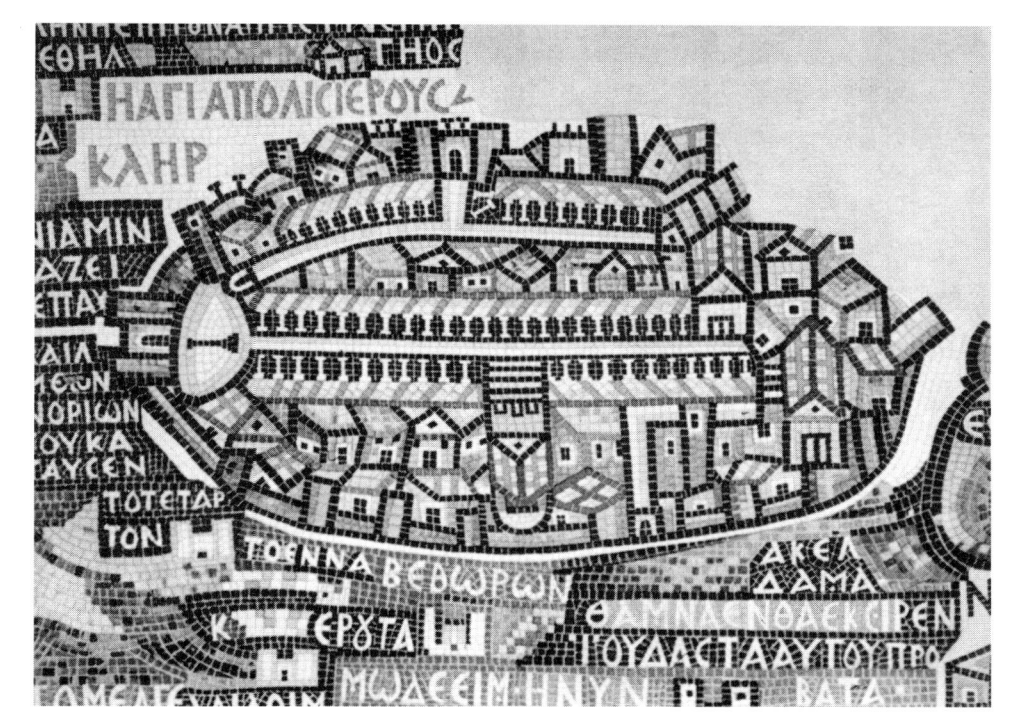

The Medeba mosaic, a Byzantine-era map of Jerusalem

throughout the Roman Empire, both West and East, were ravaged and robbed on a regular basis throughout the fourth, fifth, sixth and seventh centuries. It is not surprising, therefore, that not until the nineteenth century did Jews dare to build large, impressive and ornate synagogue buildings in Christian Europe. And it is not surprising that the beginning of the end of European Jewry on Kristallnacht in Germany in 1938 was marked by the destruction of synagogues throughout that country. The hatred towards the synagogue has deep roots in Christian countries.

Monastic Living

A FINAL STATEMENT regarding Byzantine Christianity concerns the rise of monasteries and convents during the fourth, fifth, sixth and seventh centuries. Separation from general community life existed in Judah at the beginning of the Common Era, especially amongst the Essenes and other groups that found solace and spiritual meaning in the lonely isolation of desert caves. Nevertheless, this type of ascetic life was criticized by the rabbis because of its anti-family, anti-community structure. The rabbis warned, "Separate yourself not from the community."[15] Christian

---

15. Mishnah, *Avos*, Chapter II, section 5.

asceticism and monastic living became a part of that religion and even until the modern era claimed vast numbers of practitioners.

The Byzantine Church created and operated vast and fantastic monasteries, the remains of many of which are still visible today.[16] The Church itself attempted to control the numbers of the monasteries and convents, fearing "the weakening of urban or village congregations which resulted from the exodus of the most dedicated members into special communities..."[17] The Roman Catholic Church also had a vast system of monasteries operating in Europe. During the "Dark Ages" these monasteries were the only islands of learning and literature in the sea of ignorance and illiteracy that enveloped Christian Europe.

The monastic system found no echo in Jewish life, and the monasteries of the Byzantines were not admired or imitated by the Jews.[18] The Jews would build their own places of refuge within their homes, families, communities and institutions of learning.

---

16. In the Judean desert today there are monasteries that were built in Byzantine times, such as Mar Saha, carved out of the rock, whose size and architecture are so awesome that even today they are still beyond belief. There are very few monks still living in these enormous warrens of halls and rooms.

17. *The Oxford History of the Roman World* (Oxford University Press, 1991), p. 471.

18. In the Middle Ages, however, certain forms of asceticism and self-mortification did become accepted in Ashkenazic Jewry, especially in twelfth- and thirteenth-century Germany.

19
Islam and the Jews

AS WE HAVE SEEN, the slow spread of Christianity in the Roman Empire was a steady yet painful matter, subject to intense opposition and persecution. Christianity took no less than three and a half centuries to achieve acceptance, and eventually dominance, in the Roman world. Not so with its major competitor for the minds and souls of men for the next millennia, the faith of Islam.[1]

Just as the Byzantine Church (and, to a lesser extent, the Western Roman Church) was poised to impose Christianity on all of Europe, North Africa, Asia Minor and the Middle East — having seemingly conquered all of their pagan enemies — Islam swept out of the sands of the Arabian desert and forced Christianity to make a retreat of its own, geographically, politically and psychologically. The first part of the seventh century had seen Christianity reach its highwater mark in world domination. The second part of the century would witness the unbelievably rapid expansion and penetration of Islam into the Mediterranean world at the expense of Christianity.

Historians are always tempted to play "what-if" games with the stories of the past. Most Jewish historians (until the recent revisionist-historians) are convinced that the Byzantine Church would have attempted to eradicate Judaism totally if the Church itself had not been defeated and its plan for hegemony in Asia Minor and the Mediterranean basin thwarted by the rising tide of Islam.[2] Thus, the

---
1. An Arabic word which can be loosely translated as "submission to God."
2. This is the opinion of the nineteenth-century historians such as HaLevi, Yaavetz and even the secular historian Graetz. However, more modern Jewish historians, especially in Israel, for some unexplained reason, appear to downplay the historic threat to the survival of Judaism of Byzantine Church domination of the Jews.

coming of Islam may be seen as a providential occurrence that allowed the Jews to slip between the cracks Islam made in Byzantine Church persecution. However, as is the case in all historic "gifts" in Jewish history, the rise of Islam itself would prove to be only a mixed blessing for Israel.

The Founding of Islam

THE FOUNDER OF ISLAM was Mohammed,[3] an early-orphaned young man who, after marrying a wealthy widow much older than he, lived comfortably in Mecca[4] in the center of the Arabian peninsula. However, he soon started falling into trances, announced that he was experiencing visions, and claimed to have been told from heaven that he was to be the savior of the Arab world. He also felt charged to proclaim his prophesies to the rest of the world, convinced as he was of his ability to communicate with the Divine, and of his unique mission in life.

His message, unlike that of early Christianity, was one of politics and power. He deplored the weaknesses of the Arab world of the seventh century. He saw his task to be one not only of religion-building but just as importantly, of empire-building.

The Arab society in the early seventh century was badly divided, with constant tribal warfare the norm. Although Christian missionaries from Ethiopia had been active for a century in Arabia, the population had remained overwhelmingly pagan. The once-strong, indigenous Arabic civilization had deteriorated so that there was now a marked increase in camel-nomadism and closed, exclusively tribal societies. There were strong Jewish communities in Mecca and Medina,[5] composed mainly of merchants, traders and craftsmen. These Jews were not especially learned, although, as Mohammed would ruefully discover, their loyalty to Judaism, for the most part, ran very deep. It is from these half-educated Jews that Mohammed de-

---

3. The date of his birth is reputed to be c. 571. He came from very humble origins, and his tribal clan was of very minor importance in the rigid tribal hierarchy of the time.

4. Mecca was a well-established station on the silk-and-spice route to India and Asia for centuries before Mohammed turned it into a sacred city.

5. Medina is another major Arabian oasis and way-station on the silk-and-spice route. Mohammed would make it the second holiest place in Islam. It is north of Mecca.

veloped his knowledge and viewpoint regarding Judaism and the Jews, a fact which contributes to many of the inaccuracies regarding the Bible and the beliefs of the Jews which litter the Koran.[6]

The Influence of Judaism

MOHAMMED WAS A FERVENT monotheist, determined to end the pagan ways of his fellow Arabs.[7] As all other Arabs, he saw himself as a direct descendant of Abraham through Hagar's son, Ishmael. By 610, Mohammed had convinced himself of his divine, prophetic role and began to preach his new religion publicly. He believed that Abraham's true heritage was through Ishmael and not Isaac, although Isaac (as well as other major biblical figures of the "Old" and "New Testament") was to be considered and revered as a prophet in the hierarchy of Islam (albeit relegated to a status inferior to that of Mohammed himself).

Originally, many Jewish customs and rituals were incorporated into Islam by Mohammed. The eating of pig was forbidden, the practice of circumcision was institutionalized as an act of faith, and facing[8] Jerusalem while reciting prayers was made obligatory. It was also decreed that the great annual holy fast day was to take place on the tenth day of the first lunar month of the Arab calendar, just as in Judaism, Yom Kippur falls on the tenth day of the first lunar month of the Jewish calendar. The idea of strict, almost infinitely undefinable monotheism is certainly Jewish in origin and is undoubtedly Islam's main borrowing from the Jews.

---

6. The Koran is the basic book of faith, practice and law in the Moslem religion. It contains Mohammed's recounting of the revelations he claimed were made to him by God during periods of prophecy. It was compiled over years and in numerous stages, and therefore has the tendency to be self-contradictory regarding many issues of politics, policy and worldview. It contains both high praise and sulfuric vituperation regarding the Jews. Because of this, it was never difficult for Moslem rulers to quote the Koran to justify just about any policy that they instituted regarding the Jews.

7. He was, therefore, also a fanatical anti-Christian, firmly convinced that its concept of Jesus as the son of God was blasphemous in the extreme. The Koran states unequivocally that God is singular, was not born, and is omnipotent.

8. It is almost certain that Arab males, even while remaining pagans, were circumcised as a matter of course and custom for millennia, from the time of Abraham and Ishmael onward. However, Mohammed elevated this ancient tribal custom into a new declaration of faith in the one-and-only God.

Mohammed, because of these Jewish gleanings and similarities, unrealistically expected cooperation, support and eventual acceptance from the Jewish communities of Arabia. But even at the point of a sword, precious little aid to Mohammed and his ideas was forthcoming from the Jews. Mohammed would react badly to this perceived theological snub, and he would come to annul and change many of the Jewish-based customs of original Islam and to make life terribly difficult for the Jews.

The Rule of the Sword

MOHAMMED ENCOUNTERED violent opposition in Mecca to his claim of being a prophet and to his teachings. The Quraysh tribe, the dominant clan in Mecca, looked at Mohammed as a troublemaker and a potential usurper of its power. It forced Mohammed to flee Mecca, and in the year 622 (which has subsequently become year 1 in the Moslem calendar) he took up residence in Medina. The year of Mohammed's move to Medina is known as the year of the *Hijra* (or Hegira).[9] It was in Medina, in his enforced exile, that Mohammed further formulated and publicized many of the core ideas of his new faith. Much of the Koran was also a product of his years there.

In Medina, Mohammed developed a large and loyal following. He preached conversion by the sword, and his violent cohorts relished the bloodletting, especially since it was now sanctioned by religious *diktat*. Mohammed soon overcame his pagan Arab brothers in Medina, forcing them all to accept his new religion. Finished with Medina's Arabs, he turned his attention to its Jews.

In the Koran itself, Jews are the ones who foretell the coming of the great prophet Mohammed to their wicked and disbelieving pagan Arab neighbors. But in real life the Jews would not become followers of Mohammed. In his rage at being scorned, Mohammed made war upon the Jewish community of Medina and destroyed it. It was then that he turned very anti-Jewish and discarded some of the very

---

9. The word means "journey" but is not too far in sound from the word for "migration," which is really the true sense of the word as regards Mohammed.

customs of the Jews that he had originally instituted in Islam.[10]

By 630 Mohammed and his warriors defeated the Quraysh tribe and occupied Mecca. There Mohammed destroyed the pagan gods at the ancient worship place, the *Ka'ba,* which he rededicated as the temple of Abraham and Ishmael, and which became the holiest shrine in Islam.[11] He also executed many of his former opponents, and, as he had done in Medina, he decimated the Jewish community in Mecca as well. It soon became a rule that no non-Moslem could enter Mecca, let alone dwell there. The surviving Jews of Mecca and Medina fled to Yemen and other parts of the Middle East.

Mohammed returned to Medina, there to dwell for the balance of his life as the patriarch, judge and lawgiver of the new faith of Islam. But Mohammed's sword, once unleashed, would continue to travel the world over on missions of conquest and forced conversion.

The Spread of Islam

WHEN MOHAMMED DIED in 632, only ten years after the *Hijra*, the religion of Islam was fairly confined to the cities of Medina and Mecca and some other scattered parts of Arabia. Mohammed, as other powerful and unique leaders before and after him, made no provision for his succession,[12] perhaps feeling himself immortal. His closest male relative was his cousin Ali, who had married Mohammed's daughter Fatima. However, most of the tribesmen who had supported Mohammed in his wars, and especially the people of Medina, repudiated Ali's claim to leadership and appointed Abu Bakr as their leader and successor to the prophet (caliph). He in turn was succeeded as caliph by Omar.

Omar realized that there was too much dissension within the Moslem camp. Medina and Mecca saw each other as competitors

---

10. The annual fast day now became an annual fast month, *Ramadan;* circumcision was kept, but it played a different role than it does in Judaism; the number of daily prayer periods was increased from three to five; prayer was now recited facing Mecca and no longer Jerusalem; and the Saturday Sabbath day was abolished. The Moslem holy day of the week is Friday, but it is not so much a day of rest and family gathering as it is a day of assembly for public worship.
11. One of the major religious obligations of a devout Moslem is to journey at least once during his life to Mecca, there to worship at the *Ka'ba*. This pilgrimage is called *haj*.
12. He is quoted as saying, "Prophets have no heirs."

THE JEWS UNDER ISLAM IN THE 7TH-8TH CENTURIES

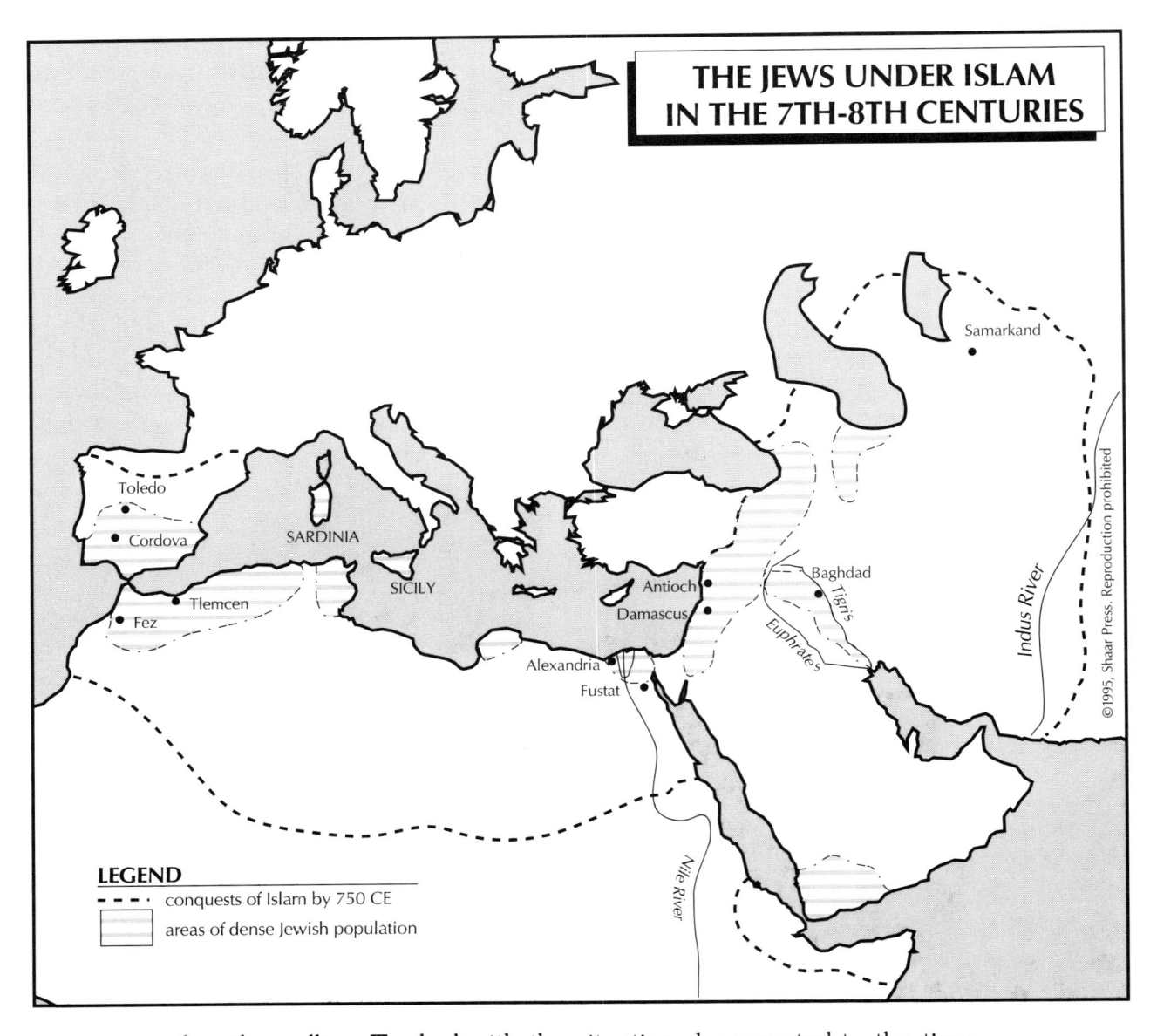

LEGEND
- - - - conquests of Islam by 750 CE
▤ areas of dense Jewish population

rather than allies. To deal with the situation, he resorted to the time-honored ploy of dictators to abort inner revolt: he embarked on foreign wars of conquest. "The results [of the wars] surpassed the caliph's highest hopes; Persia, the Fertile Crescent and Egypt were conquered for Islam."[13] Thus did Islam come to Babylonia, and more particularly to the Jews of Babylonia.

No other religion experienced as rapid an expansion in adherents and in control of territory as did seventh-and eighth-century Islam. From Africa to the Caucasus and from India to Spain, the new

---

13. John Alden Williams, *Islam* (New York, 1962), p. 80.

religion was soon dominant. Much of the Parthian and Byzantine empires, both almost bled white by their century-old war, was now taken away from them by the seemingly unstoppable Moslem tide. Christianity was thrown back on its heels, and its very existence, let alone its control of Europe, was now put in doubt.[14]

Sunnis and Shiites

THE MOSLEMS WERE SUBJECT to the same inner strife that divided Christianity. In Islam, however, it was not so much doctrine or beliefs that were contested as it was pure power and rights of inheritance. The main Moslem group, followers of Abu Bakr and Omar, became known as the *Sunnis,* the most numerous and powerful group in Islam.[15] However, a sizable number of the faithful followed Ali, Mohammed's son-in-law. They formed the base of the *Shiite* movement in Islam. The Shiites themselves are divided into two warring factions, the "seveners" and the "twelvers."[16]

Many of the violent struggles within the Moslem world have their root cause in these ancient power feuds that have persisted for almost fourteen centuries.[17] All of this division and turmoil within Islam would

---

14. It was only at the Battle of Tours (Poitiers) in 732 that Charles Martel, the Frankish king, arrested the Moslem onslaught on Europe and saved Christianity from the warriors of the Moslem caliph.

15. The *sunna* (literally, *practice*) was a type of oral tradition that helped interpret the teachings of the Koran, sometimes modifying in practice the harsh written word. It is estimated that over two-thirds of the Moslems in the world today are Sunnis.

16. Their dispute centers on which of Ali's descendants represented the true religion. They agree that Ali was the first *imam* (leader), the successor to his father-in-law, Mohammed. The "seveners" are the followers of Ismail, the oldest son of the sixth Shiite *imam,* whom they believe to be the true heir to the mantle of Mohammed. They are also called the *Fatimates* and were very powerful in North Africa and Egypt from the tenth through the twelfth centuries. The "twelvers" are followers of the twelfth *imam,* Mohammed ben Hasan Al'Askari, who disappeared mysteriously in 879 when he was but eight years old. The "twelvers" believe that he has been living in concealment since then and will appear again at the end of time to be the ruling *imam.*

17. The most serious incident of violence within early Islam occurred in 680 when Hussein, the son of Ali and the grandson of Mohammed, was killed by the forces of Yazid I, a successor to the caliphate of Omar through his father, Othman. The Shiites have never forgiven that murder.

allow the Jews to become important in Islamic society, since the Jews had much to contribute to any faction that sought or attained power. Would there have been a completely unified and monolithic Moslem world, the position of the Jewish communities under its control would certainly have been problematic. In a divided and factionalized Moslem world, however, the Jews were necessary, useful and productive. For the Jews to survive in the Moslem world, they only needed to keep within their proper place in society by outwardly demonstrating subservience and respect.[18]

Omayyads and Abbasids

THE MAIN SUCCESSORS to Mohammed, who formed the first dynasty of caliphs in the seventh century, were called the Omayyad rulers. Despite constant and serious opposition by Ali and his descendants, they persisted in their rule well into the eighth century.

Those who are in power for a long time inevitably earn many enemies. In 750, the Omayyad's Shiite foes joined those enemies and overthrew the Omayyads. Still, none of Ali's descendants were chosen to replace the Omayyad caliph. Instead, the new caliph was a descendant of Abbas, an uncle of Mohammed. This inaugurated the rule of the Abbasid dynasty, a rule that endured for over five centuries.

This dynasty transferred the main capital of the Arab world from Damascus to Baghdad, placing itself in close proximity to the Jewish community of Babylonia. This would prove to be a mixed blessing, for although the Jews were now able to wield more influence at court, all of the details of Babylonian Jewish life now came under the close and sometimes malevolent eye of the caliph of Baghdad.

Meanwhile, the few surviving Omayyads escaped to Spain where, under the leadership of the greatest of the Omayyads, Abdel-el-Rahman, they established themselves as the rulers of Cordoba. The Jews in Babylonia would eventually play a leading role in the Abbasid world, while those of Spain would help build the Omayyad rule into one of greatness. In contrast, the Shiites, the followers of Ali, were excluded from power and influence in both centers of Moslem power. They would sulk and brood over this hurt for long centuries.

---

18. See my *Herald of Destiny* (Shaar Press, 1993), pp. 27-29.

The Jews and Islam

THE ATTITUDE AND RELATIONSHIP of the Moslem leaders towards the Jews was varied and erratic. Mohammed himself did experience some initial success with some of the Jews of Medina. Unlearned and superstitious, having already adopted ways and customs of the Arabs over the centuries of living in an Arab society, many of the Jews of Medina were not repelled by Mohammed's proclamation of a new monotheistic faith that would unite mankind. Most of the favorable comments in the Koran regarding Jews emanate from this early period of Mohammed's ministry.

Soon, however, Mohammed met the hard-core Jews who not only rejected Islam but also ridiculed his claims of prophecy and his mission. These Jews, who constituted the vast majority of Jews living in Arabia at the time, were no more willing to accept Islam than their ancestors had been willing to accept Christianity six centuries earlier. Many felt Mohammed to be personally bizarre and mentally unbalanced[19] and, while accepting Islam's undoubted monotheistic base as a major improvement over the previous Arab paganism, clearly felt that Islam was not addressed or relevant to them as Jews, since they had already had a valid and vital two-millennia-old spiritual heritage of pure monotheism when Mohammed was born. Most of the terribly negative things that the same Koran has to say about Jews and Judaism are a result of this later time and the growing realization by Mohammed that the Jews would not willingly accept Islam.

Thus, at the beginning of Islam's rise, the sword presented itself as the logical solution to Mohammed's Jewish problem. The policy of Islam from its onset was to convert forcibly those who did not appreciate Islam's truth on their own. Many Christians were put to death because of their refusal to desert their faith and embrace Islam. Most of the pagan Arab tribes of the Middle East willingly converted to Islam and in fact formed the armies that would spread the new faith throughout the world. However, after the martyrdom *en masse* of a number of Jewish communities, the Moslems rethought their Jewish policy. They turned away from

---

19. Maimonides, in his "Epistle Regarding Forced Conversion" and other works, refers thusly to Mohammed.

pure genocide and instead decided to exploit the talents, position and strategic connections of the established Jewish communities now under their control.

There remained a strong trend amongst certain Moslem groups[20] to eliminate the Jews from Moslem society, either by exile or by death, but the rulers of the Moslem world generally followed a policy of exploitation of the Jews and thus, out of the necessity of their own best interests, usually protected them from the ravages of the more radical elements of Islam. True, from time to time, great persecutions of the Jews would occur in the Moslem world. Nevertheless, there would also be long periods of tolerance and cooperation between the two communities.[21]

The Effects of Islam

THE SUDDEN AND UNFORESEEN appearance of Islam on the world scene served as an effective check on the cruel persecution of the Jewish community of Babylonia by the Byzantine Christians. The Moslem world consciously attempted to erase the Christian influence from the Middle East. By the end of the seventh century it would be a mosque, not a church, that stood on the Temple Mount in Jerusalem.

The Jews in Babylonia benefited greatly from the substitution of Moslem for Byzantine rule. By dealing directly with the caliphs in Baghdad and other Middle Eastern cities, the Jews were able to revitalize their societies, and Babylonian Jewry especially experienced a rebirth and renewal in the seventh, eighth and ninth centuries.

New and great leaders would emerge to build a strong Jewish society, which would eventually become the foundation of both Sephardic and Ashkenazic European Jewry. The new age would be called the time of the *Geonim* and would mark the final institutionalization of Talmudic life[22] amongst the Jewish people.

---

20. In the modern era, they are described as "fundamentalists," a term that does not adequately describe their beliefs and goals.
21. Such as the "Golden Age" of Spanish Jewry, from the ninth to twelfth centuries.
22. Not just Talmudic study or knowledge, but Talmudic life itself.

20

The Era of the Geonim

THE MOSLEM CONQUEST of the Middle East abruptly ended the Babylonian Jewish community's struggles with the Byzantine and Persian empires. A new era then began for that community.

As described previously, Mar Zutra, the impetuous and rebellious *Reish Galusa,* was executed by the Persians in 558. For almost eighty years thereafter, under the swirl of the never-ending conflict between the Persians and the Byzantines, the position of *Reish Galusa* had languished mainly unfulfilled and, even when occupied, impotent. All effective leadership in the Jewish community had resided in the hands of the *Geonim* — the heads of the yeshivos of Sura, Pumbedisa and, for a short time, Peroz-Shavur.[1] However, under the new Arab rulers of the country this situation changed dramatically.

In the year 637, the caliph Omar defeated the Persian king Chosoroes II decisively and finally, placing Babylonia and practically the entire Persian Empire under Moslem domination. Omar immediately appointed a *Reish Galusa* to head the Babylonian Jewish community now under his Moslem rule. The man he appointed was Bustenai, one of the legendary figures in Jewish lore.[2]

---

1. The *Geonim* of this time (c. 590-640) were R' Chanan of Ashkaya, the *Rosh Yeshivah* of Pumbedisa; R' Mar bar R' Huna, the *Rosh Yeshivah* of Sura; and R' Mari Sorgo bar R' Dimi, the *Rosh Yeshivah* of Peroz-Shavur. The yeshivah of Peroz-Shavur closed in the year 660 for reasons not definitively known to us. From that time forward, the *Geonim* were always the two heads of the yeshivos of Pumbedisa and Sura alone.

2. See *Seder HaDoros* by R' Yechiel Halperin (Jerusalem, 1963), pp. 174-6, for the fantastic legend of Bustenai and how he became *Reish Galusa.* In truth, the life and career of Bustenai were fantastic enough without the need for any embellishment of legend and myth. Nevertheless, his life and deeds are enmeshed in such a powerful web of legend that they almost defy historical unraveling.

Bustenai

IT REMAINS UNPROVEN amongst historians whether Bustenai was a direct descendant of David and thus the legitimate heir to the position of *Reish Galusa*. However, Bustenai's claim to such Davidic descent went unchallenged during his lifetime, and it must be assumed that his contemporaries recognized him as a legitimate *Reish Galusa*. His ascension to the office was marked by competition from another claimant and by controversy, but Bustenai was finally confirmed in his office by Omar in c. 638.

In one of the more unlikely twists of personal fate, Bustenai then became the brother-in-law of Omar, the caliph: Omar, after defeating Chosoroes II, took one of his daughters as a wife, and then presented Bustenai with another one of them. A refusal to marry the woman would have cost Bustenai his life and perhaps brought untold tragedy on the Jewish community he headed and represented. According to the opinion of most of the contemporary and later *Geonim,* as recorded for us in *Iggeres R' Sherira Gaon,*[3] Bustenai's Persian wife converted to Judaism and conducted herself as a loyal and observant Jewess.

Bustenai also had a Jewish wife at the time and fathered sons from both women. As can be expected in such a complicated family situation, great dissension later arose between the two branches of Bustenai's descendants, and the issue of the Jewishness of Bustenai's Persian wife was raised many times over the next centuries. In any event, all of those who occupied the position of *Reish Galusa* in Babylonian Jewish life from the middle of the seventh century until the end of the eleventh century were direct descendants of Bustenai, although some were descended from his Jewish wife and others from his "Persian" wife.

---

3. R' Sherira was the *Gaon* of Pumbedisa at the end of the tenth century. His famous *Iggeres* (*Letter*) is in reality a history of Israel until his day, with special detail and emphasis on the story of Babylonian Jewry from Talmudic times. This "letter" has been republished dozens of times and translated into many languages, including English. See my *Herald of Destiny* (Shaar Press, New York, 1993), p. 20, for more information regarding R' Sherira Gaon and his "letter."

Bustenai and the Geonim

BUSTENAI WAS A VERY TALENTED and able administrator. During his reign, the *Geonim* of Sura and Pumbedisa deferred to him in almost all political and communal matters. He in turn cooperated with the *Geonim,* consulting with them and giving them free reign in the operation of the yeshivos and the Torah educational system of Babylonia.

The caliph had granted the *Reish Galusa* broad taxing, judicial and police powers. This in effect made the *Reish Galusa* the "king" of the Jews in seventh-century Babylonia. Under him, the Jews had regained full autonomy over their affairs. Jewish courts were established and empowered throughout Babylonia. The judges and procedures of the courts were subject to public complaint and the *Reish Galusa's* sporadic review. Nevertheless, in the four centuries of *Reish Galusa-Geonim* rule in Babylonia, the Jewish courts were seen by both the Jewish and the Moslem communities[4] as being just and moderate in their deliberations and decisions. The rules of Jewish law were strictly adhered to in these Babylonian Jewish courts, and in fact much of the Torah-Talmudic literature of Geonic times deals with actual court cases and decisions made by these autonomous Jewish courts.

The Courts

JEWS RARELY RESORTED TO settling their own disputes in the Moslem courts, though under Moslem law they were afforded the right to do so. The primary reason was simply that the Torah forbids Jews to take their disputes to non-Jewish courts. As a result, an overwhelming sense of community condemnation was visited upon a Jew who resorted to the Moslem courts to attempt to win his point. This attitude towards all non-Jewish courts has remained strong throughout the Exile and has always been a source of Jewish unity and self-discipline in difficult times. In addition, the basic Jewish attitude in Babylonia was that the

---

4. There are instances recorded in the literature of the *Geonim* where Moslems preferred to have their personal monetary disputes litigated in a Jewish court rather than in a Moslem government court.

Jewish courts were superior in every way to those of the Moslem government, and that the integrity of the Jewish courts was infinitely stronger than that of the Moslem courts.[5]

However, Jews did use the Moslem courts to enforce decrees or decisions that for some reason they were unable to execute themselves. The main problem regarding the Jewish court system in Babylonia arose during those not-infrequent times when there was strong friction between the *Reish Galusa* and the *Geonim*. Then the question of whom to appoint as judges, and in fact, of who had the moral as well as legal right to appoint those judges, was raised and hotly contested.

Since under the caliph's fiat the courts were under the control of the *Reish Galusa*, it is only natural that the *Reish Galusa* usually won out in these struggles, and the Jewish judges were appointed by him. However, the *Geonim* always felt themselves entitled, even obligated, to protest against poor judicial appointments. Thus, the Jewish courts, which contributed so much to Jewish stability and prestige in Babylonia under the early Moslem rulers, later became the flash point for intense personal and communal strife and pain.

The Role of the Babylonian Geonim

THE STRENGTH OF the Babylonian Jewish community, its *Reish Galusa* and its *Geonim* was of such a nature that Jews all over the world looked to Babylonia for guidance and leadership. Under the caliph Omar, the Jews were allowed to reenter and settle in Jerusalem and in other places in the Land of Israel.[6] However, the Jewish community in the Land of Israel saw itself only in the role of a valiant defender of the right of Jews to live in their homeland, not in the role of Jewish world leadership. That role belonged clearly and exclusively to Babylonian Jewry and its leaders. The *Geonim* left a wealth of responsa and writing directed to all the Jewish communities in the

---

5. Bribe-taking and other more subtle forms of graft were endemic in the Moslem court system for centuries, with violent attempts at reform and housecleaning occurring regularly throughout the first millennium of Islam.

6. Most notably in Tiberias, which again became a center of Jewish learning and life. Only seventy Jewish families were allowed to establish permanent residence in Jerusalem. Omar also began the construction of the Mosque of Omar (the Dome of the Rock) on the Temple Mount in Jerusalem, a structure which still stands today.

L-R: First page of the earliest printed Sheiltos of R' Achai Gaon (Venice, 1548); manuscript page of Halachos Pesukos of R' Yehuhai Gaon; manuscript page of Halachos Gedolos of R' Shimon Kayyara

world[7] on matters of legal and moral behavior and on Jewish public policy of the times. Of the major Torah works of the *Geonim,* three manuscripts survived and have been republished many times, with numerous commentaries and supra-commentaries added to the original texts. These three works are 1) *She'iltos* of R' Achai (early eighth century); 2) *Halachos Pesukos* of R' Yehudai Gaon, which was commited to writing by his disciples (eighth century); and 3) *Halachos Gedolos* (*B'Hag*) of R' Shimon Kayyara (about ninth century). All of these works served as written conduits of the Babylonian schools of Torah, their traditions and Talmudic interpretations for later generations of scholars who treated their words as authoritative.[8] In the nineteenth and twentieth centuries, new discoveries of manuscripts from *Geonic* times would spark a renewed interest in scholarly research regarding the *Geonim* and their works, and a new field of Jewish studies — *Geonica* — would arise.

---

7. The Jewish Exile during the period of the *Geonim* reached from Spain in the West to India in the East. There were Jewish communities in Italy, the Balkans, France, Egypt and the Caucasus. However, all of these communities, even when combined, were dwarfed by the size and strength of the Babylonian Jewish community.

8. The *Halachos Gedolos* was held in special reverence by Rashi and *Tosafos* in the Middle Ages and was accorded great authority in Talmudic interpretation and judicial decision. *Tosafos* wrote regarding *Halachos Gedolos,* "All of its words are words of authentic Torah tradition."

Chisdai and Shlomo

WHEN BUSTENAI DIED IN C. 670, he was succeeded by a son named Chisdai, whose mother was Bustenai's non-Persian wife. Although wealthy and powerful, Chisdai was personally insecure. In order to establish clearly his right and the right of his descendants to the position of *Reish Galusa*, Chisdai attempted to discredit his half-brothers by claiming that their mother, the Persian princess daughter of Chosoroes II, was never legitimately converted to Judaism, and that they therefore were of lineage that would preclude them from serving in any official leadership position in the Jewish community.

Chisdai's claim was hotly denied by his half-brothers. The matter was brought before the *Geonim* of the time, who decided against Chisdai and upheld the Jewish legitimacy of the descendants of Bustenai's Persian wife.[9] This earned the *Geonim* the unremitting enmity of Chisdai and his family, while the children of Bustenai's Persian wife never forgave Chisdai and his family over this attempt to delegitimize them.

Chisdai ruled arrogantly and high-handedly until his death in c. 690. His son Shlomo succeeded him to the office and continued in the abrasive and interfering ways of his father. He appointed a relative of his as *Gaon* of Pumbedisa, and when the rabbis of Sura did not show that *Gaon* sufficient deference, his threats of punishment forced many of them to flee Babylonia.

In c. 730, Shlomo, breaking with long-held tradition, appointed a non-Suran as the *Gaon* of Sura. This scholar, R' Shmuel *Gaon,* was nevertheless a fortuitous choice, for he was of great scholarship, sterling character and great organizational talents. For the eighteen years of his rule, Sura regained its preeminence as the major yeshivah in Babylonia.

In 756, Shlomo once again appointed a Rabbi of Pumbedisa to be the head of Sura. This was the great Mar R' Yehudai *Gaon* already

---

9. The decision was written by R' Chaninai *Gaon* of the yeshivah of Sura. Chisdai's claim was that the Persian princess converted only under duress and that no true princess would willingly forsake her family's faith, which had been the official religion of the royal house of Parthia/Persia for centuries. The rabbis disagreed, citing the sterling character and noble behavior of this woman as a Jewess throughout her life and the Jewish piety of her offspring.

mentioned above.[10] During the reign of R' Shmuel *Gaon*, the *Reish Galusa*, Shlomo, once again raised the issue of the Jewish legitimacy of the children of Bustenai's Persian wife. And once again the *Geonim* rebuffed the attack.[11]

The Abbasids

DURING THE LONG REIGN of Shlomo,[12] the Omayyad dynasty was ended and supplanted in c. 750 by the Abbasids. The seat of the caliphate was moved from Damascus to Baghdad, and the *Reish Galusa* was now forced to appear regularly and for considerable lengths of time at the court of the caliph. As such, his influence and prestige began to wane in the yeshivos of Babylonia and eventually in the general Jewish community as well.

The Abbasids generally treated the Jewish community with kindness and tolerance during their almost three centuries of rule. Most of the troubles in the Babylonian Jewish community would now spring from internal disputes and divisions unrelated to the rule of the Abbasids.

Anan and the Birth of Karaism

WHEN SHLOMO DIED in c. 760, the question of succession to the post of *Reish Galusa* arose.[13] The contest centered itself between the conflicting claims of two nephews of Shlomo, Anan and Chananyah. Even though Anan was

---

10. There are records indicating that Mar R' Yehudai *Gaon* was sightless during the time he headed Sura, but that apparently in no way dimmed his greatness and Torah leadership. At the same time that he headed Sura, his brother, R' Dodai *Gaon*, was the *Gaon* of Pumbedisa.

11. The opinion this time was authored by R' Shmuel *Gaon*, who, in spite of being a protégé and appointee of Shlomo, decided against him.

12. Over sixty years. However, there are opinions that he was *Reish Galusa* for only about thirty years. The historical dates involved are somewhat contradictory and unclear.

13. There is an opinion among some historians that Shlomo's son, Yitzchak Iskai, did indeed succeed his father for a term lasting several years. According to these authorities, the dispute regarding the next *Reish Galusa* would have to have taken place after the rule of Yitzchak Iskai.

Entrance of the ruins of a Karaite place of worship in Jerusalem

older, more brilliant intellectually and very charismatic, the *Geonim* of both Pumbedisa and Sura recommended to the caliph the choice of Chananyah as *Reish Galusa.*

Anan, ignoring the decision of the *Geonim* and the decree of the caliph, nevertheless declared himself *Reish Galusa* and attempted to depose his brother. The caliph had Anan arrested and was ready to execute him for rebellion. In his own desperate defense, Anan concocted the theory that he was really of a different religion than Chananyah and the *Geonim*, and explained to the caliph the differences between his new religion and traditional Judaism.

The caliph accepted the existence of this new religion and allowed Anan his freedom. Anan now indeed invented a new faith with emphasis only on the Written Law, discarding the Talmud and the Oral Law. Anan also introduced a new calendar for the Jewish year. Eventually Anan's machinations developed into Karaism, a heretical philosophy which plagued Jewish solidarity and Torah faith for two centuries until meaningfully bested by R' Saadia *Gaon* in the tenth century.[14]

Although Karaism was initially popular in Babylonia, its appeal soon waned as the Babylonian Jews, under sophisticated and strong *Geonic* leadership, came to realize the inherent contradictions and weaknesses of the Karaite doctrine. However, Karaism remained potent and strong in the Jewish community of Egypt until the twelfth century, when Maimonides yet struggled to eradicate it from the Jewish nation.[15]

The Waning Power of the Reish Galusa

ONE OF THE MAJOR NEGATIVE effects of the Karaite heresy was the weakening of the position of the *Reish Galusa* in the eyes of the reigning caliphs of Baghdad. The rabbinic (non-Karaite) Jews continued to pledge

---

14. See *Herald of Destiny*, pp. 7-9.

15. His attitude was to refute the Karaite ideas and beliefs while at the same time showing a benevolent and brotherly attitude to the individual Karaite Jews themselves.

their loyalty and subservience to a central *Reish Galusa*. However, that *Reish Galusa* himself no longer enjoyed blanket governmental powers, since the caliphs diluted their decrees of empowerment to allow for many different *Reishei Galusa* characters to serve at one and the same time.

In 770, Chananyah died, and the *Geonim* then chose as *Reish Galusa* Zakkai bar R' Achunai. He was another descendant of Bustenai's Persian wife,[16] and his appointment touched off another round of dispute among the warring Bustenai descendants regarding the status of Zakkai's Jewishness. Thus, the Babylonian Jewish community was caught in a number of internecine battles at the same time.

The power struggles among the contenders for the post of *Reish Galusa*, the struggles of the *Geonim* against Karaism and the rising tension between the yeshivos of Sura and Pumbedisa over priority of leadership all served to make the last centuries of Babylonian Jewish life years of strife and anguish, albeit punctuated by the appearance of great Torah figures who somehow were able to transcend the frustrations of the times.

The Legacy of the Geonim

THREE OF THE MAJOR *Geonim* of this period, whose works have been preserved for us, are 1) R' Netronai *Gaon*,[17] 2) R' Amram *Gaon*[18] and 3) R' Tzemach bar Poltoi *Gaon*.[19] R' Netronai left us a wealth of responsa, especially directed to the ever-expanding Jewish community of Spain, which was already then an important Jewish center. R' Amram prepared an entire text for a prayer book[20] which became the basis for all later Jewish books of prayer. R' Tzemach wrote a rudimentary dic-

---

16. From this time forward, until the end of the office of *Reish Galusa* three centuries later, all of the holders of that office were descendants of Bustenai's Persian wife.
17. Flourished about 850 in Sura.
18. Flourished about 880 in Sura.
19. Flourished about 880 in Pumbedisa.
20. It is called the *Siddur of R' Amram Gaon,* and since that time every Jewish prayerbook has been called a *siddur* (from the Hebrew word *seder,* meaning *order* or *arrangement;* here, one of prayer.)

Siddur R' Amram

tionary translating Aramaic names, places, phrases and obscure words that appear in the Talmud into Hebrew. It was the precursor of other famous and much larger and all-encompassing Talmudic dictionaries produced in the medieval and modern eras of Jewish life.

The *Geonim* felt that their major responsibility to the Jewish people was to pass onward the traditions of Israel, whole and undiluted, and to preserve and explain the entire Talmud. As has been stated by one of our century's great scholars on the works of the *Geonim*, Dr. B. M. Levin, "The conclusion of the Talmud was the foundation of their life's home, and the *Geonim* invited all of Israel to be their guests at the table of the Talmud. They guarded its integrity in their yeshivos with zealousness and devotion, and therefore the *Geonim* can truly be considered the true custodians of the tradition of the Talmud. All of the scholarship of the *Geonim* in Babylonia, the place where the Talmud was created and developed, stretching over centuries, should be viewed as one long signature and final editorial redaction of the subject matter of the Talmud."[21] All other matters — political, governmental, economic or social — were of secondary concern to them.

In this task they were outstandingly successful, and it is upon their foundations of scholarship and tradition that later Sephardic and Ashkenazic Jewry would build their societies.

---

21. Dr. B. M. Levin, *Otzar HaGeonim* (Haifa, 1928), pp. ii-iii.

21
Epilogue — The Echo of History

THIS BOOK HAS THE apparent drawback that it deals with ancient history. It tells a story about people, events, and societies that are 1,700 to 2,500 years old. As such, one would expect its readership to be limited to those who are true history buffs, for logically it does not speak to the average person at the end of the twentieth century of the Common Era. And when I began to write this book over three years ago, I was also of that opinion.

I had intended this book to be not much more than a bookend — the completing work of my trilogy on Jewish history, the first two volumes of which are *Triumph of Survival* on the modern era and *Herald of Destiny* on the medieval era; and thus, with this work, the entire gamut of post-biblical Jewish history would be complete. But one of the painful things about writing a book is that the author must also read the manuscript. Doing so proved to be an eye-opening surprise to me. For I was not reading a story of past events as much as dealing with a description of current Jewish life, problems, hopes and aspirations.

In many ways, our generation is similar to those of the Second Temple because there is a Jewish state, with all of the opportunities and disappointments that such a situation implies. Thus, we can make direct comparisons to the conditions and problems that faced our ancestors in the Second Commonwealth. And such a comparison is enlightening, and perhaps disturbing.

The Second Commonwealth and its five-hundred-year aftermath faced squarely the cultural struggle between Jewish traditional life and Hellenistic-Roman values and life-style. From the time of Ezra through the Hasmonean wars and kings, through Roman wars, defeat and destruction, to the times of Christian-Byzantine domination and until the Moslem hegemony over the Middle East, the main struggle for Jewish survival was never limited to the physical sphere alone. The battle was for the soul of the Jewish people; and even if Jews survived individually and physically, the Jewish people and its unique sense of mission and destiny would have been irretrievably lost had not Jewish values, life-style and observance of Torah tradition triumphed over the prevalent cultures of the day.

The story told in this book, with all of its twists of plot and fate and its cast of unforgettable characters, is basically the story of this cultural struggle. The Hellenist-Roman world eventually collapsed, weighed down with its moral, social and political iniquities and abominable aberrations. Much of the culture of that world survived, however, and in its varying forms still provides the base for Western civilization today. Thus, the struggle described in the pages of this book is not so much an ancient one, long ago ended and decided, but rather a current one in which all of us are participants and not merely observers.

Not long ago, it might have seemed surprising that the Jews of the ancient world were so easily swayed by Hellenism and its pagan, violent and wanton ways. However, when we are witness to the secularization of so many of the Jewish people in our time, with the tragic personal and national consequences involved in this process, it is much easier to understand that long-ago struggle. The issues of today — unlimited and uninhibited decadent behavior, the easy acceptance of death and violence, the removal of the "unfit" who are a burden on society and its resources, the glorification of nature combined with the downgrading of humans and their purpose, the tyranny of the majority and, in spite of all protestations to the contrary society's non-accommodation of minority opinions and groups, society's search for utopian and immediate solutions to intractable problems, the sloganeering of such words as "peace," "democracy" and "progress," the glorification of the bodies of athletes, fashion models, and beautiful people, the anti-family program of the intelligentsia — all of these issues are those of two millennia ago.

Apparently little has changed, in spite of our great progress in technology and science. We should therefore not be surprised at the appearance today of the ideological successors to the Sadducees,

Essenes, Zealots, Hebrew Christians, religious fanatics, corrupt and violent kings, leaders and politicians who are blinded by their ideas and wants, and who implement policies that destroy instead of build; we should not be shocked by longings that give rise to a climate where exotic and "spiritual" religions flourish; nor should we be shocked even by great internecine hatred among different Jewish groups. For though the Second Temple and its physical world are now the province of historians and archaeologists, the issues and problems of that world somehow still belong to our clergy, psychologists, psychiatrists, doctors, social workers, politicians and parents. That is why I feel that the story told in this book is so poignant and pertinent.

The heroes of the book and of the millennium that it covers are those individuals who swam against the current of Hellenist-Roman culture. They were exemplary people, people who were good and refined in a world that did not overly treasure these commodities. They carried the Jewish people through that age by dint of their love of fellow human beings and of God, their loyalty to God's Torah and to the destiny of His people and Land, by the strength of their personalities and leadership abilities. From Ezra through Hillel, Rabbi Akiva, Rabbi, Rav, Abbaye, Rava, Ravina, Rav Ashi and Rav Amram *Gaon*, the thread of holy and inspired humanity as represented by true Torah behavior and loyalty is what shines through as the main theme of the Jewish story in the Classical Era. Maybe that is also the true story of our own times.

Upon concluding this work, I am thankful and delighted to have been able, through the grace of God, to complete this three-volume series of books on Jewish history. What a history! What a people! Anyone who is aware of the Jewish story should and can, in my opinion, become a more firm believer in the Jewish destiny and mission. Such firm believers are the guarantee of the Jewish future, as they have been of the Jewish past. Even if they are only a relatively small number of individuals, the few against the many, all of Jewish history confirms their worth and influence. It is through the lives of such people that all of Jewish history is written.

Completed in the Holy City of Jerusalem on the happy day of the Jewish calendar, 15 Av, 5755 — 11 August, 1995

Bibliography Index

Bibliography

Assaf, S., *Tekufat HaGeonim V'Sifrutah*, Jerusalem, 1955

Belkin, Samuel, *The Alexandrian Halakah in Apologetic Literature of the First Century C.E.*, Providence, 1936

Ben Sasson, C.H., *Toldot Am Yisrael*, Tel Aviv, 1969

Bentwich, Norman, *Josephus*, London, 1914

Bichler, Avraham, *HaKohanim V'Avodatam*, Jerusalem, 1965

Bradford, Ernie, *Paul the Traveler*, New York, 1993

Comay, Joan, *The Temple of Jerusalem*, New York, 1975

Ferrill, Arthur, *The Fall of the Roman Empire*, London, 1986

Finegan, Jack, *Light from the Ancient Past*, Princeton, 1946

Flavius, Josephus, *Complete Works*, Whiston, W., trans., New York, 1969

Funk and Wagnalls, *The Jewish Encyclopedia*, New York, 1912

Gafni, Yeshayahu, *Mechkarim B'Toldot Yisrael B'Tkufat HaMishnah V'HaTalmud*, Jerusalem, 1994

Goldwurm, Hersh *History of the Jewish People, The Second Temple Era*, Mesorah Publications, Brooklyn, 1982

Grant, Michael, *The Fall of the Roman Empire*, New York, 1990

HaLevy, Yitzchok Isaac, *Doros HaRishonim*, Frankfurt Am Main, 1918

Heyman, Aaron, *Toldos Tannaim V'Amoraim*, Jerusalem, 1914

Hoenig, S.B., *Sanhedrin Gedolah*, Jerusalem, 1965

Holder, Meir, *History of the Jewish People, From Yavneh to Pumbedisa*, Mesorah Publications, Brooklyn, 1986

Hourani, Albert, *A History of the Arab Peoples*, New York, 1992

Johnson, Paul, *A History of the Jews,* New York, 1987

Keter Publishing, *Encyclopedia Judaica,* Jerusalem, 1972

Klausner, Joseph, *From Jesus to Paul,* Boston, 1943

Klausner, Joseph, *HaBayis HaSheni B'Gadluso,* Tel Aviv, 1930

Kurman, Avraham, *Zeramim V'Kitot B'Yahadut,* Tel Aviv, 1967

Levy, Eliezer, *Toldot HaHalachah,* Tel Aviv, 1953

Lewy, H., *Three Jewish Philosophers,* Philadelphia, 1960

Lieberman, Saul, *Greek in Jewish Palestine,* New York, 1942

Lieberman, Saul, *Hellenism in Jewish Palestine,* New York, 1950

Margolyos, Reuven, *Yesod HaMishnah V'arichasah,* Jerusalem, 1993

McKeon, Richard, *Introduction to Aristotle,* New York, 1947

Oppenheimer, Aaron, *HaGalil B'Tkufat HaMishnah,* Jerusalem, 1991

Oxford University Press, *The Oxford History of Greece and the Hellenistic World,* Oxford, 1986

Oxford University Press, *The Oxford History of the Roman World,* Oxford, 1986

Parker, James, *The Conflict of the Church and the Synagogue,* Philadelphia, 1961

Roth, Cecil, *A History of the Jews,* New York, 1961

Rubin, Alexis, *Scattered Among the Nations,* Toronto, 1993

Safran, Shmuel, *B'ymei Habayis U'B'ymei HaMishnah,* Jerusalem, 1994

Williams, John Alden, *Islam,* New York, 1962

Wolfson, H.A., *Philo-Foundations of Religious Philosophy in Judaism, Christianity and Islam,* Boston, 1940

Zeitlin, Solomon, *The Rise and Fall of the Second Jewish Commonwealth,* Philadelphia, 1944

Zeitlin, Solomon, *Josephus on Jesus,* Philadelphia, 1931

Index

A

Abba Aricha [Rav]   240 fn.
Abbahu   256
Abbasids   306, 315
Abbaye   267
Abu Bakr   305
Achai, R'   243
Acher, Elisha ben Avuyah   219
Acra   62
Acre   158
Acropolis at Athens   29
Aelia Capitolina   209
Aeschylus   27
Afghanastan   20, 203
Aggadah   284
Aggadata d'Bei Rav   248
agricultural tools [*illus.*]   50
agriculture   46, 48
Agrippa   148
— fortified Jerusalem   149
— [*illus.*]   138
— Coins minted by [*illus.*]   148
Agrippa II   153, 155, 200
— deposition of   200 fn.
agronomos   242
Ahasuerus   7
Akiva, R' [chapt. 13]   199 fn., 204, 208, 210 ff., 240
— martyrdom of   215
— tomb of [*illus.*]   216
Alcimus   71
Aleinu prayer   249
Alexander Balas   75
Alexander the Great,   14 fn., 59, 121,
— and calendar   22
— and Jerusalem   21
— as Jewish   219
— [*illus.*]   19
— with Shimon HaTzaddik [*illus.*]   21
Alexander Yannai   92, [*illus.*] 93, 115
— and water libation offering   98
— death of   100
— opposed by the Pharisees   95
Alexandra   136 ff.

Alexandria   29, 36, 49, 155
— Temple in   38 fn.
Alfasi, Yitzchak, R'   283 fn.
Ameimar   272
Amidah prayer   179
— nineteenth blessing of   194 fn.
Ami, R'   256
Amoraim, men of the Talmud   241
— [*chart*]   277
Amram *Gaon*   317
— *Siddur of*   317 fn., [*illus.*] 318
Anan   315
"an *eye* for an *eye*" and the Sadducees   85 fn.
Anshei Knesses HaGedolah [Great Assembly]   13
— [*illus.*]   15
Antigonus of Socho   37 ff.
Antigonus Gonatas   21
Antigonus the Hasmonean   130
Antiochus   43, 59
Antiochus III   41, 42, [*chart*]   43
Antiochus IV, [Epiphanes]   44, 62
— attempts to eradicate Judaism   62
— captures Jerusalem   62
— decrees against Jews   63
— invades Persia   65
— Jewish revolt against   64
Antiochus Sidetes   157
Antiochus V [Eupator]   66, [*illus.*]   44
Antiochus VII   80, [*illus.*]   44
— Jews in his army   82
Antipater   128
Antipatris   139
Antonia, Fortress of [*illus.*]   116, 169
Antoninus of the Talmud, identity of   224 fn.
Antoninus Pius [*illus.*]   220, 221
Antony   136
apikorus   32 fn.
Apollonius   63, 65
aqueduct at Caesarea [*illus.*]   48
Arabia   201
Arabs, circumcision   301 fn.
Aramaic   238
Archelaus   142
Arch of Titus [*illus.*]   171
Aretas   115

Aristobulus, Hyrcanus and Antipater [chapt. 8]   114 ff., 188
Aristobulus III   136
Aristophanes   27
Aristotle   20, 27, 30 f., 31
Aristotle [*illus.*]   31
Artchashashta (Artaxerxes)   7 fn.
Ashi, Rav, editor of Talmud   272
Ashkelon   51
Ashkenazic Jewry   308
Asia Minor   20, 203, 208
Asi, R'   243, 256
Assyrians   3
astronomy   31
Athens   18
Augustine   271
Augustus   106
— [*illus.*]   107, 136
Av Beis Din   37, 40, 43
Av, ninth of   169, 211
Avos manuscript [*illus.*]   15

B

Bablyonian exile, end of seventy years   1, 45
Babylonia [chapt. 15]   238 ff., 269
— fall of   1
— Jewish community   8, 203; [*map*]   239
— role of Central Leadership   238
Bacchides   73
Bais Guvrin   57
bais hashelachin   48 fn.
baptism   192
barbarian tribes   270
Bar Kamtza   154 fn.
Bar Kochba   199, 210
— artifacts from [*illus.*]   212
— letter from [*illus.*]   212
— war of   206
Baruch ben Neriyah   8
Bashan   93
Beis Choron   65, 156
Beis She'an   78

Beis She'arim   224, 230
— tombstone in [illus.]   230
Beitar   209
— fall of   211
Ben Sira, Proverbs of   14 fn.
Ben Yair [illus.]   154
Bible, canonization of   14
biology   31
Birchas HaMinim   194 fn.
Biryonim   152, 165
Black Sea   18
Bnei Beseira   131 fn.
Boethusians   38
Book of the Maccabees   70 fn.
bris amanah   16
Brutus   106
Bustenai   309 *ff.*
— and the *Geonim*   311
Bysosim (Boethusians)   38
Byzantium   261, 289
— Jews of [map]   293

Caesar and Pompey   123
Caesarea   57, 139, 153, 155, 160, 215, 256, 262
— [illus.]   147
calendar, and dating legal documents   22
calendar, Christian   264
calendar, Jewish   263
Caligula   110
Carmel   51
Cassius   106, 128
Chaggai   3, 13
Chama bar Guria, R'   250
Chana and her seven sons   63
— [illus.]   64
Chanukah and the Hasmoneans [chapt. 5]   59 *ff.*
— menorah [illus.]   68
— miracle of   66
— observance   68
Chever haYehudim   90 fn.
Chisda, R'   250, 254, 314
Chiya R'   236, 237 fn., 241
cholent pot [illus.]   85
Choni HaMe'agal   116 fn.
Chonyo   36 fn., 39, 59, 61
Chonyo II   38
Chonyo III   43
Christianity   146, 150, 178, 200, 207, 225, 239, 289, 299
— becomes official religion of Rome   260
— Jewish life under   295
— Manichaean brand   292
— opponents of   276
— rise of   191
— Roman persecution of   260
— split into two   261
— spread of [map]   193
Christian Orthodox Church   262
"Christ-killers"   192 fn.
Church, Byzantine   289
Church, Eastern   262
Church, Orthodox   289
Church, Roman Catholic   295
Church, Western   262
Cicero   106
Cicero [illus.]   106
circumcision   209
— and Arabs   301 fn.
— banned by Antiochus IV   63
— Hadrian's laws against   209
— Roman view of   183 fn., 209
City-states   18
Claudius   111, 148 *ff.*
Cleopatra   93
Colosseum, Roman   182
— [illus.]   183
Commodus [illus.]   229
Commonwealth of Judah   17, 23
Commonwealth, Second   6 fn., 9, 11, 40, 142, 144
Constantine, converted to Christianity   260
Constantine, persecutions by   262
Constantinople   289
— named by Constantine   261
— wall of   290
Constantius II [illus.]   268
Corinthian capitol [illus.]   29
Cyrus the Great   2 fn.
— [illus.]   2
— tomb of [illus.]   4
Cyprus   208
— proclamation of   2

Damascus   147, 155
Daniel   1
Darius   7, 10
— defeat of   20
— [illus.]   11
"Dark Ages"   271, 294 fn.
Dead Sea   54
"Dead Sea Scrolls"   87 fn., 88
Decapolis   93
Demetrius   99
Demetrius II   78
Diaspora   105
Diocletian [illus.]   256
Domitian   182, 199 *ff.*
dreidel [illus.]   67
Dura Europos [illus.]   5, 66

Eastern Roman Empire   270
Egypt   208
— Jewish community   36
Ein-Gedi   54
Elazar   64
Elazar ben Azaryah, R'   199 fn., 202, 208
Elazar ben P'das, R'   256
Elazar ben Shamua, R'   218
Elazar ben Shimon, R'   164
Elazar ben Yaakov, R'   177
Elazar ben Yair   154, 170
Elazar HaModa'i, R'   211
Elazar, the High Priest   37
Elephantine   36
Elephantine papyrii   12 fn.
Eliezer ben Hyrcanus, R', and *cherem*   186
— tomb of [illus.]   181
Eliezer, R'   208
Elisha ben Avuyah [*Acher*]   219
Emmaus   67
Epicurus' philosophy [*hedonism*]   31, 32
Epimanes   44
Epiphanes   44
Eretz Yisrael
— in the time of R' Yochanan ben Zakkai [map]   166
— return to [chapt. 1]   1*ff.*
— *see* Israel   238, 245
— under Alexander Yannai [map]   94
— under Herod's Rule [map]   137
— under Roman Occupation   122
see also Israel, Land of
Essenes   87, 150, 192
— caves of Qumran   88
Esther   7

Euphrates   1
Euripides   27
Exilarch; *see Reish Galusa*
Ezra   3 fn., 6,45, 46, 132, 231, 246
— decree of   9 fn.
— Great Assembly   13
— ordinances of   14
— revitalizes Jewish life in Jerusalem   10

family purity   209
fast days regarding rain and drought   48 fn.
Felix   150
Fish   54
Four Emperors, Year of the   161

Gaius   148
Galilee   49
Gallus   268
Gamla, fortress of   159; [*illus.*] 160
Gamliel *HaZaken* (the Elder), Rabban   146, 147, 167
Gamliel II, Rabban   164 fn., 167, 186, 189, 208
Gamliel III, Rabban   246
Gaza   29
Geonim   252, 253, 292, 309-311
— [definition] 259 fn.
— Era of   309
— period of   259
Germanicus   109
Gessius Florus   152
Gorgias   66
Great Assembly   13, 23, 177, 231
Greco-Roman   90
Greece and Hellenism [chapt. 2]   17*ff*
Greek City States [*map*]   18
Greek Empire, division of the   20
Greek
— language and Jews   26
— names   26
— philosphers   34
— sports   60
— gymnasium   28, 60

Hadrian   205-208, 211, 221
— and Aelia Capitolina   209
— [*illus.*]   221
— laws against circumcision, Sabbath, and family purity   209
— permission to rebuild Temple   206
— rebellion against; dating of 209 fn.
Halachos Gedolos   313
Halachos Pesukos   313
Haman   5
Hamnunah, R'   250
HaNasi Yehudah, R'   229
Hasmoneans [chapt. 6]   73 *ff.*
— civil war   114
— dynasty [*chart*]   134
— dynasty, end of   79
— empire, borders of   84
— fate of explained by Ramban   72 fn., 74 fn.
— forces   65
— Kingdom   68
— Kingdom [*map*]   69
— opposition to   84
— rule, end of   114
Hebrew   238
— alphabets   14 fn.
Hebron   57, 70, 139
Heliodorus   43
Hellenism and Hellenists   26ff, 33, 90
— and Antiochus   59
— and circumcision   28
— and view of the deity   27
— beginning of   22
— Jewish, vs. Hasmoneans   73
— Jews: "*Misyavnim*"   35 fn., 70
— Ptolemaic and Seleucid [chapt. 3] 35 *ff.*
— struggles with Rabbis   37
— vs. Judaism   34
Heraclius   294
Herod   40, 46, 107, 125, 130, 139, 147, 200
— beautification of the Jerusalem Temple   36 fn.
— construction of   128 fn.
— further atrocities of   135
— [*illus.*]   126
— palace   169; [*illus.*] 127, 130, 131, 135
— reconstruction projects   139
— stones of the Western Wall [*illus.*] 129
Herod's Temple   139
High Priesthood, corruption in the   144
Hijra   302
Hillel   132 *ff.*
Hillel and Shammai, Houses of   131-3, 154, 176
Hillel II, and Jewish calendar   264
Homer   27
Huna, R'   250, 253, 254, 258
Hutzal   243
Hyrcanus   101, 115, 121

Idi, R'   276
Idumeans   3, 70, 84, 92, 123, 163
Iran   203
Islam, and Jews   299, 307
— founding of   300
Israel, Land of, role passes to Babylonia   238, 245; *see also Eretz Yisrael*

Jaffa   57, 70, 160
James   193
Jason   59, 61
Jericho   54, 160
— [*illus.*]   81
Jerusalem   39, 57, 149, 153, 156, 160, 169, 210
— and Alexander   21
— and Hasmoneans   69, 70
— attacked by Titus   167
— besieged by Syrian-greeks   71
— breaches repaired by Yonasan   76
— Byzantine-era map [*illus.*]   297
— captured by Antiochus IV   62
— Civil War, 69 C.E. [*map*]   168
— coins depicting Vespasian's victory [*illus.*]   171
— division of [*map*]   151
— emigration to   9
— Ezra's death   10
— fall of   171

Index □ 329

— fortified by Agrippa 149
— Hyrcanus besieges 115
— leveling of 178
— liberated by Maccabees 67
— New City 167
— population of 17 fn., 57
— Ptolemy III and 39
— return of the Jews to 2
— siege of 119
— stone cornerstone 243 fn.
— three factions in 162
— Upper City and Lower City 163 fn., 167
— Wall of [illus.] 3
Jerusalem Talmud; see Talmud Yerushalmi 254
Jews
— attempts to Romanize 144
— communities in Babylonia [map] 239
— of the Roman Empire 100-300 C.E.
— population in Roman Empire 178
— under Islam in the 7th-8th centuries [map] 304
— uprisings against Rome 66-135 C.E. [map] 204
Josephus Flavius 157 ff.
Judah
— borders enlarged 82
— independent under Shimon the Hasmonean 78
— in Second Temple times [chapt. 4] 45ff
— population of 17 fn.
— Roman war against 156
— social and economic conditions [chapt. 4] 45
— trades and professions 55
Judah of Galilee 145
Judaism, converts to 6 fn., 10 fn.
Judea Capta 171
Julian the Apostate 269
Julius Caesar 106, 123, 125, 128
— [illus.] 106
Jupiter, temple to 209
Justinian 296

Kahana, R' 250
Kamtza 154 fn.

Karaism 315
Katzrin [illus.] 49
Knesset 14 fn.
Koran 301 fn.
K'savos d'Bei Rav 248 fn.
Kush 20

Latrun [illus.] 66
Lepidus 106
Libya 18
Lod 57, 201 ff.
Lysias, and Jerusalem 70
Lysimachus 61

Maccabees,
— Book of 70 fn.
— treaty with Rome 72
— Yehudah 65, 72
Macedonian 20 fn.
Machzor, and Rav 248
magi 276
Malachi 3, 13
Mani, R' 262
Mar bar Rav Ashi 277
Marcus Aurelius
— identity of 224 fn., 235
— [illus.] 223
Marcus Salvius Otho 161
Mark Antony 106, [illus.] 107, 130
Mar R' Yehudai Gaon 314
Mar Shmuel 241, 244, 247, 252, 258
— and Jewish calendar 264
Martyrs, the Ten 217 fn.
Mar Ukva 253
Mar Zutra 290, 309
Masada 139, 170
— [illus.] 127, 154
— siege of 170
Masa Mechasya 244 ff., 272
Mattisyahu and his sons 64, 80
— slaying a Hellenist [illus.] 66
Mecca 300
Mechilta 248
Mechoza 266 ff.

Medeba mosaic [illus.] 297
Medina 300
Meged, fortress of 159
Megillah, illuminated [illus.] 5
Meir, R' 178, 208, 218
Menachem ben Galilee 154
Menander 27
Menelaus 61, 63
— and Lysimachus, rabbinic revolt against 61
Menorah [illus.] 63
Mesopotamia 203
metaphysics 31
meturgaman 242
Michmash 74
Midrash 284
Mikveh
— at Masada [illus.] 155
— at Tzippori [illus.] 189
minyan shtaros 22
Miriam (Mariamne), 135, 147, 200
Mishnah, creation of [chapt. 14] 165, 177, 229 ff., 231, 238, 248
— expansion of through Talmud 246
— manuscript [illus.] 280
— of R' Akiva 234
— of R' Meir 234
— Sections of the 234
— Tractates of [chart] 232-3
— with Rambam's commentary [illus.] 235
Mishnah Rishonah 177, 234
Mitzpah 67
Modi'in 64
Mohammed 294, 300
Monastic Living 297
Mordechai 1, 13
Mount Gerizim 84, 258
Mount of Olives [illus.] 53
Mount of [the Anointing] Oil 52 fn.
Mount Tabor [illus.] 121

Nabateans 201
Nachum Ish Gamzu 215
Naresh 272
Nasi 40, 43, 166, 202
— post of abolished 270 fn.
— power of the 222

330 ☐ ECHOES OF GLORY

Nechemiah   1, 10, 13, 45
 — and Darius [*illus.*]   8
Nehardea   241, 243
 — destruction of   258
 — synagogue in   243 fn.
 — yeshivah in   244
Nero   111, 112, 150, 152
 — coin minted by [*illus.*]   161
Nerva   190, 199
Netronai *Gaon*   317
New Moon, celebration of, banned by Antiochus IV   63
Nicaea, Council of, and Christian calendar   265
Nikanor   66, 71
 — defeated by Maccabees   71
Nitai HaArbeli   43, 85

Octavian   106, 136
olive press [*illus.*]   52
Omar, caliph   303, 305, 309
Omayyad dynasty   306, 315
Onkelos   199 fn.
Oral Law (*Torah She'b'al Peh*)   7, 230
 — justification to record in writing   231 fn.
 — preservation of in Yavneh   177
 — revitalization of by Hillel   132
 — the chain of transmission [*chart*]   277

Pachda   290
Papyrus deed [*illus.*]   37
Parthenon   139
Parthia   206, 270, 275, 292
 — Byzantine war   293
Paul   192
Pelusium   29
Peroz, king   277
Persians
 — Empire   1
 — religion   12
 — tolerance   11
Pesach, massacre on   142
Peter   192 *ff.*
Pharisees   46, 85, 87, 95, 96, 102, 144, 150, 153
Phasael   130
 — Tower [*illus.*]   130
Philip of Macedonia   19, 65, 70
 — [*illus.*]   19
Philippi, Battle of   129
Philo of Alexandria   36 fn.
Philosophy, Development of   30
pig, on the Temple Mount   63, 118
Plato   31
Pliny the Elder   54
Pompeii   182 fn.
Pompey   106, 108
 — [*illus.*]   107
 — siege of Jerusalem   119
 — regime   120
Pont-Du-Gard [*illus.*]   140
Pontius Pilate   146
 — [*illus.*]   147
prayer
 — basic order esablished   14
 — for rain   48
 — institutionalization of   179
Proverbs of Ben Sira   14 fn.
Prozbul document [*illus.*]   132
Ptolemy   21-24, 23, 77, 80, 81
 — coin of [*illus.*]   25
 — Dynasty [*chart*]   41
 — Empire   24, 42, 47, 59
Ptolemy Dorimenes   66
Ptolemy II (Philadelphus)   24, 35, 38
 — and translation of the Bible   25
Ptolemy III   38
Ptolemy IV   41
Ptolemy V   42
public school system, Jerusalem   96
Pumbedisa   259, 265, 267
 — growth of   259
 — leaders of   275
Punjab   20
Purim   1, 4, 13

Quietus   204
Quraysh tribe   303

Rabbah   265
Rabbah bar Nachmani   267
Rabbah bar Bar Chana   245
Rabbeinu HaKadosh (*Our Holy Teacher*), Yehudah HaNasi, R'   229 fn.
Rachel, wife of R' Akiva   214
rain, prayers for   48
Ramadan   303 fn.
Ramban   192 fn.
Rashi   274 fn.
Rav   244, 247
 — *aleinu* prayer   250
 — and *semichah*   241 fn.
 — contributer to Siddur/Machzor   248
 — School of   248
 — *see* Abba Aricha   240
Rava   267
Rava, penitential prayer of   267 fn.
Ravina   272, 273
rebellion against Rome; three listed   208
Reish Galusa (the Exilarch)   241 242, 252, 253, 290, 311
 — waning power of the   316
Rome and Roman Empire [chapt. 7]   105 *ff.*
 — basilica in   260 fn.
 — Catapult [*illus.*]   162
 — city of, fall   289
 — Colosseum   139
 — decline of [chapt. 16]   255 *ff.*
 — division of [*map*]   261
 — "evil kingdom"   205
 — exile   178
 — Friends of   154, 162
 — Galileans revolt   126
 — Jewish population   178
 — procurators   143
 — "Romanize" the Jews   144
 — rabbinic delegation to   199
 — ravaged by fire; and Nero   112
 — revolt of Zealots   151
 — theater   108
 — trend of conversions to Judaism   199
 — Western Empire   294
Romulus and Remus [*illus.*]   105

Index □ 331

S

Sabbath 209
— Antiochus' laws against 63
— Hadrian's laws against 209
— in Jerusalem 10
Sabinus 161
Sadduccees 38, 85, 87, 96, 101, 144, 150, 154,158
— and water libation offering 96
— disdain for Torah 85
Salome 91 fn.
Samaritans 3, 7, 45, 207
— decline of the 257
— temple, destruction of 84
Sanhedrin 90 fn., 176, 199, 202
— and calendar 264
— disbanding of 123
— in the post Temple era 176
— locations of [*map*] 185
— members executed under Herod 131
— president of (*Nasi*) 37
— reconvening of, at Usha 207
— under Roman procurators 143
— Yavneh 176
Sassanian kings 266
Saul 192
Savoraim 291
school system throughout Judah 96
Schottenstein Edition of Talmud [*illus.*] 286
Sea of Galilee 54
Second Temple model [*illus.*] 47
Seleucus IV 43
Seleucids 21, 23, 43, 47, 59
— and Ptolemaic Empire (240 B.C.E) 24
— Dynasty [*chart*] 42
— Empire 41, 42
— Hellenism 43
— kingdom 22
semichah (ordination) 241 fn.
Seneca 112
Sephardic Jewry 308
Sepphoris; *see also* Tzippori 158, 262
— [*illus.*] 49
Septuagint 25, 38, 157 fn.
— date of 26
Shammai 131, 133
Shapur I, King (*Shvor Malka*) 251, 268
Sharon 51

Shas 234
Shavuos, massacre on 142
Shechem 258
Shefar'am 222
She'iltos of R' Achai [*illus.*] 313
Shemaya and Avtalyon 116, 123
Shema Yisrael 294 fn.
Sherira Gaon, Iggeres 310
Sheshes, R' 266
Shiites 305
Shiloach (Silwan) 98
Shimon 64, 73
— achieves sovereignty and independence 78
Shimon bar Giora 163 *f.*
Shimon bar Yochai, R' 217, 220
— the cave of [*illus.*] 221
Shimon ben Gamliel, Rabban 155, 158, 162, 208
Shimon ben Kosiba 211
Shimon ben Lakish, R' [Reish Lakish] 246, 254
Shimon ben Shetach 95 *f.*, 100
Shimon ben Yochai, R' 208
Shimon ben Zoma, R' 208
Shimon HaTzaddik 14, 17, 21
— tomb of [*illus.*] 20
Shimon Ish HaMitzpeh, R' 177
Shimon, son of Hillel 143
Shlomis Alexandra 91, 118
— reign of 100
Shlomzion, Queen 91 fn.
Shmuel *Gaon*, R' 314
Shomron 3, 57
Shushan, Gate of 10
Sicarii 145, 152, 154, 158, 170
Sicily 18
Siddur, and Rav 248
Siddur, Italian [*illus.*] 250
Sidon 49, 54
Sidra 242, 244
Sifra d'Bei Rav 248
Silwan, Waters of the [*illus.*] 97
slavery 56
Socrates 31
— [*illus.*] 32
Sophocles 27
Spain, Christian Reconquest 295
Spain, Visigoth bishops of 264
Sparta 18
sports, Greek 60
Stoic 31
Succos 96
Suez Canal 13
Sulla 106
Sunnis 305

Sura 242, 244*ff.*, 258, 265
— and Pumbedisa 252
— elders of 265 fn.
— leaders in 276
synagogue 296
— at Gamia [*illus.*] 180
— floor at Bet Shean [*illus.*] 180
— institutionalization of 179
Syria 18, 46, 203
— army, and the Maccabees 67
— breached Temple walls 63
Syrian-Greek soldiers, killed by Mattisyahu 64

T

Talmud — Book of the Jews [chapt. 17] 279 *ff.*
— Babylonian [Talmud Bavli] 272, 283
— editing of 245 fn., 272-3
— comparison between *Bavli* and *Yerushalmi* 281
— development of 255
— editions [*illus.*] 279-286
— organization of as explained by Rashi 274 fn.
— power of the 285
— Yerushalmi [Jerusalem Talmud] 246 fn., 254, 281
— year of the final editing of 268 fn.
Tammuz, seventeenth of 169
Tanna, a colleague of the rabbis of the Mishnah 241
— [*chart*] 277
Tarfon, R' 204, 208
tax collection 25, 38 *f.*, 39, 47
tax franchisers 43
Tekiasa d'Bei Rav, translation 249
Temple, Second
— and miracle of Chanukah 67
— attempted defilement of by Heliodorus 43
— attempted defilement of by Ptolemy IV 41
— dedication of 8
— destruction of 169
— permission to rebuild 2
— permission to rebuild, by Hadrian 206
— purified by Maccabees 67
— reconstructed by Herod 139

332 ☐ ECHOES OF GLORY

— siege   119
— year of destruction   169 fn.
Temple Mount   47 fn., 162, 169
Temple of Chonyo   36
Terentius Rufus   176 fn.
Thebes   18
Theodosius the Great   270
Tiberias   57, 109, 159, 216, 243 fn., 246, 262
— Yeshivos in   256
Tiberius Caesar   146
— [illus.]   147
Tigris   1
Tineius Rufus   176 fn., 210, 220
Tisha b'Av   169, 211
Titus   157 fn., 167, 169, 171, 182, 199
— Arch of   182
— [illus.]   171, 183
— bronze coin [illus.]   167
Torah
— education   117
— school system   100
— supremacy of reestablished   10, 16
Toras Kohanim   248 fn.
Tosefta of R' Oshiya   248
Tours, Battle of   305 fn.
Trajan   199-206
— Arch [illus.]   202
— columns [illus.]   201
Transjordan   46
Translation of the Seventy   25
Tryphon   77
Tyre   49, 54
Tyropean Valley   47 fn.
Tzemach bar Poltoi *Gaon*   317
Tzippori (Sepphoris)   57, 202, 262, 296
— [illus.]   236,

Usha   189, 199
— reconvening of Sanhedrin   207

Valerius Gratus   146

Vespasian   157 ff., 184
— meets R' Yochanan ben Zakkai   164
— campaigns of   159
Vesuvius, volcano of   182 fn.

War, explanation of rabbinic attitudes toward   95 fn.
water libation offering,
— and Alexander Yannai   98
— mocked by Sadducees   96
wine   51

Xenophanes   27 fn.

Yarchei Kallah   245
Yarchei Kallah, revived   274
Yavneh   57, 79, 160, 165, 199
— and *bo bayom*   187
— and its wise men [chapt. 10] 175 ff., 184
— changes in   188
— disbanded   201
— institutionalization of the synagogue
— leadership in   184
— replaces Jerusalem as center of Torah life   165
— restrictions by Romans   185
— Sanhedrin   176
— scholars of   165 fn.
Yazdegerd   275-277
Year of the Four Emperors   161
Yehoshua ben Gamla   96
Yehoshua ben Perachya   43, 85
Yehoshua, R'   208
Yehoshua the High Priest   13

Yehudah Aristobulus   89
Yehudah bar Yechezkel   259
Yehudah ben Beseira, R'   240
Yehudah ben Tabai   100
Yehudah HaLevi   30 fn.
Yehudah HaMaccabee   65
— [illus.]   67
Yehudah HaNasi, R'   178, 241
— and Antoninus   223
— known as 'Rabbi'   240 fn.
Yehudah Nesiah I, R'   246
Yehudah Nesiah III, R'   262
Yehudah, R' (ben Il'ai)   220
Yehudah, son of Shimon   80
Yerushalmi; see *Talmud* Yerushalmi   263
yeshivos, in Caesarea and Tiberias   256
Yeshu, execution of   192 fn.
Yirmiyah, R'   250
Yochanan   64, 73
Yochanan ben Zakkai, Rabban   146, 165 ff., 175
— meets Vespasian   164
— tomb of [illus.]   146,
Yochanan Hyrcanus, son of Shimon   80
— Coin minted by [illus.]   81
— *Eretz Yisrael* under [map]   83
Yochanan of Gush Chalav (John Gischala)   158, 163, 168
Yochanan, R'   246, 254
Yonasan   64, 73 ff.
— killed by Tryphon   78
Yonason, High Priest   152
Yose ben Yochanan   39 ff.
Yose ben Yoezer   39 ff.
Yosef ben Tovia   25 fn., 39, 43
Yossi, R'   218

Zadok   38
Zadokim (Saducees)   38
Zealots (*Kannaim*)   144, 145, 150, 154, 156, 158, 162
— revolt against Rome   151
Zechariah   3, 13
Zerubavel   2
Zoroaster   12
zugos (pairs)   40, 85, 91, 234,
— [chart]   92, 277
Zutra, Mar   290

Index □ 333